Tensions of Social History

Global History: European Perspectives and Approaches

In Association with the European Network in Universal and Global History (ENIUGH)

Series editors: Matthias Middell (Leipzig University) and Katja Castryck-Naumann (Centre for the Study of University of Leipzig, Germany)

Global history has become an increasingly common and successful way to study history over the last three decades. As this method increases in use, more attention has been paid to the historiography, theory and skills associated with doing global history. To date, research in global history is primarily visible when coming from the Anglo-American world. This series seeks to contribute also many other European perspectives in order to highlight the diversity of global histories and its historiography.

Published in association with the European Network in Universal and Global History, this series provides an overview of current trends in global history research from across the European continent. Taking a non-Eurocentric approach and anchored in the variety of area and transregional studies, it publishes research on developments in and outside of Europe along with innovative historiographical studies critiquing the value and uses of global history and histories of globalization. Exploring 'globalization-critical movements', it will question who is doing what kind of globalization, and with what interests and goals? In doing so it seeks to demonstrate that there are many types of globalization being done in different ways. Contributing to the critical reflection of Eurocentrism in global history, it positions Europe within global processes, and critically assesses European approaches to extra-European developments.

Founded in 2002, the European Network in Universal and Global History brings together more than 600 European global historians and organizes a major conference every three years. With a steering committee of around twenty elected representatives from various European countries, it represents the best research in Europe on Global History.

Tensions of Social History

Sources, Data, Actors and Models in Global Perspective

Alessandro Stanziani

BLOOMSBURY ACADEMIC
LONDON • NEW YORK • OXFORD • NEW DELHI • SYDNEY

BLOOMSBURY ACADEMIC
Bloomsbury Publishing Plc
50 Bedford Square, London, WC1B 3DP, UK
1385 Broadway, New York, NY 10018, USA
29 Earlsfort Terrace, Dublin 2, Ireland

BLOOMSBURY, BLOOMSBURY ACADEMIC and the Diana logo are
trademarks of Bloomsbury Publishing Plc

First published in Great Britain 2023
This paperback edition published 2024

Copyright © Alessandro Stanziani, 2023

Alessandro Stanziani has asserted his right under the Copyright, Designs and
Patents Act, 1988, to be identified as Author of this work.

For legal purposes the Acknowledgements on p. vii constitute an
extension of this copyright page.

Cover image: PDMPhotos / Stockimo / Alamy Stock Photo

All rights reserved. No part of this publication may be reproduced or
transmitted in any form or by any means, electronic or mechanical, including
photocopying, recording, or any information storage or retrieval system,
without prior permission in writing from the publishers.

Bloomsbury Publishing Plc does not have any control over, or responsibility for,
any third-party websites referred to or in this book. All internet addresses given in this
book were correct at the time of going to press. The author and publisher regret any
inconvenience caused if addresses have changed or sites have ceased to exist,
but can accept no responsibility for any such changes.

A catalogue record for this book is available from the British Library.

A catalog record for this book is available from the Library of Congress.

ISBN: HB: 978-1-3502-7682-6
       PB: 978-1-3502-7685-7
       ePDF: 978-1-3502-7683-3
       eBook: 978-1-3502-7684-0

Typeset by Integra Software Services Pvt. Ltd.

To find out more about our authors and books visit www.bloomsbury.com
and sign up for our newsletters.

Contents

Acknowledgements — vii

Introduction — 1

Part 1 What is a source? Archives, memory and contested contextualities

1 Revolutionary archives — 21
   Where multiple worlds meet: revolution, theatre and cosmographies — 23
   Archives and the French Revolution — 27

2 Archives in the twentieth century: from communism to the decolonization — 33
   Totalitarian archives? — 33
   Written sources against oral documents: the invention of the source and people with no history — 42
   Locating the archives — 45
   Conclusion: Part 1 — 54

Part 2 The social life of data

Introduction: archives, data and models — 58

3 When one person eats two chickens and another none, on average they eat one chicken each. The invention of social statistics under capitalism — 63
   The social construction of an artefact: questionnaires, expeditions, texts and data — 67
   Back to the future. From Russian statistics to Piketty — 70

4 Environment and social inequalities: how are data made and by whom? — 73
   Weather forecasting: science, divination or both? — 76
   Predicting future harvests — 79
   Cyclones: from travel narratives to forecasting — 85
   Cyclones in the archives — 92
   Conclusion: Part 2 — 97

Part 3   Fragments of social worlds
  Introduction 102
  How can this discussion be developed in transregional and global
    perspective? 103

5 What is a worker, what is a slave? 107
  Who is the 'real' slave? 112

6 What is a peasant? The global history of 'immobile people' 123
  Fighting for or against ideal types. Peasant studies in the Cold War 126
  Peasants in history? Pluri-activity and multiple identities 130

7 What is a consumer? Identities and alterities in the stomach 141
  Quantifying consumption and its roots: famines or speculation? 144
  Quality in consumption: Who defines it? 148
  Standardization and mass consumption 155
  Conclusion: Part 3 159

Part 4   The quest of universality: values, theories and the European model

8 Societies and their evolution: from the Enlightenments to Marxisms 163
  Marx's social actors in global context 166
  Neo-Marxism and the 'social turn' 171

9 Weberian worlds 175
  The great divergence: Weber on his head? 181
  Durkheim and the Annales School 184
  Social structures and the *longue durée* 186
  Back to anthropology? 189
  Conclusion: Part 4 193

General conclusion 195

References 202
Index 236

Acknowledgements

This book is the final product of about thirty years of discussion with colleagues, friends and students. As it would be impossible to remind all of them, I will do my best and I apologize for those whom I do not mention. Discussions on the tensions between data and sources took place during my staying at the Wissenschafts Kolleg, the Wiko, Berlin, in 2011–12. Discussions with historians, biologists, artists, philosophers and legal scholars provided an incredible arena for such a complicated topic. Among those who took part in the weekly seminar I organized were Claudio Lomnitz, Monique Borgerhoff Mulder, Samantha Besson, Bénédicte Zimmermann, Edhem Eldem, Susannah Heschel, Clemens Leonhard, Jim Hunt, Ji-Hyung, Stephen Stearn, Israel Yuval and Franz Alto Bauer. Their suggestions were incredibly useful.

I also acknowledge my intellectual debt to the Eniugh and the great opportunity of discussing several papers in its several workshops and conferences, not forgetting friends and members of the steering committees over the years, among them Gareth Austin, Matthias Middell, Marcel Van der Linden and Eric Vanhaute. Friends of the Global History Collaborative I co-managed between 2014 and 2022 (EHESS, Princeton, Tokyo Universities, Humboldt and Freie University) also helped my reflections: Jeremy Adelman, Sebastian Conrad, Andreas Eckert, Masashi Haneda, not forgetting the French 'crew': Marc Elie, Antonella Romano, Silvia Sebastiani, Emmanuel Szurek, Xavier Paulès, Corinne Lefèvre, Pablo Blitstein. Among the specialists of the history of quantification and measure with whom I had the pleasure to discuss these subjects in depth, I would like to thank Morgane Labbé, Alain Blum, Andrea Bréard, Yanni Kotsonis, Eric Brian, my first master Jean-Claude Perrot, Jean-Yves Grenier, not forgetting the very young Adam Tooze whom I had the pleasure to invite to speak in Budapest in 1993. I am specially thankful to the members of the editorial and reading boards of *Histoire et Mesure*, a wonderful journal I have contributed to for over twenty years and which I currently edit. Other friends oriented valuable discussions on the relationships between social sciences, history and quantification: Jerome Bourdieu, Gisèle Sapiro, Georg Steinmetz, Thomas Piketty, Gilles Postel-Vinay, Maurice Aymard, Robert Salais, Christian Topalov and Paul-André Rosental. Jane Burbank and Fred Cooper read and commented on the very first version of this manuscript; five anonymous referees provided amazing, decisive suggestions to improve this work. A special thank to my students, many of them under the burden of complicated discussions on sources, data and social actors. With their questions and patience, they helped me to better formulate my own reflections.

Introduction

Public debates and anxieties about illegal migrants to Europe (and the US border, between India, Bangladesh and Myanmar, etc.) focus not just on abstract considerations about the 'others' but also on empirical evidence: how many migrants are really coming? What is their social status on departure and their political status on arrival? Observers inevitably compare current trends with historical ones.[1]

The same is true for debates about social inequalities on global scale, at the very core of social studies since the beginning of the millennium and peaking with Piketty's bestseller, *Capital in the 21st Century*.[2] His book's success is closely related to the quantification in its main argument. Or consider evaluations of the social impact of global warming and environmental change: any suggestions or timetabling about the future require the measurement of multiple variables and their past trends. Attempts to put global warming into a 'natural' very long term have been made by economic and political lobbies hostile to any restriction of current lifestyles and economies.[3]

Sometimes, public debates start from attempts to quantify the past; in the United States, in recent years, historians and media have debated the proposition made by representatives of the so-called New History of Capitalism, arguing that early US economic growth relied on slavery.[4] Here, too, statistical data, social categories (slaves, free people) and explanations are extremely controversial.

These kinds of questions – who are the slaves? who are the refugees? – enter a broader questioning about the classification of social actors in contemporary societies and the past. The identification of slaves and trafficked people cannot occur without

---

[1] It seems useless just to provide an introductory bibliography on this topic. Among the others, see: Alexander Betts, ed., *Global Migration Governance* (Oxford: Oxford University Press, 2011); Anna Maria Mayda, 'International Migration: A Panel Data Analysis of the Determinants of Bilateral Flows', *Journal of Population Economics* 23 (2010): 1249–74; Lauren Mc Laren, Anja Neundorf and Ian Paterson, 'Diversity and Perceptions of Immigration: How the Past Influences the Present', *Political Studies* 1 (2020) https://doi.org/10.1177%2F0032321720922774. See also *The International Migration Review*.

[2] Thomas Piketty, *Capital in the 21st Century* (Boston: Harvard University Press, 2014).

[3] Christophe Bonneuil and Jean-Baptiste Fressoz, *The Shock of the Anthropocene* (London: Verso, 2017).

[4] Gavin Wright, *Old South, New South: Revolutions in the Southern Economy since the Civil War* (New York: Basic Books, 1986); Sven Beckert, 'Emancipation and Empire: Reconstructing the Worldwide Web of Cotton Production in the Age of the American Civil War', *American Historical Review* 109, no. 5 (2004): 1405–38; Sven Beckert, *Empire of Cotton* (New York: Kopf, 2014).

questioning who the 'free' people are. Since the 1990s, most observers have noted the end of the working class in the West and advanced countries, replaced by composite middle classes, and in some cases by social actors with multiple identities (consumer, worker, renter, etc.).[5] These considerations are part of debates about the political orientations of the major parties and also influence political and social attitudes towards the 'others'. It is no accident that much hostility towards immigrants comes from popular classes.

Finally, anxieties about social dynamics past and present converge into more general considerations about the 'path of history'. Even if the philosophy of history has repeatedly been declared dead, the meaning of history is still present in public debates. Take the two opposing interpretations of the post-1989 world, one evoking the end of history (Fukuyama), the other the clash of civilizations (Huntington).[6] To some extent, philosophical considerations of the 'laws of history' have even won new life with the emergence of 'collapse theories' relating environmental dynamics and the end of our societies.[7]

This book takes these debates seriously and seeks to identify the main postulates orienting discussions about societies and their history.[8] An oxymoron might summarize it as a social history of social history. To do so, I intend to expand arguments on the four main components of social history writing: archives, data, categories and models. Before introducing each of them, I need to specify how they will be discussed.

First, I aim to produce an 'archaeology of social knowledge' and trace the historical origins of most of the tools, schemes and categories we use nowadays to explain historical social dynamics: the way we trust or distrust documents and figures, why we are so keen to listen to experts and politicians presenting our reality in figures and data, why we can quantify everything. I also explain where the ambition of quantifying social relationships comes from and why data on the environment are so controversial. I will also reiterate the origin of the main social categories: the worker, the slave, the peasant and the consumer; I do not neglect the intellectual and social origins of the main social theories, from Marx to Weber and Durkheim. And yet, this 'archaeological deconstructivism' aims at moving beyond a mere Foucauldian approach.[9] In particular, and second, the construction and circulation of ideas, concepts, methods and sources themselves will be intertwined with each other and all related to social dynamics.[10] Instead of just 'deconstructing' models, social actors and categories, sources and data, I will show how they were identified and co-produced (by multiple actors) in

---

[5] Marcel van der Linden, ed., *Workers of the World* (Leiden: Brill, 2008); Andreas Eckert, ed., *Global Histories of Work* (Boston and Berlin: De Gruyter, 2016).
[6] Francis Fukuyama, *The End of History and the Last Man* (New York: Free Press, 1992); Samuel Huntington, *The Clash of Civilizations* (New York: Simon & Schuster, 2011, original article 1993).
[7] Jared Diamond, *Collapse* (New York: Viking Press, 2005); Pablo Servigne and Raphaël Stevens, *Comment tout peut s'effondrer* (Paris: Seuil, 2015); Alessandro Stanziani, *Capital terre. Une histoire longue du monde d'après* (Paris: Payot, 2021).
[8] George Steinmetz, ed., *The Politics of Method in the Social Sciences* (Durham, London: Duke University Press, 2005).
[9] Ian Hacking, *The Social Construction of What?* (Cambridge, MA: Harvard University Press, 1999).
[10] Jean-Claude Perrot, *Histoire intellectuelle de l'économie politique* (Paris: EHESS, 1992).

specific historical contexts. It is not an abstract epistemology of social history, its tools and artefacts, but an historical investigation of methodological debates about 'social history' deeply embedded in their social and political contexts.[11] The tensions I refer to were not only debates among scholars but also those in the wider public arena, including public officials, about the ways of identifying social classes.

Some of these tensions were simply imagined by external observers. For example, in some circumstances, class struggle did not really take place and many of those called proletarians, or even revolutionary proletarians, were not proletarians at all. And yet, one cannot merely evoke the gap between discourse and practice, representations and social reality; the two were closely interlinked. The way unions, for example, looked at workers, rightly or wrongly, influenced their social and political action and the workers' attitudes. In other words, when I speak of the tensions of social history, I intend to question not just the construction of modern knowledge about societies (is it better expressed in numbers and data or through archival or other qualitative documents? through Marxism or Weberian theory?) but also the way in which these discussions interacted with the structural transformation of societies themselves. The long evolution of peasantries over centuries, the birth of consumer society, the slow emergence of proletarians from the ashes of the peasant workers who were the vast majority for centuries, before and under capitalism, the changing impact of the environment on social life and vice versa are some of the broader historical trends we are dealing with when discussing archives, data and social theories.

Third, this investigation will be conducted in a transregional perspective; conventional tools of historiography (archives, data, concepts, models) are under attack from postmodern and postcolonial studies claiming that most of these archives are issued from particular European or Western perspectives while being used to explain the history of non-European areas. In fact, despite the ambition of overcoming Eurocentrism, most approaches historians seek to develop still are under the burden of categories and models issued from social sciences, political sciences and economics which indeed are Eurocentric;[12] for example, discussions on, say, power and society under the Mughal, despite the knowledge of ancient Persian, consider this polity according to the notions of cosmopolitanism or civil society as inherited from Kant or Habermas, the only question being whether these notions were relevant or not to study the Mughal Empire. Examples may be multiplied. The question, of course, is not to deny that Western-centric attitudes were imposed in other parts of the world – this was a fact, and still today students working on, say, the history of India or China are requested to know the fundamental of historical tools as developed in Europe and the European history itself – it is why the reverse is not true. Yet, this does not mean that

---

[11] J. G. A. Pocock, *Barbarism and Religion*, 5 vols (Cambridge: Cambridge University Press, 1999–2011); Dominick LaCapra, *History and Criticism* (Ithaca: Cornell University Press, 1985); Reinhart Koselleck, *Futures Past: On the Semantics of Historical Time* (New York: Columbia University Press, 2004); Anthony Grafton, *Defenders of the Text: The Traditions of Scholarship in the Age of Science, 1450-1800* (Cambridge, MA: Harvard University Press, 1991), are those among many others who contributed to the advances along this perspective.

[12] Alessandro Stanziani, *Eurocentrism and the Politics of Global History* (New York: Palgrave, 2018).

we need to look for some alternative to Western approaches and embark on a quest for 'Indian' or 'African' social categories and approaches.[13] In other words, mine is not an attempt to provincialize Europe by looking at some notions such as labour, the subject and so on, as many have done after Chakrabarty, but an effort to overcome this same tension between 'Western' and 'non-Western' categories and historical tools. This book intends to show that the way most Western approaches to the social sciences and history have developed owes much to transregional and colonial interaction.[14] Of course, connected histories cannot be isolated from unequal exchanges and dependency: if colonial actors strongly contributed to the construction of archives and data, they were nevertheless constrained into European approaches and models. These last followed the expansion of European bureaucracies and investigators into the Global South rather than the other way round.

In short, this is a transregional social and political history of the tensions between models and concepts,[15] sources[16] and data[17] in the writing of history and in their interplay with the social dynamics themselves. With these premises in mind, we may now turn to present the main topics under discussion: the construction of archives (Part I) and data (Part II), that of social actors and classes (Part III), and, finally, the so-called social 'models' (Part IV). There are hundreds – indeed, thousands – of titles on each of these topics, as I will describe in a moment. Yet, not only there are very few transregional histories of archives, statistics, social theories and social groups (most recent global histories simply put national scholarly work side by side), but there are almost no histories combining archives and statistics, theories on societies and philosophies of history, in their connections and in a transregional perspective. Of course, this book does not pretend to be exhaustive on each of these themes; that would be a too large and probably pointless aim. This is an essay, an attempt to launch the debate on the past, present and future of history and social history, in particular in post-postmodern and global societies. As such, this essay certainly misses titles, angles and perspectives. Some parts of the world are missing while some others – Europe, Russia – are over-represented. This partially reflects my own fields; and yet, as I have already developed elsewhere, transnational and global history is not to be confused with world history,[18] while 'the Russian case' historically was more than just a case. As we will see, it strongly influenced social theories, social statistics and contributed to the evolution of archives in the twentieth century. Some

---

[13] This argument also in Rama Sundari Mantena, *The Origins of Modern Historiography in India* (New York: Palgrave Macmillan, 2012).

[14] George Steinmetz, ed., *Sociology and Empire* (Durham, NC and London: Duke University Press, 2013); Stanziani, *Eurocentrism*.

[15] Reinhart Koselleck, *Vergangene Zukunft. Zur Semantik geschichtlicher Zeiten* (1979, English translation, *Futures Past*); Willibald Steinmetz, Michael Freeden and Javier Fernandez-Sebastian, eds, *Conceptual History in the European Space* (New York: Berghahn, 2017).

[16] Carlo Ginzburg, *Miti, emblemi e spie* (Torino: Einaudi, 1986 English translation): *Clues, Myths and the Historical Method* (Baltimore: Johns Hopkins University Press, 1989); Grafton, *Defenders of the Text*; Sheldon Pollock, Benjamin Elman, Ku-ming Kevin Chang, dir, *World Philology* (Boston, Mass: Harvard University Press, 2015); Mantena, *The Origins of Modern Historiography*.

[17] Mary Poovey, *A History of Modern Fact* (Chicago: University of Chicago Press, 1998).

[18] Alessandro Stanziani, *Les entrelacements du monde* (Paris: CNRS éditions, 2018); Stanziani, *Eurocentrism*.

would consider that I remain agnostic and do not define 'historical truth' or 'social evidence'. But this book intends to show precisely how these debates were and still are historically embedded. It will explicitly take position against some normative judgements in these fields. First, we need more than a strictly rigid division between 'civilizations' when this is turning from a mistaken theory into a confirmed prediction and a political move. And when social inequalities and environmental destruction are growing globally despite a century's progress in techniques, knowledge, science and economics, we need to overcome the simplistic opposition between statistical and archival positivisms, social and cultural history, or between Western-centred and Indo-, Afro-, Sino-centred approaches to the social implications of global warming. This essay is a first step in this direction.

Archives, memory and contested contextualities

The evolution of concepts and theories of social transformation accompanied changes in the main tools of analysis: sources and data. We cannot understand the evolution, the strength and limits of social models for history without looking at their tools. But what constitutes a source in the writing of history and specifically in the history of societies?[19]

Conventional historians may see this question as trivial; they distinguish between primary and secondary sources (archives and published titles). Yet, this distinction is historically and geographically situated;[20] this book intends to disclose not just its methodological but also its social origins and its implications. My aim is not to trace another short history of the archives, many of them are available, in both long-term (since the early modern period) and trans-national perspectives.[21] Rather, I intend to show the multi-scalar (local, national, transregional) interplay between archival construction and social dynamics.

---

[19] Among others, Daniel Woolf, *A Global History of History* (Cambridge: Cambridge University Press, 2011); Sanjay Subrahmanyam, *Aux origines de l'histoire globale* (Paris: Fayard, 2014); Georg Iggers, Edward Wang and Supriya Mukherjee, *A Global History of Modern Historiographies* (New York: Routledge, 2008); *The Oxford History of Historical Writing*, 5 vols (Oxford: Oxford University Press, 2011–15); Velcheru Narayana Rao, David Shulman and Sanjay Subrahmanyam, *Textures of Time: Writing History in South India, 1600–1800* (Delhi: Permanent Black, 2001); Edward Wang, *Inventing China through History* (New York: State University of New York Press, 2001); Israel Gershoni, Amy Singer and Y. Hakan Erdem, eds, *Middle East Historiographies: Narrating the Twentieth Century* (Seattle: University of Washington Press 2006).

[20] Sheldon Pollock, Benjamin Elman and Ku-ming Kevin Chang, eds, *World Philology* (Boston, MA: Harvard University Press, 2015); Anthony Grafton, *What Was History? The Art of History in Early Modern Europe* (Cambridge: Cambridge University Press, 2006).

[21] Among others, see the special issues on archives and empires, *Ab Imperio*, 3 (2007) and 4 (2008); also the special issue devoted to archives in *Annales HSS* 74, no. 3 (2019); the journal *Archival Science*, publishing essential forums and articles since the late 1990s; 'Historiographic "Turns" in Critical Perspective', *American Historical Review* 117, no. 3 (2012): 698–813; the special issues: 'Fabrique des archives, fabrique de l'histoire', *Revue de synthèse* 125 (2004); 'The Social History of the Archive: Record-Keeping in Early Modern Europe', *Past & Present* 230, suppl. 11 (2016). See the following notes and those in the relevant chapters for more references.

For sure, archives existed well before the eighteenth century, not only in Europe, not only in state administration but also in church institutions, private organizations and local administration, in China, as well in India, in the Ottoman and Safavid empires.[22] Yet something happened in the late eighteenth century (Chapter 1): a new relationship was settled between the invention of modern archives and revolutions. Archives were mostly accessible to the public and had to contribute to the consolidation of the 'memory of the nation'. The social life of archives and, in the archives, the organization and classification of documents and actors themselves were mediated by this central category in both social life and the life of the archives: the nation (this last including and subjugating, as we will see, the colonial worlds as well).[23]

I follow this trend during the Bolshevik Revolution (Chapter 2), focusing on the notion of the totalitarian archive and the global development of archival organization during the twentieth century.[24] In this case, the classification of documents and social actors was subject to the strict rules of Marxist, then Leninist, then Stalinist orthodoxy. Again, how people presented a public figure in the archives, the representations of social dynamics as retrieved from the archives, and social life were strongly connected. Putting the revolution on stage was one of the main aims of the Soviet archives.

Chapter 2 also discusses the long history of colonial and postcolonial archives, first in Russia and Soviet Union, then in European empires. I will start from the opposition between oral tradition and written documents,[25] between people with and without history in the nineteenth and twentieth centuries,[26] down to the decolonization of documents in the archives (which documents? how were they classified? where?)[27] from the interwar period to the 1970s, and, finally, the decolonization of archives themselves, with the disputes over the transfer of documents from the colonies to

---

[22] Arif Dirlik, Vinay Bahl and Peter Gran, eds, *History after the Three Worlds: Post-Eurocentric Historiographies* (Oxford: Oxford University Press, 2000). Thomas Lee, ed., *The New and the Multiple: Song Senses of the Past* (Hong Kong: Hong Kong University Press, 2005). On-cho Ng, Edward Wang, *Mirroring the Past: The Writing and Use of History in Imperial China* (Honolulu: Hawaii University Press, 2005). Abdallah Laroui, *Islam et histoire* (Paris: Albin Michel, 1999); Sholeh Quinn, *Historical Writing during the Reign of Shah Abbas: Ideology, Imitation and Legitimacy in Safavid Chronicles* (Salt Lake City: University of Utah Press, 2000); Harbans Mukhia, *Historians and Historiography during the Reign of Akbar* (New Delhi: Vikha Publishing House, 1976).

[23] Among others, Arlette Farge, *Le goût de l'archive* (Paris: Seuil, 1989); Pierre Nora, *Les lieux de mémoire. II. La nation* (Paris: Gallimard 1986); Jean et Lucie Favier, *Archives Nationales. Quinze siècles d'histoire* (Paris: Nathan, 1988).

[24] Sophie Coeuré and Vincent Duclert, *Les archives* (Paris: La découverte, 2011); Marc Mazour, *The Writing of History in the Soviet Union* (Stanford: Stanford University Press, 1971); Antonella Salomoni, 'Un savoir historique d'État. Les archives soviétiques', *Annales HSS* 50, no. 1 (1995): 3–27.

[25] Walter Ong, *Orality and Literacy: The Technologizing of the World* (New York: Methuen, 1982); Ann Laura Stoler, *Along the Archival Grain* (Princeton: Princeton University Press, 2009).

[26] Sean Hawkins, *Writing and Colonialism in Northern Ghana: The Encounter between the LoDagaa and 'the World of Paper'* (Toronto: University of Toronto Press, 2002).

[27] A huge bibliography cumulated during last two decades on the decolonization of the archives. Among the others, see: the special issue devoted to this topic in *Archival Science* 19 (2019); Joanne Barker, *Native Acts Law, Recognition and Cultural Authenticity* (Durham, NC: Duke University Press, 2011); Jeannette Bastian, 'Whispers in the Archives: Finding the Voices of the Colonized in the Records of the Colonizer', in *Political Pressure and the Archival Record*, edited by Margareth Procter, Michael Cook and Caroline Williams (Chicago: Society of American Archivists, 2006), 25–43.

the mainland.[28] Colonial and postcolonial studies, disputes over the classification of people[29] and of documents[30] went hand in hand, and yet the issue was not the same in Russia, in France, in Britain and in their respective former colonies.

Since the nineteenth century, archive-based studies have laid claim to an assumed objectivization of reality. The positivist method in the humanities, taking archives as a firm and unquestionable source, dominated the historical profession until very recently, although with varying success and significance according to period and country. In France, for example, a certain criticism of this posture emerged in the early twentieth century, while in the West, then worldwide, it was the postmodernist turn which generalized the criticism of archival positivism. However, as we will see, these were very different positions, the former leading to a convergence between sociology and history, the latter pushing towards literature and philosophy.[31]

Moreover, archival positivism and philology also raise another question: that of the national boundaries of history and its writing. Whereas archives were mostly built at national scale (hiding or rigidly separating them from their imperial dimension), so-called area studies developed in Europe during the last quarter of the nineteenth century, in the United States after 1945 with different purposes (empire and Orientalism in the one case, the global Cold War in the other) but with a common position that justified the presumed 'uniqueness' or 'specificity' of an area by some sorts of civilizational values.[32] Therefore, if in this book we want to overcome these barriers, we need to show the actual transregional circulation of knowledge and archives.

These chapters do not just intend to deconstruct the archives and show that they were an invention – which was probably true – but also aim at problematizing the postmodernist relationship between archives, power and historical dynamics. Archives reflect the architecture of power, as Jacques Derrida and Michel Foucault pointed out, yet by itself this architecture cannot be taken for granted.[33] If archives are a social and political construction, then so is the state, particularly the nation-state and the imperial state. It was precisely when (nineteenth–twentieth centuries) the building of the nation-state reached its peak that archive construction became a transnational, trans-imperial and global endeavour. Before and beyond this process, archives existed all over the world; this was the case in early modern and modern Eurasia, then, in the

---

[28] Ousmane Mbaye, 'Le Caom: un centre d'archives partagées?' *Afrique et Histoire* 7, no. 1 (2009): 291–9.
[29] Jean and John Comaroff, *Ethnography and the Historical Imagination* (Boulder, CO: Westview Press, 1992).
[30] Verne Harris, *National Archives of South Africa* (Pretoria: National Archives, 2000). Camille Lefebvre and M'hamed Oualdi, 'Remettre le colonial à sa place. Histoires enchevêtrées des débuts de la colonisation en Afrique de l'Ouest et au Maghreb', *Annales HSS* 72, no. 4 (2017): 937–43.
[31] Michèle Riot-Sarcey, 'Questionner l'histoire à rebrousse-poil', *Espace Temps* 82–3 (2003): 17–27; Françoise Blum, ed., *Genre de l'archive. Constitution et transmission des mémoires militantes* (Paris: Codhos éditions, 2017); Wenxian Zhang, 'Dang An: A Brief History of the Chinese Imperial Archives and Its Administration', *Journal of Archival Organization* 2, nos 1/2 (2004): 17–38; Meena Gautam, 'History of Archives and Archival Sciences from 1950 onwards Based on Indian Practices', *Atlanti* 23 (2013): 135–47.
[32] Alessandro Stanziani, *Les métamorphoses du travail contraint* (Paris: Presses de Sciences-Po, 2020).
[33] Michel Foucault, *L'archéologie du savoir* (Paris: Gallimard, 1969), English translation 2002.

twentieth century, all across the globe, well beyond the ideological tensions between communism and capitalism. In fact, this very tension was reflected in the organization itself of the archives across the two blocs, and, after 1945, in the Global South as well.[34]

In short, we need to understand not only how social actors are publicly presented in the archives ('fiction in the archives', as Zemon Davis nicely puts it),[35] but also how the encounter between people and archives is performed; social history *in* the archives and social history *of* the archives form a single bundle.[36] Where Western European States sought to build up their historical memory as issued from the French Revolution, the openly imitative attempt made in the USSR to legitimize the Revolution was at the same time more radical (creation of the archives of the Revolution) and less consistent with people's everyday lives. In its turn, decolonization was accompanied by a fight for the control of the colonial archives and the contested memories of colonialism. Yet, those claims did not exclude the rise of nationalism in newly independent countries and the still ongoing disputed validity of archival documents in both the Global South and North.

For this reason, I do not intend to limit myself to debates related to Ann Laura Stoler's work about the utility and truthfulness of colonial archives.[37] 'Against the grain' was the classic subaltern postcolonial criticism of archives: they speak only in the name of colonizers and therefore one must adapt and change them to give a voice to colonized people. Stoler argued that we may understand the multiple, sometimes contrasting, attitudes of colonizers when we read colonial archives and therefore try to extract the attitudes of colonized people as well ('along the grain').

This is indeed a crucial point – this book shares it – but I intend to add two further angles: first, we need to clarify how this debate about archives as the 'voice of power' (Foucault, Derrida, subaltern studies), or, conversely, as a 'synthesis' of multiple actors has oriented the reading of archives 'against' or 'with' the grain. This tension depends on the context and our question cannot be solved once and for all exclusively on epistemological grounds. In other words, we need to include archives themselves, and debates on them, in both hermeneutics and a contextual historical dimension. To this end, I study in detail three major moments in the history of archives: the French Revolution and its aftermath across the globe (the invention of national archives); the Bolshevik Revolution and its aftermath, in terms of archival organizations in Russia and its empire; the colonial archives of Western powers under and after colonial rule.

Second, and starting from this, I will also engage into a conversation much more material than the writing and reading documents: access to them. There were struggles

---

[34] Joan Schwartz and Terry Cook, 'Archives, Records, and Power: The Making of Modern Memory', *Archival Science* 2 (2002): 1–19; Thomas Richards, *The Imperial Archive: Knowledge and the Fantasy of Empire* (London and New York: Verso, 1993); Ann Laura Stoler, 'Colonial Archives and the Art of Governance', *Archival Science* 2 (2002): 87–109.

[35] Natalie Zemon Davis, *Fiction in the Archives* (Stanford: Stanford University Press, 1990); Roberto Gonzalez Echevarria, *Myth and Archive: A Theory of Latin American Narrative* (Cambridge: Cambridge University Press, 1990); Terry Cook, 'Fashionable Nonsense or Professional Rebirth: Postmodernism and the Practice of Archives', *Archiv* 51 (2001): 14–35.

[36] Stoler, *Along the Archival Grain*; Lynette Russell, 'Indigenous Knowledge and Archives: Accessing Hidden History and Understandings', *Australian Academic and Research Libraries*, 36, 2 (2013): 161–71.

[37] Stoler, *Along the Archival Grain*.

and eventually negotiations about archival documents themselves, their access and location: who controlled them, how did they move between the mainland and the colonies, who was in charge of these negotiations? Taken together, the histories of archival construction in the age of modern and then contemporary revolutions and decolonization lead us to examine in detail the construction of sources as a social act and a social fact.

The social life of data

Data and sources are usually contrasted: humanities scholars consider data to be a construct and often take archives for granted, while social scientists are sceptical about the 'objectivity of the archives'.[38] Quite conversely, Ann Laura Stoler, like Ginzburg before her, points out, without developing the case, the related discussions on archives and data, and more generally on the cognitive status of 'evidence' since the seventeenth century.[39] This book takes this line of reasoning further and shows that, apart from major differences, despite the tensions between social sciences and the humanities in this respect, it is the similarities between sources and data as historical artefacts that deserve attention.[40]

Like researchers in the 'hard' sciences, economists, social historians and some sociologists make significant use of data. But what exactly are data? And where did we get the idea that quantities were more reliable for producing history than discursive documents?

As I did for sources, my aim with data is not just to deconstruct them and show that they are an 'invention', but to highlight the fact that they always are unequally co-produced (by investigators, social actors and sometimes bureaucrats) while impacting social dynamics. Statistics on employment strongly influence the orientations of the government and the main social actors. Of course, many histories of statistics are available;[41] they have extensively contributed to the history of our knowledge of the historical and social construction of data in relation with broader social dynamics

---

[38] Theodor Porter, *The Rise of Statistical Thinking, 1820–1900* (Princeton: Princeton University Press, 1986); Theodor Porter, *Trust in Numbers: The Pursuit of Objectivity in Science and Public Life* (Princeton: Princeton University Press, 1995); Alain Desrosières, *La politique des grands nombres* (Paris: La découverte, 1993).

[39] Stoler, *Along the Archival Grain*; Ginzburg, *Clues, Myths*.

[40] On the contested notion of evidence, see among others, Simon Schaffer, 'Self Evidence', *Critical Inquiry* 18, no. 2 (1992): 327–62; William Roche, 'Evidence of Evidence Is Evidence under Screening-Off', *Episteme* 11, no. 1 (2014): 119–24; Alex Stein, *Foundations of Evidence Law* (Oxford: Oxford University Press, 2005); Andrew Bell, John Swenson-Wright and Karin Tybjerg, eds, *Evidence* (Cambridge: Cambridge University Press, 2008); Peter Murphy, ed, *Evidence, Proof and Facts: A Book of Sources* (New York: Oxford University Press, 2003); William Twining, *Rethinking Evidence. Exploratory Essays* (Cambridge: Cambridge University Press, 1994).

[41] Mary Poovey, *A History of the Modern Fact. Problems of Knowledge in the Sciences of Wealth and Society* (Chicago: University of Chicago Press, 1998); Steinmetz, *The Politics*; Porter, *The Rise of Statistical Thinking*; Judy L. Klein, *Statistical Visions in Time: A History of Time Series Analysis, 1662–1938* (Cambridge: Cambridge University Press, 1997); Michael Zakim, 'Producing Capitalism: The Clerk at Work', in *Capitalism Takes Command: The Social Transformation of Nineteenth-Century America*, edited by Michael Zakim and Gary John Kornblith (Chicago and London: The University of Chicago Press, 2012), 223–47.

and the emergence and transformation of capitalism in particular.[42] The relationship between statistics, social differentiation and development is particularly relevant in the many histories of GDP published in recent years.[43] The role of the state in the emergence of modern statistics has been emphasized.[44] Moreover, histories of statistics outside the Western world have recently been produced.[45]

Compared to much of this valuable scholarship, my aim here is twofold: on the one hand, I intend to infringe national and area studies boundaries and discuss instead the connections and disconnections in statistical tools and inquiries between different areas. Yet, this does not mean investigating statistics on a world scale. As Ken Pomeranz stated several years ago, global history does not necessarily require including the entire

---

[42] Jonathan Levy, *Freaks of Fortune: The Emerging World of Capitalism and Risk in America* (Cambridge, MA: Harvard University Press, 2014); Daniel B. Bouk, *How Our Days Became Numbered: Risk and the Rise of the Statistical Individual* (Chicago and London: The University of Chicago Press, 2015); Eli Cook, *The Pricing of Progress: Economic Indicators and the Capitalization of American Life* (Cambridge, MA: Harvard University Press, 2017); Michael Ralph, 'Value of Life: Insurance, Slavery, and Expertise', in Sven Beckert and Christine Desan, eds, *American Capitalism: New Histories* (New York: Columbia University Press, 2018), 257–81; William Deringer, *Calculated Values: Finance, Politics, and the Quantitative Age* (Cambridge: London: Harvard University Press, 2018), esp. 227–62; William Deringer, 'Compound Interest Corrected: The Imaginative Mathematics of the Financial Future in Early Modern England', *Osiris* 33, no. 1 (October 2018): 109–29; Jens Beckert, *Imagined Futures: Fictional Expectations and Capitalist Dynamics* (Cambridge, MA: Harvard University Press, 2016); Jill Lepore, *If Then: How the Simulmatics Corporation Invented the Future* (New York: Liveright, 2020).

[43] Diane Coyle, *GDP: A Brief but Affectionate History* (Princeton: Princeton University Press, 2014); Joseph Stiglitz, Amartya Sen and Jean-Paul Fitoussi, *Mismeasuring Our Lives: Why GDP Doesn't Add Up* (New York: New Press, 2010); Dirk Philipsen, *The Little Big Number: How GDP Came to Rule the World and What to Do about It* (Princeton: Princeton University Press, 2015); Ehsan Masood, *The Great Invention: The Story of GDP and the Making and Unmaking of the Modern World* (New York: Pegasus Books, 2016); Phillip Lepenies, *The Power of a Single Number: A Political History of GDP* (New York: Columbia University Press, 2016); Zachary Karabell, *The Leading Indicators: A Short History of the Numbers That Rule the World* (New York: Simon & Schuster, 2014); Robert Fogel, Enid Fogel, Marc Guglielmo and Nathaniel Grotte, *Political Arithmetic: Simon Kuznets and the Empirical Tradition in Economics* (Chicago: University of Chicago Press, 2013).

[44] Judy L. Klein and Mary S. Morgan, eds, *The Age of Economic Measurement* (Durham, NC: Duke University Press, 2001); Paul Studenski, *The Income of Nations, Part One: History* (New York: New York University Press, 1958); Mary O. Furner and Barry Supple, eds, *The State and Economic Knowledge: The American and British Experiences* (Cambridge: Cambridge University Press, 1990); Eric Brian, *La mesure de l'État* (Paris: Albin Michel, 1996); Adam Tooze, *Statistics and the German State, 1900–1945* (Cambridge: Cambridge University Press, 2001).

[45] Several histories of statistics outside Western Europe have been published during last two decades: Arunabh Ghosh, *Making It Count: Statistics and Statecraft in the Early Republic of China* (Princeton: Princeton University Press, 2020); Andrea Bréard, *Reform, Bureaucratic Expansion and Production of Numbers: Statistics in Early Twentieth Century China*, Habilitationsschrift (Berlin: Technische Universität Berlin, 2008); Alain Blum and Martine Mespoulet, *L'anarchie bureaucratique. Statistique et pouvoir sous Staline* (Paris: La découverte, 2003); Morgane Labbé, *La Nationalité, une histoire de chiffres. Politique et statistiques en Europe centrale (1848–1919)* (Paris: Presses de SciencesPo, 2019); Hernán Otero, 'Socio-History of Statistics on Latin America. A Review', *Histoire et mesure* 33, no. 2 (2018): 13–32; Nelson Senra, *História das Estatísticas Brasileiras: 1822–2002*, 4 vols (Rio de Janeiro: IBGE, 2006–9); Jorge Pantaleon, *Una nación a medida. Creencia económica y estadística en la Argentina (1918–1952)* (Buenos Aires: Ediciones al Margen, 2009); Jean-Pierre Beaud and Cláudia Damasceno Fonseca, 'Le chiffre et la carte. Pratiques statistiques et cartographiques en Amérique latine (du milieu du XVIII e au milieu du XX e siècle)', *Histoire & Mesure* 32, no. 1 (2017): 3–8; J. K. Ghosh, P. Maiti, Talluri Rao and B. K. Sinha, 'Evolution of Statistics in India', *International Statistics Review* 67, no. 1 (2007): 13–34.

globe, but problematizing connections, dependences and dynamics, starting from specific sites.[46] Second, and starting from this, I will escape from the division between state and civil society so widespread in histories of statistics; instead, I will present the fragmentation of statistical bureaucracies while seeking to identify accurately what forms of 'voice' different social actors had, in specific contexts, when facing data collectors. As in other parts of this book, examples chosen to discuss the historical significance of data mostly come from the long nineteenth century (*c*. 1750–1914). This is because, during this period, data for the first time became a political tool and a scientific object of debate. Social dynamics were investigated through the lens of data on social poverty, impact of climate change, health, demography, etc. Newly emerging capitalism in the West, urbanization, imperial and colonial construction, faith in science, including the rationalization of society itself, were all related, and people found in presumably 'objective data' a tool for knowing and taking action.[47] The emergence of the modern state and society, the shapes capitalism took, all were clearly expressed in 'data' and embedded in data. However, beyond those general trends, quantification did not take the same shapes and social meaning in all contexts according to the object of measurement. In order to exemplify this process, we therefore need to choose appropriate fields. Which ones?

In Chapter 3 I will start with social enquiries in the nineteenth century; they expressed the ambition of social quantification but also the less-known history of the transfer of these tools and categories across countries. What happened when social statistics and methodologies conceived in France, Britain or Germany were used to study Russia or China?

Debates on social differentiation in the countryside – the end of the peasantry – played a crucial role in Russia and strongly influenced political programmes and concrete policies. Several connected problems arose: if the notions of property, peasants and workers were easy to criticize – and they were when extended to Russia (or India or Africa) – the question was more complicated for statistical tools themselves. Were probability or correlation or statistical monographs suited to 'exotic' contexts, where, for example, statistical infrastructures (bureaus, intermediaries, qualified personnel) were lacking and the population to be surveyed could not complete questionnaires?

Yet, in many investigations since the nineteenth century onwards, in particular in agrarian and protoindustrial societies (i.e. in most of the world until the late twentieth century, in Western Europe itself until the second half of the nineteenth century), the social differentiation and statistics of well-being were related not just to markets and the economy but also to the environment. Attempts to quantitatively investigate the impact of climatic variations in order to direct public policies led to two major fields of research: weather forecasting and future harvests. I will discuss how Russian economists sought to imitate the US statistical bureau in predicting future harvests. This required an effort to overcome the peasants' presumed ignorance or, worse, deception. Of course, similar efforts took place elsewhere, in British India in particular, where colonial authorities, economists and statisticians sought to identify criteria for

---

[46] See his introduction to *The Great Divergence* (Princeton: Princeton University Press, 2000).
[47] Klein and Morgan, *The Age of Statistical Measurement*; Brian, *La mesure*; Porter, *The Rise*.

predicting future harvests and reducing the risk of famine.[48] To that end, more accurate weather forecasts were required (see Chapter 4). So-called 'social statistics' therefore sought to interact with a field 'in progress', weather forecasting.

The difficult acceptance of weather forecasting in Europe (tension between astrology and astronomy, religion, science and popular beliefs)[49] was entangled with the even more difficult recognition from a Western perspective of 'non-European' knowledge of weather, in particular maritime weather.[50] In this respect, the most difficult site which Western maritime knowledge of the time had to face was the Indian Ocean; the monsoons and local conditions of navigations made essential maritime and weather knowledge as developed in Europe and the across the Atlantic quite inappropriate. How did encounters and eventual transfers of knowledge take place? By whom? And, above all, which kind of data were produced in this context? Before any interpretation was done, data and information were co-produced by all these actors. This very same information is still the source of discussions between historians, scientists and social scientists nowadays, for example on whether the number of cyclones in the Indian Ocean was already increasing due to climate change in the nineteenth century or only afterward or not at all. Together, the historical construction of data on society, environment and food provides the setting in which we may investigate the cult of data and its criticism still nowadays.

Fragments of social worlds

One piece of our puzzle is still missing: after discussing sources and data, archives and statistics, we need to consider the identification of the social actors themselves. From the mid-1960s on, the so-called 'social turn' was presented as a new trend in historiography, as opposed to conventional history made up of influential persons

---

[48] Arap Maharatna, *The Demography of Famine* (Delhi: Oxford University Press, 1996); Mike Davis, *Late Victorian Holocausts* (London: Verso, 2000).

[49] Katharine Anderson, *Predicting the Weather: Victorians and the Science of Meteorology* (Chicago: University of Chicago Press, 2005); Fabien Locher, *Le savant et la tempête. Étudier l'atmosphère et prévoir le temps au XIXe siècle* (Rennes: Presses Universitaires de Rennes, 2008); Gwyn Campbell, ed., *Bondage and the Environment in the Indian Ocean World* (New York: Palgrave, 2018).

[50] T. N. Krishnamurti, Lidia Stefanova and Vasubandhu Misra, eds, *Tropical Meteorology: An Introduction* (New York: Springer, 2013); Grain Colten, *Perilous Place, Powerful Storms: Hurricane Protection in Coastal Louisiana* (Jackson: University Press of Mississippi, 2009); Kerry Emmanuel, *Divine Wind: The History and Science of Hurricanes* (Oxford: Oxford University Press, 2005); Stuart Schwartz, *Sea of Storms: A History of Hurricanes in the Greater Caribbean from Columbus to Katrina* (Princeton: Princeton University Press, 2015); Eleonora Rohland, *Changes in the Air* (New York: Berghahn, 2018); James Beattie, Emily O'Gorman and Matthew Henry, *Climate, Science, and Colonization: Histories from Australia and New Zealand* (Basingstoke: Palgrave Macmillan, 2014); Fiona Williamson, 'Weathering the Empire: Meteorological Research in the Early British Straits Settlements', *The British Journal for the History of Science* 48, no. 3 (2015): 475–92; Martin Mahony, 'For an Empire of "all Types of Climate": Meteorology as an Imperial Science', *Journal of Historical Geography* 51 (2016): 29–39; Angelo Matteo Caglioti, 'Meteorological Imperialism. Climate Science, Environment, and Empire in Liberal and Fascist Italy (1870–1940)' (PhD diss., University of California, Berkeley, 2017).

(mostly men), elites and ideas. E. P. Thompson, Hobsbawm and Sewell, among others, advocated this approach and sought to retrospectively present it as a major turn.[51] Yet, at the end of the 1980s another 'turn' emerged, the postmodernist and cultural turn which accused the social turn of essentializing society as a whole and social actors/classes in particular (the proletarian, the peasant, the capitalist) without considering the fact that all were cultural constructs. Both these approaches have been recently faced with the global turn, accusing previous historiography of Eurocentrism.[52] Chakrabarty was among the first who stressed the difficulties of exporting to non-European areas, namely India, such categories as working class, capital and capitalism.[53] All these approaches overlook the fact that similar discussions had been taking place since the eighteenth century[54] when the very identification of history and memory, its political and social role were at the core of intellectual and political debates.[55] The many ways of conceiving of the history of peasants, slaves, labouring classes, the bourgeoisie and the nobility, subaltern and colonized people have oriented political and intellectual debates as well as social tensions for the last three centuries. Part III will discuss how social actors (a slave, a worker, a capitalist, a peasant, a consumer) have been identified since the eighteenth century onwards. Just as for sources and data, I do not intend to claim any top-down 'invention' of social actors, but rather their co-identification at the intersection of multiple spheres and worlds. European thinkers and actors progressively identified 'peasants', 'capitalists', 'estate owners', 'consumers', 'workers' and 'proletarians'. These constructions were social and intellectual at the same time, always problematic in Europe itself and even more outside it. I intend to trace the history of some of these categories, to begin with the well-known opposition between status and contract societies (Chapter 5). This tension was and still is currently used to contrast old regime and 'modern' societies, colonial and mainland societies, freedom and un-freedom. As such, the status/contract dichotomy is prior to other social classifications. I intend to unpack this dichotomy focusing on its original inventor, Henry Sumner Maine. He wrote extensively on this point in relation to two main questions: the tension between ancient (in particular Indian) and modern (British) societies, on the one hand, and the tension between liberal societies and the new welfare state, on the other hand. Then I will show how in practice these categories were much more blurred than Maine suggested: some workers in Britain were in fact servants and peasant workers,

---

[51] Charles Tilly, 'Three Visions of History and Theory', *History and Theory* 46 (2007): 299–307; Theda Skocpol, *Visions and Method in Historical Sociology* (Cambridge: Cambridge University Press, 1985); Peter Burke, *History and Social Theory* (Ithaca: Cornell University Press, 1992); William Sewell, *Logics of History: Social Theory and Social Transformation* (Chicago: University of Chicago Press, 2005). Also William Sewell, 'The Political Unconscious of Social and Cultural History, or, Confessions of a Previous Quantitative Historian', in Steinmetz, *The Politics of Method*: 173–206; George Steinmetz, *Sociology and Empire* (Durham, NC and London: Duke University Press, 2013).
[52] Stanziani, *Les entrelacements du monde*.
[53] Dipesh Chakrabarty, *Provincializing Europe* (Princeton: Princeton University Press, 2000).
[54] Bryan Palmer, *Descent into Discourse: The Reification of Language and the Writing of Social History* (Philadelphia: Temple University Press, 1990); Andrew Abbott, *Chaos of Disciplines* (Chicago: The University of Chicago Press, 2001); Sewell, *Logics of History*.
[55] Iggers, Wang, Mukherjee, *A Global History of Modern Historiographies*; *The Oxford History of Historical Writing*, 5 vols (Oxford: Oxford University Press, 2011–15).

while emancipated slaves and new immigrants in India faced the problem of being fully recognized as 'free people'. The tension between legal status and social condition originated in this context and had huge implications in terms of exclusion, integration and social inequalities in both Britain and India and, later, in the construction of the welfare state. Nowadays, the tension between status and contract is still at the very core of debates on the welfare state, neoliberalism and capitalism all around the globe.

Most contemporary social and political theories, approaches and ideologies are dependent on these questions. Conventional approaches in the historiography provided an ideal definition of slaves, serfs and wage earners. Thus, slavery and serfdom are defined by the lack of legal rights allotted to slaves and serfs, their hereditary statute, the master's right of ownership and the coercive extraction of surplus. The major identified difference is that, unlike slaves, serfs were attached to the land.[56] Yet, clear-cut distinctions may be analytically useful, but they are not necessarily confirmed by an empirical analysis of the categories and practices. In recent decades, a new historiography in global labour history radically shifted this approach and stressed instead the uncertain boundaries between free and unfree labour in many contexts.[57] But, if this is so, then what about the notion of class? Are there still 'workers' and proletarians or rather peasant workers? Alternatively, if slaves cannot be reduced to chattel slavery on the western shores of the Atlantic, then is there still room for a clear distinction between bonded people, slaves and workers? It is symptomatic and sometimes paradoxical to see cultural relativism espoused both by academics critical of 'imperialism', 'colonialism' and now globalization and by local managers and multinational companies that exploit child labour.

As a result, the question has now become whether or not a given form of dependence, bondage, etc., found in a particular society in Africa, Asia, the Indian Ocean or the Americas could be considered 'slavery'. If the answer is yes, then by implication slavery existed before and independently of colonialism; conversely, if the answer is no, it means that these forms of dependence and bondage were specific to a particular place and 'imperialist' and revisionist culture would like to call them 'slavery' to minimize the West's 'debt' to the Third World. As already done in previous chapters and, on this particular topic, in my previous work, I do not take sides in favour of one or the other 'general' definition of labour and forced labour, but rather set the boundary line between free labour and forced labour in specific historical and institutional contexts and explain why, in a given context, this line was conceived and put into practice in one way rather than another. Instead of attempting to establish the moment when 'free labour' and 'civilization' emerged, or conversely, stigmatizing the continuation of the 'guild tradition' or even of latent forms of slavery, I want to

---

[56] For example, Michael Bush, ed., *Serfdom and Slavery: Studies in Legal Bondage* (Manchester: Manchester University Press, 1996), in particular 'Introduction' and Stanley Engerman, 'Slavery, Serfdom and Other Forms of Coerced Labour: Similarities and Differences': 18–41.

[57] Tom Brass and Marcel van der Linden, eds, *Free and Unfree Labour: The Debate Continues* (Berne: Peter Lang, 1997); Andreas Eckert, ed., *Global Histories of Work* (Oldenburg: De Gruyter, 2016); Leo Lucassen, 'Working Together: New Directions in Global Labour History', *Journal of Global History* 11, no. 1 (2016): 66–87; Sabyasachi Bhattacharya, ed., *Towards a New History of Work* (Delhi: Tulika Book, 2014).

grasp the dynamics at work in certain historical forms of labour, starting from the historically situated tension between freedom and constraint.

I will then move to peasants (Chapter 6). Often presumed to be immobile actors and therefore at the margins of global history nowadays, they were at the very core of social, political and anthropological investigation over centuries. I will present a global intellectual and social history of peasantry: first, the identification and definitions of peasants at different times and places, then the pragmatic, fundamental, multiple-occupation life of these actors who at the same time claimed to have only a single occupation as 'pure peasant'. With this definition, they sometimes met intellectual and political observers who, for somewhat different reasons, also stressed the importance of an ideal peasant who had to be defended or, on the contrary, was swept away by modernity. I will conclude with the return of imagined peasants today in the anti-globalist and environmentalist discourse.

The last chapter (7) of this section is about consumption and the world of goods. Where does the 'consumer' as an actor – different from the purchaser and from the worker – come from? How was this notion constructed, in which framework, by whom and with what consequences?

Since the 1990s, not only liberal but also social democrat experts and scholars stressed 'the end of the proletarian' and the rise of a 'consumer's republic'.[58] I will trace the slow emergence of the 'consumer' in social practices and theories, in particular at the turn of the nineteenth and twentieth centuries; this chapter will discuss the evolution of the tension between scarcity and opulence, and relate it to the evolution of social differentiation and global capitalism. At the same time, this is also a critique of the modernization and globalization paradigms in food history, as circular and ready-made explanations which actually do not explain much.

Explanations, schemes and models of social dynamics

Part IV returns to notions and 'models' of social historical dynamics. It is not by chance that this section is the final one: in usual approaches to social history and social investigations, the 'model' or general referential scheme is introduced at the very beginning, to set the intellectual and explanatory framework. Here, rather, the relevant methodological question is: how do we look at major ideas and patterns for society and its history after tracing the historically situated features of archives, data and social actors? If empirical observation and social identities are not just 'constructed' but are intimately linked to social action, how do we evaluate Marx and Weber's theories? Are they the panacea to the instability and relativity of empirical observations or do they themselves belong to the same joint action of social actors?

Obviously, my purpose is not to present a comprehensive history of these approaches, which would take an encyclopaedia,[59] nor is my aim to search for the 'real Marx' or 'real

---

[58] Elizabeth Cohen, *A Consumers' Republic* (New York: Knopf, 2003).
[59] The huge number of encyclopaedias of social sciences, in their multiple editions, as they cumulated since the 1920s, testify to the importance and complexity of these questions.

Weber' or 'real Voltaire'. My starting point here is that most of the reflections on societies and history those authors produced aspired to be 'universal', and yet their meaning needs to be investigated. If one must identify a shared ambition for these authors, it is not just their explanation of what 'society' is, but their quest for universality. This last must be found not in human behaviour itself, but in the presumed universal 'laws' orienting humankind. How were multiplicity and uniqueness reconciled into theories and visions which, even now, relentlessly surprise us in their overwhelming ambition, bright rhetoric and yet incredible falsehood, but survive in this same 'modernity' they contributed to identify? Is this failure related to Eurocentrism, as Chakrabarty and many others have stressed? And/or to a more fundamental weakness in their 'centrism' in explaining global and local historical dynamics?

For example, the main authors of the European Enlightenment were oriented by multiple connections between European and non-European worlds. Yet, this attitude fell apart at the moment when some of these authors investigate slavery, serfdom and, from this, the meaning and practices of freedom (Chapter 8). This orientation consolidated in the nineteenth century when both liberal and socialist, then Marxist, explanatory schemes of social dynamics diffused. This is a different history from Chakrabarty's 'Two Histories of Capital'. My aim is not to highlight the gap between, say, Marx's categories and non-European contexts,[60] but rather to show the mutual influences between the German, British, French, Russian and Indian contexts in shaping Marx's thought and, inversely, its reception, with particular attention paid to Russia. All the same, Weberian-style comparatism still appears as another European approach which spread all around the world in social sciences. Many historians have criticized this approach as ahistorical.[61] According to this view, the comparison is artificially set up by the observer, but ignored by the actors themselves. This is the long-standing debate between so-called emic and etic approaches to history[62] which added a further dimension to it when non-European areas were concerned. Yet, this approach produced radically heterogeneous approaches, in terms of Eurocentrism, notions of modernity and society. Russian authors (the same can be said for many Indian, Chinese, Latin American and even French and British authors, etc.), observers and politicians have made use of comparison to support their arguments. In particular, the worldwide success of Weberian style of comparison (Chapter 9) during the Cold War was a by-product of the emigration of economists and intellectuals from Central and

---

[60] Said, followed by several subaltern studies' authors, criticized Marx along this line.
[61] Among others, Sanjay Subrahmanyam, 'Du Tage au Gange au XVIe siècle. Une conjoncture millénariste à l'échelle eurasiatique', *Annales. Histoire, Sciences Sociales* (2001): 51–84; 'Connected Histories: Notes towards a Reconfiguration of Early Modern Eurasia', *Modern Asian Studies* 31, no. 3 (1997): 735–62; Michael Werner and Bénédicte Zimmermann, eds, *De la comparaison à l'histoire croisée* (Paris: Seuil, 2004); Michel Espagne, 'Sur les limites du comparatisme en histoire culturelle', *Genèse* 17, no. 1 (1994): 112–21; François Dossé, *La marche des idées: histoire des intellectuels, histoire intellectuelle* (Paris: La découverte 2003); Romain Bertrand, *L'histoire à parts égales* (Paris: Seuil: 2011).
[62] Simona Cerutti and Isabelle Grangaud, 'Sources and Contextualization: Comparing Eighteenth Century North-Africa and Western European Institutions', *Comparative Studies in Society and History* 59, no. 1 (2017): 5–33; Heinz-Gerhard Haupt and Jürgen Kocka, *Comparative and Transnational History* (New York: Berghahn, 2009).

Eastern Europe. Not only did authors move beyond the Berlin Wall and the Cold War divide, but so did their approaches. The success of comparisons based upon ideal types was widespread and adapted in Africa, Asia and Latin America. Quite paradoxically, the debate on the 'great divergence', while denouncing Weber, still preserves his main categories (the town, the role of market, investment, the state in the process of modernization) while radically reversing his conclusion (in particular Europe as a leader and Asia as a follower).

Yet unlike German-based comparisons, other models of social history developed in France, mostly related to Durkheim. If class struggle or the Enlightenment are far from being universal notions to explain social dynamics, is solidarity a better one? Unlike Marx's class struggle or liberal individualism, Durkheim and historians under his influence, from Bloch to Braudel, place solidarity at the very core of their reflections. This particular political philosophy of society went hand in hand with an epistemological project seeking a unified vision of the social sciences.[63] During the second half of the twentieth century, these debates fragmented and produced some unexpected outcomes such as microhistory, on one hand, and the social turn, on the other. These perspectives deserve close examination: what kind of interplay with non-European worlds – if any – did authors like Durkheim, Bloch or Braudel experience?

The identification of capitalism, the very notion of Europe, changes and continuities, revolutions and structures in history were among the main intellectual and political issues during those years. The Annales School and the social turn in Britain sought to answer these questions by putting the focus on Europe: the Mediterranean, the French and British Revolutions and the Industrial Revolution. Even Braudel's world systems, later reformulated by Wallerstein, imagined a centre and a periphery.

Yet, this approach was challenged from the outset by another, mostly related to anthropology. In particular, from the 1920s on, Mauss, Malinowski, Polanyi and many others studied forms of economic rationality and values in non-Western societies not so much to explain their 'backwardness', but, quite the contrary, to stress the contested and debatable 'mentality' of Western capitalism as it was affirmed in mainstream economic analysis.[64] Meanwhile, hybridity and unilinear historical development was at the very core of several strands in anthropology and sociology; both went beyond static comparison as well as classical 'global' structuralist perspectives.[65] This approach provided a valuable tool for understanding social historical dynamics which still today produces many related although different outcomes (connected history, trans-imperial sociology, etc.). Economic anthropology in particular is crucial for inserting economic behaviours into a social and historical dimension, transcending the very ideal of 'progress' and modernization, as well as functionalist and structuralist interpretations of history. Tensions between, say, economic and anthropological perspectives on

---

[63] Fernand Braudel, *La Méditerranée et le monde méditerranéen à l'époque de Philippe II* (Paris: Flammarion, 1949).
[64] Steinmetz, *Sociology and Empire*.
[65] Steinmetz, *The Politics of Method*.

value and exchange would be hard to understand without inserting them into global structural dynamics: decolonization and the fate of newly independent countries, the international economic order and its main institutions, and the globalization of the last few decades. These dynamics have inspired and fed methodological debates while, conversely, the way anthropologists and economists identify 'economic rationalities' has strongly influenced politics and economic policies in both the Global South and North, and the global order itself.

Part One

What is a source? Archives, memory and contested contextualities

The opposition between comparison and connection – the first is supposedly subjective, the second objective and source-based – undermines *l'histoire croisée* and connected history in general. The connections found in archives are just as subjective as the comparisons made by an historian. Archives and documents are never ready made, lying in wait of discovery; they are produced first by the historical actors in administrations or companies that originally provided them, then by the archivists who classified them and finally by historians who select a given document and present it in an equally individual manner. I argue that this debate must be put into appropriate historical context in order to understand who associates archives and truth, why and with which outcomes, and which actors, by contrast, claim 'invention in the archives'. I will focus on the three main moments that mostly contributed to shape the role and meaning of archives in the modern and contemporary world: the French Revolution, the invention of 'national archives' and their diffusion worldwide in the nineteenth century; then the Soviet Revolution, the new meaning of archives and its impact on twentieth-century major debates on totalitarianism and 'truth'. Third, I will discuss the origin and transmutation of colonial archives before, during and after decolonization. As explained in the Introduction, for each part, and for the history of archives as a whole, huge bibliographies are available. I do not intend to add another list to those histories, but instead seek to identify long and short trends, local and global dynamics in the social history of archives as a contested place of memory and history writing.

1

Revolutionary archives

During recent years, new approaches put the revolutionary moment of the turn of the eighteenth and nineteenth centuries into a global perspective.[1] The main attempt consisted in escaping from national and Eurocentric vision of revolutions; thus, the American and the French Revolutions are presented as the consequence and the origin of global economic, political and social transformations of the world, while revolutions in Saint-Domingue, India or Latin America responded to local as well as to global factors.[2] If this is so, then the historical notion of revolution itself must be put under scrutiny as well. Here, the main reference is, of course, Koselleck's analysis.[3] The main lines of this study are well known: echoing Hannah Arendt,[4] Koselleck argued that the notion of revolution moved from astronomy (the Copernican revolution) to politics and history. The shift from cyclical to linear time in the notion of revolution was expressed by Hobbes (among the others) in the 1640s, then again by Locke forty years later. In both cases it was associated with the restoration of the crown.[5] However, in order to make this evolution possible, in political terms, the qualification of conflicts had to be moved from civil war (and the restoration) to revolution. As such, cyclical time was replaced by unilineal time and progress.[6] Time as expecting horizon was succeeded by time as return. As such, revolution became an irreversible shift, a radical

---

[1] Suzanne Desan, Lynn Hunt and William Max Nelson, eds, *The French Revolution in Global Perspective* (Ithaca and London: Cornell University Press, 2013); David Armitage and Sanjay Subrahmanyam, eds, *The Age of Revolutions in Global Context, c. 1760-1840* (New York: Palgrave Macmillan, 2010).

[2] Jeremy Adelman, *Sovereignty and Revolution in the Iberian Atlantic* (Princeton: Princeton University Press, 2006); D. A. Brading, *The First America: The Spanish Monarchy, Creole Patriots and the Liberal State, 1492-1867* (Cambridge: Cambridge University Press, 1991).

[3] Reinhart Koselleck, *Futures Past: On the Semantics of Historical Time* (Cambridge, MA: MIT Press, 1985; orig. Germany, 1979). Chapter on revolution originally published, not by chance, after 1968: *Zeitschrift für die Einheit der Wissenschaften im Zusammenhang ihrer Begriffsbildungen und Forschungsmethoden Stud Gen (Berl).* 22, no. 8 (1969): 825–38.

[4] Hannah Arendt, *On Revolution* (New York: Viking Press, 1963).

[5] Reinhart Koselleck, 'Revolution ', in *Geschichtliche Grudbegriffe: Historisches Lexicon zur Politisch-Sozialen Sprache in Deutschland*, edited by Otto Brunner, Werner Conze and Reinhart Koselleck, 9 vols (Stuttgart: Ernst Klett Verlag, 1972–90), vol. 4: 653–788.

[6] On this, see Alexandre Escudier, 'Temporalisation et modernité politique: penser avec Koselleck', *Annales HSS* 64, no. 6 (2009): 1269–301.

change in society and politics. This shift expressed the change from an *ancien régime* society based on estates to a bourgeois society.[7]

This approach strongly influenced historians in their investigation of the shifting perception and organization of time, not only in intellectual but also in social and economic history.[8] These interpretations preserved the breaking impact of the Enlightenment and the Industrial Revolution and related the organization of time to that of the new society.

However, more recently, several authors have criticized this interpretation; some, like David Armitage, empirically contested Koselleck's argument by arguing that the idea of revolution as a change has been widespread since antiquity, and therefore the building of the British Empire expressed less the tension between restoration and revolution than a coexistence of multiple forces over the long run.[9] This approach found a broader support in a recent edited book in which several authors stressed the coexistence of the two meanings of the revolution in Britain over the longer term.[10]

The strength of this work consists in its effort to escape from historical determinism and from the clear-cut opposition between the history of ideas and the social-economic history of the revolution. Its main limitations are located in the lack of global synchronic connections and the quick dismissal of any structural explanation of the revolutions.

Along a more general perspective, François Hartog argued that since the turn of the eighteenth and nineteenth centuries the obsession with the present coexisted and, to a given extent, overburdened Koselleck's future-past in the social construction of (historical) time.[11]

Anthropologists also advanced different orientations from Koselleck:[12] on the one hand, structuralist perceptions of time and Braudelian *longue durée* focused on continuities in culture, politics and society. On the other hand, Geertz and several other anthropologists insisted (like Armitage) on the multiplicity of time perceptions in the same society and the same temporal space.[13]

In the following pages, I would like to pursue this conversation along the following lines:

1. Were perceptions and practices of the revolution in the seventeenth and eighteenth centuries a purely German, French, Anglo-Saxon affair? Or, in other words, how Eurocentric were the aforementioned approaches to revolution and time?

---

[7] For further interpretations of Koselleck, see the excellent synthesis by Willibald Steinmetz, 'Nachruf auf Reinhart Koselleck (1923–2006)', *Geschichte und Gesellschaft*, 32–3 (2006): 412–32; Willibald Steinmetz, Michael Freeden and Javier Fernandez-Sebastian, eds, *Conceptual History in the European Space* (New York and Oxford: Berghahn, 2017).

[8] Witold Kula, *Les mesures et les hommes* (Paris: EHESS, 1985); E. P. Thompson, 'Time, Work Discipline, and Industrial Capitalism', *Past & Present* 38 (1967): 56–97.

[9] Keith Michael Baker and Dan Edelstein, eds, *Scripting Revolution. A Historical Approach to Comparative Study of Revolution* (Stanford: Stanford University Press, 2015). Also, David Armitage, *The Ideological Origins of the British Empire* (Cambridge: Cambridge University Press, 2000).

[10] Baker and Edelstein, *Scripting Revolutions*.

[11] François Hartog, *Régimes d'historicité* (Paris: Seuil, 2003).

[12] Johannes Fabian, *Time and the Others: How Anthropology Makes Its Object* (New York: Columbia University Press, 1983).

[13] Clifford Geertz, *Local Knowledge* (London: Basic Books, 1985).

I will show that the identification of the notion and practices of the revolution were not just a Western and transatlantic, but a global, affair.
2. Can we still hold that the notion of revolution moved from cosmology to society and politics?

   I will argue that the answer is not so clear, and that not only in Asia but also in the 'West' this transition persisted over time. However, unlike Armitage's argument, I will put this persistence into a Euro-Asiatic space related to history writing and the changing meaning of 'historical truthfulness'.
3. Was the notion and practice of the revolution related to the raise and transmutation of the modern (nation) state?

   In fact, the revolutionary momentum was the basis of not only political and social transmutations, but was also a major shift in history writing itself: revolutions created the modern notion of archives, in which the construction of collective memory was and still is crucial. The French Revolution seized all the documents and classified them, separating pre-revolutionary and post-revolutionary files. The revolutionary break was in the archives themselves, which were at the same time acquiring the status of 'primary source' as opposed to other (private) sources, myths and oral sources. This process was globalized and most countries around the world adopted this same scheme: national independencies had to be certified in the archives starting with the classification of documents. The Bolshevik Revolution, as we will see, marked the apogee of this process, in which fiction in the archives, to reiterate Natalie Zemon Davis's celebrated expression, took a state dimension.
4. How do we connect the revolution of the archives and the revolution in the archives?

   In other words, although the French and Bolshevik Revolutions and later decolonization greatly contributed to creating the modern archive, they also produced documents in which the revolution was staged. 'Fiction in the archives' became revolution in the archives: whole sets of documents were produced, preserved and classified in order to suggest a particular representation of the revolutionary moment. I begin with the development of the notion of revolution itself across Eurasia in the seventeenth and eighteenth centuries; then I show how this development influenced the organization of the French and other archives in the nineteenth century. I then follow continuities and changes in the meaning of archives and of the revolution itself in the Soviet archives, before concluding with the decolonization of the archives.

Where multiple worlds meet: revolution, theatre and cosmographies

In late 1658, François Bernier arrived in Sourat, a port city on the coast of Gujarat. By the spring of 1659, he had joined the circle of associates surrounding Crown Prince Dara, who was to succeed Shah Jahan to the Mughal throne. Bernier remained at the Mughal court for three years. There he became the official imperial chronicler for all of

Europe, seeking to 'expose' the false elements in the histories of the Moghul monarchs, and the erroneous notions about India entertained by Europeans.[14]

An increasing bibliography on Bernier is available, covering his attitude towards the Moghul, the impact of Gassendi and Spinoza, his Orientalism, his role on the French colonial ambitions, his notion of race, etc.[15] Here I will focus on a more modest concern, that is, his notion of revolution in connection with historical writing. His experiences with Dara, and later Aurangzeb, prompted him to reflect on the notion of 'revolution', a term he readily employed to describe Aurangzeb's overthrow of the Crown Prince. The using of this term by Barnier derived from both French and Moghul influences. Thus, on 13 November 1661, Jean Chapelain wrote to Bernier that he encouraged his desire to travel and suggested he get to know 'l'histoire et les revolutions de ce royaume', not only since Tamerlan (Timur) but since Alexander the Great.[16] In this letter, unlike Koselleck's argument, revolution already meant political changes which were not cyclical but irreversible.[17]

There were important mutual influences between the French and the Indian contexts and these were clear in Bernier's approach. Like most Indian chroniclers of the period, Bernier presented several versions of the same event, drawing at the same time on Gassendi for the probabilistic approach to history.[18] Multiple interpretations and variations were all equally possible and, instead of presenting one as real and unique, Bernier (like Gassendi) translated the statistical principle of probability and likelihood (*vraisemblable*) into a style of history.[19] Bernier combined his critique of geocentric thinking with a critique of historicity: the Copernican revolution and the search for historical truth were one and the same process.[20]

In this respect, historical writing was produced at the interface with statistics and astronomy on the one hand, literature and theatre on the other hand. Bernier drew on Racine for stylistic inspiration (in particular the principles Racine outlined in the second preface to Bajazet, where he stressed the advantage of writing on distant

---

[14] François Bernier, *Un libertin dans l'Inde Moghole* (Paris: Chandeigne, 2008); Michael Harrigan, 'Seventeenth-Century French Travellers and the Encounter with Indian Histories', *French History* 28, no. 1 (2014): 1–22.

[15] P. Bulle, 'François Bernier and the Origins of the Concept of Race', in *The Color of Liberty: Histories of Race in France*, edited by Sue Peabody and T. Stovall (Durham, NC and London: Duke University Press, 2003), 11–27; Peter Burke, 'The Philosopher as Traveller: Bernier's Orient', in *Voyages and Visions: Towards a Cultural History of Travel*, edited by Jas Elsner and Joan-Pau Rubiés (Chicago and London: the University of Chicago Press, 1999), 124–37; Nicholas Dew, *Orientalism in Louis XIV's France* (Oxford: Oxford University Press, 2009); Joan-Pau Rubiés, 'Oriental Despotism and European Orientalism: Botero to Montesquieu', *Journal of Early Modern History* 9 (2005): 106–80.

[16] Quoted in *Un Libertin dans l'Inde Moghole: 18.*, A Jean Chapelain Lettres, tome 2nd (2 janvier 1659–20 décembre 1672), edited by P. Tamizey de Larroque (Paris: Imprimerie Nationale, 1883).

[17] *The Age of Revolutions in Global Context*, introduction xv–xvi.

[18] José Freches, 'François Bernier, philosophe de Confucius au XVIIe siècle', *Bulletin de l'Ecole française d'Extrême-Orient* 60 (1973): 385–400.

[19] Sylvia Murr, 'Bernier et les gassendistes', *Corpus* 20–1 (1992): 115–35.

[20] Paolo Francesco Mugnai, 'Ricerche su François Bernier filosofo e viaggiatore (1620–1688)', *Studi filosofici* 7 (1984): 53–115; Joan-Pau Rubiés, 'Race, Climate and Civilization in the Works of François Bernier', in *L'Inde des Lumières:Discourse,histoire, savoirs (XVIIe–XIXe siècle)*, edited by Marie Fourcade and Ines Zupanov (Paris: EHESS, 2013): 53–78.

people and times).²¹ In Athalie, Racine put on the stage the British Glorious Revolution transposed in a mythical antiquity. King's legitimacy descend from the law and by God, and the exercise of power in itself is not a valuable legitimation of it.²² Actually, the using of the theatre in historical representation and analysis was extremely widespread in Western Europe (from Camillo, through Lull, down to Giordano Bruno and Rameau)²³ and in Russia.²⁴

Yet, Bernier's approach also found its inspiration in the way, in the Mughal world, dynastic changes were incorporated into the framework of cosmography. These aspects have been brilliantly studied by a number of authors, notably Muzzafar Alam.²⁵ In fact, universality accompanied the writing of history in Mughal India, a synthesis of Hindu and Muslim elements. Cosmographies and the writing of history were part of this synthesis. Persian and Islamic interpretations of history were well known in the Mughal court and state. Along with these documents in Persian, many others were produced in Hindi, Marathi, Rajasthani, Punjabi, Sindhi and Bengali. These attitudes reflect the cosmopolitanism of the Mughal Empire.²⁶

Through the interaction among these various influences, Bernier's work became a model of the Eurasian crossroads of historical and scientific knowledge. Thus, histories of the evolution and use of the term 'revolution' based entirely on French sources miss an essential aspect, namely its transnational and global dimension. Revolution as a political and historical category did not come into being with the French Revolution, but much earlier, in the context of knowledge circulating in Eurasia, and it was connected to the questions of truth and authenticity in history which we have previously discussed. Erudition and scepticism first, followed by the 'invention of archives', contributed to assess the idea of time and revolution as supported by 'objective artefacts'. In fact, archives existed all across early modern Eurasia. In China, under the Song, history became one of the required sections in the training of elites during the eleventh century. The production of history became a centralized activity under state control. A central bureau was supposed to compile 'true events' that could constitute the memory of the current dynasty, and stabilize that of preceding dynasties in order to avoid any proliferation of interpretations other than its own.²⁷ Historians compiled the 'Veritable Records' of each emperor; they also produced six comprehensive histories of the regime and their territories, annals and monographs. The Ming inherited practices

---

[21] 'Lettre envoyé à Monsieur Chapelain', 4 Octobre 1667, in *Un Libertin dans l'Inde Moghole*, 301–44.
[22] Jean-Marie Goulemot, *Le règne de l'histoire* (Paris: Albin Michel, 1996), 102 ff.
[23] Frances Yates, *The Art of Memory* (Chicago: University of Chicago Press, 1966).
[24] Richard Stites, *Serfdom, Society, and the Arts in Imperial Russia* (New Haven: Yale University Press, 2005).
[25] Muzzafar Alam, *The Languages of Political Islam, 1200–1800* (Chicago: University of Chicago Press, 2004); Louise Marlow, *Hierarchy and Egalitarianism in Islamic Thought* (Cambridge: Cambridge University Press, 1997); Tarif Khalidi, *Historical Thought in the Classical Period* (Cambridge: Cambridge University Press, 1994).
[26] Satish Chandra, *State, Pluralism, and the Indian Historical Tradition* (Oxford: Oxford University Press, 2008); Corinne Lefèvre, Ines Zupanov and Jorge Flores, eds, *Cosmopolitismes en Asie du Sud. Sources, itinéraires, langues (XVIe–XVIIIe siècles)* (Paris: EHESS, 2015).
[27] Thomas Lee, ed., *The New and the Multiple: Song Senses of the Past* (Hong Kong: Chinese University Press, 2005).

from preceding dynasties; the compilation of official history mobilized approximately a thousand people across a number of ministries; 'veritable documents' (*Ming shilu*) contained all of the relevant elements on which official history was supposed to be written. These documents were produced in two copies, one under seal and another preserved by the grand secretary. These two copies were deposited in the imperial archives, while the original documents were often (not always) burned.

Despite this control, critical analysis of sources and the multiplication of non-official histories experienced a considerable rise. These different sources and approaches encouraged the philological analysis required to identify authentic documents and to attest to their authenticity.[28] Historical volumes and studies increased to such an extent that a bibliography from the period identifies ten genres for writing history, which were organized into 1,378 categories, and numbered 28,000 booklets.[29] Connections were important between China and Japan. Here, historical texts had been produced since the Nara period (710–94), in particular the *Kojiki* (Records of Ancient Matters) and the *Nihon Shoki* (Chronicles of Japan). Both texts related the creation of the world and the foundation of Japan. Chinese history was both a model and a source.[30] In the following century a different type of history, written in Japanese, appeared in the form of *monogataries*'stories in which fiction, myth and chronicles were mixed. The *Gukansho* (Jotting of a Fool) and *Okagami* (Great Mirror) were written in Japanese and looked for reason (both divine and human) and predictability in history, starting from past experience.[31] In particular, Hanawa Hokiichi, strongly inspired by Motoori Norinaga's philological approach, believed that the study of the past should be based on reliable materials, subject to careful, textual criticism. With this aim, he examined and classified hundreds of historical materials published in the *Gunsho ruiju* (Great Collection of Old Documents) since 1786.[32]

In the Islamic worlds, historiography expressed a sense of temporal progress from Creation through the prophets, culminating with Muhammad. The attention given to the original texts of the Prophet gave rise to analyses seeking to reconstruct the chain of transmission of the texts themselves. In the ninth century a 'science of traditions' henceforth identified the rules for evaluating and authenticating texts, with the possibility of distinguishing between the authentic and the fake (*hadiths*).[33] The convergence of the Indian, Persian and Islamic historiographies in India were expressed in the forms, genres and sources of historical writing. Islamic traditions in chronographies and biographies added to chronicles and annals. Sultanate chroniclers

---

[28] Pamela Kyle Crossley, *A Translucent Mirror: History and Identity in Qing Imperial Ideology* (Berkeley: University of California Press, 1999).

[29] Franke Wolfgang, *An Introduction to the Source of Ming History* (Kuala Lumpur: University of Malaya Press, 1968).

[30] John Harrison, ed., *New Lights on Early Medieval Japanese Historiography* (Gainsville, FL: University of Florida Press, 1959).

[31] Delmer Brown and Ichiro Ishida, trans. and eds, *The Future and the Past: A Translation and Story of the Gukansho, an Interpretative History of Japan, Written in 1219* (Berkeley: University of California Press, 1979).

[32] Motoori Norinaga, *Gunsho ruiju* (Great Collection of Old Documents), comp. Hanawa Hokiichi, 30 vols (Tokyo: Kanseikai, 1959–60).

[33] Franz Rosenthal, *A History of Muslim Historiography* (Leiden: Brill, 1968).

developed several genres of historical writing that were often influenced by the Arab-Muslim world. Along with these documents in Persian, many others were produced in Hindi, Marathi, Rajasthani, Punjabi, Sindhi and Bengali.[34] These attitudes reflect the openness of the Mughal Empire, which took care to integrate the traditions and religions of different groups.[35] Alongside these documents produced in the Mughal court, numerous other texts saw the light of day both in different regions – in languages that were equally different – as well as in the principalities that emerged during the eighteenth century from the ashes of the Mughal Empire, especially Mysore and the Maratha in the south, and Punjab in the north. Legal and mystical documents were produced, as were chronicles and biographies.[36] This was the context in which Bernier developed his reflections on history and revolution. In other words, archives existed all around the world well before the French Revolution and connections between these worlds were important. It is from these Eurasian encounters with the source of history that we can now pass to evaluate the novelties introduced by the French Revolution in the organization and meaning of the archives.

Archives and the French Revolution

Topics such as breaks vs. continuities, myth vs. history and philosophical vs. scholarly history, frequently debated in the eighteenth century, took on new significance after 1800. Revolutionary changes and restorations raised the issue of breaks and continuities in history, leading in turn to the question of whether a few general principles could be derived from historical experience, and hence to the philosophy of history. Enlightenment thinkers had put forward a notion of history often rooted in a Eurocentric political philosophy with universalist aims. It was a history that expressed the globalizing ambitions of the West. The nineteenth century maintained this universalist outlook, but sought to detach it from its previous revolutionary claims, highlighting instead the nation as the subject of history, archives as its source and philology as its instrument. With the French Revolution, archives became a public institution and a place of remembrance.[37]

The very organization of the archives testifies to this fact: the new regime constructed its own memory as well as that of the previous regime; archival documents were entered and classified in accordance with this requirement.[38] However, instead of locking up the original documents in the state secretariat and destroying those from the previous dynasty like archivists in China, post-revolutionary France allowed public access to state archives.

The main countries of Europe followed suit, building their own national archives almost everywhere during the second half of the nineteenth century. Setting up public

---

[34] Sunil Kumar, *The Emergence of the Delhi Sultanate, 1192–1286* (New Delhi: Permanent Black, 2007).
[35] Mantena, *The Origins*.
[36] Rao, Shulman and Subrahmanyam, *Textures of Time*.
[37] Nora, *Les lieux de mémoire*.
[38] Krzysztof Pomian, *Sur l'histoire* (Paris: Gallimard, 1999)

archives sometimes became a synonym for independence, even before it was achieved. This was the case in Hungary, for example,[39] whereas in Italy the creation of national archives and libraries was seen as a milestone in establishing the legitimacy of the new state after the wars of independence and unification.[40]

Archives usually became synonymous with the nation and diametrically opposed to a global view of history; this attitude sometimes surfaced in the way the archives were organized. In France, documents were divided between those pertaining to the *ancien régime* and those concerning the modern era. Archival classifications signalled institutional breaks and covered up the continuities.[41] Inventories and documents of the *ancien régime* (invented precisely at this moment) were opposed to modern archives, *en train de se faire*, in the spatial organization of the archives themselves. The so-called conservative, provenance principle of classification was supposed to confirm this approach. French archivists love stressing the full adherence to this principle.[42] Documents were classified and ordered according to their 'producer'.[43] The nineteenth century constructed its own memory as well as its imagination, which has influenced the perceptions of virtually all historians ever since.

The adopted solutions varied from one country to another; in Russia, after the reforms implemented by Peter the Great in 1718–20, each central institution had its own archive (closed to the public), which was organized either chronologically or according to the 'case', topic or region concerned. In 1765, two scholars, Gerard F. Miller (real German name: Gerhard Friedrich Müller, 1705–83) and Nikolai N. Bantich-Kamenskii (1737–1814), proposed to group documents together in a single archive housed at the College of Foreign Affairs, under the ministry of the same name. However, this principle proved difficult to apply to all ministry sections; the archivists therefore decided to complete the regional criterion with a classification according to the geographical origin of the document, and, within that framework, sub-classifications into thematic categories.[44]

In the United States, the state archives were inventoried relatively late and the National Archive founded only in the 1930s.[45] As in the Netherlands, the classificatory principle per keywords and concepts was introduced from the very onset. This did not mean that history legitimizing the nation was not developed. During the first half of the nineteenth century, considerable efforts were made to establish and publish local archives of the revolution by local historical societies (in Massachusetts, Wisconsin, Kentucky, Louisville, Chicago, etc.). However, it was only at the end of the nineteenth

---

[39] Monika Baàr, *Historians and Nationalism: East-Central Europe in the Nineteenth Century* (Oxford: Oxford University Press, 2010).
[40] Giuseppe Di Costanzo, ed., *La cultura storica italiana tra Otto e Novecento* (Napoli: Liguori, 1990).
[41] Paul Delsalle, *Une histoire de l'archivistique* (Saint-Foie: Presses Universitaires du Québec, 2000).
[42] Claire Béchu, ed., *Les Archives nationales. Des lieux pour l'histoire de France. Bicentenaire d'une installation, 1808–2008* (Paris: Archives nationales-Éditions Somogy, 2008).
[43] Lucie Favier, *La mémoire de l'État. Histoire des Archives nationales* (Paris: Fayard, 2004).
[44] Victoria Prozorova-Thomas, 'Le classement selon le principe de pertinence comme reflet de la commande d'État: les archives soviétiques', *Matériaux pour l'histoire de notre temps* 82, no. 2 (2006): 58–64.
[45] Ian Tyrrell, *Historians in Public: The Practice of American History, 1890–1970* (Chicago: University of Chicago Press, 2005).

century that a national system of research universities began to be settled and professional historians emerged.[46] The American Historical Association was founded in 1884; in 1899, the profession established a high school curriculum in history that distinguished a sequence of ancient, medieval and modern European, English and American history.[47] Time scale and history meanings were strictly Eurocentric. While rejecting philosophy of history, most historians stressed 'Anglo-Saxon' racial superiority. Authors such as John Burgess justified the end of reconstruction and denied any rights to Afro-Americans, Indians and many immigrants.[48] In 1893, Turner advanced his celebrated history and theory of the frontier as a founding myth of US history.[49]

A strong connection developed in the nineteenth century between archives and the nation-state.[50] This connection is still visible in historians' practices – witness the predominance of national history – and in the continued acceptance of nineteenth-century notions about what constitutes a legitimate, authentic source. From the standpoint of political ideology and administrative organization, the nation-state unquestionably triumphed in the nineteenth century. However, it was less successful in terms of practices, where the strength and significance of the state changed, e.g. in federalized and centralized states, in the role assigned to local authorities, in its social recognition (which was weak in Italy, for example), and ultimately in its actions. Despite the emphasis on the nation-state, empires still largely dominated the nineteenth-century political scene. These aspects were reflected in the way archives were constructed and organized, as the complicated relationships between the various central, municipal, regional and colonial archives attest.[51]

This fact leads to question the overall interpretation of archives, in Foucault's wake, as just an expression of power.[52] If archives are a social and political construction, then so is the state, particularly the nation-state. The archives express both the presumption of factualness and an ideal: the well-ordered classification of documents according to the principle of provenance credits the state with much greater coherence and rationality than it has in reality. Institutions – governments, ministries, departments and agencies – certainly think[53] and this behaviour reflects the underlying social order and procedures for making records. However, institutions do not form a homogeneous

---

[46] Thomas Bender, *Intellectual and Public Life: Essays on the Social History of Academic Intellectuals in the United States* (Baltimore: Johns Hopkins University, 1993).
[47] William Dunning, *Reconstruction, Political and Economic, 1865–1877* (New York: Harper, 1907); Edward Eggleston, *The Beginning of a Nation: A History of the Sources and Rise of the Earliest Settlements in America, with Special Reference to the Life and Character of People* (New York: Appleton, 1896).
[48] John Burgess, *Reconstruction and Constitution* (New York: Scribner's Son, 1902).
[49] Frederick Jackson Turner, 'The Significance of the Frontier in American History', reprint in *Frontier and Section: Selected Writings of F.J. Turner* (Englewood Cliffs, NJ: Prentice Hall, 1961).
[50] Anne-Marie Thiesse, *La création des identités nationales: Europe XVIIIe–XIXe siècle* (Paris: Seuil, 1999).
[51] Jean-Yves Rousseau and Carole Couture, eds, *Les fondements de la discipline archivistique* (Québec: Presses Universitaires du Québec, 1994).
[52] Foucault, *L'archéologie du savoir*.
[53] Mary Douglas, *How Institutions Think* (Syracuse: Syracuse University Press, 1986).

block, much less a rational whole as Weber imagined.[54] Quite the contrary, in fact; most public institutions and their archives manifest competition and confusion rather than Weberian rationality. Documents and information circulate poorly, not only between institutions but also within a single agency or department. Two types of document 'label' reveal the complexity of this process. First, copies of a given document indicate the circulation of information: documents bearing the word 'copy' indicate the characteristics and limits of information circulation. Copies are supposed to inform other institutions or other levels and offices within the same agency/department. However, before the introduction of carbon copies, it was possible to observe way a document – and hence its information – may have been amended both in 'horizontal' circulation between institutions and 'vertical' circulation within an organization. The 'copy' was not really a true copy until the invention of reprographic techniques. Disagreements between, say, the ministry of commerce and that of foreign trade, or between the latter and that of agriculture during the second half of the nineteenth century attest to this point. These institutions accuse each other of holding back information. When the original document and its copies are found in the archives it is possible to validate (most often) or invalidate these accusations.[55]

The other indication found on documents is the 'secret' stamp, which in principle aims to limit circulation.[56] These documents are common not only in totalitarian states and in police archives,[57] but almost everywhere. However, this 'secret' status tends to become quite commonplace, especially in the Soviet Union where almost all the documents were secret.[58] As a result, institutions end up producing self-generating information (staff members write what their hierarchical superior expects to receive) and reveal a lack of knowledge about the field they are supposed to evaluate. Legions of historians have confused the organization of the archives with that of the State and its control over social life. This is to confuse ambition with reality.[59] Big brother wants to control everything; whether he succeeds is another matter.

This gap is even more evident in the organization of colonial archives.[60] In France as in Portugal, in Great Britain as in Spain, the classification of colonial archives seems to suggest a clear imperial organization 'from above'. This organization has long underpinned colonial history, then postcolonial history, each accepting the ambitions of administrators and elites as realities.[61] Granted, the construction of colonial archives largely expresses the colonialist ambition, the desire to dominate, to control and to

---

[54] Blum and Mespoulet, *L'anarchie bureaucratique*; Adam Tooze, *Statistics and the German State, 1900–1945* (Cambridge: Cambridge University Press, 2001).
[55] Alessandro Stanziani, *Histoire de la qualité alimentaire* (Paris: Seuil, 2005).
[56] Sébastien Laurent, ed., *Archives 'secrètes', secrets d'archives? Historiens et archivistes face aux archives sensibles* (Paris: CNRS Éditions, 2003).
[57] Jean-Marc Berlière, 'Richesse et misère des archives policières', *Les cahiers de la sécurité intérieure* 3 (1990–1): 165–75.
[58] Coeuré and Duclert, *Les archives*.
[59] Schwartz and Cook, 'Archives, Records, and Power'.
[60] Richards, *The Imperial Archive*; Isabelle Dion, 'Les archives coloniales', *Histoire et archives* 13 (2003), 1–26.
[61] Richard Price, *Convict and the Colonel: A Story of Colonialism and Resistance in the Caribbean* (Boston: Beacon Press, 1998).

repress,[62] while inventing imagined communities that are not confined to the nation but also include the empire. Thus, the repression and exploitation of colonies and their inhabitants, the profits obtained and the most brutal civilizing instinct appear in the archives, notably in policy documents, decrees and official orders. Yet, if one takes a closer look at the correspondence, the transmission of documents and information, one finds that confusion and the lack of information and knowledge prevail.[63] From this point of view, the archives and the way they are classified are, for us and today's students, less a tool for discovering the 'truth' in the positivist sense of the term than one for constructing an ethnography of state knowledge. The archives, their classification, confusion and faulty circulation of information help us to understand the way 'the power' thinks but also how this same power is not an homogeneous block and how the actors involved affect the final outcome.[64] Of course, this does not mean that colonialism, dependence and the exploitation of human beings and resources are just policy goals, but rather that if we avoid studying the archives only 'from above' we can produce a more complex picture of historical dynamics. Between archives that offer a source of truth and archives that only convey the arrogance of the colonizers, it is possible to find a middle road: treating the archives not only as documents to extract or as fiction, but as acts negotiated between multiple powers. The complex production of archival documents is a field that allows us to understand the way power, knowledge and historical construction are intertwined. The classification of documents reflects the ongoing day-by-day construction of historical memory. For example, the separation in France by the nineteenth century, between national archives and colonial archives, led to the classification of separate files on slaves and files on wage earners. For sure, the authorities and institutions at the origin of archives and in charge with these different topics were themselves distinct. At the same time, this clear-cut distinction between the ministry of labour or industry on the one hand, the ministry of the colonies on the other hand, put in the shadow the mutual legal, social and economic interconnections between slaves and wage earners, as we will see in Part III. The same was true in Britain, with archives of the Colonial Office being separated from the others. In fact, it was precisely in this period, when discussion of the nation-state reached its peak, that archive construction became a transnational, trans-imperial and global endeavour. Conferences on archival topics and meetings of historical and archive societies drew participants from other countries. The growing number of libraries, history journals and scholarly societies reinforced this circulation. The invention of national archives was indeed a transnational process made of strong similarities and local adaptations, but that, particularly in the West, hid the imperial, not just national and metropolitan, structure of power and knowledge.

---

[62] Richards, *The Imperial Archive*.
[63] Christopher Bayly, *Empire and Information: Intelligence Gathering and Social Communication in India, 1780–1870* (Cambridge: Cambridge University Press, 1996).
[64] Stoler, 'Colonial Archives and the Art of Governance'.

2

Archives in the twentieth century: from communism to the decolonization

Totalitarian archives?

It would be impossible to understand the meaning of social history in the twentieth century without the Russian Revolution. During much of the twentieth century, Marxist approaches to social history responded to the political and intellectual question on whether the 'Soviet path' conformed, or did not, to Marx's scheme. The interpretations of the 'West' and, even more, of the 'Third World' were directly related to this original quandary. Indeed, the Bolshevik Revolution fundamentally altered the way we conceive of history, even beyond political judgements: for the first time, it moved away from universalistic versus particularistic notions of history and progress; even if the original ambition was to export revolution to the rest of the world, in a very few years after 1917, the notion of socialism in one country prevailed and with it the idea that opposite blocs could persist in time. The construction of temporalities hinges in large part on this revolution, the images it evokes and its political role. Among the issues surrounding the October Revolution and its history, we find future-oriented history; Russia as a model or an exception, and thus the nature of 'historical laws'; the possibilities of seeing the revolution reproduced elsewhere, above all outside Europe; the absolutely central role of history in justifying or criticizing the revolution, and conversely its role in political debate. Even today, this influence is obvious in the shift in focus from a forward-looking history, capable of predicting the future, to a history of its failure and the attempt to explain it without falling into the trap of historical necessity yet again. In the end, the Bolshevik Revolution reopened the debate concerning 'truth' in history, along at least three main quarrels: whether these theses can be proven without access to archives; the role of propaganda in historiographical construction, only to end, after 1989, with almost blind faith in the archive documents finally available. For the past century, all these problems arising from within the notion of history and of its methods have been heavily conditioned by the Russian Revolution. In every case, the connections to the globality of history are clear: revolution, by its very nature, raises the question of whether it is exceptional or supposedly universal, local or worldwide.

The revolution of 1917 had a radical effect, in Russia first of all, where the use of history was crucial to legitimize the seizure of power by the Bolsheviks. Trotsky and

Menshevik authors saw the revolution as a deviation from the 'normal' path of historical development. Liberal and socialist authors held the same view.[1] Lenin, however, altered his earlier position and henceforth justified Russia as an exceptional case, demonstrating the possibility of carrying out a revolution and arriving at a socialist society without going through capitalism. Mikhail Pokrovskii, an official historian of the revolution and of the regime in its early years, tried to reconcile 'the universal laws of history' with the revolution of 1917.[2] 'Before 1917', declared Pokrovskii,

> I maintained that the same regularity (*zakonomernost'*) existed in the field of social phenomena as in the field of chemical and biological phenomena, and that there was no difference between these disciplines. Today my position has changed. There is an essential difference between the natural sciences and the science of society. While in fact all science expresses the development of the forces of production, the social system and class struggle, it is also true that these phenomena are expressed differently by the different disciplines. Unlike the natural sciences, the science of society directly expresses class struggle.[3]

The Russian Revolution and the civil war eliminated many of the historians from the Tsarist period through death or exile.[4] Among those who were left, very few were critical of the new regime. The most notable was Sergei Platonov (1860–1933),[5] one of the greatest Russian historians since Vasilii Kliuchevskii.[6] Reputed for his knowledge of European historiography and philosophy, Platonov specialized in the study of seventeenth-century Russian history, employing philology and Ranke's methods in a broad philosophical framework. Others, like Yevgeny Tarle (1875–1955), made greater use of Marxist categories.[7] These authors, both of them experts in archival research, helped to set up the Soviet archives, aided by archivists trained before the war.[8] Tarle drew on the history of the French archives and their classifications.[9] The French had

---

[1] John Barber, *Soviet Historians in Crisis, 1928-1932* (New York: Holmes and Meier, 1981).
[2] Mikhail Pokrovskii, 'Obshchestvennye nauki v SSSR za 10 let' (Social Sciences in the USSR in the Past Ten Years), *Vestnik kommunisticheskoi akademii* 26 (1928): 3–30.
[3] Pokrovskii, 'Obshchestvennye', 23.
[4] Konstantin Shteppa, *Russian Historians and the Soviet State* (New Brunswick: Rutger University Press, 1962).
[5] Sergei F. Platonov, *Ocherki po istorii smuty v Moskvoskom gosudarstve XVI–XVII v* (Studies on the Times of Trouble in the Muscovite State, Sixteenth–Seventeenth Centuries) (Saint Petersburg, 1899, edition Vremia, 1923).
[6] Vasilii Kliuchevskii, *Drevnerusskie zhitiia sviatykh kak istoricheskii istochnik* (Old Russian Saints Lives as Historical Sources) (Moscow, 1871); *Kurs russkoi istorii* (Lessons of Russian History), (Moscow: Tipografiia Lissnera i Sobko, 1904–21).
[7] Robert Byrnes, 'Creating the Soviet Historical Profession, 1917–1934', *Slavic Review* 50, no. 2 (1991): 297–308.
[8] Viktor N. Samoshenko, *Istoriia arkhivnogo dela v dorevoliutsionnoi Rossii* (History of Archives in Pre-Revolutionary Russia) (Moscow: Vysshaia Shkola, 1989).
[9] A. I. Alatortseva and Galina D. Alekseeva, eds, *50 let sovetskoi istoricheskoi nauka: Khronika nauchnoi zhizni, 1917–1967* (50 Years of Soviet Historical Science: Chronicles of The Scientific Life, 1917–1967) (Moscow: Gosizdat, 1971).

faced the same problem after 1789. How could documents classified for the use of government administrations or companies, associations and private individuals be transformed into sources for historians and other readers? Like France and other countries in the early nineteenth century, Russia, too, had to deal from the outset with the question of the break and continuity between the old regime and the new in the process of document classification itself.[10] Starting from this question, Soviet archivists had three objectives: first, to classify and make available Tsarist documents; second, to highlight the revolutionary documents, i.e. the actions of the Party, workers, trade unions and peasants; and third, to determine how the new regime's documents should be organized.[11] Does this mean that the notion of totalitarian archives is as valuable as many Western and Russian post-Soviet authors claimed?[12]

Although, even recently, some authors claimed central, direct control of Soviet power on archive production, classification and use,[13] the reality was much more complicated. First, the organization of the archives was disputed: some Russian historians and archivists recommended organizing documents based on their origin and transposing the classification used in Tsarist ministerial archives to the people's commissariats.[14] Others favoured dividing up the documents according to their destination, the solution favoured by Soviet managers in order to highlight the revolutionary break. For this purpose, the establishment of new Marxist archives was deemed necessary, to be supported by the creation of archives of the revolution, emphasizing the role of the Party and the revolutionaries. Citing the example of the French Revolution, many Russian authors stressed the crucial political role of archives in shaping the revolutionary memory. However, achieving this aim was impeded by the fact that the archives were widely dispersed, with most of them abroad. Recovering the documents then became one of the main tasks of the Soviet diplomatic and archivist apparatus. On 1 June 1918, a decree constituted the EGAF (Unified Central State Archive) whose purpose was to gather all documents. Initially, the EGAF was subordinated to the Narkompros (People's Commissariat for Education). In 1922 it was transferred to

---

[10] Shteppa, *Russian Historians*.
[11] On the critics of totalitarian archives: Salomoni, 'Un savoir historique d'État'; Mark Von Hagen, 'The Archival Gold Rush and Historical Agendas in the Post-Soviet Era', *Slavic Review* 52, no. 1 (1993): 96–100; Werth, 'De la soviétologie'. Recent works on the fabrication of the revolutionary archives: Vera Kaplan, 'Two Archives of the Russian Revolution', *Archival Science* 20 (2020): 361–80; Francis Blouin and William Rosenberg, eds, *Processing the Past: Contesting Authorities in History and the Archives* (New York: Oxford University Press, 2013); M. S. Chudakova, 'Organy politicheskogo syska nakanune i v period Fevral'skoi revoliutsii' (The Political Investigation Organs on the Eve and during the February Revolution), *Vestnik KGU im. N. A. Nekrasova* 3 (2006): 132–7; Stephen Kotkin, 'The State – Is It Us? Memoirs, Archives, and Kremlinologists', *The Russian Review* 61, no. 1 (2002): 35–51.
[12] Grimsted, *Archives and Manuscript*; Vladimir E. Korneev and Olga N. Kopylova, 'Arkhivisty na sluzhbe totalitarnogo gosudarstva 1918-nachalo 1940-kh godov' (Archivists at the Service of the Totalitarian State, 1918–Beginning of the 1940s), *Otechestvennye Arkhivy* 1 (1992): 13–24.
[13] Sophie Coeuré, 'Le siècle soviétique des archives', *Annales HSS* 74, no. 3 (2019): 657–86.
[14] A. V. Chernov, *Istoriia organizatsiia arkhivnogo dela SSSR. Kratkii ocherk* (History and Organization of Archives in the USSR. Small Essay) (Moscow: Gosizdat 1940); V. V. Maksakov, *Istoriia organizatsiia arkhivnogo dela SSSR 1917–1945 gg.* (History and Organization of Archives in the USSR, 1917–1945) (Moscow: Nauka, 1969).

the VTIK (the All-Russian Central Executive Committee).[15] One must be careful about the meaning of 'centralization': in the Soviet case, the fact that archives came under a single authority did not mean that documents were transferred and centralized in a single place as was done in the French national archives (not including departmental and communal archives, of course). Quite the contrary: in Russia, archives of the economy were separated from archives of the revolution, to which were added the archives of ancient Russia (RGADA) and the archives of imperial Russia (RGIA). As in pre-revolutionary Russia and in all other countries, debates focused on the classification of documents: should the principle of conservation be adopted? Which continuities and breaks between Tsarist and Soviet institutions should be emphasized in the classification of files?

While the majority of archivists supported the principle of conservation, a second group was favourable to a system of classification based on the content of documents.[16] They were backed by state representatives arguing that the principle of conservation had been invented by 'bourgeois' archivists, while the socialist archives were oriented towards the future and thus towards a current political use and classification of documents.

Archivists in place, mostly inherited from the Tsarist period, initially sought to conciliate these two orientations, but, of course, this attitude gave birth to different solutions according to the fond, the political pressure on the materials concerned, etc.; thus, the national archives in Moscow and Petrograd-Leningrad made use of the same major sections: Supreme power (laws, decrees, monarchy); Judicial archives; Finance; Army and Navy; Culture (education, print); Interior and administration. While waiting the formation of 'red archivists', the power in place decided to launch the publication of selected materials in order to orient discussions and historical interpretations. The journal *Kransii archiv* (Red Archives) was created in 1922 with the purpose of showing 'the historical necessity of the revolutionary process, since Pugachev to 1917'. In the first issue, the introduction recalled the French principle of Messidor, 7, year 2 (25 June 1794) on public access to archives. Revolutionary archives were supposed to be a special section. Strong conflicts opposed 'bourgeois archivists' and representatives of the power over decisions to take in the classification of documents, in particular in the entirely created archives of the revolution, issued from documents imported from abroad and documents displaced from already settled files.[17] 'Bourgeois archivists' insisted on keeping the conservatory principle, while Soviet leaders and the historian Pokrovskii wanted to adopt a thematic classification in order to show the historical necessity but also the major break brought by the revolution.

To achieve this aim, major importance was given to oral sources and the testimonies of selected actors of the revolution. Their memories had to be collected in order to

---

[15] E. V. Starostin and T. I. Khorkhordina, 'Dekret ob arkhivnom dele 1918 goda' (The Decree on the Archives of 1918), *Voprosy Istorii* 7–8 (1991): 41–52.

[16] A. S. Nikolaev, 'Glavnoe Upravlenie Arkhivnym Delom (aprel'–oktiabr 1918 goda) (General Direction of the Archives, April–October 1918)', *Istoricheskii Arkhiv* 1 (1919): 5–6.

[17] V. Maksakov, 'Piat let Arkhiva Oktiabr'skoi revoliiutsii, 1920–sentiabr' 1925 g.' (Five Years of Revolutionary Archives, October 1920–September 1925), *Arkhivnoe delo* 5–6 (1926): 3–13.

confirm the strong ideological lines of the party, such as the revolutionary attitude of the peasantry, and their relationship with Lenin and the Bolsheviks rather than 'populists', with the exception of course of 'rich peasants'. The role of the party was also central to the debate and therefore to the selection and presentation of archival documents. These were supposed to show the coherent activity of the party under Lenin both in Russia and abroad, despite counter-revolutionary action and deviations from the line by some Bolshevik leaders. The archives of the Okhrana, the Tsarist political police, were a major body of revolutionary archives. The Historical Archives of the Revolution were at the centre of a battle that ended in late 1926 with the transfer of the Moscow fonds to the Central Archives – against the advice of the archivists. From that moment onward the classification of archives gradually stabilized along with the new regime, as Stalin progressively took control.[18] The centralization of the archive institutions came with the increasing control and influence of the Communist Party itself on these matters. Between 1938 and 1960, the national archives were a branch of the powerful Ministry of the Interior and the state police. Most of the archivists who had taken part in their national conference in 1929 were arrested in the 1930s. However, because of the lack of 'revolutionary archivists', a number of 'bourgeois archivists' inherited from the Tsarist regime were kept in place until the 1960s, although in subordinate positions or even the local archives of the 'provinces' (the socialist republics of the USSR).

History underwent a profound renewal in the USSR after Stalin's death. This research naturally began with the criticisms that Lenin and Marx levelled at capitalism and its ideologues. Western approaches were nevertheless increasingly presented and diffused, under the pretext of being able to criticize them better. A new generation of historians strove to change conventional Soviet interpretations, notably with regard to national history. Stalin's collectivization was criticized, while Lenin's New Economic Policy (NEP) enjoyed considerable support that called for similar reforms in the USSR of the 1960s.[19] A new journal, *Voprosy istorii* (Questions of History), founded in 1953 and headed by Anna Pankratova, became the mouthpiece for increased liberty in history.[20] Its board was quickly dismissed after the events in Hungary in 1956. One of the reactions of Soviet historians in the face of repression, in particular that of Mikhail Tikhomirov, was expressed in the rediscovery of *istochnikovedenie* – or source analysis – developed by Lappo-Danilevskii in the early twentieth century, and then taken up by a first generation of Soviet historians during the 1930s. This return to sources was justified by a desire to base oneself on 'genuine documents' as opposed to the arbitrariness of

---

[18] Tat'iana Khorkhordina, *Istoriia otechestva i arkhivy: 1917–1980-e gg* (History of the Nation and the Archives, 1917–1980) (Moscow: RGGU, 1994); Id., *Rossiiskaia nauka ob arkhivakh: Istoriia. Teoriia. Liudi* (The Russian Archival Science: History, Theory and People) (Moscow: RGGU, 2003); François-Xavier Nérard, 'Quelles archives soviétiques? Réflexion sur la constitution des archives du pouvoir stalinien', *Territoires contemporains* 2 (2011), http://tristan.u-bourgogne.fr/CGC/publications/historiographie/ FX_Nerard.html.

[19] Liubov Sidorova, *Ottepel' v istoricheskoi nauke: sovetskaia istoriografiia pervogo poslestalinskogo desiatiletiia* (The Thaw of the Historical Science: The Soviet Historiography during the First Decade after Stalin) (Moscow: Pamiatniki istoricheskoi mysli, 1997).

[20] Reginald Zelnik, *Perils of Pankratova: Some Stories from the Annals of Soviet Historiography* (Seattle: University of Washington Press, 2005).

official history.²¹ From this point forward historians produced a great many collections and editions of archival documents, which would serve as a basis and essential starting point for historiography after the fall of the USSR. Between 1955 and 1962, the journal *Istoricheskii arkhiv* published many archival documents that were often controversial in nature, to the extent that the journal was shut down in the early 1970s. However, the publication of archival documents would continue until the end of the communist regime, and then developed in a new form beginning in the 1990s. Under Gorbachev, archivists were among the most active supporters of the new course.²²

Since the 1990s, the publication of archival documents has continued in Russia, following the tradition that was developed during the Soviet period.²³ Fundamental domains were covered, including the archives of Stalin and the Politburo, the gulag, collectivization, purges and the secret police, the Comintern, etc.²⁴ A new generation of Russian historians embarked upon these activities. The approach remained 'classic', as the archives were discussed from the perspective of the origins and validity of the documents, with philology and erudition guiding these approaches. Criticisms of the 'positivism of sources' remained marginal.²⁵ As during the Soviet period, this attitude can partly be explained by the education of historians, and partly by the Russian context, in which arbitrary interpretations imposed by authorities were too often still present after the fall of communism. Over decades, history in the Soviet Union had served propaganda, and archival materials had been concealed or distorted for that purpose. Since the 1990s, and indeed even earlier, Russian historians who claimed to be 'sticking to the archives' were actually seeking to escape censorship and propaganda. To their ears, Derrida and Foucault's archival deconstructivism, which was being 'discovered' at that time in Russia, sounded like a surrender to the claim that history could not be anything but an 'invention'. The journal *Ab Imperio* was one of the exceptions: its editors sought to establish a dialogue between postmodernist thought and Russian historiography. It is no accident that this conversation took place because of the close relationship between those editors and some Western, mostly US, historians.

In this way professional historians defended the 'truth' and 'objectivity' of archives. This has been an important issue in Russia, now more than ever, with the political and nationalist use of history by media that is often close to power. The Cold War served as a justification for the persisting secrecy of entire folds of archives; this is where debates and worries about 'totalitarian' archives joined those concerning colonial archives. In both cases, 'concealed' historical memories lay at the core of political and historiographical debates; in both cases the 'appropriate' source (which archives,

---

[21] Viktor A. Chernyk, 'Tsentr izucheniia minuvshikh vremen: k 50-letiiu Arkeograficheskoi komissii RAN' (The Centre of the Study of 'small affairs': 50 Years of the Archaeographical Commission of the Academy of Science), *Vestnik Rossiskoi Akademii Nauk* 76, no. 9 (2006): 837–42.

[22] Khorkhordina, *Istoriia otechestva*.

[23] Patricia Grimsted, *Archives of Russia Five Years after: 'Purveyors of Sensations' or 'Shadows Cast to the Past'* (Amsterdam: International Institute of Social History, 1997).

[24] Oleg V. Khlevniuk, *Stalinskoie Politburo v 30-ye gody* (Stalin's Politburo during the 1930s) (Moscow: Airo-XX 1995).

[25] Nicolas Werth, 'De la soviétologie en général et des archives russes en particulier', *Le Débat*, November–December (1993): 127–44; Blouin and Rosenberg, *Processing the Past*.

which language, written vs. oral sources) became crucial evidence for this wider debate on historical trends and memory. But, unlike the colonial worlds of Western powers, in post-imperial Russia movement beyond the previous official historiography was achieved by using evidence from the archives rather than by denying it as in the postcolonial approach. In other words, in post-Soviet historiography, the critics of official history and propaganda did not necessarily engage in a denial of archives ('against the grain'), but, on the contrary, looked for 'hidden documents' or read already known archives in a quite new light ('with [or along] the grain').

It is no accident that, after 2000, it was mainly Western scholarship which sought to transpose Edward Said's analysis of knowledge, archives and Orientalism to the Russian and Soviet case. The debates concerned both whether Said's argument was applicable to Russia,[26] and whether Russia was to a certain extent 'distinct' from European empires.[27] This last point led to several others, related to the question of identifying specific Russian and then Soviet features in terms of empire building.[28]

On the Russian side, attitudes also differed partly because of their somewhat different traditions of 'Orientalism'. After the 1917 Revolution, two approaches emerged on Oriental studies, one in Leningrad, led mostly by historians inherited from the previous regime using ethnography and Oriental languages as their main tools of investigation.[29] The other school, in Moscow, was much closer to the new regime and sought to elaborate theories and empirical studies on the various ethnicities in the Soviet Empire according to Marxist-Leninist theory.[30] To this one

---

[26] Daniel R. Brower and Edward J. Lazzerini, eds, *Russia's Orient: Imperial Borderlands and Peoples, 1700-1917* (Bloomington: Indiana University Press, 1997); Michael Kemper and Stephan Conermann, eds, *The Heritage of Soviet Oriental Studies* (London: Routledge, 2011); Adeeb Khalid, 'Russian History and the Debate over Orientalism', *Kritika: Explorations in Russian and Eurasian History* 1, no. 4 (2000): 691–9; Nathaniel Knight, 'Grigor'ev in Orenburg, 1851–1862: Russian Orientalism in the Service of Empire?' *Slavic Review* 59, no. 1 (2000): 74–100.

[27] Vera Tolz, *Russia's Own Orient: The Politics of Identity and Oriental Studies in the Late Imperial and Early Soviet Periods* (Oxford: Oxford University Press, 2011); Maria Todorova, 'Does Russian Orientalism Have a Russian Soul? A Contribution to the Debate between Nathaniel Knight and Adeeb Khalid', *Kritika: Explorations in Russian and Eurasian History* 1, no. 4 (2000): 717–27.

[28] Alexander Morrison, '"Applied Orientalism" in British India and Tsarist Turkestan', *Comparative Studies in Society and History* 51, no. 3 (2009): 619–47; Aleksei Miller, ed., *Rossiiskaia imperii v sravnitel'noi perspektive: Sbornik statei* (Moscow: Novoe izdatel'stvo, 2004); Alexei Miller and Alfred J. Rieber, eds, *Imperial Rule* (Budapest: Central European University Press, 2004); Kimitaka Matsuzato, *Imperiology: From Empirical Knowledge to Discussing the Russian Empire* (Sapporo: Slavic Research Center, 2007); Geoffrey Hosking, *Russia: People and Empire, 1552-1917* (Cambridge, MA: Harvard University Press, 1997); Andreas Kappeler, *Rußland als Vielvölkerreich: Entstehung, Geschichte, Zerfall* (Munich: C. H. Beck, 1992); Alexander S. Morrison, *Russian Rule in Samarkand, 1868-1910: A Comparison with British India* (Oxford: Oxford University Press, 2008). See also the special issues on this topic, *Kritika* 7, no. 3 (2006) and 12, no. 2 (2012). Thomas Barrett, *At the Edge of Empire: The Terek Cossacks and the North Caucasus Frontier, 1700-1860* (Boulder, CO: Westview Press, 1999); Alexander Etkind, *Internal Colonization: Russia's Imperial Experience* (Cambridge: Polity Press, 2011); Steven Sabol, *The Touch of Civilization: Comparing American and Russian Internal Colonization* (Boulder, CO: University Press of Colorado, 2017).

[29] Francine Hirsch, *Empire of Nations: Ethnographic Knowledge and the Making of the Soviet Union* (Ithaca, NY: Cornell University Press, 2005).

[30] Irina Filatova, 'Indoctrination or Scholarship? Education of Africans at the Communist University of the Toilers of the East in the Soviet Union, 1923-1937', *Paedagogica Historica: International Journal of the History of Education* 35, no. 1 (1999): 41–66.

must add the Communist University of Toilers of the East (KUTV), for students from the Middle East and beyond. The organization of the 'local' archives was supposed to reflect the main principles of accepted Marxist theory; therefore, the question was whether 'Oriental' and 'African' countries had to pass through the general main stages in history, as indicated in Marxist theory (ancient, medieval, pre-capitalist, capitalist, socialist and communist) or if they could skip some of them and 'jump' directly to socialism. Even if the 1920 Baku Congress of the Peoples of the East firmly came out against the necessity of the colonial world passing through the capitalist stage, debates about the Asiatic mode of production continued during the 1920s and early 1930s. Those who supported the existence of such a mode came close to the Trotskyists; so, in 1934, the Party Congress excluded this theory from Marxism.[31]

In this context, archives again played a crucial role. The organization of local archives was put under the strict control of the central state, and most forms of brutal colonialism, ethnic cleansing and massive displacement of populations were kept secret.[32] It is no accident that, after the October Revolution, each Soviet Republic's central archive was named 'Central State Archive of the October Revolution and Socialist Construction'. There were three sets of archives in each former republic of the USSR: archives of organs of the state, those of the Communist Party and its various organs, and the archives of security organs.[33] The party archives were crucial because the party, rather than state organs, took the most important decisions.

Local archives preserved important major files not only in Russian but also in local languages (in particular in the correspondence between local authorities and the local population), not to mention the long tradition of translation of diplomatic and political sources between Russian, Turkic and Mandarin, and in the many languages spoken inside and outside the Russian and Soviet Empire.[34] Naturally there were debates on the meaning of translation and mediation in Tsarist, then Soviet, and post-Soviet Russia. Mediation was important in the production of documents themselves, and this process has been well studied for Central Asia and the Muslim areas.[35] For example,

---

[31] Stephen Dunn, *The Fall and Rise of the Asiatic Mode of Production* (London: Routledge & Kegan Paul, 1982); Joshua A. Fogel, 'The Debates over the Asiatic Mode of Production in Soviet Russia, China and Japan', *American Historical Review* 93, no. 1 (1988): 56–79.

[32] Serhy Yekelchyk, *Stalin's Empire of Memory* (Toronto: University of Toronto Press, 2004); Douglas Northrop, *Veiled Empire* (New Haven: Yale University Press, 2016); Sean Pollock, 'Historians and Their Sources: Discourses of Russian Empire and Islam in Eurasian Archives', *Ab Imperio* 4 (2008): 234–52.

[33] Adeeb Khalid, 'Searching of Muslim Voices in Post-Soviet Archives', *Ab Imperio* 4 (2008): 302–12.

[34] Natalia F. Demidova and Viktor S. Miasnikov, eds, *Russko-kitaiskie otnosheniia v xvii veke: materialy i dokumenty* (Russian-Chinese Relations in the Seventeenth Century: Materials and Documents), 2 vols (Moscow: Nauka, 1969–72); Natalia F. Demidova, ed., *Materialy po istorii russko-mongol'skikh otnoshenii: russko-mongol'skie otnosheniia, 1654–1685 sbornik dokumentov* (Materials for the History of Russian-Mongol Relations: Russian-Mongol Relations, 1654–1685, Collection of Documents'), (Moscow: Izdatel'skaia Firma Vostochnaia Literatura, 1995, 1996, 2000) with archive documents. The original documents in Persian are also translated by Scott Levi, *The Indian Diaspora in Central Asia, 1550–1900* (Leiden: Brill, 2002), Appendix 1.

[35] See the forum in *Ab Imperio* 3 (2007) and 4 (2008).

judicial archives in the Central Asian republics are mostly in Russian.[36] The Muslim populations of Central Asia, who in the Tsarist archives appeared mostly either as supplicants (to the Soviet authorities) or as objects of suspicion,[37] also turned during the Soviet period into local bureaucrats speaking with the same voice as in Moscow. Dissident Muslim voices mostly figured in the secret police archives.[38]

Some major questions emerge in this relationship between archives, historical memory and the management of the empire: was the Russian, then Soviet, central state similar to or different from Western empires in terms of archive production and control, and, therefore, as regards the organization and power of the state, and the role of local powers and local populations? Were 'local actors' silent in these sources? These questions are related: one might consider that the Soviet Empire (and the Russian before it) was similar to the Western ones, and therefore argue that the voice of subject peoples is somewhat 'lacking' in the archives. Of course, this interpretation starts from the hypothesis that the Western and the Russian empires worked as the postcolonial interpretation of them argues: knowledge, language and memory are tools in the colonizers' hands against the colonized.[39] But one may also argue that the Soviet Empire (and the Russian before it) was not so brutal as the Western empires: integration and assimilation of local populations were more extensive and so it was the 'voice of the subaltern'.[40] In this case, archives may be read 'with the grain' and not necessarily 'against the grain', as for Western empires.[41]

However, a third view is also possible: both the above attitudes, and therefore the reading of colonial archives in Russia and the Soviet Union, suppose that the postcolonial interpretations of the European empires are those depicted in postcolonial studies (unequal powers of the colonial state and the subalterns). The Russian-Soviet Empire was therefore compared and studied on the ground of this hypothesis. But what if we start from the alternative hypothesis that the European empires lacked information and authority and were mostly, as it were, 'broadcasting' powers, claiming strength and efficiency while actually lacking them?[42]

Some scholars, such as Sophie Coeuré, firmly argue that the Soviet Empire was not like the European empires as Stoler and Herbst depicted them: centralization and brutality were a reality and this is the major difference with the European empires.[43] This is the opposite of the initial orientation of some Russia specialists arguing that the Russian Empire was milder than the Western European one; quite the contrary, the 'unorganized' European empires are contrasted with the strongly centralized and

[36] Svetalana Gorshenina, 'Krupneishie proekty kolonial'nykh arkhivov Rossii: utopichnost' ekzostivnoi Turkestaniki general- gubernatora Konstantina Petrovicha fon Kaufmana', *Ab Imperio* 3 (2007): 291–35. See also the Forum on the Imperial archives in *Ab Imperio* 3 (2007) and 4 (2008).
[37] Khalid, 'Searching of Muslim Voices'.
[38] Northrop, *Veiled Archives*.
[39] Morrison, *Russian Rule*.
[40] Burbank and Cooper, *Empires* (at least for the Russian, not the Soviet Empire).
[41] See on this point and different attitudes in the special issue of *Ab Imperio* 3 (2007) and 4 (2008).
[42] Stoler, *Along the Archival Grain*; Frederick Cooper and Anne Laura Stoler, *Tensions of Empire* (Berkeley: University of California Press, 1997); Jeffrey Herbst, *States and Power in Africa: Comparative Lessons in Authority and Control* (Princeton: Princeton University Press, 2000).
[43] Coeuré, 'Le siècle soviétique'.

brutal Soviet Empire. This conclusion seems to overlook that most studies of Soviet power have stressed the gap between its formal centralization and its actual lack of coordination. In this case, the fact that both the European colonial powers and the Russian state were 'broadcasting' powers, claiming strength well beyond reality, is not in contradiction with the fact that, indeed, brutality and violence took place, in part precisely because of the lack of real authority over the populations concerned.

The most appropriate answer to this question would be to differentiate by period and region. For example, the attitudes the Russians and Soviets had vis-à-vis the Muslim populations were not the same as regards other populations. Languages in the archives, and 'the voice of subalterns', varied accordingly.[44] In particular, the presence of the state in Muslim affairs greatly increased under Soviet rule.[45] Nevertheless, we still need a careful, comparative analysis of the European and Russian empires which considers their variability by region and period.

One further point deserves attention: in post-Soviet Russia, access to colonial archives, already extremely limited under Soviet rule, became relatively easy in the 1990s and early 2000s, before major restrictions in recent years. How far is this limited access different from that of the colonial archives in other areas of the world? It is from this decentralized Russian perspective that we may turn now to the history of colonial and postcolonial archives in the 'Western' realm.

Written sources against oral documents: the invention of the source and people with no history

In the nineteenth century, Ranke and his followers promoted philology and language; they succeeded in imposing their particular use of language as the only acceptable way to write history. The distinction between primary and secondary sources made it possible to separate archives from oral traditions as well as from existing historiography. This differentiation, Ranke claimed, would enable future historians, unlike their predecessors, to present facts rather than opinions. In other words, archives were simply equated with 'facts' and historical truths, without any critical reflection on principles governing archive development or the selection of documents by historians.[46] Eurocentrism, already present in the seventeenth century

---

[44] See in particular the special issue devoted to these questions in *Ab Imperio* 4 (2008). Also: Jane Burbank and Mark von Hagen, 'Coming into Territory: Uncertainty and Empire', in *Russian Empire. Space, People, Power, 1700–1930*, edited by Jane Burbank, Mark von Hagen and Anatolyi Remnev (Bloomington: Indiana University Press, 2008): 1–29; Jane Burbank and David L. Ransel, eds, *Imperial Russia: New Histories for the Empire* (Bloomington: Indiana University Press, 1998); Robert Geraci and Michael Khodarkovsky, eds, *Of Religion and Empire: Missions, Conversion, and Tolerance in Tsarist Russia* (Ithaca and London: Yale University Press, 2001); Dominic Lieven, ed., *The Cambridge History of Russia, Vol. 2. Imperial Russia, 1689–917* (Cambridge: Cambridge University Press, 2006).

[45] Khalid, 'Searching of Muslim Voices'.

[46] Leopold Ranke, *Die Römischen Päpste in den letzten vier Jahrhunderten*, 3 vols (Leipzig: Duncker und Humblot, 1834–6).

and consolidated during the eighteenth, became so dominant in the nineteenth century that it was easily exported outside Europe. Reformers in Japan,[47] Russia and Indonesia,[48] as well as in the Ottoman Empire[49] and Latin America, were eager to produce European-style history, using its methods and adopting its categories as universal. Imperialist Eurocentric thinking ended up producing its opposite: the defenders of local and national languages contrasted the enthusiasm of certain more or less Europeanized reformers. No doubt there was a good deal of cross-fertilization, for translation always involves appropriation and encounter; the hybridization of concepts indeed played a significant role.[50] At the same time, cultural exchange was never symmetrical: historical works written in European languages were translated into the national languages of other countries such Japan after the Meiji reforms and in Latin American and Asia, rather than the reverse. Also, the bibliographies circulating at the international level were in French, German and English, and only in part in Spanish and Portuguese, and the rest of the world was expected to adapt. The European conquest of the world, in its strengths and its weaknesses, was perfectly expressed in the languages of historians.[51]

For sure, the mediation of local actors was indispensable for investigations of religious texts, legal documents, inscriptions, maps and botany; and the works produced by the Europeans were a synthesis of their own perceptions and knowledge and those of local actors.[52] The problem in the nineteenth century was not so much interaction, but the fact that it was concealed on both sides due to colonialism and Western dominance. This is where the opposition between oral tradition and written documents came in.[53] Archives and the dominant historical culture transformed history and radicalized it at the same time. By giving priority to written documents and records, everything derived from oral sources was removed from history.[54] A global process was at work here: nineteenth-century historical culture excluded everyone either not engaged or only marginally involved in the production of documents, who therefore remained on the sidelines of progress and modernity – in other words, the peasants inside Europe and the 'peoples without a history' outside it.[55] The solution in these cases was to compile customs, practices and oral traditions. In India, Indonesia, Africa and Central Asia, local customs became the subjects of scholarly anthologies ranging from law to religion and folklore, and gradually evolved into anthropological and ethnographic

---

[47] Margaret Mehl, *History and the State in Nineteenth-Century Japan* (New York: St. Martin's Press, 1998).
[48] Anthony Reid and David Marr, eds, *Perceptions of the Past in Southeast Asia* (Singapore: Singapore University Press, 1979).
[49] Khalidi, *Arabic Historical*.
[50] Stanziani, *Les entrelacements*.
[51] Gopal Balakrishnan, ed., *Mapping the Nation* (London: Verso, 1998).
[52] Mantena, *The Origins of Modern Historiography in India*; Kapil Raj, *Relocating Modern Science* (Basingstoke: Macmillan, 2007).
[53] Jack Goody, *The Domestication of the Savage Mind* (Cambridge: Cambridge University Press, 1977).
[54] Ong, *Orality and Literacy*.
[55] James Clifford, *The Predicament of Culture: Twentieth-Century Ethnography, Literature, and Art* (Cambridge, MA: Harvard University Press, 1988); Hawkins, *Writing and Colonialism in Northern Ghana*.

studies.[56] Colonial law was a complete fabrication, presenting Western law and courts in opposition to those of local populations. This approach inherited from the very invention of the archives of the nation in post-revolutionary France, then in the rest of Europe and the Americas.

The twentieth century dramatically changed this landscape; connected events such as the end of 'central Empires' in Europe, the Bolshevik Revolution, first independentist and nationalist movements in Asia, Africa and Latin America subverted the notions and practices of archives and the definition of 'source' itself. In India, nationalism and the independence movement gained strength, while riots broke out in Punjab and Bengal during the war. In this context, the writing of Indian history became a crucial political issue, generating debates over sources, methods and proposed theories. In the preface to the *Cambridge History of India*, Henry Dodwell described the revolt of the Sepoys as a demonstration of ingratitude for the benevolent changes brought about by Britain.[57] Such works generated strongly nationalistic studies in Indian history,[58] emphasizing Indian democratic traditions, the strength of the Indian economy prior to the arrival of the East India Company (EIC).[59] Conventional tools of historiographical investigation were challenged, starting with the validity of 'local' Indian sources in vernacular languages. Several British historians characterized these sources as 'mythology', suited to the study of literature and folklore but not serious history. Yet some of these sources had been translated by 'Orientalists' at the end of the eighteenth century and throughout the nineteenth century.[60] The issue was thus raised during the interwar period: can these sources be considered legitimate? Are they genuine expressions of 'Indian traditions' or merely another variant of Orientalism?

After the First World War, the context of the debates changed in the face of rising nationalism in India and even in Britain. In London, Sanskrit and Indian history were henceforth taught at the School of Oriental and African Studies (SOAS), which was founded in 1916 to train colonial administrative personnel, military forces and businessmen looking to work in Asia or Africa.[61] However, when Indian nationalism started expanding in the mid-1920s, SOAS professors also put their expertise to work in opposing what they considered increasingly ideological interpretations of history being expressed in India. SOAS was thus a scholarly institutional response to the transformations under way in the British Empire.

Indeed, in India, the history department at the University of Allahabad launched a series of translations from vernacular languages as well as the *Journal of Indian History*,

---

[56] Mantena, *The Origins*; Stoler, *Along the Archival Grain*; Nicholas Dirks, Geoff Eley and Sherry Ortner, eds, *Culture, Power, History: A Reader in Contemporary Social History* (Princeton: Princeton University Press, 1994); Price, *The Convict and the Colonel*.

[57] Verney Lovett, *A History of the Indian Nationalist Movement* (London: Murray, 1920).

[58] Rakhal D. Banerjii, *The Age of the Imperial Guptas* (Benares: Benares Hindu University, 1933); Dipesh Chakrabarty, *The Calling of History: Sir Jadunath Sarkar and His Empire of Truth* (Chicago: The University of Chicago Press, 2015).

[59] C. H. Philips, ed., *Historians of India, Pakistan and Ceylon* (New York: Oxford University Press, 1961); Siva Pada Sen, ed., *Historians and Historiography in Modern India* (Calcutta: Institute of Historical Studies, 1973).

[60] Mantena, *The Origins*.

[61] Ian Brown, *The School of Oriental and African Studies. Imperial Training and the Expansion of Learning* (Cambridge: Cambridge University Press, 2016).

which focused from the start on handwritten sources from Indian states during the pre-colonial and colonial periods. Sarkar, one of the leading actors in the movement, helped with the publication of several Marathi documents and the history of the Marathas.[62] Did such documents constitute 'genuine history'?

To answer these questions would require not only linguistic but also historical knowledge: it would have required determining who developed a particular usage of Indian languages in the past and how this was done prior to and under colonial rule. Unfortunately, such an investigation was impossible during the interwar period because archives in India were closed to Indian students and researchers. Thus, the attitudes of the British authorities and Indian researchers towards constructing and granting access to archives developed in reaction to each other.[63] After the war, new dynamics took place in a different context, where the process of decolonization went along with a struggle over the sites and content of archives.

Locating the archives

As mentioned in the general introduction, a rich historiography has been produced in recent decades on colonial archives and the process of decolonization of history and those archives. As regards the main subject of discussion, the use of archives, the very possibility of extracting the 'voice' of colonized, subaltern and marginal people has probably been the most hotly debated. Not just the argument, but above all the categories (social, political, anthropological, even the notions of space and time)[64] adopted in the colonial archives have been subjected to radical criticism. The classical postcolonial and subaltern criticism focusing on the partiality of colonial sources and the special light in which colonized people were presented has been flourishing for decades now. Archives have been extensively discussed as instruments of power and imperialism, tools for controlling and counting local actors, re-writing their history and creating imagined communities.[65] This criticism has been particularly virulent in South Asia and Africa.[66] In Africa, the opposition between written archives and oral sources, so dear to colonial power and colonial history, has been adopted by postcolonial

---

[62] Jadunath Sarkar, *History of Aurangzeb*, 5 vols (Calcutta: Sarknar, 1912–52); *Fall of the Mughal Empire* (Calcutta: Patna, 1932–50).

[63] Robin Winks, *The Historiography of the British Empire-Commonwealth: Trends, Interpretations, and Resources* (Durham, NC: University of North Carolina Press, 1966).

[64] Kimberly Anderson, 'The Footprint and the Stepping Foot: Archival Records, Evidence, and Time', *Archival Science* 13, no. 4 (2013): 349–71; Jan Rüsen, ed., *Western Historical Thinking: An Intercultural Debate, Making Sense of History: Studies in Historical Culture and Intercultural Communication* (New York: Berghahn, 2002).

[65] Richards, *The Imperial Archive*; Benedict Anderson, *Imagined Communities* (London: Verso, 1991).

[66] Marie-Aude Fouéré and Lotte Hughes, 'Heritage and Memory in East Africa Today: A Review of Recent Developments in Cultural Heritage Research and Memory Studies', *Azania: Archaeological Research in Africa* 50, no. 4 (2015): 542–58; Marie-Aude Fouéré, *Remembering Julius Nyerere in Tanzania: History, Legacy, Memory* (Dar es Salaam: Mkuki na Nyota, 2015); Verne Harris, *National Archives of South Africa* (Pretoria: National Archives, 2000); Florence Arès, *Rapport final sur le développement des archives nigériennes* (Paris and New York: ONU, 1991); Albert Mban, *Les problèmes des archives africaines. A quand la solution?* (Paris: L'Harmattan, 2007).

studies, while reversing the value given to each.⁶⁷ In the absence of any reliable picture provided by colonial powers, oral history has been presented as the main well-founded source to rely on and, sometimes, the idea of African history by African historians has been advanced.⁶⁸ More recently, however, this dichotomy has been partially overcome by historians of Africa, close to Stoler's epistemological posture,⁶⁹ who advocate the possibility, if not the necessity, of reading colonial archives along the grain in order to capture the complexity of the relationships between 'colonizers' and 'colonized' in the construction of those sources.⁷⁰

In the case of India, the critics of colonial archives took a somewhat different orientation, insisting not only, as in Africa, on the partiality of views of the archives and their role as a tool of domination,⁷¹ but also, rather than on orality, on the necessity of relying on vernacular published sources.⁷² Other contributions urged either a return to social history⁷³ or reconstruction of the co-writing of archival sources by colonizers and colonized.⁷⁴ Similar debates took place on the history of China, South-east Asia and Latin America.⁷⁵ In other words, since the 1960s at the latest, the debates that took place in Western countries on the meaning of the archives as text, artefact and tool for power were mutually pollinating with the tensions of decolonization. This was not just

---

[67] Eric Woolf, *Europe and the People without History* (Berkeley: University of California Press, 1982); Echevarria, *Myth and Archive*.

[68] Comaroff, *Ethnography and the Historical Imagination*; Pierre Singavarelou, 'Des historiens sans histoire? La construction de l'historiographie coloniale en France sous la Troisième République', *Actes de la Recherche en Sciences sociales* 184, no. 5 (2010): 30–43; Jan Vansina, *De la tradition orale: essai de méthode historique* (Tervuren: Musée royal de l'Afrique centrale, 1961); Daniel McCall, *Africa in Time Perspective: A Discussion of Historical Reconstruction from Unwritten Sources* (Boston: Boston University Press, 1964); Toyin Falola, *Sources and Methods in African History: Spoken, Written, Unearthed* (Rochester, NY: University of Rochester Press, 2002).

[69] Ann Laure Stoler, *Capitalism and Confrontation in Sumatra's Plantation, 1870–1979* (Ann Arbor: University of Michigan Press, 1995); Shahid Amin, *Event, Metaphor, Memory: 1922–1992* (Berkeley: University of California Press, 1995).

[70] Lidwien Kapteijns, *African Historiography Written by Africans, 1955–1973* (Leiden: Brill, 1973); Catherine Coquery-Vidrovitch and Odile Goerg, *Des historiens africains en Afrique* (Paris: L'Harmattan, 1998); Caroline Neale, A *Writing Independent History: African Historiography, 1960–1980* (Westport, CT: Greenwood Press, 1985); Catherine Coquery-Vidrovitch, 'A l'origine de l'historiographie africaine de langue française', *Présence africaine* 173, no. 1 (2006): 77–90; Andreas Eckert, 'Fitting Africa into World History: A Historiographical Exploration', in *Writing World History 1800–2000*, edited by Benedikt Stuchtey and Eckhardt Fuchs (Oxford: Oxford University Press, 2002): 99–118; Erik Gilbert and Jonathan Reynolds, *Africa in World History from Prehistory to the Present* (Upper Saddle River, NJ: Pearson, 2004).

[71] Sumit Guha, 'Speaking Historically: The Changing Voices of Historical Narration in Western India', *American Historical Review* 109, no. 4 (2005): 1084–103; Gyan Prakash, 'Subaltern Studies as Postcolonial Criticism', *American Historical Review* 99, no. 5 (1994): 1475–90; Gayatri Chakravorty Spivak, 'The Rani of Sirmur: An Essay in Reading the Archives', *History and Theory* 24, no. 3 (1985): 247–72.

[72] Supriya Mukherjee, 'Indian Historical Writing since 1947' in *The Oxford History of Historical Writing*, edited by Alex Schneider and Daniel Woolf, vol. 5: 515–38 (Oxford: Oxford University Press, 2015); Vinay Lal, *The History of History: Politics and Scholarship in Modern India* (Delhi: Oxford University Press, 2003).

[73] Sumit Sarkar, *Writing Social History* (Delhi: Oxford University Press, 1997).

[74] Rao, Shulman and Subrahmanyam, *Textures of Time*.

[75] Edward Wang, *Inventing China through History* (New York: State University of New York Press, 2001); Gershoni, Singer and Erdem, *Middle East Historiographies*; Iggers, Wang and Mukherjee, *A Global History of Modern Historiographies*.

a move from the 'centre' to the 'periphery' but a two-way road: if Derrida or Foucault looked South, from the other direction the question of the appropriate categories not just for investigation (we will discuss them in Part IV) but in the archives themselves spread from India, African and Latin American countries towards the 'Global North'. Since then, the question has not just been that of the categories of the observers now and in the past, but also that of the commensurability of valid categories from different area studies. These debates certainly reflected some major trends: the difficult, painful reflection on historical memory after the Second World War in Europe, decolonization and the end of European empires.[76] Note that the impact of Foucault and Derrida was not the same in the 'Global South'. While, as we have seen, in Russia, most historians opposed 'deconstructivism', this was not the case in India and Africa. In India, Spivak translated Derrida in 1967 and, therefore, Derrida's criticism of archives greatly influenced the second generation of subaltern studies (which was under the influence of Said and Foucault instead of Gramsci, as for the first generation) down to Prakash and Chakrabarty. Archives as a political site of power were their main credo. This transfer was more difficult in places like South Africa where, despite Derrida's strong influence on Verne Harris, one of the chief archivists,[77] the major political issues in post-apartheid society led to doubts about deconstructivism, as in Russia, and for similar reasons: the silence of a distorted official history had to be overcome through the 'truth' discovered in the archives.[78] The postcolonial critique of 'distorted' history and 'mediated archives', as expressed not only in India but also among archivists and historians in the Netherlands, Canada (Terry Cook was the leading archivist in this transfer) and the United States, reached South Africa. Those archivists urged leaving the narrow-focused examination of the single document and considered instead whole sets of files and their social and political origin and elaboration.[79] More importantly, these authors consider that documents are not just passive items, but living artefacts; archivists themselves strongly contribute to this life: they do not merely classify and preserve but continuously transform archives and documents, and focus research and the public memory. In this version, postmodernism went far beyond the critique of archives as power or the mere deconstructivism of sources and argued instead for actively reimagining the past through the appropriation of documents and their meaning.

And yet, the fact that debates mostly focused on the origin and interpretation of the archives helped conceal another, no less central, question on the location of the archives and the classification of documents.[80] If archives and power are related,

---

[76] Stanziani, *Eurocentrism*.
[77] Harris, *Archives and Justice*.
[78] André Du Toit, 'La Commission Vérité et Réconciliation sud-africaine. Histoire locale et responsabilité face au monde', *Politique africaine* 92, no. 4 (2003): 97–116; Marie-Aude Fouéré, 'L'effet Derrida en Afrique du Sud. Jacques Derrida, Verne Harris et la notion d'archive(s) dans l'horizon post-apartheid', *Annales HSS* 74, no. 3 (2019): 745–78.
[79] Joan Schwartz and Terry Cook, 'Archives, Records, and Power: The Making of Modern Memory', *Archival Science* 2 (2002): 1–19.
[80] Alistair Tough, 'Archives in Sub-Saharan Africa Half a Century after Independence', *Archival Science* 9 (2009): 187–201; Nathan Mnjama, 'Dealing with Backlog Accumulation of Archival Materials in Eastern and Southern Africa', *Information Development* 22, no. 1 (2006): 48–56; S. McKemmish and others, eds, *Archives: Recordkeeping in Society* (Wagga Wagga, NSW: Center for Information Studies, Charles Sturt University, 2005).

then, how can we possibly dismiss the importance of gaining access to documents and their very location? And if the classification of documents, not just their content, orients research and interpretation, how can one possibly escape from the organization of colonial archives in the homeland and that of archives in the former colonies?[81] These points, in particular the second one, have been too easily neglected and mostly made by archive staff,[82] as if historians were limited to talking about textuality and interpretation and not the role the classification of documents plays in their research.

For example, in the British colonies, historians such as Richards have argued that the organization of the archives was a major tool in the management of the empire itself, a place where reality and fantasies met.[83] At the same time, he adds that archives were a major tool of British imperialism. However, at least in the colonial capitals, record keeping was built around the concept of registry: the secretariat ran the record keeping and its organization; registers were organized following the branches of the administration. In principle a register of registers should have been produced, but in many cases this never saw the light. As a consequence, new officials in charge modified the attribution of records to one register or another. In general, well-organised archives were not established until just before independence (exceptions were the archives of central African colonies set up in the 1930s). During independence, in particular in areas like Kenya where this was a violent process, the destruction of archives was massive. However, destruction of documents was part of ordinary archival policy in South Africa throughout apartheid. Elsewhere, this attitude persisted after independence due to lack of resources. After independence, most expatriate British officials did not help at all. In some cases, they did, as in Kenya. However, newly born states had difficulties training and retaining archivists, either because of low wages or because there were no archivists at all, and this was part of the broader trend of corruption.

In France, the history of colonial archives is primarily that of the artificial separation of records in locations other than the national and metropolitan archives.[84] This was quite explicit in France where Colbert created the Dépôt des Archives de la Marine et des Colonies in 1680, located in Saint-Germain-en-Laye near Paris. It was moved to Paris in 1699 and to Versailles in 1763. Three years later the Dépôt des Chartes des Colonies was transferred there as well. In 1778 a new Dépôt des Chartes et Plans des Colonies was established and then placed under the authority of the Naval Ministry three years later. All these archives were gathered together in Paris in 1837, but not in the same place as the national archives. Only some of the

---

[81] Brian Axel, ed., *From the Margins: Historical Anthropology and Its Future* (Durham, NC: Duke University Press, 2005).

[82] Abiola Abioye, 'Fifty Years of Archives Administration in Nigeria: Lessons for the Future', *Record Management Journal* 17, no. 1 (2007): 52–62; Jeannette Bastian, 'Reading Colonial Records through an Archival Lens: The Provenance of Place, Space and Creation', *Archival Science* 6, no. 3–4 (2006): 267–84; Carolyn Hamilton, Verne Harris, Michèle Pickover, Graeme Reid and Razia Saleh (eds), *Refiguring the Archive* (Dordrecht: Kluwer Academic, 2002).

[83] Richards, *The Imperial Archive*.

[84] Barker, *Native Acts*; Procter, Cook and Williams eds, *Political Pressure and the Archival Record*.

colonial records were transferred to the national archives in 1899 when a general shift towards centralization took hold in France (central state vs. municipalities, confirmed hierarchies between national and regional authorities, etc.). It was in this context that, on the eve of the First World War, M. Schefer was placed in charge of the organization and classification of the archives. He suggested doing away with the 'sacred' principle of conservation and reorganizing the records according to their topics and objects. He began these transfers, but they were interrupted by the war. Ever since, archivists in France have deplored the 'damage' caused by this subversive action, which is quite unacceptable from the standpoint of the '*principe de conservation*' – more or less idealized, as we have seen. However, as for the metropolitan archives, the 'sacred principle' was not always enforced – right from the very production and first collection of documents. In particular, directors of one or another section, commission or organization took a large number of relevant documents to their own office or even their home, instead of transferring them to their own cataloguing department. This widespread behaviour weakened the 'principle of conservation' by provenance. A major shift occurred in the 1950s and 1960s when decolonization was accompanied by the transfer to Paris of all or some of the records that had been hitherto preserved in the colonies (we will return to this crucial event shortly). In 1966, all the documents recovered from the colonies were stored in Aix-en-Provence where, twenty years later, they were finally joined by all the other documents already available in Paris.[85]

This story suggests several interconnected questions. First, it confirms the extreme flexibility of the principle of provenance. It is not so much a matter of contrasting this principle to cataloguing by keyword or topic, as archival history usually relates, but understanding the way the two principles constantly overlapped and the reasons for that. During the *ancien régime* in France, for example, the separation of the colonial archives from the others – for the exclusive use of the administration, let us not forget that – was consistent with the idea that the settlement of colonies and sovereignty were connected, as shown in previous chapters. In the nineteenth century, with the opening of public archives, the principle of provenance took on a peculiar meaning: the history of the French nation, preserved in the newly created national archives, must be kept separate from that of its empire, more or less in the shadows with frequent shifts between republic and empire and their respective meanings in post-revolutionary France. It is not by chance that the consolidation of colonial and metropolitan archives took place only at the turn of the twentieth century when the centralized state metamorphosed under the Third Republic. This happened at the moment when republican values were ultimately affirmed, but, at the same time, France launched into a new colonial venture in Africa. Old colonial archives, from the 'first colonial empire' as it is referred to nowadays, were therefore put in the same place as the metropolitan archives, but still kept in separate files and with no connections between them in the inventories, nor consequently in historians' approaches at that time. Even more important, new

---

[85] Charles Laroche, 'Les archives de l'expansion française outre-mer conservées en métropole', *La gazette des archives* 55 (1966): 235–52.

archives in the African colonies, not forgetting Indochina,[86] were still preserved *in situ* and they scarcely appeared in the central archives. More than ever, empire was embarrassing to the nation, in particular under the French republicanism of that time, and is still very much so today.[87] In short, the sacred principle of provenance (sacred to archivists, and sometimes to historians) is not only blurred in practice, but the way this is done is an indicator of the political and social construction of historical memories themselves. This was true in the organization of the archives back in the nineteenth century when archival classifications celebrated the 'birth of the nation'; this was also the case in the USSR with the constitution of fully invented 'revolutionary archives'. Colonial archives also dropped the 'principle of provenance', on the one hand, by presenting a well-organized colonial state (which was hardly the case) and, on the other hand, by collecting and translating 'local', 'oral' or 'vernacular' sources in a well-established idiom and putting them into appropriate classification boxes. Then, postcolonial archives also constantly mentioned the principle of provenance while constantly seeking to evade it, except when it was needed to show the 'power' of the colonial state (in this case, the same colonial classifications in the archives were kept alive).

A number of new states adopted the same classification systems as colonizing countries in order to facilitate comparison with corresponding archives in the metropole. Numerous authors contested the relevance of this solution, which was supposed to obscure the role of 'subalterns', the colonized and those on the margins. As a result, there were suggestions to use classifications by keywords in order to offer different perspectives from those of colonial history.[88] Postcolonial interpretations openly call for a general overruling of the principle of provenance in the name of the fight against Eurocentrism.[89] Why is this important? As we have already mentioned, social scientists and historians have usually distinguished between archive-based categories and social theories and models. This clear-cut opposition is based upon the idea that archives simply reflect historical realities and that their very classification and order respect the 'principle of provenance'. However, we have just seen that this principle is not often respected, and that social categories and models influence the ordering of files, inventories and, therefore, research. We further develop this point in Part III, where we examine the social categories themselves as embedded in the archives, social theories and social dynamics.

We may also observe that the strict separation between colonial and metropolitan archives influenced whole generations of French historians and commentators extremely keen to specialize either in the history of France or in that of its colonial empire. Apart from some general remarks 'to set the context', any interplay between the two is strikingly absent. To a certain extent, this divide mirrored that between

---

[86] Féréol de Ferry, 'Les archives en Indochine', *Gazette des archives* 8 (1950): 33–41; Jacques Borgé and Nicolas Viasnoff, *Archives de l'Indochine* (s. l., M. Trinckvel, 1995).
[87] Frederick Cooper, *Citizenship between Empire and Nation* (Princeton: Princeton University Press, 2014).
[88] Bastian, 'Reading Colonial Records'.
[89] Cook, 'Fashionable Nonsense or Professional Rebirth'; Bastian, 'Reading Colonial Records'.

specialists of the *ancien régime* and historians of contemporary France. Classifications in the archives as well as the institutional framework for history teaching in France strongly influenced its historiography: clear-cut divisions between metropolitan and colonial worlds and between pre-revolutionary and contemporary France orient much of the historiographies. Although continuities across the revolution have been the subject of several studies (albeit always a small minority), the colonial and national worlds are still separate. And yet, one can hardly separate these two worlds and their strongly interrelated histories. This is true in the ordering of archives themselves. In fact, the transfer of documents from the colonies to metropolitan France was a dramatic story. The way this transfer was done depended on the history of each colony and its documentation, and then on the process of decolonization itself, taking different paths in Madagascar and Algeria, Reunion and Indochina. For example, Algeria already had a well-established archival service in 1962, where classifications did not exactly match those of the national archives but presented some innovations in terms of files, institutions and classifications introduced in 1927.[90] At the moment of decolonization only a few archives were transferred to Paris, and some of them, as we will see, have only lately been declassified. Archives available in Aix included those of the central authorities in Paris and Alger, and those of the governors of Alger, Oran and Constantine. In Indochina, the archives were organized in 1934 with specific series not corresponding to those in either Algeria or Paris. The most astonishing case was that of French West Africa (AOF) where almost all the archives were kept in place when it acquired its independence from Paris. Now, the general criterion that specialists of French archives and government officials and archivists of the 1950s and 1960s followed was that archives of so-called 'current affairs' were kept in place, while documents of the 'sovereign administration' were transferred to France.[91] This argument was based on an agreement signed in 1949 in Indochina in which this policy was proposed in view of independence. In fact, this distinction is acceptable only at first sight: first in the classification of the archives themselves – how can one clearly set the boundary between politics and administration? – and second in the transfer process. The latter mostly depended on the political sensitivity of the files and the specific process of decolonization. For instance, the *état civil* (register of births, marriages and deaths) of Algeria was not transferred, while all military archives were. The French authorities sent exploratory missions to the main colonies starting in the late 1940s to identify the importance and organization of their archives (Laroche mission to sub-Saharan Africa in 1948, Ménier mission to Pondicherry in 1949–50 and to Brazzaville in 1952, mission to Dakar and Abidjan in 1953–4, Laroche and Ménier mission to Indochina in 1954). However, a real, detailed history of the negotiations, political and diplomatic pressures and military interventions concerning the archives colony by colony is still to be written. Such a history should identify documents in the so-called directors' (of archives) files, in the Foreign Affairs archives and, to some extent, at the Ministry of War and in the cabinets of the French prime minister and

---

[90] Sylvie Clair, 'Le Centre des Archives d'Outre-Mer', *La Gazette des archives* 142–3 (1988): 5–17.
[91] Etienne Taillemite, 'Les archives de la France d'outre-mer', *La Gazette des archives* 22 (1957): 6–22; Mbaye, 'Le Caom: un centre d'archives partagées?'.

president. Surprisingly, this history has been ignored by all those who, in the wave of postcolonial history, have just focused on categories of colonial archives.

It is with this huge limitation in mind that we may turn now to the question of reconstructing postcolonial histories. We have already mentioned the arguments of subaltern studies and their attempt to reveal the bias of Western history and thought. These tensions have a long history and convey the political relations between former colonies and colonizing countries, which remain challenging today. Memory as denunciation and claims of colonial crimes were the subject of a great many debates. In France, this debate exploded during the 2000s concurrently with the history of the Algerian War and the history of slavery. These demands echoed those of African countries that had already been addressed to Great Britain and the United States during previous years. In France, however, the debate took on a particularly virulent dimension due to the silence surrounding the Algerian War and slavery, along with resistance to such openings, as shown by the nationalism of Sarkozy and the historian Pierre Nora when they were asked questions on the subject. Again, access to archives was crucial. It took until the 1990s for the French Army archives on the Algerian War to be opened to the public. It was only ten years later, in 2004, that a collective work, *La fin de l'amnésie*, finally saw the light of day.[92] It was followed by an increasing number of works, and subsequently even by a 'war of memories' over the 'benefits' of colonization and its destructive effects.[93] In other words, the 'declassification' of files did not just bring access to 'truth' but, as should be expected, engendered a real 'battle' of memories.

These tensions surrounding archives and memory were not limited to Algeria, but cut across the entire field of colonial studies. Decolonization was accompanied by a synchronous process of implementing archives in ex-colonies and reorganizing colonial archives in metropolitan France. In the first case, the fact of having national archives took on almost as much importance as having an airline and a currency. In practice, however, this operation depended on the forms taken by decolonization, violence and tensions, along with the appropriation of documents by new authorities. Sometimes, as in East Africa, archives were quite simply burned during wars of independence and civil wars to heat or clean oneself. Sometimes colonial authorities were able to repatriate a large part of the documents, but this was not always the case.[94] Senegal and French West Africa generally represent a good example of this latter outcome, while French Equatorial Africa fell in the first category. Algerian archives were also in large part repatriated, even though they were subsequently not very accessible for a long time.

While taking into consideration the constructed nature of archives, their use not only for historical reconstruction but also for 'justice' and 'national reconciliation' is altogether central. Thus, in South Africa, unlike in Algeria, the organization and

---

[92] Mohammed Harbi and Benjamin Stora, *La guerre d'Algérie, 1954–2004. La fin de l'amnésie* (Paris: Laffont, 2004).

[93] Olivier Le Cour Grandmaison, *Le 17 Octobre 1961. Un crime d'État à Paris* (Paris: La dispute, 2001); Sylvie Thénault, *Une drôle de justice: les magistrats dans la guerre d'Algérie* (Paris: La Découverte, 2001).

[94] Tough, 'Archives in Sub-Saharan Africa'.

recovery of archives expresses not only tension with the metropole but also in the country itself that arose from the ashes of civil war.[95] In most African countries, the customs and issues surrounding archives often came up against a lack of specialized staff, the instability of such staff due to limited salaries, the phenomenon of corruption[96] and, finally, the exertion of control over archives in connection with internal political tensions. Beginning in the 1990s, the situation improved in a number of African countries, with increased national and international resources being allocated to archives for staff training, document preservation, digitization and cataloguing. Personnel transfers, often between the former metropole and its colonies, also accompanied the transfer of resources. New connections were also put in place outside the postcolonial framework; for instance, in Sudan, where Chinese financing played a role in the construction and preservation of national archives.[97]

Although the classification of archives influences research and its conclusions, the colonial legacy and the European attitude of associating Africa, orality and 'peoples without history' was reproduced within a certain postcolonial thought, and later in nationalist thought in Africa itself.[98] Western anthropologists were the first to oppose local knowledge with colonial constructs, including archives.[99] Criticism, when not rejection, of colonial archives was thus expressed just as well in India as in Africa.[100] Numerous works have highlighted the existence of a genuine African civilization and economy, which was subjected and annihilated by colonial authorities. Oral sources have multiplied for lack of sufficient colonial sources on this subject, and they have been asserted as the 'true sources' of African history.[101]

These tensions over sources are reproduced when it comes to the background of authors: must one be African to write a proper history of Africa?

In Europe, decolonization translated into support for African history (e.g. African history at SOAS in London, centres for African history in France). In 1962, the United Nations Educational, Scientific and Cultural Organization (UNESCO) evoked the need to develop African history throughout the world. However, in new African states, emphasis was increasingly placed on the need to have African historians. These historians were often educated in Europe or the United States, and had a tendency to adopt nationalist postures. This positioning was even more widespread among historians educated in Africa itself, and often critical with regard to their colleagues educated elsewhere, who were accused of being under the influence of

---

[95] Harris, *National Archives of South Africa*.
[96] Kenya Anti-Corruption Commission 2007. Kenya Anti-Corruption Commission presents training certificates to records management committee members. Available via http://www.kacc.go.ke/archives/PressReleases/PRESS-RELEASE-RECORDS.pdf.
[97] Mban, *Les problème des archives africaines*.
[98] Echevarria, *Myth and Archive*.
[99] E. E. Evans-Pritchard, 'Social Anthropology: Past and Present, The Marett Lecture, 1950', *Social Anthropology and Other Essays* (New York: Free Press, 1951); Claude Lévi-Strauss, *La pensée sauvage* (Paris: Plon, 1962).
[100] Comaroff, *Ethnography and the Historical Imagination*.
[101] Vansina, *De la tradition orale*; Falola, *Sources and Methods*.

colonial thought.¹⁰² In reality, nationalism and pan-Africanism were mixed; while the homogeneity of Africa was sometimes denied depending on the context, nationalism was a constant in several African historiographies.¹⁰³ In this context, archives became the object of strong suspicion among Africanists in Africa as well as outside it, while oral sources were often presented as 'real African' sources.¹⁰⁴ This was not counting the role of mediators, mostly Europeans, and African elites as the origin of oral sources.¹⁰⁵

Conclusion: Part 1

In the West, since the emergence of historical sciences, the notion of 'sources' has mostly been associated with archives, with an established opposition between primary and secondary sources on one hand, and between written and oral sources on the other. Although these oppositions are porous and quite often called into question, they have nevertheless guided the historian's craft for several centuries. A social and intellectual history of sources reveals unexpected tangles and problems, such as the relation between the demise of a person, an institution, a regime and the creation of documents and archives. In France, as in other countries, the birth of what is known as 'modern' historiography is often associated with that of the modern state, the latter being identified with the nation-state. This interpretation calls for qualification, because during the period studied and well beyond it was empires that dominated the world stage. This connection is often lost in Eurocentric histories of European historiography, which tend to underestimate not only the importance of similar dynamics in non-European worlds but also the very early interface between empire and nation in Europe itself, and its role in the emergence of a historiography known as 'modern'. Both translating from and learning the languages of colonized peoples were part of imperial management, and influenced the constitution of modern historiography. Said saw this clearly for Europe, and linked it to European domination; however, this process also took place in Russia, China, India and the Ottoman Empire. In all of these cases, the identification of 'historical method', the content of history and the legitimizing of empires were linked.

The same was true for revolutions and decolonization: these have been major turning points in the definition of sources and their interconnectedness with the history of societies whose archives have been much more than testimonies. The construction of memory and the classification of documents are themselves part of this history. These relations are fluid, sometimes tense: the desire to permanently establish document classification coexists with inevitable changes in the institutions that produce the documents, which calls into question the suitability of the classification system. National archives are arranged and organized according to principles that

---

[102] Kapteijins, *African Historiography*.
[103] Coquery-Vidrovitch, 'A l'origine'.
[104] Mamadou Diawara and others, eds, *Historical Memory in Africa* (New York: Columbia University, 2010).
[105] Mantena, *Artifacts of History*; Stoler, *Along the Archival Grain*.

were consolidated and became universal during the nineteenth century, in an effort to establish the principle of *classification by provenance* – considered to be the only correct approach – over *classification by topic*, which was accused of being artificial as it was based on 'a-historical' social sciences. In practice, there is no reason for such an opposition, and archives classify and reclassify their documents in response to institutional and historical changes. The archives themselves have been the focus of battles and conflicts – during revolutionary times, but also during decolonization and following the Second World War. Following these events, the very definition of sources became a cause of conflict and discussion. This is why oral sources have become so important in the history of Africa and that of 'people without history', and also for the survivors of the Shoah and the purges and repressions of the twentieth century. This is also why texts that used to be deemed fiction and myth are now offered as perfectly adequate sources in India, Africa, several countries in Asia and even in Europe and the Americas. Rather than reproduce the debates that continue to the present day between colonial archives as an expression of the governing power (and therefore unusable) and colonial archives as an expression of resistance by the colonized, we have shown how these archives were jointly written by actors who, although they possessed very different powers, all participated in the creation and classification of documents. The social history of colonial archives (and archives in general) confirms this overlap and the lack of differentiation between 'practices' and 'discourse'. The battle for the archives, their production and control, accompanies and contributes to the construction of the world. Which world? In the nineteenth century, national archives and the emergence of liberal nation-states in Europe went hand in hand. Liberal ideals and the constitution of national archives were not just joined together, but expanded well beyond the boundaries of Europe, to Latin America in particular. The identification of history with the history of the nation was one of the greatest successes of liberalism. And yet, this apparently homogeneous attitude hid the persistence of colonial empires and, with them, the very fact that a colonial memory was built, artificially distinct from national memory. Separate archival collections and, increasingly over time, even distinct places for national and colonial archives concealed this strong interrelationship between the emergence of the nation-state and the persistence of empires. It is no accident that, in places like France, colonial history and general history (i.e. national history) are distinct fields in historiography, just as the archives themselves are kept separated.

The twentieth century partially disrupted this order, first with the Russian Revolution and then with the process of decolonization. In archive building, the Russian Revolution was initially inspired by the French Revolution and its archives: a clear-cut break between 'before' and 'after' oriented the organization of archives. At the same time, the Soviets added something new: they openly invented thematic archives named 'the archives of the revolution'. The principle of provenance was therefore completely overruled, and the reconstruction of national revolutionary memory was oriented by pre-established archival categories and collections of documents. Continuities through the revolution were concealed in the organization of files which, at the same time, put into separate collections 'real revolutionary' and 'counter-revolutionary' actors.

These new tensions between the provenance and thematic classification of documents further developed during the decolonization process, when the building of national archives in most emerging countries again concealed the mutual relationship with the previous colonial homeland in both the categories and classification of documents. Although the principle of provenance was officially claimed by archivists, new collections celebrating the end of the colonial yoke were put together as well. These ambiguities also found expression in debates about categories: subaltern interpretations of the colonial archives sought to overturn the dominant categories, and yet they remained prisoners of those categories. Postcolonial archival and historical categories merely reversed the colonial ones, while keeping the same epistemological and analytical framework. However, all these social and political tensions around historical memories and societies in the archives cannot be fully understood without their complement, namely, the political economies of capitalism, imperialism and socialism. In this case, it was not well-classified texts and documents, but well-ordered data and graphics that were the main sources of tensions.

Part Two

The social life of data

Introduction: archives, data and models

We have already discussed one solution that modern thinking on epistemology has offered to the question of knowing how to prove a statement, beyond its philosophical and possibly logical relevance: the invention of the archive as a source for established 'facts'. This approach is usually contrasted to those that many social scientists, economists, sociologists and some historians, but also anthropologists and political scientists, espouse, mostly based on quantities as a proxy for reality. A huge bibliography is available on these themes: histories of statistics – both in their positivist, scientific version and in a reflexive approach[1] – and political and social histories using statistics.[2] We need to make a distinction between two main points; on the one hand, the history of statistics, and on the other, the use of data in social history. On the first point, we have already mentioned in the Introduction the main themes and focuses of histories of statistics: their epistemological background, their social, political and economic justification and origin, the role of the state, the different national histories of statistics. The following pages illustrate my deep indebtedness to these studies; at the same time, I also intend to distance myself from some of their postulates and interpretations. Thus, instead of contrasting, say, the British, French or Chinese ways of producing statistics, I will show the connections (and disconnections) in the circulation of statistical knowledge and statistical infrastructure (administration, literacy, training of statisticians). Second, the state will not be seen as a monolithic entity, and as such opposed to (civil) society in statistical production, but, rather, I will stress the fragmentation of state agencies and their different interactions with social actors. This implies that, instead of simply relating the emergence of statistical reason to the role of the state in social and economic life (which was certainly true), I will seek to identify which was the form of state for which statistics and economic-social policies emerged. Third, even if structural dynamics (i.e. the emergence and transformations of capitalism) seem to be relevant in explaining the emergence of statistical thinking, I will avoid any simple causal link between capitalism and statistics. This approach is tempting, and I am certainly keener on it than a pure intellectual history of statistics. At the same time, I will stress the cognitive and empirical interplay between structures and ideas: not just capitalism, defined *a priori*, influencing statistics, but a particular form of capitalism giving birth to a particular form of statistics and, vice versa, a possible reformulation of the historical definition of capitalism based upon statistics. This is where we need to take position vis-à-vis modern social history. After all, E. P. Thompson was not so keen on making use of statistics and data, quite the contrary: he relied more on cultural anthropology. However, he was an exception and most social historians of the 1970s and 1980s made wide use of data. This attitude paved the way for the cultural turn which, by the way, had among its forerunners earlier social quantitative historians such as William Sewell and Lynn Hunt.[3] I will discuss

---

[1] Just a few references: Stephen Stigler, *The History of Statistics: The Measurement of Statistics before 1900* (Boston: Belknap Press, 1990); Peter Bernstein, *Against the God: The Remarkable Story of Risk* (New York: Wiley, 1996); Andrew Dale, *A History of Inverse Probability* (New York: Springer, 1999).

[2] Porter, *Trust in Numbers*; Desrosières, *La politique des grands nombres*.

[3] Sewell, 'The Political Unconscious'.

these trends in detail in Part IV. Here it suffices to mention them and the social turn in order to raise a broader methodological question: how did the study of society make use of data? Was it a form of positivism (and which one)? Was it incompatible with or complementary to the use of archives? Unlike what some historians supporting the cultural turn in the late twentieth century asserted, the first option was not always the right one: data and archival sources have more in common than not.

Let us take the examples of the infinite discussions on the profitability of slavery. This is where the connections between Parts II and III (data and social categories) become relevant: the historiography pointed to several topics reflecting these connections, and we may mention one – the profitability of slavery. In this particular case, the identification of social actors and the attempts to move from archival analysis to databases testify to the relationships between epistemology and social practices, at the very core of this book. Eric Williams set off this debate in 1944 with a twofold argument, claiming that slavery had financed the Industrial Revolution and that its abolition had contributed directly to the transformation of capitalism.[4] Ever since, many scholars have taken part in this debate and we need to examine each argument in detail: the number of slaves, the profitability of the slave trade and of the plantations, their role in capital accumulation in Britain and the United States, and finally the role of cotton in the Industrial Revolution. Thus, during last decades, a team of scholars invented and updated a database on the slave trade across the Atlantic. The team made use of ships and other information as identified in British, French, Spanish, Portuguese and Dutch archives.[5] Furthermore, in view of the extremely high number of valuable works produced on this subject, there is no need to discuss in detail the history of slavery and of transatlantic slavery in particular. Instead, let us move to the crucial question here: was this trade profitable?

Very few authors radically deny the role of the slave trade and slavery, while stressing the role of domestic demand and innovation as the prime origins of the Industrial Revolution and accumulation.[6] According to this interpretation, the rise of the Atlantic and the slave trade was a consequence of British economic growth, not its cause.[7] This argument is purely hypothetical and starts from the premise that markets were perfectly competitive, which was absolutely not the case at that time. Recently McCloskey radically attacked along a similar line tenants of the role of international trade and argued that cotton in itself was not fundamental and that Britain would have achieved its Industrial Revolution even with beer, given the role of democracy, innovation and domestic markets.[8] This is an important move in our perspective: it

---

[4] Eric Williams, *Capitalism and Slavery* (Chapel Hill: North Carolina University Press, 1944).
[5] http://www.slavevoyages.org/tast/assessment/estimates.faces. David Eltis, Stephen D. Behrendt, David Richardson and Herbert S. Klein, *The Trans-Atlantic Slave Trade: A Database on CD-ROM* (Cambridge and New York: Cambridge University Press, 1999).
[6] Sheridan, *Sugar and Slavery*.
[7] C. Knick Harley, 'Slavery, the British Atlantic Economic and the Industrial Revolution', *University of Oxford Discussion Papers in Economic History* 113 (2013) http://www.nuff.ox.ac.uk/economics/history/paper113/harley113.pdf.
[8] Deidre McCloskey, *Bourgeois Dignity. Why Economics Can't Explain the Modern World* (Chicago: University of Chicago Press, 2011).

shows that, in order to 'hold the line' (slavery did not contribute much to the Industrial Revolution), some authors are ready to overcome not only archives but also data and make use of a 'model'.

Recently, Burnard and Riello also insisted on the marginal role slavery and the slave trade played in the Industrial Revolution.[9] According to them, slave cotton expanded only after the Industrial Revolution had taken place. Klas Rönnbäck also considered that the contribution of slavery and the slave trade to British economic growth was marginal.[10] Evaluating the profits from the slave trade is difficult for multiple reasons; first, we need to know, for each vessel, the number of slaves, the price of each one and their costs. Ship ledgers must be supplemented with traders' accounting books, including the cost of insurance, freight, etc. It has been estimated that errors of about 5 per cent in the evaluation of sales (quantity and prices) lead to errors of about 55 per cent of the final value. Added to a standard 5 per cent error in the estimation of costs (slaves, ships, insurance, freight), net profits are likely to have been underestimated or overestimated by … 100 per cent![11] Last but not least, profitability depended on the return trip or, even worse, on the triangular trade, involving at least two other trips by the same ship, for which we also need to know the costs, revenues, etc.

All these uncertainties help to explain why each of the many historians involved in this debate over decades has produced her or his own weighting and correction of the data and why they have come up with extremely different results. Thus, Richard Sheridan and Roger Anstey criticized Williams;[12] so did David Richardson, who argued that Williams overestimated the slaves' prices while underestimating costs.[13] According to Richardson, the rate of profit in the slave trade was 4–5 per cent, and, starting from that amount, he reduced the contribution of the slave trade to British capital formation, which he explained mostly by domestic demand. Stanley Engerman preferred to adopt a macro-economic approach: he started from the correct assumption that one could not evaluate the profits from every single voyage and still less their reinvestment in industrial activities. He took the number of transported slaves, multiplied it to obtain

---

[9] Trevor Burnard and Giorgio Riello, 'Slavery and the New History of Capitalism', *Journal of Global History* 15, no. 2 (2020): 225–44.

[10] Klass Rönnbäck, 'On the Economic Importance of the Slave Plantation Complex to the British Economy during the Eighteenth Century: A Value-Added Approach', *Journal of Global History* 13, no. 3 (2018): 308–27.

[11] Guillaume Daudin, 'Profitability of Slavery and Long-Distance Trading in Context: The Case of Eighteenth-Century France', *The Journal of Economic History* 64, no. 1 (2004): 144–71; Guillaume Daudin, *Commerce et prospérité: la France au XVIIIe siècle* (Paris: PUPS, 2005); Guillaume Daudin, 'Empires et économie' http://spire.sciencespo.fr/hdl:/2441/5l6uh8ogmqildh09h4dqk0kai/resources/empireseteconomieversionpreliminaire.pdf; Guillaume Daudin, 'Comment calculer les profits de la traite?', *Outre-mer* 89, no. 336-7 (2002): 43–62.

[12] Roger Anstey, 'Capitalism and Slavery: A Critique', *Economic History Review* 21 (1968): 307–20; Roger Anstey, *The Atlantic Slave Trade and British Abolition* (London: Macmillan, 1975).

[13] B. Anderson and David Richardson, 'Market Structures and the Profits of the British African Trade in the Late Eighteenth Century: A Rejoinder Rebutted', *Journal of Economic History* 45 (1985): 705-7; David Richardson, 'Market Structures and the Profits of the British African Trade in the Late Eighteenth Century. A Comment', *Journal of Economic History* 43 (1983): 713–21; David Richardson, 'Accounting for Profits in the British Trade in Slaves: Reply to William Darity', *Explorations in Economic History* 26 (1989): 492–9.

their average price and deducted the cost of the voyage and insurance. He concluded that the rate of profit in this trade was not very different from that in other trades. In 1770, slave trade profits amounted to 0.54 per cent of British national income, 7.8 per cent of total investment and 38.9 per cent of total commercial and industrial investment. Between 1688 and 1800, the contribution of the slave trade to capital formation in Britain was between 2.4 per cent and 10.8 per cent.[14] This conclusion supported Williams's thesis and found further confirmation in the works of Inikori, Barbara Solow[15] and William Darity, who went even further, arguing that the rate of profit in the slave trade was as high as 17 per cent.[16] These authors concluded that the slave trade between the 1660s and the end of the eighteenth century played a crucial role in financing the English, then British, economy.[17]

This is relevant to us: it means that models discussed in Part IV of our investigation are not necessarily based upon archives (Part I) or data (Part II) or a critical discussion of social categories (Part III), but they may seek to contest all of them on pure theoretical considerations. The following chapters examine these questions, starting with the history of quantitative social surveys, before moving to the identification of social categories. This study will range from the local to the transnational in scope. Different but related kinds of data will be discussed: statistics of social differentiation (nowadays called studies of inequalities) first, and then environmental-social statistics. Together, they cover two of the current major fields of public debate making use of data where the boundary between politics and knowledge, human, social and 'hard' sciences is thinnest. These data need to be examined closely in terms of their assumptions and methodology; it is not just a matter of simply deconstructing the data, but showing the interrelation – or even co-identification – between the construction of figures and social dynamics in their situated historical anchoring. To that end, I will trace the multiple steps of data building, from the questionnaires and their responses, to the processing of qualitative information into quantitative artefacts and, finally, their mutual influence on social dynamics.

---

[14] Stanley Engerman, 'The Slave Trade and British Capital Formation in the Eighteenth Century: A Comment on the Williams Thesis', *Business History Review* 46 (1972): 430–43.

[15] Joseph Inikori, 'Market Structures and the Profits of the British African Trade in the Late Eighteenth Century. A Rejoinder', *Journal of Economic History* 43 (1983): 723–8; Barbara Solow, 'Caribbean Slavery and British Growth: The Eric Williams Hypothesis', *Journal of Development Economics* 17 (1985): 99–115.

[16] William Darity, 'The Number Game and the Profitability of the British Trade in Slaves', *Journal of Economic History* 45 (1985): 693–703; William Darity, 'Profitability of the British Trade in Slave once Again', *Explorations in Economic History* 26 (1989): 380–4.

[17] For instance: Williams, *Capitalism and Slavery*; Joseph Inikori, *Africans and the Industrial Revolution in England* (Cambridge: Cambridge University Press, 2002); Beckert, *Empire of Cotton*.

3

When one person eats two chickens and another none, on average they eat one chicken each. The invention of social statistics under capitalism

Nowadays, even among the general public, the use of data and quantitative evidence to confirm theories has become increasingly popular, as Piketty's worldwide bestseller attests. Data are widely used to validate social and economic dynamics and one cannot even imagine asserting any political claim without it being supported by 'data'. Indeed, this approach does not make any distinction between sources and data. Just as in the natural sciences, figures are simply accepted and any critical scrutiny of data as historical sources – that is, using historical and not statistical methodology – is qualified as deconstructionism. In order to assess judgements, comparisons and policies, equivalences must be made between regions, countries, continents and possibly different epochs. How is this achieved? How can equivalences be made between societies, properties, forms of labour or production?

Piketty claims – first in the introduction and then throughout the book – that he is not putting forward opinions, but rather facts based on data. This assertion can be made as long as the 'data' are not distinguished from 'sources'. It is precisely because data are considered the ultimate source of knowledge that their systematization can be presented as an expression of 'facts'. Piketty is right to remind his economist colleagues that abstract models and empirical experiments tend to overlook the complexity of social relations and the difficulty of apprehending historical causality. He is also right when he points out that the simple deconstruction of quantitative data – as often affirmed in the social sciences – is insufficient to produce an articulate analysis of society and its history. However, it must also be pointed out that the criticism of quantitative data stems from another methodological position, one that is much older than postmodernist approaches, the critical analysis of sources. Determining how and why sources were produced and their cognitive hierarchy is part of the historian's toolkit and allows them to make a distinction between 'data' and sources that eludes Piketty. Like most economists and scientists nowadays, Piketty makes the data he uses available to readers. This transparency is important; several economists have made comments and even criticisms about the relation between Piketty's data, model and conclusions. I will not go into those aspects. However, what remains in the shadows is the relation between the data and the sources they were taken from. Indeed, the latter are quite heterogeneous, ranging from the exhaustive examination of departmental archives to figures simply spat out by Maddison and even those produced in an equally uncertain manner by Boisguilbert and other eighteenth-century commentators. And that is the where the problem arises: there is an inexorable gap between these sources: the data coming from the archives mainly concerns assets and estates (on limited samples), while those coming from secondary sources pertain to capital and revenue. In reality, the various investigations conducted in such and such a region, village or province by historians are hardly cumulative, as each employs a different methodology from the others. Since the eighteenth century down to Piketty one of the central statements consists in opposing 'facts' to 'opinions', the former being identified with statistical data.[1] The identification of social 'facts' with quantities and the separation between science based on quantities and opinion based on qualities and 'discourse', have been part of this debate. Some have described this last orientation as the invention of the modern fact.[2]

Experimental moral philosophy (from William Petty to David Hume), conjectural history (the Scottish Enlightenment from Dugald Stewart to John Stuart Mill), political economy (classical economics in Britain and France) and statistics (from Jacques Bertillon to Adolphe Quetelet and then Karl Pearson) converged into a single epistemological enterprise giving birth to the 'empirical fact'. Pierre Simon Laplace (1749–1827) is generally considered one of the fathers of (inverse) probabilities, mainly applied to astrophysics. The application of probability to social sciences was mostly due to the Belgian Adolphe Quetelet (1796–1874). He adopted the law of large numbers and therefore supported the general census rather than studies using what he considered an arbitrary selection process. Social scientists were thus pushed to collect as much as data as possible. Quetelet's name is usually tied to the notion of the average man: the statistical average was turned into an ideal social type, e.g. the average height of the soldier, the average income, age, etc., of a criminal or a drunk. He used probabilities to estimate the propensity of the average man to commit a crime. Quetelet saw in the regularity of crime the proof that statistical social laws are true when applied to society as a whole, although they may be false for a single individual.[3] The liberal notion of social justice was reflected in the average man: no *a priori* distinctions were made between individuals. However, their social attitudes, as 'scientifically' identified, could prevent society from deviance. In this view, statistics confirmed the stability of bourgeois society (Quetelet wrote about this immediately after the 1848 revolution), while trying to identify regularities in the apparent chaos following the fall of the *ancien régime* and the Industrial Revolution.[4]

However, during the second half of the nineteenth century, increasing criticism of positivism encouraged attacks against social and statistical determinism. Individual

---

[1] Piketty, *Capital*.
[2] Mary Poovey, *A History of the Modern Fact: Problems of Knowledge in the Sciences of Wealth and Society* (Chicago: University of Chicago Press, 1998).
[3] Adolphe Quetelet, *Du système social et des lois qui le régissent* (Paris: Guillaumin, 1848).
[4] Porter, *The Rise of Statistical Thinking*; Desrosières, *La politique*; Alessandro Stanziani, 'Statistics', in *Encyclopedia of Europe, 1789–1914*, edited by John Merriman and J. M. Winter (New York: Scribner, 2006).

free will was opposed to 'social laws' and statistical averages; Wilhelm Lexis and Georg Friedrich Knapp (1842–1926) in Germany and their students as well as most of the Russian statisticians criticized universal statistical laws. They identified national paths of economic and demographic growth and by the same token stressed the role of individual freedom in social dynamics. According to Knapp, as every individual is different from the others, the notion of variation should replace that of statistical error.[5] In short, the credibility of numbers was a social and a moral problem, not just an epistemological one.[6]

But, if this is so, then we may ask whether this question and the answers brought to it were to become 'universal', as in physics or natural sciences, or whether they must be adapted to local contexts and how. Was it possible, for instance, to adapt the same Prussian categories to study peasants in Russia, Britain or even Africa and India?

The answer depends, among other things, on whether we refer to methods of measuring or categories of analysis or both. At the turn of the nineteenth and twentieth centuries, statisticians were divided upon the fact of knowing whether they managed just a 'tool' or a discipline and whether this was a 'natural' or a 'social' science. In first two cases, universality was claimed, while the last approach eventually stressed the incommensurability of societies and, thus, of statistical categories themselves. As already mentioned in the general introduction, histories of statistics on non-European worlds have been intensively produced during recent years.[7] Broader considerations on the transferability of statistical methods has been investigated as well.[8]

Let us take the case of Russia, on the border of the 'Western realm'. Here, these debates took place in a particular context: the period of the 'great reforms' (abolition of serfdom, creation of local representative institutions, *zemstvo*, creation of a legal order somehow open to the middle classes and even peasants) encouraged the intervention of both the state and local institutions, and they required information about the life of local society in order to adopt policies. Meanwhile, the liberal and radical revolutionary intelligentsia also praised policies based on 'local knowledge', in some cases justified by broader social and political theories (in the case of liberals and Marxists). The convulsions of the old regime in Russia, the transformation of the peasantry, the appearance of the first urban workers all contributed to the emergence of social statistics. According to the positivist credo of the time, data were a must to orient politics.

At the same time, the historical example of social statistics on Russia also relates to major methodological challenges: the transfer of presumed 'scientific investigation' of societies, the construction of social statistics in non-Western contexts, and the tension between data and qualitative investigation, statistics, political economy and

---

[5] Georg Friedrich Knapp, *Theorie des Bevölkerungs-Wechsels: Abhandlungen zur Angewanden Mathematik* (Braunschweig: Friedrich Vieweg und Sohn, 1874).
[6] Porter, *Trust in Numbers*.
[7] Among the others: Ghosh, *Making it Count*; Bréard, *Reform, Bureaucratic Expansion and Production of Numbers*; Blum and Mespoulet, *L'anarchie bureaucratique*; Senra, *História das Estatísticas Brasileiras*.
[8] Steinmetz, *The Politics of Method*; Stanziani, *Eurocentrism*.

society. Indeed, the majority of Russian economists set the methods of the natural sciences against those of economics, which was considered a social science.[9] Most Russian statisticians criticized not only Léon Walras and neoclassical economics but also Auguste Comte's general positivist paradigm. Chuprov, Professor at the University of Moscow, wrote that induction alone, based on empirical observation, cannot determine economic laws inasmuch as social events, unlike natural sciences, are related to multiple and often concomitant causes.[10] In his view, statistics could only be used as a scientific tool if they complied with Adolphe Quetelet's law of large numbers.

Iulii Ianson, Professor of Economics and Statistics in Saint Petersburg, argued that social phenomena are not the result of multiple, simple causes but of webs of 'complex, multiple causes'. He thus criticized Quetelet's notion of the *individu moyen* and more generally of any statistical mean. He drew a distinction between 'typical' and 'a-typical' (arithmetical) averages. The former are the result of variations of the same object, e.g. the heights of a building at different times. The latter express the variation of different objects, e.g. the heights of buildings in a given street. Ianson considered the first type of average a useless fiction for social science. He therefore adhered to the theory of probability in its classical version (Laplace) and to the subsequent theory of sampling as a level of representativeness starting from a given population.[11]

At the turn of the twentieth century, probability theory underwent significant development, particularly in Russia, where several authors gave birth to a new approach – induction in probability – based on ex-ante probability and Bayesian theory (we will see in later chapters that it was largely used in weather forecasting). These improvements had considerable influence on the theory of sampling: hypotheses had previously been made to justify the selection of an area, a village, households, etc. Henceforth, the use of random selection became the best way to avoid observer bias. How were these different approaches to statistics used?

Closely linked to national specificities, regional and monographic analysis enjoyed increasing success from the last quarter of the nineteenth century onwards. These studies were mostly developed in Germany and Russia, where federalism (in the former case) or local governments (the *zemstva*, in the latter case) encouraged studies of local economic conditions. Thus, a considerable number of surveys and studies of ethnography and statistics were produced between 1861 and 1914. Several reasons justified this interest; in particular, the abolition of serfdom in 1861 and the 'agrarian question' pushed central and local administrations to finance surveys with fiscal, military or socio-economic aims.[12]

---

[9] Aleksandr I. Chuprov, *Kurs Politicheskoi ekonomii* (Handbook of Political Economy) (Moscow, 1885, 1924 edition, Moscow: Gozizdat), 1, 2, 20; Mikhail I. Tugan-Baranovskiy, *Osnovy politicheskoi ekonomii* (Fundamentals of Political Economy), 2 vols (Saint Petersburg, 1905–11, reprint Moscow: Rosspen, 1998), vol. 1, 1.

[10] Chuprov, *Kurs*: 3, 17, 20, 37, 40, 45.

[11] Iulii Ianson, *Teoriia statistiki* (Statistical Theory), 3rd ed. (Saint Petersburg: Landau, 1886).

[12] Stanziani, *L'économie en révolution*; Martine Mespoulet, *Statistiques et révolution en Russie un compromis impossible (1880-1930)* (Rennes: PUR, 2001); Wayne Vucinich, ed., *The Zemstvo in Russia: An Experiment in Local Self-Government* (Cambridge: Cambridge University Press, 1982).

Of course, these studies would have been inconceivable without the influence of Europe. This influence was expressed in epistemology and scientific theories as well as in the new role science, and scientific rhetoric was called to play in the public sphere.[13] Thus, surveys and investigations 'in the field' gained increasing importance in ethnography, sociology and statistics. However, in the Russian context, these studies raised a serious theoretical problem: in the absence of a regular, homogeneous census, academic statisticians were rather sceptical about inferences drawn from samples obtained mainly by (usually local) administrative statistical offices. In the following years, the best method for selecting samples was discussed at the meetings of Russian statisticians and in the international conferences of statistics. The first solution envisaged was totally random selection; unfortunately, this approach required an up-to-date general census to test how representative it actually was.[14]

At the same time, political considerations intervened not just in the interpretation of data, but in the very organization of surveys. Thus, 'populists' seeking to stress the strength of the peasant commune contrasted surveys (led by Marxists) showing its disintegration and the advance of capitalism in Russia. The former group focused its investigations on central rural areas (more isolated from the markets), the latter on protoindustrial regions; groupings could be made according to one or another indicator (amount of land, number of members, livestock, etc.).[15] Populist-oriented statisticians considered the amount of land and the number of consumers to be the basic indicators, while Marxist authors (including Lenin) highlighted capital and labour relations. In other words, even if it was true, for example, that central agrarian areas and protoindustrial regions expressed different historical trends, the statistics and economic analysis froze those differences into a preconceived selection of areas, villages and households to be studied.

Instead of just stressing the ideological influence on statistical methods, I would highlight the far more complex process of the social construction of an artefact: how the multiple social actors intervened in the construction of a source, namely, statistical tables. To this end, I will reconstruct all the different stages investigators went through, starting with the questionnaires, then their distribution, completion, possible correction and the ultimate passage from qualitative to quantitative based information.

The social construction of an artefact: questionnaires, expeditions, texts and data

Except for the data concerning emigration available in the files of the district authorities, *zemstvo* statisticians gathered information themselves. This could be done either by organizing a field trip or through a network of correspondents. During

---

[13] Brian, *La mesure de l'État*.
[14] Stigler, *The History of Statistics*.
[15] Anton P. Shlikevich, *Podvornaia opis' Kozeleskogo uezda* (The Household Census of Kozeleskii District) (Chernigov, 1882).

the 1870s and the 1880s in particular, *zemstvo* statisticians borrowed much of their information from the studies conducted by geographers and ethnologists and relied on field trips. Thus, statisticians had to solve two problems: first, they had to choose the area, villages and possibly households to be studied and test their statistical and social representativeness; second, they had to build a network of correspondents able to fill out the questionnaires. This solution had originally been developed in the 1870s in the US, where statisticians randomly selected correspondents among farmers in different regions. However, in Russia this solution was impossible due to the lack of literacy among peasants.[16] They therefore came up with the idea of mobilizing all the local elites (priests, teachers, peasants, traders, official representatives, landowners, etc.) as 'correspondents'. They would visit the countryside, fill out questionnaires and send them to statistics offices. Here we find a first tension between social groups in the construction itself of the information: most statisticians regarded those elites with suspicion and asserted that they sometimes filled out questionnaires without even visiting the villages, and in any case 'distorted' the data according to their own perceptions. Statisticians were particularly suspicious of landowners, *zemskii nachal'nik*, and, to a certain extent, priests and rich peasants. Whenever possible, they sought to change the social composition of their correspondent network to increase the presence of people they trusted (teachers, agronomists, 'ordinary peasants') and reduce that of other categories. When this was not possible, then statisticians corrected the answers provided by the correspondents, according to their social status. For example, they presumed that landowners and Tsarist officials exaggerated peasant well-being, both in terms of possession of land, cattle or tools and of income. As is well documented in the archives of the investigations,[17] they therefore modified the answers they got by reducing these values.

Interestingly, this attitude was clear not only towards local elites –whom statisticians usually disliked for ideological and political reasons – but towards 'ordinary' peasants. Did peasants tell the truth when questioned? And if not, why not?

Most Russian statisticians fully examined these questions and answered that peasants tended to underestimate production, the extent of their *nadel'* (the allotment received at the time of the Emancipation) and their income[18] for fear of excessive fiscal and other pressure from Tsarist officials.[19] Peasants did not know 'scientific' measurement and adopted other criteria to evaluate the amount of land ('from here to the top of the hill; the brown valley', etc.).[20] Statisticians were therefore required to translate customary criteria into scientific units of measurement. This was done in stages. First, the information delivered had to be submitted for verification within the peasant community itself. When visiting villages, statisticians gathered all the people in

---

[16] Jeffrey Burds, *When Russia Learned to Read* (Princeton: Princeton University Press, 1985).
[17] Count V. N. Tenishev, *Byt velikorusskikh krest'ian-zemlepashtsev* (The Life of Grand Russian Peasants) (Saint Petersburg: Izdatel'stvo evropeicheskogo doma, 1993).
[18] O-skij, 'V Russkoj glusi', *Russkaja mysl* 3 (1910): 121.
[19] O-skij, 'V Russkoi'.
[20] Nikolai A. Kablukov, *Posobie pri mestnyh statisticheskikh obsledovaniiakh* (Methods for Local Statistical Investigations) (Moscow, 1910): 54.

front of the *skhod* to compare and verify information. In this process, the statisticians relied on the notion of evidence in oral societies and cultures they had borrowed from ethnologists of that time.[21]

According to this view, the investigator was supposed to meet and 'understand' people, unlike bureaucrats, Tsarist officials and estate owners considered to be unable to communicate with the peasants. At a first glance, this attitude seemed close to Boas's influence in Russia, according to which the proximity between the investigator and the investigated went along with cultural relativism (the different concepts were not the same in Russia and Germany, or even, within Russia, between the town and the countryside). In fact, it turned into its opposite: most statisticians considered themselves able not only to decode but also to correct the answers in order to provide a 'scientific view'.

The social construction of time and its standardization have become the subject of many investigations in history, anthropology and sociology. Social historians produced the main work in this field: on the one hand, following E. P. Thompson, several studies focused on the transformation of economic time during the industrialization process. The passage from irregular, i.e. seasonal, daytime, to standard industrial time is at the core of this sort of investigation. A second body of literature was inspired by Kula and his study of the gradual standardization of harvests and cultivated surface area in modern Poland. The time budget within the household was one of the main innovations introduced by Russian statisticians. Indeed, it was first necessary to solve the question of the running period of time: did the relevant year begin at the harvest or at sowing?[22]

If the first solution was adopted, then the yearly time budget began in July and ended in June. In this case, the business cycle had to distinguish sold production from consumption and from the portions set aside for future sowing. Savings and consumption rather than investment were the crucial variables. The peasant economy resembled Marx's simple market economy.

However, if one opted for the second solution, then the yearly time budget started with sowing in March–April. This solution took into account credit and the problem of financing production, and thus the important development of credit cooperatives at the turn of the century. In this view, the peasant economy was much closer to market economies.

Investigators who adopted the first approach were led to emphasize the lack of land and the excessive fiscal burden. This approach was widespread among most statisticians both before and after the revolution of 1917.[23] The second approach led analysts to stress not so much the lack of land as lack of capital, including management.

---

[21] Ong, *Orality and Literacy*; Thomas Charlton, Lois Myers and Rebecca Sharpless, eds, *History of Oral History* (Lanham: Altamira Press, 2007); Jack Goody, *The Interface between the Oral and the Written* (Cambridge: Cambridge University Press, 1987); Ruth Finnegan, *Literacy and Orality* (London: Callender Press, 2014); Jonathan Skinner, ed., *The Interview: An Ethnographic Approach* (London: Bloomsbury, 2013); H. Russell Bernard, *Research Methods in Anthropology: Qualitative and Quantitative Approaches*, 6th ed. (Lanham: Rowman & Littlefield, 2018).

[22] Kablukov, *Posobie*.

[23] A. V. Peshekhonov, *Statisticheskoe opisanie Kaluzshkoj gubernii* (Statistical Description of the Province of Kaluga) (Kaluga, 1898).

In short, statisticians made use of 'scientific' notions of time not only to impose urban, academic values on peasants' attitudes but also to project their own social and political utopias. Reconstructing time was not confined to the past; it influenced future trends and, as such, projected statisticians' images of the 'new' world: a perfect peasant economy, a socialist world or, to some extent, a 'Western' market society. Economic policies adopted in Tsarist Russia, then in the Soviet Union, sought to make 'realities' closer to these models, either by ordinary fiscal and price policies or by coercion.

Back to the future. From Russian statistics to Piketty

The nineteenth century was a period of increasing enthusiasm for statistics as a tool for the scientific management of politics. The positivist ideal and the reformist attitude of most European governments contributed to this success. International conferences aimed to offer the image of an international 'objective' and homogenous science, and, as such, appealed to the desire to 'scientifically' manage national politics. Statisticians complained about the 'ignorance' of professional politicians and the differences in the organization of national statistics. In most nineteenth-century societies, this problem was aggravated by the fact that statisticians generally came from a different social group than top-ranking bureaucrats and politicians. The construction of statistics was thus first affected by the existing relationship between those who produced the figures and their principal financiers and users, the administrators. The institutional context had an impact on statisticians' working conditions as well as on their perceptions of their own role and of the objects of their research. These same institutional factors affected their hypotheses and working methods. The perceptions of Russian statisticians, and to some degree peasants as well, can only be made explicit by connecting them to corresponding phenomena (the application of quantitative analyses to the social sciences, the growing intervention of public authorities in the economic realm, the war economy and the crisis of democracies) in the Western world to which they were constantly compared.

Statisticians made use of 'scientific' notions of time not only to impose urban, academic values on peasants' attitudes but also to project their own social and political utopias. Reconstructing time was not confined to the past; it influenced future trends and, as such, projected statisticians' images of the 'new' world: a perfect peasant economy, a socialist world or, to some extent, a 'Western' market society. Indeed, in nineteenth-century Russia and Europe, statistics, their production and usage, were already political and normative tools. The nineteenth century was a period of increasing enthusiasm for statistics as a tool for the scientific management of politics. The positivist ideal and the reformist attitude of most European governments contributed to this success. International conferences sought to offer the image of an international 'objective', homogenous science, and, as such, appealed to the desire to 'scientifically' manage national politics. Statisticians complained about the 'ignorance' of professional politicians and the differences in the organization of national statistics.

Russia expressed an extreme version of these tensions. Here, contrary to Weber's theory, conflicts between 'specialists' and 'bureaucrats' were political and professional at the same time: statisticians criticized their superiors for their lack of competence and for the fact that they mostly belonged to other *soslovie* (estates) and supported autocracy and its reforms. In this context, it is not surprising that statistical data reflected the normative ambition of their authors: local authorities, mediators and statisticians all translated space, time and peasant land and organization into categories and data that fit their own preconceptions and political ambitions. Statisticians were therefore required to translate customary criteria into scientific units of measurement; this was a clear anti-anthropological approach developing in this same period: cultural elites did not seek to decode 'savages', isolated peasants and 'customary' rules, but, quite the opposite, they sought to educate those people, bring them to civilization. We still today find this epistemological tension between studies seeking to bring various forms of 'primitive' and 'other' cultures to 'modern' people, urban cultural elites and, conversely, those who believe in the universality of culture and values, namely those of 'modernity'. In both cases, there is an unequal co-authorship of information and co-authored production of categories themselves between all the involved actors – statisticians, local intermediaries and elites, bureaucrats, peasants, themselves divided. All these actors contributed to conceiving, organizing, completing and interpreting statistical investigation.

As peculiar as it was, the history of economic statistics in Russia nevertheless offers a wonderful heuristic to examine a global (not only Russian) question: from the late nineteenth century up to today, empirical statistics, presumed to be falsifiable, and economics have been called to play a role in current politics.[24] As such, do they provide a descriptive or rather a normative tool? Are the trends they construct the result of past behaviours or the projection of preconceived models?

The construction of social historical dynamics as 'facts', as expressed by statistics, was a crucial concern in Tsarist Russia and remains so today. Economic historians recall the huge rate of growth Russia experienced after 1861 as a result of the emancipation of the serfs; this growth, we are told, was comparable to that of Western Europe. If any limitation persisted, it was due to the continuing strength of the peasant commune, which impeded efficiency and the optimal use of production factors. This interpretation stems from blind confidence in the figures produced at the time; they were considered experimental data from scientific laboratories, while the need for critical historical assessment of sources was forgotten. This approach goes hand in hand with another epistemological concern, namely, comparison with an idealized Western European economy. Economic historians and economists tell us which institutions limited the economic growth of Russia and which reforms should have been adopted. From this perspective, the main feature of Russia over the long term has been not so much 'economic backwardness' as continuing strong social inequality within an industrializing economy and society. On a global, comparative scale, the new, difficult relationship, if not the divorce, between democracy, capitalism and social rights is an ongoing issue, as the cases of Russia and China testify today. The problem is that ahistorical economics and economic history do not seem concerned

---

[24] One very last work on this: Fabio Giomi, Celia Keren and Morgane Labbé, eds, *Public and Private Welfare in Modern Europe: Productive Entanglements* (London: Routledge, 2022).

about it. Like economic liberalism, the social state travels poorly over time and space: the solutions adopted by the United Kingdom or France at the end of the Second World War seem difficult to maintain in Europe; they have shown all their limitations from decolonization to today, in Indian and numerous African and Latin American countries. In Africa as in India, attempts to transplant 'European-style' social states gave rise to resistance on the part of local elites as well as workers.[25]

Any answer to these questions pertains to economic models and to the other variables mentioned, namely the form of politics and sovereignty, and consequently the scales of intervention. Piketty first evokes a utopia (global regulation), then a more modest goal (European regulation) and finally an even more limited solution (an agreement between the strong countries in the eurozone). These last solutions would risk producing capital flight away from more heavily taxed areas, not to mention their impact on emerging countries. And what of emerging countries? Must they adopt the same policies as Europe? Piketty suggests a convergence between the West and Asia in the next few decades, and from that point the possibility of arriving at common policies. Unlike Piketty, Esther Duflo concentrates on the hyper-localism of public policies as an alternative to the generalizations of classic development economics.[26] Whether it be public health, credit or employment, local actors make decisions based on local values and balances, all while being henceforth inscribed in global dynamics. Duflo also focuses her analysis on the 'poor', who are outside the tax sources utilized by Piketty. In fact, these approaches are less contrary than they are complementary, in certain cases global policies being necessary to frame their local implementation. Also, whether it involves inequalities in connection to the wealthiest in Europe or the poorest in India, attention is not given to the sources of growth – which both Piketty and Duflo balk at identifying – but rather to the policies that should be adopted in order for growth to benefit the largest number of people.

---

[25] Frederick Cooper, *Decolonization and African Society: The Labour Question in French and British Africa* (Cambridge: Cambridge University Press, 1996).
[26] Abhijit Banerjee and Esther Duflo, *Poor Economics: A Radical Rethinking of the Way to Fight Global Poverty* (New York: Public Affairs, 2011).

4

Environment and social inequalities: how are data made and by whom?

Social statistics seem to comfort hard scientists, the general public and textual oriented scholars that social data are a political tool and as such constructed according to short-term interests of a ministry of a government and/or to ideological claims. What if we move to other cases, for example, environmental data? Are these a construction as well?

These questions are particularly relevant nowadays in debates about the global warming and the Anthropocene. How do we measure them and when do they begin? For some, the answer lies in the Industrial Revolution in the eighteenth century; for others, at the beginning of the twentieth century; and for still others with globalization and the consumption of fossil fuels starting in the 1950s.[1] These interpretations are all legitimate and are based on different data. At the same time, they reveal the self-confirming nature of the notion of Anthropocene: we look for data that confirm our initial hypothesis. Thus, the Anthropocene is a strictly Eurocentric category; the extravagances and misfortunes of the planet are linked to the West, to its Industrial Revolution and its dominance. These are the same problems that affect broad categories like modernization or globalization. They all point to the West either to praise or criticize, implying that the rest of the planet is simply passive. Consequently, can the solution to our current troubles only come from the West?

Indeed, this approach is based on what I would call 'the paradigm of modernization'. Since the eighteenth century, this paradigm has associated modernity with science and knowledge, with urbanization and then industrialization, with the market, bourgeois society and the end of famines. The modernizing paradigm in its liberal variants offers clear answers: yes, capitalism and economic liberalism have made it possible to overcome the famines of preceding eras and societies; yes, globalization makes it possible to improve the well-being of humanity and reconcile social justice with economic growth; no, egalitarianism is not compatible with growth; yes, science and the competitive economy will find a solution to environmental problems and inequalities.

---

[1] Simon Lewis and Mark Maslin, 'Defining the Anthropocene', *Nature* 519 (2015): 171–80; Jan Zalasiewicz et al., 'When Did the Anthropocene Begin? A Mid-Twentieth Century Boundary Level Is Stratigraphically Optimal', *Quaternary International* 383, no. 5 (2015): 196–203.

Of course, numerous currents have criticized this faith in growth and progress: anti-machine and anti-privatization movements, nature conservationists, the fight against inequalities and critics of consumerism who over the centuries have spurred the opposition to industrialism and capitalism. The anti-globalization movement and collapse theorists are the most recent incarnations of these attitudes.

Yet these criticisms are based on the same categories and *épistémè* as their opponents: the tension between science and technology, on one hand, the depletion of resources on the other; the excessive attention accorded to progress, modernization and Western capitalism. The difference is that while some idealize these elements, others reject them. How can we conceive of a different world if we keep these paradigms unchanged?

Very recently some efforts have been made to 'decolonize' the Anthropocene and environmental studies more generally.[2] Two propositions are extremely important: first, the importance of thinking about ecology in terms that transcend Western patterns and categories. The human vs. nature relationship found in Western thinking is one of them[3] and it is not possible to generalize it, especially when seeking to develop solutions in the face of current globalization. Second, the environmental question cannot be dealt with separately from the social one, which is indeed heavily influenced by colonialism. For centuries Asia dominated, then Europe and the West came to the fore, and finally, in the present day, their domination is being challenged by Asia and, in part, by Africa.

These changing hierarchies are part of what Braudel called the 'common waves' of capitalism and the market, which lift but also bring down multiple parts of the world. Waves are not just the result of markets, states and societies. Environmental transformations – the impact of El Niño and La Niña in particular – have played and continue to play a decisive role. It is the interaction between the environment, economies and societies that set the tempo of the world. On which scale?

The answer depends on the lens that we choose: geological time, biological time or social time. If we look at biological time, then the history of humanity belongs to the Palaeolithic (3 million years), not to the Neolithic (12,000 years), and certainly not to the past two or three centuries.[4] However, if we look at the weight of numbers and society, of the 80 billion humans who have lived on the planet in the past 3 million years, only 12 per cent lived prior to the past 12,000 years, 68 per cent between 12,000 and 250 years ago and 20 per cent in the past 250 years.

Those who opt for the very long term, from the Palaeolithic to the present, have the advantage of thinking beyond the past twenty to thirty years. It is possible for them to understand the long historical roots of our problems and to avoid thinking of them as something completely new. However, when using such a long time frame, one ends up lumping together agriculture, sedentary civilization, humanity and the end of the planet. Everything is predetermined since the Pleistocene (100,000 years). For example, Jared Diamond, one of the founding fathers of collapse theory, claims that the die was

---

[2] Malcom Ferdinand, *Une écologie décoloniale* (Paris: Seuil, 2019); Arturo Escobar, *Sentipensar con la tierra* (Medellin, Colombia: Ediciones Unaula, 2014).
[3] Philippe Descola, *Par-delà nature et culture* (Paris: Gallimard, 2015).
[4] Jean Guilane, *Abel, Caïn, Ötzi. L'héritage néolithique* (Paris: Gallimard, 2011).

cast as early as the Neolithic owing to the planetary distribution of easily domesticated species, both animal and vegetable. Progress and modernity originated in the Near East, he would say, because the main domesticated plants and animals happened to be found there.[5] The biological and environmental constraints were there from the start – there is no point in denying it. The anachronism is obvious: Neolithic people reasoning as if they were New Yorkers at the stock exchange. The general public and specialists from numerous disciplines loved this type of narrative, while biologists criticized it. The latter advance their conclusions based mainly on laboratory experiments that are reproducible and verifiable. In contrast, evolutionary biologists like Diamond borrow knowledge from science that they then treat in an anthropocentric fashion: ants and bees cooperate and succeed, as do certain qualities of rice and wheat. Regret, hope, jealousy and other categories taken from social psychology are generalized to interpret the behaviour of other species. The problem is not so much about erasing the human-animal barrier, but that the points they share constitute an extension of certain human characteristics, rather than the reverse. The main criticism that empirical biologists levelled against their evolutionary colleagues is that their conclusions are not based on laboratory observations, but on scattered information, on questionable data which they later link through equally dubious statistical correlations. In statistics, of course, correlation is not causation; the fact that two series are linked does not mean that one is the cause of the other. The fact that numerous species were present in the Near East at a given moment does not give us any information about the origin of this diffusion. More importantly, it can hardly be transposed through a causal chain that stretches to the massacres perpetrated by the Spanish in the Americas.

At the other end of the spectrum, 'presentists' focus on new phenomena that have occurred in recent decades. To their credit, they do point out the urgency of taking radical measures. The most striking case is that of Pablo Servigne and Raphaël Stevens, two authors who are likeable, brilliant and, above all, successful.[6] Their argument, though repetitive at times, is clear. Nevertheless, numerous researchers and academics have criticized them in specialized journals, on the radio and in the press with rather shallow arguments: contradictory data (I challenge anyone to find objective data that are accepted by everyone!), doom-mongering and, consequently, suggesting we simply give up. False accusations, especially coming from experts in economics and management, who for their part have only offered rather conventional solutions, like a bit of green taxation to save the planet, and, of course, business. The main problem with Servigne and Stevens's work is that they make no use of history. Focusing their attention on just the past few decades prevents them from identifying the link between collapse and the historical dynamics of capitalism. There is a risk of idealizing the decades and centuries 'of before' and exaggerating the new phenomena of recent years. *The World We Have Lost*[7] is a famous book by the anthropologist Peter Laslett, who advanced this type of argument during the 1960s and attracted the same sort of criticism.

---

[5] Jared Diamond, *Guns, Germs, and Steel* (New York: W. W. Norton, 1997).
[6] Servigne and Stevens, *Comment tout peut s'effondrer*.
[7] Peter Laslett, *The World We Have Lost: England Before the Industrial Age* (London: Methuen, 1965).

Weather forecasting: science, divination or both?

I suggest focusing on the interplay between empirical observations on the environment, general epistemological considerations on weather forecasting under capitalism (is it a science or a kind of divinatory explanation?) and socio-economic dynamics. How did weather forecasting emerge in the eighteenth and nineteenth centuries with improvements of navigation, the ambition of overruling, if not predicting, weather fluctuations and avoiding famines? Finally, how did these tensions travel across the world? Which kind of weather forecasting did the Europeans seek to produce when confronted with non-European worlds?

These questions are the core of a quickly increasing historiography, mostly concerned with the European and the US meteorology, but also expanding to include other parts of the world.[8]

Weather observation and forecasting not only concern epistemology but also the cognitive philosophy of knowledge: the tension between observation and predictions set at the crossroads of three distinct, though related, debates. First, the relationship between religion and science, that is, the tension between divination and predictions based on regular laws of nature. Until the very end of the nineteenth century at least, between these two extremes, astrology[9] was quite an awkward field, where scientific and religious influences tended to overlap. The problem was that many astro-meteorologists were also astrologers, and the cleavage between the two fields involved the criminalization of astrology, which took place only during the last quarter of the nineteenth century. It is not by chance that in Victorian Britain certain religious milieus that were hostile to Darwin and scientific positivism in general tried to make a comeback during the last quarter of the nineteenth century by attacking weather forecasting, whose uncertainty and lack of reliability were seized upon to point out the fallacy of science and the role of the divine in human affairs.[10]

Second, meteorology also harnessed 'popular knowledge' in its relationship with religion and 'real science'. Weather predictions were employed in pragmatic approaches, not only in maritime occupations – sailing, fishing – but also in many activities where climatic conditions were an essential determinant: agriculture, of course, and activities where natural drying determined the quality of the product – wine, indigo, fresh pasta, among others. This knowledge depended upon skills and set an uncertain boundary with popular knowledge about weather as it was developed in almanacs during the

---

[8] Among others: Anderson, *Predicting Weather*; Rohland, *Changes in the Air*; Campbell, *Bondage and the Environment*; Greg Bankoff, *Cultures of Disaster: Society and Natural Hazard in the Philippines* (London: Routledge, 2003); Matthew Hannaford and David Nash, 'Climate, History, Society over the Last Millennium in Southeast Africa', *Wiley Interdisciplinary Review: Climate Change* 7, no. 3 (2016): 370–92; James Rodger Fleming, *Meteorology in America, 1800–1870* (Baltimore: Johns Hopkins University Press, 1990); Mike Hulme, *Weathered: Cultures of Climate* (London: SAGE, 2016); Jan Golinski, *British Weather and the Climate of Enlightenment* (Chicago: University of Chicago Press, 2007).

[9] Anderson, *Predicting the Weather*: 51–4.

[10] William Fowler, *Mozley and Tyndall on Miracles* (London: Longman and Green, 1868); Peter Harrison, 'Prophecy, Early Modern Apologetics and Hume's Argument against Miracles', *Journal of the History of Ideas* 60 (1999): 241–56.

nineteenth century. It is not by chance that several economists were interested in weather forecasting, such as Stanley Jevons and John Stuart Mill. Mill considered that nature was one of the fields where scientific predictions were possible, and this included weather forecasting.[11] Predictions of future harvests, for instance, could help in the fight against famine in the colonial worlds (India was the subject of huge debates),[12] but also in Europe, in order to avoid speculation about crop outputs and social instability.

Third, weather forecasting raised the question of whether meteorology was like physics and mathematics, leading to predictable outcomes, or whether it was closer to the social sciences. The answer to this question depended on whether the social sciences were considered distinct from the natural sciences. As for statistics in general, 'scientific' meteorology (opposed to 'popular' beliefs on weather) sought to distinguish theory from empirical observation. The first seeks to explain the physics of the atmosphere while the second produces weather forecasts. As such, some claimed meteorology to be an inductive rather than a deductive science (unlike philosophy or religion).[13] But this passage also needed a new approach to statistics and probability.

As mentioned before, direct probability indicates the chances one has of drawing a black or a white ball when we only know the number of balls in a basket. On the contrary, inverse probability makes use of previous experience so it is possible to estimate the likelihood of a particular later situation. Adolphe Quetelet sought to extend this theory to social phenomena. In this, he drew inspiration from astronomy. The so-called law of error (errors in observation could be estimated and corrected) was first developed in the early nineteenth century by philosophers and mathematicians such as Gauss, Laplace and Fourier, and then by Quetelet himself. In 1828 he was appointed director of the Royal Observatory in Brussels and he presided at the first international conference on maritime meteorology in 1853. In 1838, he cited examples from meteorology to explain his theory of probability. While major statisticians like Laplace and Condorcet had already expressed their interest in weather forecasting and climatic effects such as lunar cycles on terrestrial weather,[14] Quetelet sought to apply the laws of probability to weather forecasts. After him, Francis Galton, Darwin's cousin, devoted much time to meteorology,[15] while economists like Jevons were strongly influenced by it, and some produced theories of economic activity related to solar activity. Galton strongly criticized meteorology for the lack of precision in instruments and for the improper use of statistics, as he claimed. Yet, Galton himself treated each condition independently and ignored the possibility that rules might be related each other and to a third variable. He would overcome this difficulty only in the late 1880s when he advanced his theory of correlation.[16]

Like social statistics, weather forecasting had both social and insurance implications: the impact of weather on harvests or on maritime activities are two concerns among

---

[11] Anderson, *Predicting the Weather*: 35.
[12] Mark Harrison, *Climate and Constitution: Health, Race, Environment and British Imperialism in India, 1600–1850* (Delhi: Oxford University Press, 1999).
[13] John Herschel, *Meteorology* (Edinburgh: Black, 1862).
[14] Walter Browne, *The Moon and the Weather*, 2nd ed. (London: Balliere, Tyndall and Cox, 1886).
[15] Francis Galton, *Metereographica* (London: Macmillan, 1863).
[16] Theodore Porter, *The Rise of Statistical Thinking* (Princeton: Princeton University Press, 1986).

many. Like social statistics, weather forecasting in nineteenth-century Europe had to face the scepticism of growing scientific societies that associated weather forecasting with divination and non-scientific practices. Meteorology eventually emerged as a physical science; the study of weather linked seamen observing storm signals with scientists and instruments. The standardization of measurements and instruments was a pre-condition for this relationship to develop.[17] Like statistics in general and social statistics in particular, meteorology raised a debate about the tools, methods and results of observation. It was a field of empirical observation and a reflection on observation itself. As such, meteorology also led to the same debate we find in social statistics and political economy about induction and deduction, with a preference for the former over the latter. The multiplicity of experiences and the great number of 'causes' favoured this approach in both meteorology and social statistics.

Marine insurance firms had developed these kinds of studies since medieval times. In the nineteenth century, however, the questions went beyond maritime occupations to include several other activities. Weather-related risks were assessed by private insurance companies, but it was with the rise of the welfare state that this question became central in public debates: should the state help farmers and peasants struck by weather events?

This question was linked to the reliability of weather forecasting: if forecasts were reliable, then farmers should take adequate preventive measures, otherwise they would not be compensated. The problem was that 'exceptionality' seemed to be the rule where weather was concerned, and to get reliable forecasts a completely different kind of statistics had to be developed, Bayesian statistics. Unlike classical statistics and probability, the Bayesian approach does not link probability to a frequency but to a belief, mostly based upon previous experience. For example, we may ask: what is, according to you, the probability that Donald Trump will be reappointed? Then, at a second stage, we add: and what chance do you think you have that your prediction is correct?[18]

Weather forecasting in the media constitutes the perfect example of Bayesian statistics: they show first whether there will be rain, then they add a 'confidence index' and, finally, as everybody knows, at home, you can evaluate the chances that forecasts were well founded. With regard to social statistics and social sciences, Gaussian statistics assume that random variables have a 'normal distribution': the more the cases we observe, the more they form a normal bell curve. Conversely, Bayesian statistics do not require massive observation but take into account the degree of belief in an event.[19] Social and economic statistics almost never relied on this approach, preferring

---

[17] Bruno Latour and Simon Schaffer are among those who have the most contributed to develop this topic. Bruno Latour, *We Have Never Been Modern* (Cambridge, MA: Harvard University Press, 1992); Simon Schaffer, 'Les cérémonies de la mesure', *Annales HSS* 70, no. 2 (2015): 409–35.

[18] Nassim Nicholas Taleb, *The Black Swann: The Impact of the Highly Improbable* (New York: Random House, 2010).

[19] O. B. Sheynin, 'On the History of Statistical Method in Meteorology', *Archive for History of Exact Science* 31 (1984): 53–95; Vladimir Jankovic, *Reading the Sky: A Cultural History of English Weather* (Manchester: Manchester University Press, 2000); Amy Dahan Dalmedico, 'History and Epistemology of Models: Meteorology (1946–1963) as a Case Study', *Archive for History of Exact Science* 55 (2001): 395–422. See also the journal *History of Meteorology*.

the ordinary Gaussian one. The consequence is that, despite economists' and social scientists' claims, the predictability of social events and economic crisis is a mirage, and economists systematically miss forthcoming crises. According to some heterodox traders and economists, the so-called 'black swans', considered to be extremely rare by Gaussian statistics, are actually 'normal events' in a Bayesian approach. In other words, crises are far from being exceptional under capitalism.

However, beyond Bayesian statistics, a further tool was required to produce modern weather forecasting: the telegraph. It played a central role, bringing about a major scientific breakthrough in the science of weather forecasting that would only be superseded with satellites. The telegraph provided quick information on the weather in different parts of the world and therefore facilitated efforts to develop meteorology. In the early 1860s, bureaus of meteorology were established or reorganized in Britain, Belgium, France and several other countries and began collecting regular data. Of course, these institutions were immediately confronted with related questions about the standardization of instruments and measures. In order to compare data, one needs to have established tools and measurement criteria. Vigorous debates took place in institutes, within national boundaries (for instance, between Kew and Greenwich) and finally at the international level. Again, this was a crucial step in transforming 'beliefs' into science and the sciences into a tool for public policy and private insurance. Governments and companies had to know whether the impact of climate and weather in particular could be considered predictable or unpredictable events in order to decide whether or not to compensate the affected people.

To make things worse, these problems – already complicated enough in Europe – became almost impossible to solve in 'exotic places'. Even today, it is astonishing that, unlike earthquakes, cyclones and hurricanes are not evaluated according to an international standard. Instead, each national weather office developed its own scale to classify these events. The Australian, Japanese, US, Canadian, Australian, French or British meteorological offices do not classify so-called 'tropical cyclones' the same way. Thus, the Beaufort scale requires winds at least at 118 km/hours to be classified as 'hurricane', while for the Australian meteorology bureau cyclones begin at 90 km/h but then they are classified into five categories (from weak to severe), the strongest having winds at 280 km/h. How can these differences be explained?

In order to answer, I will take two examples: harvest statistics in Russia, cyclone investigations in the Indian Ocean. In both cases, debates about forecasting were intense: could statistics foresee the feature? And were statistical and meteorological tools valid all around the globe?

Predicting future harvests

Let us take the example of an apparently easy problem: the quantification of future agriculture production in connection with climatic changes. Over centuries this was the main concern of all social actors and political rulers; even nowadays, not only in developing countries but also in most advanced countries, due to climate change, shifts in the production of main cereals heavily influence global economic trends.

This is where statistics intervene and seek to evaluate both current and future harvest starting from past experiences and, of course, weather forecasting. After the 1870s, an increasing interest in predicting future harvests emerged in most Western countries. This was for many reasons: first, the increasing size of the international market went along with global price speculations. Commodity exchanges were established in Europe and North America, with offices in Africa, China, India and Latin America. In these organizations, future products were traded. Speculators and traders sought to make their profits in gambling on future harvests. Produce exchanges and their internal logic expressed the transition from real to virtual trade. Transactions involving wheat, flour and cooking oil markets were no longer solely concerned with supplying cities but became an integral part of capital trading. The real subject of the exchanges was information on future products and transactions. Wholesale merchants seldom intervened directly in trading at the exchange; instead, they had recourse to commission actors and brokers. Indeed, the actual development of forward transactions at produce exchanges owed a great deal to the control of international transactions. It was no accident that the method per *filière*, that is, model contracts for standardized products, was developed at the Le Havre market in the 1870s. The *filière* was a written document which could be transferred by endorsement. It indicated the name of the trader and the characteristics (grades) of the product, the date of delivery and the place at which the produce was stored. On this ground, it became synonymous with a product of a given kind and quality, exchanged on forward markets. The acceptance of goods at the market required detailed classification involving a statement that the commodity received was identical to the previously recorded specified standard.[20] Thus weather forecasting and expectations of future harvests were extremely valuable; they were requested by traders and speculators and also public authorities, precisely with the aim of reducing market fluctuations and social instability.

As a complement to global speculation in developed countries, famines in less developed areas also entered into the focus on weather forecasting. The British in particular were much concerned with famines in India and their Empire more generally. It was no accident that famines multiplied in the Global South, Asia and even Eastern Europe and Russia after the 1870s: drought, floods, monsoon failure and the El Niño cycle played a role.[21] However, as there was little global climate change at that time, these events could have not produced famines without concomitant political and economic processes, namely, global speculation and colonialism.[22] In their colonial possessions, both the French and the British encouraged export and speculation despite bad harvests, and contributed to transforming them into famines. However,

---

[20] Alessandro Stanziani, *Rules of Exchange: French Capitalism in Comparative Perspective, Eighteenth–Twentieth Centuries* (Cambridge: Cambridge University Press, 2012).

[21] Richard Barber, Michael Glantz, *Currents of Change: El Nino's Impact on Climate and Society* (Cambridge: Cambridge University Press, 1996); Peter Webster and Song Yang, 'Monsoon and ENSO: Selective Interactive Systems', *Quarterly Journal of the Royal Meteorological Society* 118, no. 507 (1992): 877–926.

[22] Davis, *Late Victorian Holocausts*; Arap Maharatna, *The Demography of Famine* (Delhi: Oxford University Press, 1996); Paul Bohr, *Famine in China* (Cambridge, MA: Harvard University Press, 1972).

the solution was found not in regulating speculation but in building infrastructure, or free markets and weather forecasting. The first avenue led the British to destroy the traditional systems of irrigation in India, replacing them with their own systems, barely appropriate to the subcontinent's ecological and social systems, and ultimately increasing famine. The other solution was strongly supported by economists such as Stanley Jevons, one of the most influential neoclassical and liberal economists of all times, who argued for weather forecasting and its use in political economy.[23] This suggestion was reflected widely in both colonial and homeland policies. In home countries, systematic inquiries were launched into weather variations and the expected harvest. This was the case in India in particular, where several famines and epidemics struck in the 1870s and the 1880s, with 10 million deaths in 1876-8, and the same ten years later. Harvest failure due to a weak and late northern monsoon was in part at the origin of the famines; but, much more than harvest failure, British economic policies were determinant. British authorities continued to pressure the local population with taxes and export requirements despite the lack of produce.[24] A number of British observers, such as Jevons and Strachey, insisted on the necessity of letting the market operate while obtaining at the same time accurate information on weather. More weather stations and meteorological inquiries in India were the result of this trend.

During last quarter of the nineteenth century, these kinds of enquiries were also developed in the United States to anticipate the evolution of prices. A set of correspondents was established, and they sent regular reports to the US Department of Agriculture and local business associations such as the Chicago Board of Trade. Other countries sought to imitate this initiative but had to confront important difficulties. The international conferences of statisticians devoted most of its attention to the criteria to be used for harvest forecasts. And almost every country resorted to estimates 'by type of harvest' as they had been advanced by Russian statisticians and authorities. Russia played a crucial role in the development of these statistics precisely because it depended on the two sides of the problem: the development of markets and speculation, the persistence of famine and, of course, the link between them.[25] Political debates concerned the 'modernization' of agriculture and the appropriate economic policies to adopt in order to reach market and economic development but

---

[23] Mauro Gallegati and Domenico Mignacca, 'Jevons, Sunspots Theory and Economic Fluctuations', *History of Economic Ideas* 2, no. 2 (1994): 23-40.

[24] R. Neelakanteswara Rao, *Famines and Relief Administration: A Case Study of Coastal Andhra, 1858-1901* (Delhi: Oxford University Press, 1997); Tim Dyson, ed., *India's Historical Demography: Studies in Famine, Disease, and Society* (Cambridge: Cambridge University Press, 1989).

[25] Nikolai M. Dronin and Edward G. Bellinger, *Climate Dependence and Food Problems in Russia 1900-1990: The Interaction of Climate and Agricultural Policy and Their Effect on Food Problems* (Budapest/ New York: CEU Press, 2005); Tom Scott-Smith, *On an Empty Stomach: Two Hundred Years of Hunger Relief* (Ithaca and London: Cornell University Pres, 2021); Stephen G. Wheatcroft, 'The 1891-92 Famine in Russia: Towards a More Detailed Analysis of its Scale and Demographic Significance', in *Economy and Society in Russia and the Soviet Union, 1860-1930, Essays for Olga Crisp*, edited by Linda Harriet Edmondson and P. Waldron (New York: St. Martin's Press, 1992), 44-64; Richard G. Robbins Jr, *Famine in Russia 1891-1892: The Imperial Government Responds to a Crisis* (New York and London: Columbia University Press, 1975).

without its worst social drawbacks (famines, social unrest). That said, we need to know how these figures were obtained.

Indeed, most of statisticians argued on the one hand that peasants tend to underestimate their harvests for the reasons mentioned earlier (tax burden, landowner exploitation), and on the other hand that it was difficult for both peasants and statisticians to translate local measures (in terms of *sagen*, the height of wheat balls) into weight. They therefore used a qualitative evaluation of the harvest. There were six possible answers: excellent, very good, good, poor, very poor, no harvest at all. Each answer was assigned a number: 5 for excellent, 4 very good, etc. – then the statisticians would convert the numbers into weights. How?

Using available statistics (which they knew – as we do – to be unreliable), they evaluated the average yield (harvest per unit of surface area) over the last ten years for the region and village under investigation. This period of time was inspired by Juglar's works on the relationship between the harvest and sun cycles (ten years long) as the source of ten-year economic cycles. The result corresponded to a good or normal harvest (number 3). Thus, the other answers (excellent, very good, etc.) and their numbers (5, 4, etc.) were translated into weights according to the following system of equivalences:

5 excellent harvest = 2/3 above the average (normal = 3)
4 very good = 1/3 above the average
3 good harvest = normal = ten-year average
2 poor harvest = 2/3 average (1/3 below)
1 very poor harvest = 1/3 average
0 No harvest

It is possible to obtain any equivalence. For example, if in a given district or village the average subjective evaluation based on correspondents' answers is 3.2, then the provisional future harvest will be:

3/ten-year average = 3.2/x

x will be the production per unit of cultivated surface area in the district. By multiplying this value by the estimated cultivated surface area, statisticians obtained the estimated harvest in this area.

This method led to lively discussions. Some statisticians, notably Russian and French, stressed that the significance of the 'average value' depended on the rate of data variability. Thus, when harvests were prone to strong seasonal and yearly oscillations, which was the case in Russia, the average value was not very meaningful for statisticians, while the notion of a 'normal harvest loses its significance for peasants'.[26] It was also suggested that, when questioning peasants, statisticians should associate a 'normal harvest' not with a ten-year average but with a simple

---

[26] RGIA, fond 1290, opis 2, delo 628; D. A. Timiriatsev, 'Rapport sur l'unification de l'enregistrement de la statistique des récoltes', *Bulletin de l'Institut International de Statistique* 99 (1899): 142–8.

comparison between the current and the previous year. Statisticians would then weight this measure in the yearly average.[27]

Other statistical solutions were put forward to improve future harvest evaluation. For example, to determine the accuracy of estimates 'by type of harvest', some statistical bureaus observed that the accuracy of data depended on the concerned region and that differences in this concern reproduced over years.[28] Data also show that the estimates were in general more accurate for the winter harvest and for the most 'stable' spring harvests such as oats compared with spring rye, corn and millet. This fact would seem to indicate that weather conditions occurring between the flowering period (when the producers were surveyed) and the harvest might affect the accuracy of the estimates.[29]

Should we therefore conclude that the producers systematically underestimated the coming harvest? This hypothesis was not made explicit or quantified, however. Actually, discussions were ultimately conditioned more by political concerns (the opposition between the Tsarist administration and local self-management organizations) than by more strictly statistical considerations. As a result, despite interesting technical manipulations (think, for example, of the widespread use of coefficients of correlation), these studies remained doubtful as to the data used and the results obtained. Data was obtained using very different sampling procedures and drawn up in very different ways.

The questions raised by the harvest statistics reflect a broader phenomenon, namely the growing influence of public authorities in economic activity. This raises two interrelated problems: first, the need to have projection data available to orient state interventions; second, the difficulty of making a clear-cut separation between economic studies and tax surveys in the strict sense. Hence the wariness of the population with regard to surveys.

These problems did not arise solely in Russia, tough. If almost every country resorted to estimates 'by type of harvest', this method was applied in different ways. Thus, while Hungary adopted the same system as Russia, France preferred to avoid any mention in the questionnaire of a 'normal harvest' (over a ten-year period). On the other hand, the producer was asked if he foresaw an 'equal', 'better' or 'worse' harvest than that of the previous year 'which was still fresh in the mind of the peasant'.[30] In any case, this solution did not keep statisticians from referring *afterwards* to a ten-year average.

In the United States, as in France, the questionnaire proposed a comparison with the previous year. The system of equivalence was, on the other hand, structured on a scale of 100. This figure corresponded to the *full average crop*. According to the

---

[27] Ibid., speech by Tisserand. See also, for other countries, for example, David N. Livingstone, 'Reading the Heavens, Planting the Earth: Cultures of British Science', *History Workshop Journal* 54 (2000): 236–41.

[28] TsSK, *Veroiatnyi sbor khlebov v … godu* in *Ezhegodnik Rossii* (The Evolution of Wheat Harvest in … Year) (Ministry of internal affairs: Saint Petersburg: 1904–17).

[29] RGIA, fond 1290, opis 2, delo 430, 456.

[30] Tisserand, in the discussion following Timiriatsev's presentation, 'Rapport sur l'unification de l'enregistrment de la statistique des récoltes', *Bulletin de l'Institut International de Statistique* 9 (1899): 147.

American statisticians, it was in the producers' interest to cooperate because the selected 'correspondents' would then receive statistical bulletins to help them make better business decisions.[31] What kept Russian statisticians from adopting the same solution?

Two factors played an essential role here. First, in the United States, the possibility of also benefiting from the statisticians' estimates gave peasants an incentive to cooperate. For the information to be of use to producers, they had to be integrated in a market economy and know how to read the bulletins. In Russia, those two requirements were difficult to meet. Tsarist wheat exports came above all from the estates of nobles, who employed a peasant workforce whose services were usually provided against payment in advance and loans in kind (tools, wheat). The rest of peasant commercial activity was mainly to pay taxes.[32]

Second, statistical theory suggested, already at that time, that the 'representative' cases that made up the sample had to be selected based on studies of the entire (statistical) 'population'. But in Russia, as mentioned, only one general census of the population was ever conducted – in 1897. In fact, there was no real Central Institute of Statistics. The rivalry among the various branches of the administration prevented the creation of a real central statistics office, which was seen as a form of control over the ministries by the central administration and the Interior Ministry in particular.

The problems posed by harvest statistics were therefore resolved according to the logic of a war economy. Instead of 'forecasts' on the state and dynamism of the markets, it was indeed a question of 'estimates' made according to the demands of the administration, whose objectives became in the end the real target, no matter the real level of agriculture production. This approach persisted and further enhanced under the Soviet rule.

Yet Russia was not the only place where the tension occurred between markets and state regulation, or that between economic information to orient economic activity or to control and repress local populations. During the same period, i.e. between the 1860s and the First World War, these same tensions affected the colonial systems. Global speculation and market connections mentioned played a role in this overall tension between climate, markets and social inequalities. The construction of information and data on weather, harvests and prices were major scientific and political issues. In the following pages, I will focus on cyclones and their impact in the Indian Ocean. Again, I am not attempting here to establish whether there was climate change or not or how these economies worked; I have already discussed these points elsewhere.[33] Instead, my aim here is twofold: on the one hand, to understand how, from the present, we can reconstruct past relationships between climatic, economic and social dynamics: this involves archives, past documents and currently simulations reconstructed by scientists. In what way? On the other hand, to historicize these data and artefacts and

---

[31] Institut International de Statistique, VI Session de l'Institut International de Statistique. Saint-Peterbourg, 1897, *Bulletin de l'Institut International de Statistique*, vol. 11 (Saint Petersburg, 1899); XI Session, Copenhagen, 1908 in vol. 17 (Copenhagen, 1908).

[32] RGIA, fond 1290, opis 1, delo 625.

[33] On these points see Stanziani, *Capital terre*.

detail how the actors themselves of that time sought to capture cyclones and their impact: the tension between 'science' and 'common knowledge', and, even more complicated, in a transregional perspective, British, French and 'local' knowledge about cyclones.

Cyclones: from travel narratives to forecasting

In 2013, the *American Journal of Climate Change* published an interesting paper by two French scientists.[34] Sponsored by the Institut Universitaire de France, the paper responded to an inter-governmental mission and a scientific collaborative project seeking to understand whether global warming was responsible for the increasing number of cyclones in the Indian Ocean.[35] In turn, this project entered a wider debate about the global warming, the Anthropocene and extreme weather events.[36] In order to reconstruct meteorological events in the past, the huge bibliography produced during last fifteen to twenty years adopted several methods, among them the reconstitution of past events made with the help of statistics and models simulating past evolution of main variables. Rainfall, draughts, shifting of delta rivers, archaeobotanics, geology and other disciplines have been mobilized.[37] In particular, in the northern Indian Ocean, they identified from 1860 onwards an increase in the temperature of the water, a reduction in rainfall and weaker summer monsoons. Weaker summer monsoons led to drought and poor rice harvests, which in turn often resulted in famine.[38]

In their quest for data, some scholars decided to enter the archives for information from the periods concerned. This is where the story becomes relevant to us: the 'ordinary' use of scientific measurement and data, normally discussed by scientists only according to their scientific relevance and statistical well-foundedness, has been added to the archive research that historians do.

This is what our two scientists did: they made use of data found in the archives and they mention the places (London, Reunion, Mauritius Island), not the files and numbers, as is custom among historians. The authors justified their attitude with the

---

[34] Emmanuel Garnier and Jérémy Desarthe, 'Cyclones and Societies in the Mascarene Islands, Seventeenth–Twentieth Centuries', *American Journal of Climate Change* 2 (2013): 1–13.
[35] IPCC, 'Managing the Risks of Extreme Events and Disasters to Advance Climate Change Adaptation', *Special Report of Intergovernmental Panel on Climate Change* (Cambridge: Cambridge University Press, 2012).
[36] For an introduction: Stanziani, *Capital terre*; Brian Fagan, *Floods, Famines and Emperors: El Niño and the Fate of Civilization* (New York: Basic Books, 1999).
[37] Andrew Schurer, Gabriele Hegerl, Michael Mann, Simon Tett and Steven Phipps, 'Separating Forces from Chaotic Climate Variability over the Past Millennium', *Journal of Climate* 26 (2013): 6954–73; Brendan Buckley, Roland Fletcher, Shi-Yu Simon Wang, Brian Zottoli and Christophe Pottier, 'Monsoon Extremes and Society over the Past Millennium on Mainland South-East Asia', *Quaternary Science Review* 95 (2014): 1–19.
[38] Hai Xu, Y. Hong and B. Hong, 'Decreasing Asian Summer Monsoon Intensity after 1860 AD in the Global Warming Epoch', *Climatic Dynamics* 39 (2012): 2079–88; C. Fu and J. Fletcher, 'Large Signals of Climatic Variation over the Ocean in the Asian Monsoon Region', *Advances in Atmospheric Sciences* 5, no. 4 (1988): 389–404.

usual argument made by scientists, that is, protection of data base they had built, which is still under discussion for laboratory investigation, not for archives! Yet here we do not deal with ethical questions but rather with that of knowing which kind of data the archives contain. If so, then, how can we possibly classify these events according to current scales of winds?

The archives list eighty-nine cyclones that hit the Mascarene Islands between 1656 and 2007, with a clear increase in the incidence of cyclones in the twentieth century (forty-three compared with seventeen in the nineteenth and twenty in the eighteenth century) that cannot be explained by improved recording. Focusing on the nineteenth century, we see a peak in the number of cyclones between 1870 and 1879.[39] What do these data mean?

In part, there is scientific uncertainty about the dynamics of cyclones and their evolution. Mathematical models are still unable to fully resume cyclone formation and evolution.[40] Social stakes are equally important: in the past two centuries, private insurance and public aids depended on the classification of the event. Nowadays, debates about the global warming add another major stake, the importance and strength of hurricane and cyclones during last centuries being mentioned in the global understanding of warming.[41] That is what this chapter is about: the production of supposedly reliable statistics and information on cyclones in the Indian Ocean world (IOW). This topic has been the subject of several studies, beginning with historians' narratives of weather forecasting in colonial India as it had developed since the 1870s. This topic drew attention to the relationship between the environment in India (and thus diseases, bad harvests and the like) and the policies to adopt (whether development policies of 'modernization' or relying on so-called local communities and their mutual help). In this chapter, I will not delve too deeply into this topic as I will discuss the impact of cyclones not in India but in the Mascarene Islands. Moreover,

---

[39] N. Mimura et al., 'Small Islands', in *Climate Change: Impacts, Adaptation and Vulnerability. Contribution of Working Group II to the Fourth Assessment Report of the Intergovernmental Panel on Climate Change*, edited by M. L. Parry et al. (Cambridge: Cambridge University Press, 2007).

[40] Just a few examples within a huge scientific bibliography: Krishnamurti, Stefanova and Misra, *Tropical Meteorology*; Kieran Hickey, ed., *Advances in Hurricane Researches. Modelling, Meteorology, Preparedness, and Impact* (Rijeka: In tech, 2012); Schwartz, *Sea of Storms*; Beattie, O'Gorman and Henry, *Climate, Science, and Colonization*; Williamson, 'Weathering the Empire'; Mahony, 'For an Empire of all Types of Climate'.

[41] Raymond Arsenault, 'The Public Storm. Hurricanes and the State in Twentieth Century America', in *American Public Life and the Historical Imagination*, edited by Wendy Gamber, Michael Grossberg and Hendrick Hartog (Notre Dame: University of Notre Dame Press, 2003); Michael Chenoweth, 'A Reassessment of Historical Atlantic Basin Tropical Cyclone Activity, 1700–1855', *Climate Change* 76 (2006): 169–240; Colten, *Perilous Place*; Emmanuel, *Divine Wind*; Romain Huret, *Katrina, 2005. L'ouragan, l'État et les pauvres aux États-Unis* (Paris: EHESS, 2010); Erik Larson, *Isaac's Storm: A Man, a Time and the Deadliest Hurricane in History* (New York: Crown, 1999); José Carlos Millas and Leonard Perdue, *Hurricanes of the Caribbean and Adjacent Regions, 1492–1800* (Miami: Academy of the Arts and Sciences of the Americas, 1968); R. J. Murname and K.-B. Liu, *Hurricanes and Typhoons: Past, Present and Future* (New York: Columbia University Press, 2004); Chris Mooney, *Storm World: Hurricanes, Politics and the Battle over Global Warming* (Orlando: Harcourt, 2007); Matthew Mulcahy, *Hurricanes and Society in the British Greater Caribbean, 1624–1783* (Baltimore: Johns Hopkins University Press, 2006); Schwartz, *Sea of Storms*; James Wescoat, 'Water, Climate and the Limits of Human Wisdom: Historical-Geographic Analogies Between Early Mughal and Modern South Asia', *Professional Geographer* 66, no. 3 (2014): 382–9.

I will start much earlier than the 1870s, several decades before, and trace the collection of information and organization of knowledge before meteorology was accepted as a science in Europe and then exported to the colonial worlds. The chosen chronology therefore offers a different angle other than just colonial and development studies; it is concerned instead with the difficult interplay between maritime skills, observation and the identification of 'storms' (cyclones) that were quite unusual for Western observers.

I will begin by setting out what is known about cyclones and storms in the Indian Ocean in the period under investigation. I will then detail the impact of climatic disturbances on Reunion Island, on planters and colonial elites. The focus on Reunion Island requires some clarification. It leads us to investigate the environmental impact on an area which is much neglected compared to the northern (for storms and droughts) and eastern (typhoons, volcanoes) parts of the Indian Ocean, and this even though, as we will see, analyses of storms and cyclones were improved in Reunion and Mauritius Islands. One major peculiarity of Reunion Island (and Mauritius) is that instead of monsoon, rain and/or drought, it endures violent storms. Small islands are particularly exposed: changes in sea level, variations in rainfall regimes and winds have a strong impact. The same is true for external market shocks and food security problems in a context where small crops are marginal and dependent on a major sugar monoculture. However, this does not suffice to explain the highly differentiated impact of cyclones depending on the crop (rice and maize) and the socio-economic group (planters and indentured immigrants): environmental determinism cannot replace social explanations; it is in the interplay between the two that the solution to our problem lies.

Located in the intertropical zone, the south-west of the Indian Ocean is one of the world's seven cyclogenesis basins. Tropical cyclones make their appearance at the beginning of the austral summer, around 15 November. The cyclone season generally lasts until 15 April.[42] Winds can reach up to 300 km/h, with the released energy quadrupling when wind speed doubles. The north-eastern and extreme southern zones are the most exposed.[43] Indeed, monsoon, cyclones and the great variety and abundance of river landscapes along an immense coastline running from the Zambezi in East Africa to the Irrawaddy and the Mekong are all distinctive features of the IOW; we might add river instability, volcanoes and earthquake intensity. Various sub-regions can also be distinguished.

In contrast to trade wind regions like the Atlantic, the pattern of monsoons is quite regular. These were the winds that largely determined when and where people could sail. Regional specificities have to be considered as well. The north-east monsoon starts in November and one could leave the Arabian coast at that time and sail at least as far as Mogadishu. During the south-west monsoon period, this current reverses, going east. In the far south we are out of the monsoon system and the south-west monsoon becomes weak and unpredictable.

---

[42] Jean Ecormier, *Cyclones tropicaux du Sud-ouest de l'Océan Indien, le cas de l'Ile de la Réunion* (La Réunion: S. M. R., 1992): 7.

[43] Prospère Eve, *Ile à peur, La peur redoutée ou récupérée à La Réunion des origines à nos jours* (Saint André, La Réunion: éd. Graphica, 1992).

The situation is different between the Red Sea and western India. Ships left Calicut in January and arrived there from the Red Sea between August and November. Moving west, the western coast of Malaysia becomes a lee shore during the south-west monsoon, making it very difficult to sail or land. The monsoon pattern dictated the passage from the west of the ocean, for example the Red Sea, to Malacca in the Far East. Indeed, the China Sea has a monsoon pattern that does not exactly correspond to the timing of the Western Indian Ocean. Ships on the way to and from Canton or ports further north needed a lengthy stay in South-east Asia before favourable winds set in. Chinese junks trading with Malacca from the beginning of the fifteenth century followed the mainland coast to Indochina and then crossed over to the Malay Peninsula.

A fourth area is located south of the monsoon region; it connects the Cape of Good Hope to southern Madagascar. In this region, as in the previous ones, ocean currents combine with winds to create constraints as well as opportunities for travel by sea. Off the East African coast, during the north-east monsoon from November to April, the weak counter-clockwise gyre produces a westward current that travels as fast as one knot. During the south-west monsoon, this current reverses, going east and then north along the coast of Somalia. Below the monsoon zone, there is a steady anti-cyclonic gyre and the south equatorial current flows west and divides at Madagascar.

How can we possibly connect current scientific knowledge on monsoons and cyclones with historical sources? The first problem is that of obtaining sufficiently accurate information on the cyclones; in local sources, terminology is vague. For example, in Reunion Island, a cyclone can be referred to as a '*coup de vent*' (or *koudvan*), as 'mauvais temps' (or *mové tan*), as an '*ouragan*' (sometimes written with an 'h' in the nineteenth century); sailors refer to it as '*gros temps*' or as a '*bourrasque*', a '*trombe*', an '*avalasse*' or an '*avalaison*' – though the latter variations tend to relate to heavy rainfall without there being any cyclone. In one book dated 1869 it is even referred to as a 'typhon' in the Indian Ocean.[44] The number of different terms is not simply a question of the way people speak; even nowadays, unlike earthquakes for which a worldwide scale has been adopted, the different national weather stations (in Australia, the US, Japan, France, India, etc.) name and classify hurricanes, cyclones and typhoons in different ways.[45] So, it is easy to see why there was so much uncertainty and inaccuracy regarding cyclones in the nineteenth century. The scientific identification of tropical cyclones was slow to progress. In the eighteenth century and the first half of the nineteenth century, most information came from travel narratives and nautical logs. At that time meteorologists in both France and England were finding it hard to be taken seriously. Scientific circles considered meteorology to be akin to popular prophecy, or at best the professional know-how of sailors and planters.[46] The rise of

---

[44] Elie Pajot, *Simples renseignements sur l'Ile Bourbon* (Paris: Challanel Aîné, Librairie Coloniale 1887): 307.
[45] Centre canadien de prévision d'ouragan (16 septembre 2003), *Comment catégorise-t-on les ouragans?* http://www.ec.gc.ca/ouragans-hurricanes/default.asp?lang=Fr&n=AB062B74-1; Bureau of Meteorology (2008) *Guide to Tropical Cyclone Forecasting* http://www.bom.gov.au/cyclone/about/names.shtml
[46] Anderson, *Predicting the Weather*; Locher, *Le savant et la tempête*.

meteorology was thus relatively slow – the second half of the nineteenth century – and was due to a combination of events, beginning with the interest in the weather shown by public administrations, essentially in order to limit the effects of poor harvests, and by the colonial elite in relation to problems of famine, especially in Africa and the Indian Ocean.

This rise was less easily implemented in the colonies, due to both the lack of knowledge about the local environment and to the high cost of obtaining such knowledge. In the Indian Ocean in particular, meteorological analysis remained the domain of scientists and explorers; the British and French Navies gradually compiled charts for currents, tides and winds, but these analyses were concentrated in the north of the Indian Ocean, leaving its southern areas relatively neglected. This state of affairs meant that progress in the understanding of cyclones was slow. It was mainly officers and seafarers who were the first to attempt to gather information from logbooks in order to arrive at more general analyses. In this attempt, they largely relied upon local seamen and observers; technical progress in shipbuilding as well as knowledge of local conditions of navigation, including cyclones, located at the overlap of multiple local and European skills. Sir Francis Beaufort (1774–1857), hydrographer and officer of the Royal Navy, devised his famous scale in 1806: he measured the strength of wind through the observation of ripples, their size and frequency, and estimated its impact on the various kinds and sizes of sails. His scale goes from 0 (calm) to 12 (cyclone). Beaufort improved his scale while travelling across the globe and conversing with local seamen. In 1824, another English captain, Locke Lewis, suggested that the British authorities in Mauritius and the French officers in Reunion Island should unite their efforts and share their information on cyclones. No such collaboration took place. The first research of this type was carried out in 1838 by Colonel Sir William Reid. He used newspaper articles and logbooks which he collected in Reunion Island, Mauritius, England and Barbados, where he had been posted. He provides highly detailed descriptions of hurricanes, their paths, how they formed, their direction and strength, changes in pressure and levels of rainfall. He described in great detail the main hurricanes to hit Barbados, Mauritius, Reunion Island and certain parts of India over previous decades. He proposed what he referred to as a 'Law of storms'.[47] This was in fact a set of general principles compiled from examples mentioned in his work. Reactions were mixed: some felt the work to be totally unsuitable and unscientific, whilst others saw it as a real step forward. Among the latter was Henry Piddington (1797–1858), another English captain. Whilst Reid's interest in tropical storms had developed during his time in Barbados, Piddington had served in Calcutta and in the region of the Brahmaputra estuary. When studying the history of the cyclones which had devastated these regions, he immediately grasped the link – highly innovative for that period – between tropical storms at sea and devastation on land. He invented the term cyclone to describe the whirlwind characteristics that he compared to a snake winding itself into a circle – 'kyklos' in Greek. He correctly distinguished between the anti-clockwise rotation of cyclones in the northern hemisphere and the clockwise

---

[47] Sir William Reid, *An Attempt to Develop the Law of Storms* (London: John Weale, 1838).

rotation of those in the southern hemisphere.[48] Piddington's work was to remain the ultimate reference for sailors in the tropics for half a century.

In France, whilst the works of Reid and Piddington were well known, the study of tropical cyclones was based on research carried out on Reunion Island. It was no seafarer, but a botanist and naturalist from Reunion Island, Joseph Hubert (1745-1825), famous for having introduced cinnamon and cloves to Reunion Island, who in 1818 suggested that tropical storms did not move in straight lines but turned.[49] He talked about a simultaneous movement of rotation and translation which was to be confirmed fifteen years later by German meteorologist Dove.[50]

This same idea was later developed by another Reunion man, Gabriel Hilaire Bridet, who set down in his *Étude sur les ouragans de l'hémisphère austral* (Study of Hurricanes in the Austral Hemisphere) the factors that sailors and landsmen should use to establish the eye and course of a cyclone. According to him, they establish the position of the eye using wind directions and their variations.[51] Bridet, a harbourmaster on Reunion Island, used Hubert's notion of circular rather than convergent winds (Meldrum's theory) to explain the parabolic course of cyclones along a west–south-west trajectory and then south–south-east as the cyclone gradually moves into the southern hemisphere. It was indeed Bridet who ensured the liaison between naval officers, meteorologists and administrative authorities. As harbourmaster on Reunion Island from 1850 to 1860, he encouraged observation, analysis and the constitution of extensive archives on cyclones and the damage they caused. British meteorological observation in the Indian Ocean naturally focused also on India and sought to connect it with the broader climatic condition of the Himalayas on one side and the Indian Ocean on the other. In the 1850s, a member of the Board of Directors of the East India Company, Colonel William Henry Sykes, published a long paper on the climate and meteorology of the Deccan. Meanwhile Piddington's work on cyclones saw the light and Richard Strachey produced meteorological observations on the Himalayas and Tibet. He had supported the creation of an Indian meteorological station since the 1850s. However, his project did not find a response from the administrative authorities until the mid-1860s, when several cyclones hit India and Calcutta in particular, taking 50,000 lives and destroying much property. Meteorological stations were therefore established in Madras, Bombay and Bengal presidencies.

Maps and their accuracy were, of course, crucial to this task. Again, British and French officers relied upon local actors to draw maritime maps of winds, currents,

---

[48] Henri Piddington, *The Sailor's Horn-book for the Law of Storms* (London: Smith Elder, 1848); A. K. Sen Sarma, 'Henry Piddington (1797–1858): A Bicentennial Tribute', *Weather* 52, no. 6 (2012): 187–93.

[49] Gabriel Gérard, *Un grand créole, Joseph Hubert, 1747–1825* (Saint-Denis, La Réunion: éditions Azalée, 2006).

[50] Henry Dove, *The Law of Storms Considered in Connection with the Ordinary Movement of the Atmosphere* (London: Longman, 1886).

[51] Hilaire Gabriel Bridet, *Étude sur les ouragans de l'hémisphère austral. Manœuvres à faire pour s'en éloigner et se soustraire aux avaries qu'ils peuvent occasionner* (Saint-Denis, La Réunion: Rambosson, 1861); John Cox, *Storm Watchers. The Turbulent History of Weather Prediction from Franklin's Kite to El Niño* (Hoboken, NJ: John Wiley & Sons, 2002).

seas and shores. Meteorology also part of a huge project of a trigonometrical survey of India. This enterprise, launched in the early 1800s, recorded the geodesic details of the Indian landscape.

At the same time, knowledge of cyclones also interacted with general studies of winds, in particular hurricanes in the Western Atlantic. William Redfield mapped the West Indies hurricanes of 1835 while Elias Loomis explored the value of synoptic maps of storms.[52] His storm maps brought together the main features of the future standard representation of the weather: isothermal lines, connecting points of usual deviation from average temperature, isobars, and arrows giving the wind direction. In his presentation to the American Philosophical Society in Philadelphia in 1843, Loomis also compared the two rival theories of storms, one presenting winds whirling around a centre, the other imagining them blowing in toward the centre from all directions. Loomis did not close the debate, but he made clear the huge advantage of transferring mass observations to synoptic charts.[53] It was not until the 1870s that Francis Galton offered a map of winds with barometric pressure. He revealed that high pressure areas were calms and surrounded by clockwise winds, a condition he named 'anti-cyclone' in reference to the cyclone pattern of low pressure. The problem was that, for some decades still, maps were often inadequate to convey distinctions between 'scientific' and 'popular' weather forecasting. For example, in 1887, one Ralph Abercromby put on his map for cyclone prognostics not only isobars and winds but also animal behaviour, bodily sensations and the like.[54] Moreover, even among 'scientific' accounts of meteorology a major problem persisted: the lack of standardization of measure (at what speed a wind becomes a cyclone) and of instruments themselves. Indeed, this was a more general question strongly disputed in England itself, and, thus, even more across its empire. As late as the 1870s, the two main observatories in Kew and Greenwich disagreed on the methods and instruments of observation and together criticized the multiplication of criteria among local regional observatories. Like other branches of science, meteorology was therefore confronted with the need to standardize instruments and techniques of observation if it wanted to move from the status of amateur hobby to a 'real science'. Of course, standardization was necessary to produce weather forecasting. However, this process took decades because the trouble came not just with instruments but also with the collection and exploitation of observations. The new insights in the theory of probability, mentioned above, entered this general transformation and acceptance of meteorology as a science. Still, in this case as well, as in many other branches of scientific knowledge, the question was whether this new 'science' (from a Western perspective and definition) was applicable to the tropics.

It is now time to take a closer look at the archival documents. If actors themselves named and evaluated differently the various cyclones, how can we possibly rely on these sources?

---

[52] Gisela Kutzbach, *The Thermal Theory of Cyclones: A History of Meteorological Thought in the Nineteenth Century* (Boston: American Meteorological Society, 1979).
[53] Anderson, *Predicting the Weather*: 193.
[54] Ralph Abercromby, *Weather: A Popular Exposition of the Nature of Weather Changes from Day to Day* (London: Kegan Paul, 1887).

Cyclones in the archives

The analysis of Reunion Island archive sources on cyclones allows us on the one hand to understand their impact and the impressions of people at that time and on the other hand the interests and stakes at the origin of these documents. In other words, if we want to make an appropriate reading and use of these documents, we need first to understand why they were produced; maybe their motivation did not lie in studies on 'global warming' as ours does nowadays, but in something else. What was it? Why did records on cyclones multiply in the archives during the nineteenth century? Why was there this interest in the conditions of production, in particular in those years? After all, cyclones always hit the island; there were major setbacks for coffee producers, especially the smaller ones. In fact, the increasing presence of cyclones in the archives was less related to their objective multiplication during this period than to the political and social context, namely the tensions related to slavery and its abolition, and the role colonies such as the Reunion Island played in the French Empire. The production of archives on cyclones and the needs for meteorological knowledge were consequences of these broader stakes.

With the conquest of Mauritius by the English and the evolution of the slave trade in the Atlantic (English embargo), the worldwide sugar market took off. Prices soared and, wishing to profit from the situation, Reunion producers abandoned coffee for sugar cane. This conversion went hand in hand with a significant increase in the importation of slaves, despite the English embargo.[55] However, following a period of relative respite during the 1820s, sugar production also found itself facing climate issues. These social and economic stakes in a quickly changing world (from slavery to post-slavery; increasing world market for sugar) contribute to explain the major interest in reporting and measuring cyclones. In the 1830s, assessments by experts, gendarmes and the botanist from the island's Department of Internal Affairs reported losses equivalent to one ninth of the manioc harvest, one third of maize, three quarters of rice and almost all fruit and cloves. Coffee and sugar, however, suffered losses of between one eighth and one ninth of the total crops.[56] In other words, the assessment of both the strength of cyclones and the damage they caused could not be separated from the social cost and social policies to be adopted.

This scenario was repeated in an even more dramatic fashion in 1844–5: the extremely violent cyclone of 21 December 1844 was followed by floods on 4 January 1845 and then by a further cyclone on 8–9 March 1845.[57] The governor asked for special

---

[55] Monica Schuler, 'The Recruitment of African Indentured Labourers for European Colonies in the Nineteenth Century', in *Colonialism and Migration: Indentured Labour before and after Slavery*, edited by Petr Emmer (Dordrecht, Boston and Lancaster: Martinus Nijhoff, 1986): 125–61; Herbert Gerbeau, 'Quelques aspects de la traite illégale des esclaves à Bourbon au XIXe siècle', in *Mouvements de populations dans l'Océan indien* (Paris: Imprimerie Champion, 1979): 273–96; Richard Allen, *European Slave Trade in the Indian Ocean, 1500–1850* (Athens: Ohio University Press, 2015).

[56] ANOM (Archives Nationales d'Outre-Mer, Aix-en-Provence), FM SG/ Reu c 124 d 931, Coup de vent du 5 mars 1832, Rapport au ministre du 13 mars 1832.

[57] ANOM, FM SG/Reu c 124 d 932, Inondation du 4 janvier 1844, Rapport du gouverneur du 6 janvier 1845.

aid and for the law on the colony's tax allocations to be modified.[58] The lack of rice led to its price rising from 16–17 francs per 75 kg to 25 francs. Five ships from India were expected over the next two months, transporting approximately 20,000 75-kg sacks of rice. But these were imports that had already been scheduled and purchased for a 'normal year', due to the island's now chronic deficit in rice as a consequence of production strategies (more land being used for sugar cane to the detriment of other crops). The arrival of these ships would therefore not suffice to meet food requirements and those of the slaves in particular.[59] The result was that food on the plantations was scarce and the conditions of the slaves and 'free' immigrants were deteriorating.[60]

The abolition of slavery in 1848 only slightly changed this situation, and not for the better. In order to compensate for the increased costs caused by the move from slavery to indentured work, planters once again increased the amount of land used for sugar and looked for ways to reduce the food rations of their workers, at a time when their numbers were constantly increasing. The lack of available labour encouraged several landowners to call for the arrival of additional recruits, but this time from Africa, especially since France was moving towards the abolition of slavery.[61] In all, 43,958 Indian recruits arrived on Reunion Island between 1849 and 1859.[62] This growing population increased the pressure on food resources precisely at the moment when the amount of land devoted to maize, cassava and rice was being reduced in favour of sugar (which rose from 50 per cent to 68 per cent of cultivated land between 1850 and 1860).

It was within this context of latent shortage and virtual sugar monoculture that further cyclones hit the island. Whilst the sugar plantations were hit, generally speaking they came through it quite well, unlike the maize and rice crops and the foodstuff reserves which, as usual, were almost entirely destroyed. The island's Council asked for 10,530 francs in aid and 2,480 sacks of rice. But due to lack of resources, the governor only agreed to half of the requested aid and 2,000 sacks.[63]

Cyclones seemed to intensify in the 1860s and the 1870s.[64] Instead of detailing each file, we must now ask: what do these records tell us? We have already mentioned the fact that meteorology and its diffusion responded to the needs of expanding international markets and their need to face the risks of transportation (insurance) and harvest failure, in particular the use of futures (future contracts on goods to be

---

[58] ANOM, FM SG/Reu c 124 d 934, Coup de vent du 8 et 9 mars 1845, Rapport au ministre du 31 mars 1845.
[59] ANOM, FM SG/Reu c 124 d 934, Coup de vent du 8 et 9 mars 1845, Mars 1845: Lettre de la direction de l'intérieur (Réunion) au gouverneur.
[60] ANOM, FM SG/Reu c 124 d 935, Coup de vent du 25 janvier 1847.
[61] ANOM, FM SG/Reu c 454, d 5042 à 5074, Réunion, tableau de l'immigration africaine à la Réunion de 1848 à 1869. See also Ho Hai Huang, *Histoire économique de l'île de la Réunion, 1849–1881: engagisme, croissance et crise* (Paris: Lavoisier, 2004).
[62] Jacques Weber, 'L'émigration indienne à la Réunion: "contraire à la morale" ou "utile à l'humanité"', in *Esclavage et abolition dans l' Océan Indien, 1723–1869*, edited by Edmond Maestri (Paris: L'Harmattan, 2002): 309–28.
[63] ANOM, FM SG/Reu c124 d 937, Ouragan du premier mars 1850.
[64] ANOM, FM SG/Reu c 124 d 941 and c 942, Cyclones des 11 et 26 février 1860, inondation du 11 février, ouragan du 27 février 1861.

produced). Public authorities as well were concerned insofar as harvest failure and climatic variations had not only economic but also social and political impacts. The question was whether local populations, in the colonies in particular, should benefit from any public aid and in what form. We have mentioned the case of India, where the British answer to natural calamities was more market, more economic information and eventual investment in infrastructure (roads, canals). Faced with a series of natural catastrophes, some observers began to wonder about a possible climate change; some others replied that, without previous constant observations, no such conclusion could be drafted. However, in both cases, unlike nowadays concerns, no one imagined questioning human action; the only relevant question was whether it would be possible to foresee the weather and, if possible, climate evolution, in order to adopt appropriate economic and social policies. In his report, the harbourmaster – none other than Bridet, author of the famous work on cyclones mentioned above – observed that, according to cyclone theory, between May and November cyclones are unable to grow during the first part of their course, but that they become more powerful afterwards, throughout the second part of their parabolic track, thus forming the gales found in the Cape of Good Hope and south of Reunion Island. During this season, the northern part of the island is almost always windy. On the other hand, the Saint Pierre tidal waves tend to occur during the summer months. Yet recent cyclones, and that of 1863 in particular, seemed to be an exception to this rule, as they struck parts of the island which were usually spared and did not occur during the cyclone season – facts which puzzled the governor, harbourmaster and botanist. The governor renewed his request for a proper meteorological station. In the meantime, damage assessment was becoming more detailed. The reports relating to the 1863 cyclone provide a region-by-region, village-by-village account of damage to plantations, infrastructures, industries, transport and communications.[65]

This constantly repeated damage exacerbated tensions both between the colony and central government and within the colony itself. On behalf of the central authority, the authorizing officer declared that in Reunion Island the intention was to evenly distribute the financial aid, whereas in Martinique and Guadeloupe the money had been given to the most needy. He suggested allocating 200,000 francs to the most unfortunate, 200,000 to the colonial coffers and 100,000 to municipal coffers.

Local representatives – and small landowners in particular – were quick to respond: the situations in Guadeloupe, Martinique and Reunion Island were not comparable. If in Reunion Island they began by allocating aid to those who declared themselves to have suffered the greatest losses, they would end up favouring the biggest landowners, those who had been most affected by the most recent hurricane. They should prioritize the municipalities, who would use the money to repair infrastructures and thus benefit everyone. Others added that the heavy rainfall following the cyclone had allowed many of the plantations to be rebuilt, which meant that they should not take into consideration the damage assessed immediately after the cyclone had passed. Finally, others concluded that the most affected domains were those already

---

[65] ANOM, FM SG/Reu c 124 d 942.

in difficulty prior to the cyclone and that they should not use the latest cyclone as an excuse to help incompetent owners.[66]

Of course, the scarcer the resources, the greater the tensions. French colonies such as Reunion Island received very little aid from central government; in principle they were expected to pay from their own resources, but these were limited. Until 1848, poll tax and customs duty were the main sources of revenue. When slavery was abolished, the registration duty on recruits (paid by the landowners), taxes on wages and customs duties were the main sources of revenue. Yet during the 1860s, this revenue fell – taxes on sugar exports in particular.[67]

When yet another cyclone struck the island in March 1873, France's central authorities recommended the introduction of a system of aid which took into account not only direct victims of the disasters but also the islanders as a whole. Civil servants divided the population into three categories:

- 'natives who the cyclone has left without resources and unable to work' and whose needs were estimated at 521,106 francs;
- 'needy persons to whom aid may be granted with a view to helping them to rebuild their small crops, small businesses and workshops, and to reconstruct their dwellings'. Needs were estimated at 879,508 francs;
- 'details of losses provided by landowners not asking for any aid'.[68]

This proved to be a turning point: with the sugar crisis, both immigrants and the 'poor whites' fell into the 'native' category. To these were added those who still intended to restart a small farming or commercial business. In reality, many small properties disappeared. The 'poor whites' moved to the highlands and ended up simply selling their land. Whilst the largest properties were merging, an increasing number of former immigrants, Indians for the most part, were buying land from former white landowners. In sum, the cyclones had a strong impact on social hierarchy and economic relationships in Reunion Island, in as much as they affected workers' (slaves and then immigrant recruits) access to food and the strategies employed by planters and the colonial elite. We can objectively observe that cyclones became more violent during the second half of the nineteenth century. It is also true that sugar cane has a better resistance to strong winds than maize and cassava; finally, we can confirm that the price of rice increased in the region due to the weakening of summer monsoons in India during the exact same period as rice imports became most vital to Reunion Island. At the same time, the impact of these events on Reunion Island was even greater in that the planters had already shifted production over to a sugar cane monoculture (vulnerable to floods), that food reserves were insufficient and poorly protected and preserved, and that the mistreatment of workers continued despite the standards which the English wished to see introduced. The lack of rice on the plantations was

---

[66] ANOM, FM SG/Reu c 124 d 945, Cyclone du 12 et 13 mars 1868.
[67] ANOM, FM SG/Reu c 124 d 945, Cyclone du 12 et 13 mars 1868.
[68] ANOM, FM SG/Reu c 124 d 947, Cyclone du 7 et 8 janvier 1873.

due to far more than just cyclones and could not be justified by them alone. Famine never is just a consequence of bad harvests.

This said, the most interesting point to us is the connection between these social and economic historical concerns and the epistemological questions related to the production of sources and data. The archives document an increase over time in the number of cyclones and possibly of their strength, particularly from the 1860s onwards. The political use of natural catastrophes was on the increase at that time, given the sugar crisis, the difficulties encountered by planters and the development of meteorology on the one hand, and government aid on the other. The lack of food and the inappropriate use of the colonial fund demonstrate the attempts by planters and colonial authorities to pass on to the workers the cost of lower sugar prices and competition with Mauritius and the beet market, not to mention loan and rebuilding costs in the aftermath of the cyclones.

It is in this context that the question of knowing why and how documents and evaluations of cyclones were produced became relevant. Over recent years, with the help of archaeologists, meteorologists have recreated past climatic events in impressive detail. In particular, in the northern Indian Ocean, they identified an increase in the temperature of the water, a reduction in rainfall and weaker summer monsoons as from 1860. Weaker summer monsoons led to drought and poor rice harvests, which in turn often led to famine.[69] These phenomena had numerous effects on the Mascarenes: weaker monsoons in the northern part of the Indian Ocean were accompanied by a larger number and greater strength of cyclones in the southern region. Therefore, recent meteorological studies seem to confirm the details we found in the archives.[70] But what about the meaning of archives and current modelling of the past?

The difficult acceptance of meteorology, as a science or not, its transposition in the Indian Ocean, along with several other European forms of knowledge, and colonial policies were the three main stakes in the origins of the consulted documents. Yet, in the discussions between sources and data, this hermeneutic approach and conforming to humanities is different from another approach, consisting in measuring with current criteria past environmental dynamics. The question in this case does not consist in knowing the origin of a source and past ways of identifying meteorology, but a radically different one: has the global climate been changed during the last centuries by human action? This is a completely different approach to the same question, and, therefore, scientists including some social scientists seek to fabricate their own data in response. In other words, the fabrication of data enters a normative approach, which consists in putting aside archives or, at best, curbing their meaning in accordance with current scientific theories and meteorological models. In fact, the twentieth century changed the notion of climatic risk and the strategies to cope with it: on the one hand, major planters sought to transfer the risk to small producers of Indian origin; this

---

[69] Hai Xu, Y. Hong and B. Hong, 'Decreasing Asian Summer Monsoon Intensity after 1860 AD in the Global Warming Epoch', *Climatic Dynamics* 39 (2012): 2079–88; Fu Congbin and J. Fletcher, 'Large Signals of Climatic Variation over the Ocean in the Asian Monsoon Region', *Advances in Atmospheric Sciences* 5, no. 4 (1988): 389–404.

[70] Garnier and Desarthe, 'Cyclones and Societies'.

was achieved through contracts for machine rental, share-cropping, etc. On the other hand, up until the mid-twentieth century the new welfare state was highly selective and did not necessarily benefit workers. In this context, the construction of statistics was crucial: on the one hand, the number of cyclones and their previsibility determined the very possibility of anticipating damages and then evaluating and eventually compensating for them. On the other hand, the quantification of available products for consumption (rice, manioc) and of those available for manufacturing (sugar) was essential to set prices, customs and eventually need for import. These data made the object of negotiations, eventually fraud, in their own construction, and then of conflicts in their manipulation and interpretation. It is worth saying that this does not mean that data were pure 'invention', but that their construction was a social action itself which influenced market and institutional behaviours; in the present case, these data determined the destiny of different estates, their owners and working people.

From this perspective, we find both similarities and analogies with social data. In both cases, political and economic interests lie at the very origin of data and their interpretation. In both cases, the effort consists in putting current information into a long trend perspective, as the cases of Piketty and many others confirm. In both cases, scholars look for continuities and changes: in climate and or in societies. In both cases, co-production of information and data is important: intermediaries played a decisive role between peasants and statisticians in Russia and Western Europe, as well as between Western scientists and seamen and their equivalent in the IOW. In both cases, a large majority of authors and observers conclude that social inequalities increase over time and that the same is true for the global warming. These are probably 'facts' which rely nevertheless on a strong enough trust in numbers.

Conclusion: Part 2

For decades, discussions centred on whether an instrument considered to be technical, such as that of correlation, could be distinguished from the social categories to which it is applied and therefore whether statistics are a purely technical tool or a discipline. This methodological discussion took place at a moment when, in Western Europe in particular, public administrations increasingly used statistics to orient their policies. Thus, the underlying debate was who were in charge of the identification of 'technical' criteria, the interpretation of data and political aims: 'experts' or administrative and political leaders? Of course, unlike Weber's clear-cut distinction, these oppositions hide the fact that several experts were politicians and that the very same distinction between 'statistics as mathematical theory' and statistics as a social construct was a by-product of this same tension about the identification of knowledge, the distinction between 'natural' and 'social sciences', and, therefore, the political role of knowledge itself. The outcome of this global questioning depended on the location we look at and its connections with other areas of the world. Thus, quantitative social history was first challenged in Russia, India and Latin America at the end of the nineteenth century, then reinstated in the middle of the twentieth century on the condition that 'local' social categories be used. In return, these discussions have influenced the way social statistics were conceived and practised, even in the West. For example, the time budgets of Russian statisticians were used as a model for similar instruments developed in Europe and supported most expressions of the welfare state during the twentieth century. At the same time, when confronted by Russian peasants, these statistics raised two related questions: first, did peasants and colonial people evolve along Western lines, that is, turn into capitalists and proletarians (or, in the opposite jargon, into independent producers)? Second, and starting from this, did the household protect peasants who therefore did not need a welfare state?

The Soviets sought to transform peasants into proletarians, while, by contrast, in most Western countries the welfare state did not include 'independent producers' such as peasants and craftsmen.

All the same, forecast weather statistics was aimed at private insurance, rather than the welfare state. At a global scale, these data were constructed at the crossroad of Western and local forms of knowledges on weather. In practice, initial forms of welfare state excluded 'natural catastrophes' from its range of action and preferred to rely either on private insurance or (in particular in colonial areas) to local 'spontaneous' forms of solidarity – i.e. coerced labour.

The history of statistics is related to structural trends such as: the emergence and transformation of capitalism;[71] the growing intervention of the state in social and economic life (for political and social control[72] and/or promoting welfare);[73] the rise of modern science and the process of modernization.[74] Thus from the eighteenth century calculations accompanied both the rise of capitalism and increasing faith in the modernization paradigm. To some extent, the transformations of capitalism itself relied upon, and further enhanced, those of statistics as a political tool.

However, these relationships require some further explanation. The passage from the liberal to the welfare state and regulation was certainly a turning point in the West; at the same time, a concomitant trend was expressed by the rise of authoritarian states, in theory to enhance the welfare of their populations, in practice to better control them. Does this mean that it would be misleading merely to just contrast Western social-democrat states with authoritarian polities (China, URSS, Nazi Germany)? Without erasing the huge distance between statistics as a totalitarian tool and statistics as an instrument of public policies, a number of studies adopted a Foucauldian posture and argued that in the West, too, statistics express a form of surveillance and control. There is some truth in this assertion: police control, for instance, makes wide use of statistics. However, the problem with this top-down vision is that, as we have seen, statistics are always an unequal collaborative tool between multiple actors: various state and local agencies, often in competition, intermediaries, local populations (themselves

---

[71] Zakim Kornblith, *Capitalism Takes Commands*; Levy, *Freaks of Fortune*; Bouk, *How Our Days Became Numbered*; Cook, *The Pricing of Progress*; Deringer, *Calculated Values*; Coyle, *GDP*; Masood, *The Great Invention*.
[72] Tooze, *Statistics and the German State*; Ghosh, *Making it Count*; Blum and Mespoulet, *L'anarchie bureaucratique*; Brian, *La mesure de l'État*.
[73] Alain Desrosières, *Gouverner par les nombres* (Paris: Presses des Mines, 2008).
[74] Poovey, *The Invention of the Modern Fact*; Latour, *We Have Never Been Modern*; Porter, *Trust in Numbers*; Porter, *The Rise of Statistical Thinking*.

pursuing different aims and therefore adopting different attitudes vis-à-vis the state and statistics). In this respect, statistical paradigms and categories express an unequal, hierarchical collaboration between these actors; the construction of data is not only a form of oppression and domination but also, when possible, a tool for negotiation. Social and cognitive agreements between actors are reached in this particular form of mediation, translation and equivalence which, to some extent, parallels the 'translation' of local people's words and acts by national and colonial elites, as seen in the archival documents. The standardization of language and measurement proceeds together; at first glance, the main difference is that, unlike archives, statistics as a tool and expression of the modernization paradigm are highly normative and not just descriptive: they seek to orient public policies. The use of the word *descriptive* in statistical teaching usually aims at contrasting figures with analytical statistics. This distinction is misleading: statistics, in particular social, economic, environmental statistics are never purely descriptive: they always suggest a policy. This, by the way, is confirmed by the continual complaints politicians and officials make to statisticians, that they do not provide 'pure' data. Of course, pure data never exist, and the criticism mentioned actually expresses the fact that data do not necessarily express what politicians or officials want them to express. Statistics therefore confirm Latour's argument that we have never been modern, precisely because the separation between science and normativity has been never achieved, far from it. Of course, as we saw in Part I, archive building also has normative dimensions: it is not just a neutral classification of documents waiting for historians to read and interpret them, but has precise political aims: the consolidation of the nation-state, the celebration of the revolution, the strict separation between the homeland and its colonies, etc.

And yet, in both archival documents and statistics some fundamental categories were kept undefined: the social actors themselves. Peasants, workers, capitalists, artisans: who were they? How were they identified and how did they publicly present themselves?

The following chapters will seek to answer these questions; I start with the definitions of slaves and workers, and then move to peasants and conclude with consumers.

Part Three

Fragments of social worlds

Introduction

How can we think about society in its relations with the economy? Individual actors, classes (or even class struggle), social groups, temporary groupings?

For several centuries, these questions have accompanied the debates on how market economies function and their outcomes in terms of inequalities, social relations and political conflicts. For example, in the nineteenth century, for so-called 'classical' thinkers and Marxists, ideal types and social classes are indispensable to the study of how production is organized and its impact on distribution, whereas – for opposite reasons – neoclassical, utilitarian and liberal thinking seeks to emphasize the perfect interchangeability between worker and capitalist. However, in both cases, the economic actor or group is identified by their economic function (consumer, worker, capitalist). These approaches therefore neglect the links between these individuals or groups, on one hand, and institutions and economic norms, on the other. Ricardo's worker or Marx's proletarian is not defined by a particular employment contract, but according to an economic function that precedes and determines all institutional relations. These nineteenth-century conceptions were shaped by several logics: those of economic reasoning (neoclassical theory, classical theory, Marxist theory, etc.), political philosophy or just politics. The identification of social actors was therefore important to furthering societal projects, such as the abolition of corn tariffs for Ricardo, the advent of socialism for Marx or stock market reform for the first neoclassical economists.

During the second half of the twentieth century, these social categories were contested: the greatest upheaval was experienced by proletarians and their class consciousness, both by observations from the political world and by socio-economic realities: the adoption of bourgeois behaviour by workers and the emergence of the consumer (the republic of consumers). However, even the 'bourgeois' and the 'capitalists' were subjected to significant change, with the increased complexity of the middle class on one hand, and the formation of employee-owned companies on the other. The fall of the Berlin Wall and the end of real socialism dealt the final blow to these analyses in terms of class. However, once the old paradigms had collapsed, the question of identifying actors and social groups remained open. One solution commonly adopted to get out of this impasse – without falling into economic determinism – was to disaggregate forms of social identification and recognition. Following this approach, the identification of social actors by class – to the extent it had ever existed – would disappear, just like that of isolated individuals, in keeping with an ultra-liberal representation of capitalism. The emphasis is increasingly placed on the multiplicity of characteristics that each individual has in relation to their profession, gender, age (retiree), physical condition (access to healthcare), residence (owner, tenant) or actions (consumption, service, etc.). Ulrich Beck and Anthony Giddens were among those who moved in this direction with the greatest force. The advantage of this approach is that it steers clear of economic determinism. At the same time, shattering the characteristics that qualify each actor also presents a risk: that of neglecting the hierarchy and the interrelations between these characteristics. While it is true that social integration is achieved through employment, access to housing, membership in a sports club, marriage, etc., it is also true that these multiple characteristics are dependent on each other. For example, the relations that individuals have as tenants with respect to their landlord are influenced by whether they can produce proof of employment and income. Similarly, during a job interview, candidates would be wise to highlight their skills, professional training, accumulated experience, etc. Finally, access to marriage is predicated on prior social and institutional conditions, and once the marriage contract is signed it generates not only economic and social consequences but also statutory ones (the limited rights of the married woman and children). Once these hierarchical dimensions have been taken into account, social characteristics must be inscribed in precise institutional and historical contexts in order to determine the link between hierarchy, social integration and economic dynamics. In a capitalist economy, do these characteristics exist prior to the market exchange or are they a consequence of it?

The answer to this question is both historical and epistemological. Social history, as it was developed in the 1970s, owed a lot to sociology: social groups were identified by researchers who then searched for empirical proof. The cultural turn criticized the precedence of the model over the sources; researchers might be looking for 'proletarians' where there were only servants, worker peasants or any other form of wage labour. This criticism joined that of numerous historians who sought to highlight the historically situated scope of social categories which for the most part were conceived in the nineteenth century and to which we are still bound today. Micro-history provided a complementary argument by revealing the complexity and multiplicity of social identities – in a dialogue with anthropology, but also the irreducibility of the individual to a given group, usually from the outside, by the historian. Nowadays, this traditional way of apprehending social history is in difficulty for several reasons: these numerous criticisms, which have only received partial responses, but also the difficulty of drawing on numerous, often scattered archives that are difficult to apprehend in comparison with other approaches (political history, history of knowledge). For example, verifying the actual extent of the famous privatizations (enclosures) of common land in Great Britain at the turn of the nineteenth century required at least twenty years of research in the local archives to produce the first results. The same goes for most other classic subjects of social history, most of which still require a comprehensive and detailed examination of the archives.

How can this discussion be developed in transregional and global perspective?

Global labour and social history, as developed since the 1990s, largely inherits previous conventional Marxist-Weberian approaches.[1] Following the same line of reasoning, more recently a vast international group based in Amsterdam has been producing a

---

[1] Brass, van der Linden, *Free and Unfree Labour*; Andreas Eckert, ed., *Global Histories of Work* (Boston and Berlin: De Gruyter, 2016); Leon Fink, *In Search of the Working Class: Essays in American Labour History and Political Culture* (Champaign, IL: University of Illinois Press, 1994); *Sweatshops at Sea: Merchant Seamen in the World's First Globalized Industry, from 1812 to the Present* (Chapel Hill: University of North Carolina Press, 2011); Jürgen Kocka, *Arbeitsverhältnisse und Arbeiterexistenzen. Grundlagen der Klassenbildung im 19. Jahrhundert* (Bonn: Dietz, 1990); *White Collar Workers in America 1890–1940. A Social Political History in International Perspective* (London: SAGE, 1980); 'New Trends in Labour Movement Historiography: A German Perspective', *International Review of Social History* 42 (1997): 67–78.

still ongoing project of global nomenclatures of forms of labour. No fewer than twenty main labour relationships have been identified (including wage earners, slaves, serfs, domestic workers), each with several sub-categories (time-wage and piece-work earners; domestic, rural, industrial slaves, etc). To each category is ascribed a 'kind of labour relationship': reciprocal, tributary, market, non-market. Innumerable historical cases from all around the world from the sixteenth century to the present day are then placed into boxes in the matrix.[2] As with all taxonomies, this one is static and based upon unhistorical categories taken from a certain Marxist-Weberian approach and then imposed on different contexts. They are sorts of ideal types, useful for raising questions, much less for providing unexpected answers (unexpected under the model). During a person's life, they can experience multiple, sometimes coexistent labour relationships: an indentured migrant can turn into a slave or a worker. On the other hand, anthropologists have persistently criticized the market/non-market distinction. Finally, this nomenclature does not explain connections, and possible disconnections between periods and areas, except for radical revolutionary breaks.

A complementary approach, although not necessarily incompatible, is the so-called global microhistory.[3] This label confusingly joins together two distinct approaches: regional and local monographies, and microhistory. Unfortunately, this confusion has been extremely widespread in the English-speaking academic world. During the 1970s and 1980s, original microhistory, as an analytical and epistemological method, radically contested the notion of statistical representativeness, whereas it was constantly present in local studies (is this area, village representative?). Microhistory, rather, advocated the notion of the relevance of the chosen case in raising questions appropriate to the context, this last being mobile and, at the end of the day, not opposite to the investigation itself.[4] Unfortunately, these dimensions are lacking in the new global microhistory of labour which combines the two different approaches mentioned. Moreover, this approach has difficulties in reconciling individual lives and structural trends; authors simply seek to include life stories in broader categories (workers, proletarians, capitalism) which finally downplays all the initial emphasis on the complexity of lives.

A third possibility is explored in a recent co-authored book on the 'global bourgeoisie'.[5] One of the editors' main aims, as announced in the Introduction, is to show that the 'bourgeois century' (i.e. the nineteenth century), usually depicted as a European specificity, was actually global, and middle classes emerged all around the globe. Contrary to Chakrabarty, who claims the impossibility of exporting the Marxist notion of class and working class in particular to India, the authors affirm their willingness to stress the universality of the 'bourgeoisie' itself, with, of course, multiple

[2] https://collab.iisg.nl/web/LabourRelations/
[3] Christian De Vito and Anne Garritsen, *Micro-Spatial Histories of Global Labour* (London: Palgrave, 2018); *Annales HSS* 73, no. 1 (2018), in particular the introduction by Romain Bertrand and Guillaume Calafat: 1–18; *Past & Present* 242, supplement 14 (November 2019), in particular the introduction by de Jan de Vries: 23–36.
[4] Giovanni Levi, 'Les usages de la biographie', *Annales ESC* 44, no. 6 (1989): 1325–36.
[5] Christophe Dejung, David Motadel and Jürgen Osterhammel, eds, *The Global Bourgeoisie: The Rise of the Middle Classes in the Age of the Empire* (Princeton: Princeton University Press, 2019).

variations. The use of the word is provocative, since the underlying idea and aim are to adopt an opposite angle to the subaltern and civilizationist approaches: instead of rejecting a category as European-born or Eurocentric, one can suggest its universality. Markets, the bourgeois, cosmopolitanism, the Enlightenment, etc., would no longer be a Western exclusivity.[6] Here we find a crucial theme of our investigation: whether to name social groups according to a 'universal' scheme or follow 'local' cultural and historical specificities. In the following chapters, I suggest a different path; instead of deciding whether we can call the Indian labouring people 'workers' or the African rural population 'peasants', I trace two interrelated paths: the ways external observers qualify these actors and the multiple identities these same actors claimed for themselves. As for archives and data, my ambition is not so much to contrast theories with historical realities but to reveal their interrelations, convergences and possible divergences and the social historical implications of these. For example, if some British workers did not consider themselves as proletarians, what did this imply in terms of their political and social behaviours?

---

[6] This line of reasoning also animates Pomeranz's Great divergence or Conrad's global enlightenment.

5

What is a worker, what is a slave?

Social statistics, censuses and other quantitative artifacts are based upon categories without which it could not be possible to count slaves, wage earners, peasants, etc.

Having already discussed statistics, we need now to understand how their social categories were identified. On this, legal scholars provide ideal, ahistorical types and express the relationships between labour and freedom in terms of status and contract.[1] A slave is defined by their legal status, and so is a free worker. Indeed, this longstanding opposition has been widely diffused in history and the social sciences since the last quarter of the nineteenth century, when Henry Maine and A. V. Dicey opposed unfree societies (*ancien régime*, feudalism, slavery) to free societies. In the former, the actors' social, political and economic actions were conditioned by their legal status, while in the latter the contract dominated. What legal scholars seem unable to catch is the fact that this view emerged in response not only to the abolition of slavery in the United States and serfdom in Russia but also to the transformation of labour institutions in Europe and the United States. In particular, the rise of collective bargaining and the welfare state was considered synonymous with the decline of freedom of contract and a resurgence of status, the latter being a distinctive feature of 'old regimes'. Since then, several authors have developed this argument.[2]

My argument will be double: on the one hand, it is my intention to reveal the origin of the opposition and its role in shaping labour hierarchies and inequalities in colonial worlds and in the mainland itself. It is historically untrue that ancient regimes and

---

[1] Unicef, *The State of the World's Children* (Oxford: Oxford University Press, 1991); ILO, *International Labour Conference, Papers and Proceedings, 89th Session* (Geneva: ILO Press, 2001); ILO, *Every Child Counts: New Global Estimates on Child Labour* (Geneva: BIT Press 2002); Henri Cunningham and P. Viazzo, *Child Labour in Historical Perspective, 1800-1985: Historical Studies from Europe, Japan, and Colombia* (Florence: European University Press, 1996); ILO, *La fin du travail des enfants: un objectif à notre porté* (Geneva: OIT, 2006); and Suzanne Miers, 'Contemporary Forms of Slavery', *Canadian Journal of African Studies* [Special Issue on Slavery and Islam in African History: A Tribute to Martin Klein], 34, no. 3 (2000): 714–47.

[2] Henry Maine, *Ancient Law: Its Connection with the Early History of Society, and Its Relation to Modern Ideas* (London: John Murray, 1861); Albert V. Dicey, *Lectures on the Relation between Law and Public Opinion in England during the Nineteenth Century* (London: Richard Vandewetering, 1905); Frank Tannenbaum, 'Contract versus Status', *Political Science Quarterly* 65, no. 2 (1950): 181–92; Otto Kahn-Freund, 'A Note on Status and Contract in British Labour Law', *Modern Law Review* 30 (1967): 635–44; and Patrick Atiyah, *The Rise and Fall of Freedom of Contract* (Oxford: Oxford University Press, 1979).

'despotic societies' ignored contractual arrangements while liberal societies erased differences in status. In *ancien régime* France, for example, the division of society into 'old orders' and corporative regulation has been shown to have already weakened considerably and to some extent disappeared by the early eighteenth century,[3] while, on the other hand, important status markers persisted under the liberal regime (e.g. in relation to the legal status of married women, children and merchants). This was true not only in France but also in Britain and Germany.[4] From this standpoint, the return of status in the twentieth century cannot be compared with old regime status insofar as it appeals to rules and rights in order to reduce inequalities rather than increase them. The world of labour, in particular the rights of workers under collective agreements in Europe and their fate on the one hand and the harsh conditions endured by coolies, bonded people and immigrants on the other, shows quite clearly the importance of this point for understanding past and present societies.[5] The perpetuation of differences in legal status – some of them longstanding, some new – was the chief failure of the eighteenth-century revolutionary projects: first slaves, then indentured immigrants, colonial subjects, women and children, among others, were pushed to the sidelines, if not excluded altogether from these notions of rights and their universality. Starting from this, I also intend to show that its origins lay in the experiences Henry Sumner Maine had in India before exporting them to Britain; his colonial experience led him to re-conceptualize the world of labour and rights in Britain itself.

Is it true, as so many legal scholars argue, that liberal societies are based on contract while ancient societies and welfare state societies give priority to status and, thus, formal inequalities?

Here I do not intend to discuss the theories or the intellectual history of the definition of classes, working class and proletarian in particular. Instead, I wish to reveal how these identifications were made in industrializing British society during the eighteenth and nineteenth centuries. We need to understand the origins and social consequences of these classifications for the actors themselves and not just discuss whether one or another model of historical societies we have in mind today fit with these past realities.

The idea that capitalism and in particular the English Industrial Revolution was made possible thanks to institutions that facilitated free contracts and (according to some) a proletarianized peasantry is supported by a long tradition. It dates back to at least the nineteenth century and the classical economists (Smith, Marx), continuing through Tawney and Polanyi and through most works of historical sociology and

---

[3] Michael Sonenscher, *Work and Wages: Natural Law, Politics and the Eighteenth-Century French Trades* (Cambridge: Cambridge University Press, 1989); Steven L. Kaplan, *La fin des corporations* (Paris: Fayard, 2002); William Sewell, *Gens de métier et révolution. Le langage du travail de l'Ancien régime à 1848* (Paris: Aubier, 1983); and Maxine Berg, *The Age of Manufactures, 1700–1820* (London: Routledge, 1985).
[4] Willibald Steinmetz, ed., *Private Law and Social Inequality in the Industrial Age: Comparing Legal Cultures in Britain, France, Germany and the United States* (Oxford: Oxford University Press, 2000).
[5] On Indian coolies, see for example Jan Breman, *Timing the Coolie Beast* (Delhi: Oxford University Press, 1989); Utsa Patnaik and M. Dingwaney, eds, *Chains of Servitude: Bondage and Slavery in India* (Hyderabad: Sangan Books, 1985); and Hugh Tinker, *A New System of Slavery: The Export of Indian Labour Overseas 1830–1920* (London: Hansib, 1974).

economic history in the twentieth century. Even the world-system approach, while stressing the existence of mixed forms of labour and exploitation on the periphery and quasi-periphery, has always assumed that free wage labour typified the 'core'.[6] However, in recent decades, several pieces of research have contested the impact of enclosure and the existence of a truly free labour market in industrializing Britain.[7] Thus, it is not correct to speak of capitalists and proletarians; texts of that time, even in Britain, spoke instead of masters and servants. Workers, daily labourers, servants, servants in husbandry, apprentices and the like were subject to quite similar laws under the Statute of Labourers (1351), the Masters and Servants Acts and the Statute of Artificers of 1562.[8] The Statute of Labourers (1350–1) was enacted two years after the Ordinance of Labourers had been put in place and was followed by a set of laws gathered under the umbrella of the Masters and Servants Acts, which multiplied in the sixteenth century and accompanied the Statute of Artificers and Apprentices (1562). During the term of service, the labour of servants was legally reserved for their masters. Even at the expiration of the term of service, servants were not allowed to leave their masters unless they had given 'one quarter's warning' of their intention to leave. As such, the labour of servants was considered the legitimate property of the master. In fact, in early modern Britain, resident servants were like wives and children: all were members of the household and all were the legal dependants of its head. This implies, on the one hand, that servants, children and wives were entitled to be maintained by the head of the household; on the other hand, all of them were supposed to be under his authority, the family head benefiting from a higher legal status and more legal entitlements and rights than his dependants and family. Both marriage and labour contracts were actually status contracts: they gave rise to a different legal status for wives and servants, on the one hand, and for masters and husbands on the other. Dependency was a normal part of a differential system of rank and degree in which everyone, adult and child, man and woman, had and knew their place. In general, labour was seen as akin to domestic service, with the employer purchasing the worker's time.

However, the word 'servant' took on different meanings at different times, and the labour relationship did not consist of a single homogeneous legal status. For example, between the fourteenth and sixteenth centuries, contemporaries restricted the word 'servant' to particular wage workers who resided with their master, so labourers and artificers were not included under this rubric. However, from the sixteenth century on, 'servant' was increasingly used to define any sort of wage earner and thus included

---

[6] Marc Steinberg, 'Capitalist Development, the Labor Process, and the Law', *American Journal of Sociology* 109, no. 2 (2003): 445–95.

[7] Among others, Robert Steinfeld, *The Invention of Free Labor: The Employment Relation in English and American Law and Culture, 1350–1870* (Chapel Hill: University of North Carolina Press, 1991); Robert Steinfeld, *Coercion, Contract, and Free Labour in the Nineteenth Century* (Cambridge: Cambridge University Press, 2001); Simon Deakin and Frank Wilkinson, *The Law of the Labour Market: Industrialization, Employment, and Legal Evolution* (Oxford: Oxford University Press, 2005). Douglas Hay and Paul Craven, eds, *Masters, Servants, and Magistrates in Britain and the Empire, 1562–1955* (Chapel Hill: University of North Carolina Press, 2004).

[8] Ann Kussmaul, *Servants in Husbandry in Early Modern England* (Cambridge: Cambridge University Press, 1981).

journeymen, artificers and other workmen.[9] From the late eighteenth century on, judicial decision excluded domestic servants from the scope of master and servant statutes – at least in England; although in the colonies they usually were included.[10] As the leading British legal doctrine of that time put it, the difference was that by owning slaves and war captives you owned things, whereas labour services meant that you owned a certain person's time.[11] It was a lease of labour in which the lessee had the right to benefit from all the time and capacities of their labour force. Labour as service reflected 'an influential legacy of the overlap between labour and recruitment, on the one hand, and personal service (domestic and other kinds of labour) on the other. A father had the right to claim his children's labour, it was a duty and a service and family rules overlapped with labour rules. A master had a strong resemblance to a father as well and as such he could treat servants and above all apprentices as people under his personal tutelage. Again, the notion of service was clearly expressed in most documents related to these affairs in early modern and modern Britain. Of course, this notion of labour as service was adopted by extension in all other forms of labour relationships – in agriculture, mines, manufacturing – where master, father and military officer coalesced into a legal and social actor having full rights over labouring people. As long as contracts for the hire of labour continued to be understood as conveyances of property in labour, contractarian individualism would continue to furnish support for unfree labour. Criminal proceedings accompanied the emphasis placed on contractual free will as a foundation of the labour market. Criminal sanctions were provided for because labour was free and the worker freely agreed to them.

Thus, the long-term movement of labour rules in Britain hardly confirms the traditional argument that early labour freedom in the country fuelled the Industrial Revolution. On the contrary, the Industrial Revolution was accompanied by increasingly strict regulations and criminal sanctions on workers. Masters and Servants Acts were a powerful tool in the hand of masters/employers in meeting the increasing demand for labour in the eighteenth and nineteenth centuries. Criminal law became harsher for workers during the Industrial Revolution, and the prosecution rate increased as well. The new Masters and Servants Acts were not vestiges of feudal times but a clear response to the new industrializing context. Moreover, these rules were enforced; between 1857 and 1875 (when the Masters and Servants Acts were repealed): 5–8 per cent of servants were prosecuted, but the percentage rose as high as 17 in some areas and even 20 in London in certain years.[12]

And in practice? If legally speaking wage earners were servants, in economic and social relationships were they 'proletarians'?

Before 1914, employment in agriculture, in absolute terms, declined only in the UK, Belgium and France. The decline did not start in the UK until after 1850 or, according

---

[9] Steinfeld, *The Invention*: 17–22.
[10] Hay and Craven, *Masters*: 7.
[11] William Blackstone, *Commentaries on the Laws of England*, 4 vols (London: Strahan, Woodfall, 1793–5), booklet 2: 402.
[12] Douglas Hay, 'England 1562–1875: The Law and Its Uses', in *Masters, Servants and Magistrates in Britain and the Empire, 1562–1955*, edited by Douglas Hay, Paul Craven (Chapel Hill: University of North Carolina Press, 2004): 67.

to Clark, after 1869; in France and Belgium after 1870; and in the rest of Western Europe only after 1918. For the rest of Europe, the decline was not perceptible until after the Second World War.[13] This picture is different when it is expressed in relative terms: in this case, the percentage of agricultural employment declined in Britain in the sixteenth century when men already made up 55 per cent of agricultural workers, but then did not decline any further until the last quarter of the eighteenth century.[14]

Between 1701 and 1831, the absolute number of workers employed in agriculture remained roughly constant and then increased until the 1870s. Between 1801 and 1851, the number even rose slightly as new techniques in husbandry demanded more labour, not less.[15] Even though the percentage of the population employed in agriculture fell from 60 per cent to 30 per cent, agriculture did not retain more than a small portion of the increase in total labour supply that became available as a result of population growth in the countryside.[16]

Due to the persistent need for labour in agriculture, dual employment (rural and urban) was the rule until the mid-nineteenth century. Careful analyses have uncovered major errors in the censuses and data used by conventional historians: in fact, in mid-nineteenth-century censuses, the statistical margins of error for large occupational groups such as agriculture, commerce and manufacturing trades are probably within the range of 40 per cent to 66 per cent![17] This means that, at the time, most people still found it convenient to maintain dual residency in order to move seasonally between the countryside and the town.

The requirement of advance notice was intended to afford employers enough time to replace departing workers and avoid sudden stoppages. Day labourers were often employed at will for a few weeks. However, the frequency of departures, mostly in connection with the harvest, demonstrated the relatively limited impact of the law on workers' behaviour. In short, there were few proletarians in Britain, even by the mid-nineteenth century, while pluri-activity and peasant workers dominated the scene. It is no accident that most members of the First Socialist International were artisans and peasant workers and not the proletarians Marx expected to meet. It is also no accident that, ever since, most observers and commentators have debated 'class consciousness', its existence or not, and how and where to find it: the problem was that most proletarians actually were not proletarians at all, as we have just seen.

At the same time, labouring people were subject to strong social and institutional rules that sought to compensate for their pluri-activity with coercion and low wages. From this perspective, contract enforcement was a substitute for higher wages: masters

---

[13] Federico, *Feeding the World*: 57.
[14] Gregory Clark, 'Agriculture and the Industrial Revolution, 1750–1850', in *The British Industrial Revolution: An Economic Perspective*, edited by Joel Mokyr (Boulder, CO: Westview Press, 1993), 227–66.
[15] Charles Timmer, 'The Turnip, the New Husbandry, and the English Agricultural Revolution', *Quarterly Journal of Economics* 83 (1969): 375–95.
[16] O'Brien, 'Agriculture and the Industrial Revolution'.
[17] Peter Lindert and Jeffrey Williamson, 'Revising England's Social Tables, 1688–1867', *Explorations in Economic History* 19, no. 4 (1982): 385–408; Peter Lindert and Jeffrey Williamson, 'English Workers' Living Standards during the Industrial Revolution: A New Look', *Economic History Review* 36, no. 1 (1983): 1–25.

used it as long as they could, in order to secure labour. This complex, ambiguous attitude vis-à-vis wage labour helps explain the uncertain attitudes British actors and commentators had towards slavery.

Who is the 'real' slave?

Anthropologists, sociologists and historians differ considerably in their assessments of what precisely constitutes slavery, highlighting variously issues of social status (membership of or exclusion from the clan, family and local community), religion, legal status (forms of dependence, freedom of movement, hereditary nature of constraints), economic conditions and political, legal and procedural rights.[18] The debate has sharpened even more over the last two decades as *cultural* and *subaltern studies* scholars have highlighted the relativity of notions of freedom and coercion. As a result, the critical question currently asked is whether the different forms of servitude found in various societies in Africa, Asia, the Indian Ocean world or the Americas can all be considered to constitute 'slavery'. If the answer is yes, then by implication slavery existed before and independently of colonialism. Conversely, if the answer is no, it means that these were forms of 'imperialist' dependence and bondage specific to a particular place.

My argument here is that it is strictly impossible, nowadays as in the past, to identify and define 'free' or 'wage' labour alone without taking into consideration the contextual definition of unfree and slave labour in particular. The two are historically and socially defined in relation to each other, to the point that the evolution of one (because of abolition, for instance) immediately impacts the definition and practices of the other. And, vice versa, reforms of labour in advanced countries have an impact on the identification of unfree labour in their colonies, and former colonies. So, how did different historical actors identify wage labour and slavery, why and with which consequences in terms of political and social dynamics?

During the second half of the eighteenth century, legal commentators met difficulties in justifying the existence of slavery in the British colonies and its interdiction in the mainland. This attempt to establish continuities and discontinuities in space (between English law and colonial law) and over time (the precedents went as far back as the Middle Ages) was no mere academic exercise, for major political and social issues were at stake.[19] Abolitionists stressed that serfdom (*villeinage*) had been abolished because English had evolved and gradually come to defend individual liberties and rights. The defenders of slavery, however, saw serfdom as a legal precedent that

---

[18] Alain Testart, *L'esclave, la dette et le pouvoir* (Paris: Éditions errance, 2001); Claude Meillassoux, *Anthropologie de l'esclavage* (Paris: PUF, 1986); Moses Finley, *Ancient Slavery and Modern Ideology*; Suzanne Miers and Igor Kopytoff, eds, *Slavery in Africa: Historical and Anthropological Perspectives* (Madison: University of Wisconsin Press, 1977); Stanley Engerman, ed., *Terms of Labor: Slavery, Freedom and Free Labor* (Stanford: Stanford University Press, 1999); Orlando Patterson, *Slavery and Social Death* (Cambridge: Cambridge University Press, 1982).

[19] William Blackstone, *Commentaries on the Laws of England*, 4 vols (consulted edition: Chicago: University of Chicago Press, 1979; orig. 1765–9): vol. 2, 92.

legitimated slavery.[20] It is interesting to note that, unlike what we might imagine today or even what most actors stressed during the nineteenth century, the abolitionists added racial considerations to the argument from history: race was an argument to support abolition. The blood ties among English serfs, who were necessarily white, were not the same in the slavery practised on other races or individuals often without any family ties.[21] For this reason, slavery was something other than serfdom and should therefore be abolished, even in the absence of a judicial precedent.[22] As a result, slaves residing on British soil were increasingly emancipated: by 1807, only 15 of the 4,000 individuals identified as people of colour were still formally slaves; all the others had been freed either voluntarily by their masters upon their arrival in Great Britain or by the courts.[23]

Brion Davis argued that the abolitionist movement had drawn public attention away from the tensions surrounding British wage earners;[24] in fact, Jeremy Bentham claimed that the difference between a servant and a slave was that the slave master had unlimited power and the slave had no rights. In his view, slavery was defined as unlimited, compulsory labour. The condition of the slave could be improved, as shown in the differences between slavery in the ancient world, Russian serfdom and American slavery, which was by far the harshest, most extreme form of dependence.[25] Ultimately, he concluded, the conditions of wage earners might be worse than those of slavery, even though one could not confuse the one with the other. Thus, Bentham decided the abolition of slavery must make a clear distinction between these aspects and, in line with utilitarian theory, take into consideration both its usefulness and its disadvantages for the community. From there, Bentham went on to draw an interesting connection between criticism of slavery, the obligation for the poor to work and the limits on the wages of free workers: they were all justifiable based on the comparison between utility and pain.

We find similar links between servants, the poor and slaves in the thinking of Thomas Malthus, William Pitt and Edmund Burke.[26] All of them called for revision of the paternalism and gratuitousness of the Poor Laws while criticizing slavery.[27] Reverend Joseph Townsend, a leader of the abolitionist movement, noted that, like slaves, the

---

[20] Helene T. Catterall, ed., *Judicial Cases Concerning American Slavery and the Negro*, 5 vols (Washington: Carnegie Institution, 1926–37).

[21] Roxann Wheeler, *The Complexion of Race: Categories of Difference in Eighteenth-Century British Culture* (Philadelphia: University of Pennsylvania Press, 2002); Dror Wahrman, *The Making of the Modern Self: Identity and Culture in Eighteenth-Century England* (New Haven: Yale University Press, 2004).

[22] Catterall, *Judicial Cases*, vol. 1: 20, 22.

[23] Kathy Charter, 'Black People in England, 1660–1807', in *The British Slave Trade: Abolition, Parliament and People*, edited by Stephen Farrell, Melanie Unwin and James Walvin (Edinburgh: Edinburgh University Press, 2007).

[24] David Brion Davis, *The Problem of Slavery in the Western Culture* (New York: Oxford University Press, 1966).

[25] Bentham, *Principles*, ch. 2, On slavery, para. 3310; *Works of Jeremy Bentham*, edited by J. Bowring, vol. 1 (Edinburgh: William Tait, 1838–43).

[26] Edmund Burke, *The Works of the Right Honourable Edmunde Burke*, vol. 5 (London: Bell, 1889): 84.

[27] Brion Davis, *The Problem of Slavery*.

poor work only if they are forced to do so by 'hunger and deprivation'.[28] In other words, wage labour and slavery were discussed and defined in relation to each other. Debates over the Poor Laws and the conditions of workers in Great Britain took place at the same time and in the same arena, and sometimes even in the same works, that discussed the abolition of slavery.

This fundamental ambiguity was also characteristic of the positions adopted by famous entrepreneurs of the period such as Richard Arkwright and Josiah Wedgwood. Both men were at once solid abolitionists and free market supporters, who also upheld the need to limit workers' wages and control them as Bentham suggested in his Panopticon.[29] This convergence of elements is what best describes British abolitionism at the time: criticism of slavery did not imply that free persons could be allowed to work whenever and however it suited them; on the contrary, it meant that subsistence wages, surveillance and a good deal of coercion were necessary. The slave's lack of motivation was an argument against slavery; in the British 'classical' economic thought it was no longer valid when discussing wage labour. Thus, as Jeremy Bentham explained, 'Only by offering his service can a man find happiness'.[30] In short, according to Bentham, wage earners were not slaves, but they were legally servants.

In opposition to these views, some authors linked slavery to wage labour by insisting that wage labourers were the real slaves. In 1768, Dr Daniel Burton, former Chancellor of the Oxford diocese, wrote that it was impossible to dissociate slavery from the Masters and Servants Acts, as they both deprived man of his freedom.[31] Two different attitudes are expressed here: the first one associates wage labour with slavery, and proceeds to remind the reader that one must not forget the 'true slaves', i.e. British wage earners. At first sight, this was a universalist position, but it could be quickly transformed into a way of protecting domestic workers against the invasion of former slaves. By contrast, the other attitude makes a clear-cut distinction between the slave and the wage earner and calls for gradual abolition, leading to one and the same practice of freedom: the master is not the owner of the workers, but only of their working time. Wage earners as well as former slaves must be put to work; they have no right to exempt themselves; if they do so, they will be subject to criminal prosecution. The first attitude seeks to protect local or even national labour, whereas the second aims to establish law and order. Taken together, these views show that British abolitionism initially grew out of resistance to capitalism and only later converged with it. This convergence took place during the first half of the nineteenth century, after the abolition of the slave trade (1807) and the end of the Napoleonic Wars. In this context, the link between wage labour and slavery resurfaced: should wage labour and industrialization be seen as progress and freedom or as a new kind of slavery?

The responses of economists did not always coincide with those of the labour movement. The debate over labour (the rapid development of wage labour, the status

---

[28] Joseph Townsend, 'A Dissertation on the Poor Laws'; orig. 1786; reprint in J. R. McCulloch, *A Select Collection of Scarce and Valuable Economic Tracts* (London: SN, 1859): 404.

[29] Neil McKendrick, 'Josiah Wedgwood and Factory Discipline', *The Historical Journal* 4 (1961): 30–55.

[30] Jeremy Bentham, *Principles of Morals and Legislation*, ch. 43, sec. 1, par. 1433 in *Works of Jeremy Bentham*, edited by J. Bowring, vol. 1.

[31] Prince Hoare, *Memoirs of Granville Sharp, Esq* (London: Colburn, 1828): 262.

of workers) lay squarely at the centre of a reflection on the values of bourgeois capitalist society; criticism of wage labour as a new form of slavery pervaded political and intellectual circles in Europe. The topic was embraced by socialists such as Fourier, Owen and Saint-Simon, who Marx and Engels (particularly the latter) described as 'utopians', as well as by Christian socialists and French ultra-Catholics. They all spoke of wage labour as a new version of slavery, usually citing examples of adolescent and child labour to support their assertions. Criticism of unbridled and immoral capitalism laid the groundwork for promoting cooperative fraternal organizations, fostering a return to Christian morality or a combined critique of capitalism and the regimes that grew out of the French Revolution.

Marx, too, fell victim to the same rhetoric, even though he was critical of economists who associated wage labour with slavery. He likened domestic servants to the household slaves of antiquity,[32] described child labour in factories as genuine slavery and saw slavery as barely disguised capitalism. In short, for Marx, the only difference between slavery and wage labour was how the surplus value was extracted.

The main liberal and utilitarian currents were similarly ambiguous on the subject. After condemning slavery from a moral standpoint, Jean-Baptiste Say went on to declare that the master's property right over the slave protected both master and slave. According to the rules, when a slave was officially declared the master's property, his master could not put him to death or even flog him unduly without damaging his own property. Say thought slavery could reinforce the division of labour as well as efficiency.[33] Herman Merivale added that, in the colonial context, the labour of wage earners was less productive than that of slaves in the colonial context.[34]

The labour movement, which stirred up Lancashire between 1830 and 1833, revealed the conflicting positions of abolitionists regarding the fate of British wage earners. The radical abolitionists and those in Yorkshire emphasized the connection between slavery and wage labour and demanded reforms for both.[35] From 1832 onwards, it was impossible to find a petition, a meeting or an abolitionist tract that did not associate the fate of slaves with that of child labourers in Great Britain. Among the working classes and in Protestant circles, no distinction was made between the wage earner and the slave.

However, moderate abolitionists saw the condition of slaves as grounds for imposing harsher standards on free labour in Great Britain. For Frederick Douglass, it was out of the question to speak of 'industrial slavery': wage earners were not slaves. Similarly, apprentices in Great Britain or in the colonies were not slaves.[36] Yet, in his opinion, both groups needed coercion to make them work properly.

---

[32] Karl Marx, *Das kapital*, Italian translation, vol. 1 (Roma: Einaudi, 1972): 491–2.
[33] Jean-Baptiste Say, *Cours d'économie politique* (Bruxelles: Meline, Cans et Compagnie, 1843): 522.
[34] Herman Merivale, *Lectures on Colonization and Colonies* (London: Orme, Brown, Green and Longmans, 1841).
[35] *The Poor Man's Guardian*, 17 November 1832; *Manchester Guardian*, 8 September 1832.
[36] Alan Rice and Martin Crawford, eds, *Liberating Sojourn: Frederick Douglass and Transatlantic Reform* (Athens: Ohio University Press, 1999).

The success of the abolitionist position strengthened the latter attitude.[37] It was no accident that when the abolition of slavery was declared in the colonies (1833), British wage earners lost all forms of traditional assistance: the New Poor Law, adopted in 1834, forced indigents to choose between work or being sent to a reformatory. Debates in Parliament brought out the clear connection between the eradication of slavery and the changes in mainland labour institutions.[38] The introduction of apprenticeship in the colonies encouraged discussion of the practice in Britain and helped to promote the Poor Law reforms. This assimilation of quasi ex-slaves to child labourers and apprentices was made evident in parliamentary discussions.[39] A 'transitional' period of six to twelve years, described as 'apprenticeship', was imposed on slaves; this was not a coincidence, as the period of individual enfranchisement of slaves was identical to the length of the apprenticeship contract in England. Slaves thus became apprentices, with a contract resembling the conventional apprenticeship contracts that were widespread in Great Britain. Like minors in the mainland, quasi-freed slaves had to go through a period of transition prior to their final emancipation.[40] Slaves and children were not recognized as full-fledged legal subjects and were therefore subject to their masters or fathers. During the 'transition' years, slaves were thus characterized as apprentices; they were not expected to learn a trade but rather to conduct themselves as free persons.[41]

The choice of transitory apprenticeship as the solution for abolition was based on the assumption that Blacks lacked any 'natural' economic incentive, an argument that reopened debate over the Poor Laws in Great Britain.[42] The same hypothesis was invoked in both cases: workers, like ex-slaves, were not spontaneously inclined to maximize their work effort.[43] It was therefore necessary to pay them minimal wages and resort to more or less legal methods of coercion to overcome their 'indolence'.[44] The New Poor Law consequently reduced the support provided for the poor and forced vagrants to enter workhouses. Indeed, this was the argument originally put forth by Bentham, whose name was invoked to justify the measures: the old laws concerning the poor were too costly, when in fact they served no useful purpose for society or for the workers themselves; assistance should therefore be replaced by putting the poor to work. This same principle applied equally to British wage earners and ex-slaves.[45]

---

[37] BL, MSS Brit. Emp. S 2o, E2/4 (Anti-Slavery Papers, minute book of the Committee of the Anti-Slavery Society).

[38] C. R. Dod, *Electoral Facts 1832–1853 Impartially Stated*, edited by. H. J. Hanham (London: Harvester Press, 1972); *Hansard Parliamentary Papers*, 2nd series, 15 April 1831, III, 1425–45.

[39] Brion Davis, *The Problem of Slavery*.

[40] The National Archives (TNA), Kew, CO (Colonial Office), 318/116.

[41] House of Commons, *Papers in Explanation of the Condition of the Slave Population*, 5 November 1831, *Parliamentary Papers*, 1830–1 (230), 16, no. 1: 59–88.

[42] David Eltis, *Economic Growth and the Ending of Transatlantic Slave Trade* (New York: Oxford University Press, 1987).

[43] Hansard, *Parliamentary Papers*, 1833, vol. 19: 1252–72; 1834, vol. 22: 938; vol. 25: 435–56.

[44] Hansard, *Parliamentary Papers*, 1833, vol. 18: 1378, 976; vol. 19: 2549.

[45] Tom Franzmann, 'Antislavery and Political Economy in the Early Victorian House of Commons: A Research Note on "Capitalist Hegemony"', *Journal of Social History* 27, no. 3 (1994): 579–93.

Let us summarize: contrary to the common view, past and present, 'workers' as we know them today were rare in eighteenth- and nineteenth-century Britain; instead, from an institutional, legal and social historical perspective we find servants and peasant workers with seasonal employments. Both were subject to strong legal and social constraints. At the same time, labour unions and some observers even put slaves and workers into the same basket. Quite paradoxically, they joined planters and anti-abolitionists who argued that proletarians were the real slaves. Against this indeterminacy stood the majority of the abolitionist movement, philosophers and political economists who contrasted the slave to the worker. We therefore must be cautious: if we look at the social conditions of labouring people in the eighteenth and nineteenth centuries, then the distance between slaves and workers was not huge and a grey zone of coercion and bondage dominated the whole world of labour. At the same time, this grey zone did not exist at all in theories and policies contrasting the slave and the worker, and in social practices. Although some workers might claim they were 'like slaves', no slave could claim she/he was a worker and could therefore leave or demand a wage.

So, what happened when British notions and rules met a world different from the Anglo-American Atlantic, where ideal types of wage earners and chattel slaves were identified as mentioned? In particular, how did the British interpret labour in India? Was there 'slavery'?

As I have mentioned, this question is still important nowadays in debates about slavery; in India, other Asian and African areas, many scholars refuse to assimilate local forms of bondage to slavery. As usual, I will examine this question through history's lens and show that in the eighteenth and nineteenth centuries, the British pondered this very same question, but that, unlike current presumptions, they were themselves strongly divided on this topic while being deeply influenced by the Indian context and Indian actors.

In 1782 Jeremy Bentham urged lawmakers to take the conditions peculiar to India into account before trying to impose British rules.[46] He agreed that the laws of England should serve as the standard; at the same time, he pointed out that, unlike Russia and Canada, Bengal was so completely different from England that a transfer of British law could not be achieved *in toto*.

This observation can be applied more broadly: the circulation of institutions was never unilateral – from the 'centre' to the 'periphery' – but always bilateral, although their impact was of course unequal. These mutual influences were also different from what we tend to imagine starting from ideal types of 'European' and 'British' or 'Indian' and 'African' societies. Indeed, in the 1970s, the cultural turn, and in particular Geertz, Foucault, Said and subaltern studies, stressed the relationship between culture and power. Starting from this premise, British rule in India was viewed above all as control over language. Many historians and social scientists have talked about 'kidnapped language' and language-based or 'cultural' dependence, etc. According to

---

[46] Jeremy Bentham, 'Essay on the Influence of Time and Place in Matters of Legislation', in *Works of Jeremy Bentham*, edited by J. Bowring, vol. 2 (Edinburgh: William Tait, 1838–43): 171.

this view, Western perceptions of the 'other' reduce civilization to positively valued institutions, behaviours and accomplishments associated with the West.[47] Within this context, Utilitarianism in India has been viewed as a major expression of this attitude, consisting of imposing rules, legal notions and criminal codes in order to control India. The ideals and approaches to the law[48] formulated by Bentham and James Mill, as well as the famous utilitarian analysis of status and contract, were to a large extent inspired by Indian regulations and jurisprudence.[49] The underlying question was whether legal and economic categories could apply universally or whether they had to be rooted in local culture. The transfer of British values and institutions to India became in fact a core issue in political debates and administrative governance between the 1760s and the 1810s.[50]

For sure, the British did not create slavery in India, where debt bondage and other forms of servitude were extremely widespread.[51] In Hindu areas, caste origin played a role. Caste was not the hypothetical system described in British reports, which tended to identify slavery with low castes and translate various forms of dependency into European terms (slaves, serfs). In reality, slaves kept their caste identity and masters deliberately identified and publicized their slaves' castes. In fact, there was not only a continuum of conditions between the free and the unfree, but rituals and caste also influenced the process of enslavement and emancipation. Caste was correlated with occupation, but not exclusively, and the same was true for the relationship between caste and servile status. And, in contrast to European accounts and perceptions, slaves did not always come from lower castes. Most slaves did not remain locked into slavery for a lifetime. These forms of slavery and bondage did not disappear under colonial rule, but they evolved in connection with it. Indeed, both the British and local powers made use of slaves and forced labour and competed for manpower.

In Bentham's opinion, deciding the question of British influence and Indian 'specificity' was secondary to establishing good laws everywhere. It was from this standpoint that he condemned Indian forms of slavery.[52] In the same vein, the British anti-slavery movement thus claimed it was necessary to extend the abolitionist campaign to India. Supporters of local customs and pragmatic colonial elites replied that what existed in India was not real slavery, but merely forms of family dependence and domesticity. They won the backing of the English planters in India, who claimed

---

[47] Christopher Lloyd, *The Structures of History* (Oxford: Blackwell, 1993); Roy Preiswerk and Dominique Perrot, *Ethnocentrism and History: Africa, Asia and Indian America in Western Textbooks* (New York: Nok. Print, 1978).
[48] Kartik Kalyan Raman, 'Utilitarianism and the Criminal Law in Colonial India: A Study of the Practical Limits of Utilitarian Jurisprudence', *Modern Asian Studies* 28, no. 4 (1994): 739–91.
[49] Eric Stoke, *The English Utilitarians and India* (Oxford: Oxford University Press 1959).
[50] Alessandro Stanziani, *Bâtisseurs d'Empires. Russie, Inde et Chine à la croisée des mondes* (Paris: Liber, 2012) and *Seamen, Migrants and Workers: Bondage in the Indian Ocean World, Eighteenth-Nineteenth Centuries* (New York: Palgrave Macmillan, 2014).
[51] Gwyn Campbell and Alessandro Stanziani, eds, *Debt and Bondage in the Indian Ocean World* (London: Pickering and Chatto, 2013).
[52] Lea Campos Boralevi, *Bentham and the Oppressed* (Berlin and New York: Walter de Gruyter, 1984); Fred Rosen, *Bentham, Byron and Greece: Constitutionalism, Nationalism, and Early Liberal Political Thought* (Oxford: Clarendon Press, 1992).

their enterprises were not comparable to the plantations in the West Indies. Even within the abolitionist movement, many held that bondage in India was different from slavery, either because they genuinely believed it or for tactical reasons, i.e. to stop the transatlantic slave trade first. The fact that there was nothing in the subcontinent comparable to the transatlantic slave trade – the use and trade of slaves in and from India took place on land and was therefore much more difficult to quantify and control – also helped to support this view. Bentham argued that it was not the condition but the duration of the obligation that constitutes the real difference between free and unfree labour. The living conditions of a free worker were not assumed to be necessarily better than those of a slave or a serf. According to utilitarian principles, if one could show that the enslavement of a minority group increased the sum of total happiness, then there was a rationale for slavery. Bentham thought that offering a service was the only way a man could find 'happiness or security'.[53]

Even though slavery was officially outlawed in India in 1843, local governors and elites espoused quite different attitudes depending on their own definition of slavery. As in other British dominions, the official abolition of slavery in India was followed by extremely coercive rules regarding vagrants, issued in the name of public order and economic growth as an antidote to poverty. The enforcement of anti-slavery rules was compromised by the wide use of forced labour by the British themselves. The EIC employed this type of labour digging canals and on other public work projects as well as for porterage. It was in this context that, in 1861, Maine published his famous work on ancient law, based on a series of lectures at the University of Cambridge and subsequently under the influence of the Sepoy rebellion in India, which was widely debated in Britain.[54] His main argument was a late expression of utilitarianism: legal principles are universal but must be adapted to local contexts through procedure. He therefore opposed status-based societies – India, Asian societies, ancient Europe – to contract-based societies in modern Europe. Progress consisted precisely in reducing state influence and state discrimination. Maine identified 'three ways by which law can be adapted to improvements in society: Legal Fiction, Equity, and Legislation'. Legal fiction referred to altering the interpretation of the law without changing the wording; Equity involved adding new rules to the existing central body of law; while Legislation entailed the evolution of the body of law itself. Maine associated each form of legal change with a higher form of civilization. This hierarchy reflected his original Benthamite orientation, giving priority to legislation over jurisprudence. Of course, legislation was supposed to express universal principles and above all the autonomy of free individual will over that of the state.[55]

The dissolution of traditional Indian society had to be managed through indirect rule and basic British principles.[56] Unlike Bentham, who believed in the superiority

---

[53] Jeremy Bentham, *Principles of Morals and Legislation*, chapter XVIII, section 1, para. 1433, edited by J. Bowring, vol. 1.
[54] Mantena, *Alibis of Empire*.
[55] Henri Sumner Maine, *Ancient Law, Its Connections with the Early History of Society, and Its Relation to Modern Ideas* (Createspace Independent Publishing Platform, 2013).
[56] Henri Sumner Maine, 'India', in *The Reign of Queen Victoria: A Survey of Fifty Years of Progress*, edited by Humphrey Ward (London: Smith, Elder, 1887): 460–528, in particular 478.

of the Enlightenment, Maine was concerned with the disintegration of 'traditional societies';[57] he believed that India and England shared the same Indo-European heritage, but India was the 'living past' of Europe.

It was precisely on this ground that Maine advocated the repeal of the Masters and Servants Acts in Britain in 1875. This was a fundamental step, proving that the imperial connections did not work one way only (from the mainland to the colonies) and that the colonial experiences strongly impacted the evolution of societies and institutions (of labour in the occurrence) in the mainland itself. The evolution of the labour law in Britain owed much to the Indian experience. According to Maine, criminal rules for labour were valuable for colonial worlds, where legal statuses and despotism still permeated social life; instead, British workers were regulated by free wage contracts and, as such, they could not be submitted to criminal procedures; only in time, argued Maine, these rules could be extended to the colonial world.

We find here the real origin of the opposition between legal status and contract: Maine formulated it after his experience in India and his idea that 'ancient people' and civilizations were fundamentally different from civilized people. The opposition between the mainland and the colonial worlds took place at the very moment when socialist parties and unions claimed more protection to workers; in the 1870s they supported the abolition of the Masters and Servants Acts but also the introduction of new rules protecting social welfare. Liberals like Maine supported the former but not the latter disposition: criminal rules reflected the long heritage of legal status societies, while free contract expressed liberal ideas. There was no way, from this standpoint, to introduce new statutes in the name of the social welfare.

This story has several implications. First, it provides a very different picture of colonial Orientalism as depicted by Said, Chakrabarty and postcolonial studies: instead of European (British) categories imposed on the rest of the world and on India in particular, we have uncertainties related to this same approach among British officers, some supporting this view and many others criticizing it. Maine was one among those who believed that indirect rule and local adaptations of British categories were necessities. But his story also reveals a second major insight: the encounter between 'British' and 'Indian' categories of servant, labour, etc., produced not only labour rules for colonial India but was also at the origin of the reforms of labour in Britain itself.

The removal of criminal sanctions from the individual employment relationship in the 1870s was soon followed by the first legislative interventions of the welfare state. From this small beginning, the first Workmen's Compensation Act was introduced in 1897, and the first National Insurance Act in 1911. They imposed liability on employers for workplace-related injuries and disease, and they prompted the widespread use of employers' liability insurance to spread the risks in question.[58] These changes meant that the Poor Law remained in place but dealt only with residual cases that fell outside

---

[57] Henri Sumner Maine, *Village-Communities in the East and the West* (London: Murray, 1876), Lecture 1.
[58] Deakin and Wilkinson, *The Law of the Labour Market*: 86–7.

the range of the statutory social-insurance scheme.[59] Most important, these new provisions were not extended to the colonial worlds, still supposed to be backward and not ready to receive these new rules protecting labour. Colonial people, it was said, had not the taste for money and increasing well-being, and were pushed to work only with minimum wages. Many added that, because of the lower cost of production and reproduction of labour, colonial workers would have exerted an unfair competition vis-à-vis British workers.

To conclude, most studies on slavery, abolition and human rights mix historical and normative attitudes: they look for the 'contradictions' in emancipation ideologies and processes and suggest what should have been done. For example, both the anti-slavery movement and current African-American studies persistently remind us that the American Enlightenment defended the rights of settlers and forgot those of slaves; the same was apparently true of the French Enlightenment and English political philosophy in the eighteenth century.[60] Many others have pointed out the contradictions in liberal philosophy and its formal egalitarianism. This is a normative approach, which is useful in our civic commitments today, but less relevant for historical analysis. The point developed in previous pages is not to reproach, say, Thomas Jefferson for having had slaves despite his commitment to universal human rights, but rather to understand how, in the late eighteenth and early nineteenth centuries, a slave owner could legitimately speak of universal rights. It is not so much a question of contradictions as of different worlds. Thus, abolitionism in India points out the shortcomings of utilitarianism: Bentham, Maine and several British officers sought an answer to slavery and un-freedom in the utilitarian principle; the outcome was the persistence of formal inequalities before the law, which compounded real inequalities and discrimination in political, economic and social terms. These approaches combined statutory bias with market discrimination in the name of freedom. Therefore, the distinction between slaves and wage earners was sometimes clear in theory – and even there, not always – and much more blurred in practice. The separation between social norms and practices of work and coercion would be slow and painful, and would take several centuries. This outcome is explained by the social acceptability of these norms and also by the profitability of coercion at a time when, from the seventeenth to the mid-nineteenth century, capital was expensive and capital-intensive technical innovations were not very accessible. In Britain itself, innovations were labour intensive not capital-intensive until the mid-nineteenth century. The reason for this is that capital was expensive while labour was cheap because of coercion. At the end, the welfare was initially limited to a small minority of workers and excluded not only the colonial world but also women and peasants. The question was: how were these last to be identified?

---

[59] Gilbert Bentley, *The Evolution of National Insurance in Great Britain: The Origins of the Welfare State* (London: Joseph, 1966); Jose Harris, *Unemployment and Politics: A Study in English Social Policy, 1886–1914* (Oxford: Clarendon Press, 1972).

[60] Jürgen Habermas, *The Structural Transformation of the Public Sphere* (Cambridge: Polity, 1989; orig. 1962).

6

What is a peasant? The global history of 'immobile people'

Even more than proletarians, capitalists or bourgeois, the peasantry has evinced the classificatory ambitions of a certain historiography and socio-political thought since at least the eighteenth century.[1] Legions of researchers, commentators, activists and politicians, not to forget journals specifically devoted to peasants (*Journal of Peasant Studies*), have endeavoured to formulate a definition of the peasantry, some emphasizing their economic behaviour,[2] others their access to land, still others focusing on social[3] or legal norms or their political orientations.[4] Appearing in erudite and political arguments long before other social categories such as the bourgeoisie and the proletariat, the peasantry has outlived them and is now at the heart of the alter-globalization movement[5] – proof that this category possesses great flexibility as an intellectual and political tool that transcends revolutions, political, economic and social transformations, world wars, decolonization, the Cold War and the fall of the Berlin Wall. This very persistence constitutes a phenomenon worthy of study.

---

[1] Theodor Shanin, *Defining Peasants: Essays Concerning Rural Societies, Expolary Economies, and Learning from Them in the Contemporary World* (Oxford: Blackwell, 1990); Henri Mendras, 'L'invention de la paysannerie. Un moment de l'histoire de la sociologie française d'après-guerre', *Revue française de sociologie* 41, no. 3 (2000): 539–52.

[2] Frank Ellis, *Peasant Economics: Farm Households in Agrarian Development* (Cambridge: Cambridge University Press, 1988).

[3] Theodor Shanin, *Peasants and Peasant Societies* (New York: Penguin, 1971); James Scott, *The Moral Economy of the Peasant: Rebellion and Subsistence in Southeast Asia* (New Haven: Yale University Press, 1976); Eric R. Wolf, *Peasants* (Englewood Cliffs, NJ: Prentice Hall, 1966); Henri Mendras, *Les sociétés paysannes: éléments pour une théorie de la* paysannerie (Paris: Gallimard, 1995).

[4] James Scott, *Weapons of the Weak: Everyday Forms of Peasant Resistance* (New Haven: Yale University Press, 1985); Sidney W. Mintz, 'A Note on the Definition of Peasantries', *Journal of Peasant Studies* 1, no. 1 (1973): 91–106; Christopher R. Boyer, *Becoming Campesinos: Politics, Identity, and Agrarian Struggle in Postrevolutionary Michoacán, 1920–1935* (Stanford: Stanford University Press, 2003); Barrington Moore, *Social Origins of Dictatorship and Democracy: Lord and Peasant in the Making of the Modern World* (Boston: Beacon Press, 1966).

[5] Marc Edelman, *Peasants Against Globalization: Rural Social Movements in Costa Rica* (Stanford: Stanford University Press, 1999); Michael Kearney, *Reconceptualizing the Peasantry: Anthropology in Global Perspective* (Boulder, CO: Westview Press, 1996); Jan Douwe Van der Ploeg, *The New Peasantries: Struggles for Autonomy and Sustainability in an Era of Empire and Globalization* (London: Earthscan, 2008); Tony Weis, *The Global Food Economy: The Battle for the Future of Farming* (London: Zed Books, 2007).

Erudite and political definitions of the peasantry encapsulate the fears and hopes that have accompanied transformations of the world. In the political sphere first, from the middle of the seventeenth century and the peasant wars, through the French Revolution and the upheavals of the nineteenth century, to the uprisings of the early twentieth century and the revolutions in Russia[6] and China,[7] historiography and commentators often view the participation of peasants in these events as revolts and uprisings that are unable to transform themselves into a new order.[8] Peasants have therefore been identified sometimes as insurgents, sometimes as socially excluded, sometimes simply as 'others' in relation to the town, the state, the nobility or the bourgeoisie or even finance.

Economic theories of the peasantry have sought to identify the specificity of this mode of production in relation to capitalism. In the eighteenth century, the physiocrats spoke less about peasants than about agriculture and agrarian social groups – reform-minded landowners, essentially.[9] Later, small landowners and peasants appear in the neoclassical arguments of the nineteenth century as the expression of the rationality of the small independent producer.[10] In their numerous variants, these two orientations live on in the debates between agrarian economists and proponents of 'alternative' modes of development.

However, in the socialist approach to political economy in both the nineteenth and twentieth centuries, the question is whether a peasant mode of production in its own right is conceivable. For Simon de Sismondi[11] or, a century later, Alexandr' Chayanov,[12] the answer is yes. Depending on the stream of thought, the peasant economy makes it possible to reconcile growth and ethics without falling into speculation and capitalist utilitarianism.[13] But for socialists, especially after Marx, historical laws are hard to reconcile with the existence of a peasant mode of production, which disturbs the shift from feudalism to capitalism.[14] Even Marx, at first inclined to see the peasantry as a conservative force destined to disappear with the privatization of common land and the rise of capitalism, began to have doubts toward the end of his life. It was not until the end of the nineteenth century that we would see, in socialist and Marxist political arguments, the peasantry appear as a potentially progressive political force. At first critical of these currents of thought, Lenin partially espoused this view after the revolution of 1905.

---

[6] Theodor Shanin, *The Awkward Class; Political Sociology of Peasantry in a Developing Society: Russia 1910–1925* (Oxford: Clarendon Press, 1972).

[7] Moore, *The Social Origin*; Skocpol, *States and Social Revolutions*.

[8] Eric R. Wolf, *Peasant Wars of the Twentieth Century* (New York: Harper & Row, 1969).

[9] Perrot, *Histoire intellectuelle de l'économie politique*.

[10] William Jevons, *The Theory of Political Economy* (London: Macmillan, 1979); Richard Weitz, *From Peasant to Farmer* (New York: Columbia University Press, 1971).

[11] Jean-Charles Léonard Simon de Sismondi, *Nouveaux principes d'économie politique* (Paris: Delanauy, 1819); Francesca Dal Degan and Nicolas Eyguesier, "Jean-Charles Léonard Simon de Sismondi", in *Handbook of the History of Economic Analysis*, edited by Gilbert Faccarello and Heinz Kurz, vol. 1 (Cheltenham: Edward Elgar online, 2016) https://doi.org/10.4337/9781785366642.00026

[12] Aleksandr V. Chayanov, *On the Theory of Peasant Economy* (Homewood, IL: Illinois: Richard Irwin, 1966).

[13] Scott, *The Moral Economy*; Shanin, *The Awkward Class*.

[14] Plekhanov, Kautsky and initially Lenin defended this orientation. Stanziani, *L'économie*.

At the turn of the century, a synthesis was being sought within European socialist cooperative milieux. Émile Vandervelde in Belgium, Daniel Zolla in France and Chayanov in Russia were among the best-known authors in this movement, which sought to reconcile neoclassical theory and the socialist approach.[15] Peasant utopias no longer aimed just to be conservative, but aspired to bring together the ancient and the modern. However, even in positive representations of the peasant world, as early as the seventeenth century and until the 'social' agronomy of those promoting cooperatives between 1870 and 1914, the peasantry remained a population to educate.[16] The appropriation of knowledge by the town led to reflections about the rural world and its activities. This developing agronomy was never just a simple technical discipline; it was a normative science from the outset. It was not just a matter of teaching peasants how to cultivate the land, but also inculcating them with lessons on how to live in society.[17] Indeed, the irruption of peasants onto the political scene sparked fears among these enlightened circles that would intensify at the turn of the twentieth century with the expansion of voting rights. The civilizing mission of agronomists brought them closer to actors involved in the colonization of Africa (political elites, anthropologists, ethnologists) during this same period.[18] The education of peasants and of Africans were two facets of the same movement, as was their political marginalization.

Beyond Western Europe, reflections on the rural world expressed similar dynamics. In Russia, as early as the eighteenth century, the learned debate on peasants divided those who viewed the village commune as a rational economic organization and those who only found vestiges of the past. Proletarianization was the evil to be avoided. While the debates between populists and Marxists are quite well known, two aspects are less often highlighted. First, while almost all of them saw the peasants as a population to educate, they did see (as elsewhere in Europe) the actions of urban agronomists as an engine of technical and civilizational development.[19] Second, we must not neglect the importance of imperial expansion. In Russia, at the end of the seventeenth century, the political elites justified the occupation of the steppes – considered to be deserted or inhabited by pillaging nomads – by invoking the benefits of sedentary agriculture and thus the superiority of the peasant.[20] Starting in the eighteenth century and gaining in strength, these arguments were reprised by Russian agronomists and intellectuals – often critical of Tsarism, except its imperial and national components – and carried into the USSR of Stalin in the twentieth century.

In North America, however, 'peasants' disappeared from political arguments and intellectual debates. Instead, the North American rural world was made up of 'farmers'.

---

[15] Stanziani, *L'économie*.
[16] Eugène Weber, *Peasants into Frenchmen* (Stanford: Stanford University Press, 1976); Yanni Kotsonis, *Making Peasants Backward* (New York: St. Martin's Press, 1999).
[17] Aleksandr I. Chuprov as well as Chayanov travelled several times to Italy. They both met and worked with local itinerant co-operators.
[18] Allen Isaacman, 'Peasants and Rural Social Protests on Africa', *African Studies Review* 33 (1990): 1–120; Sara Berry, 'The Food Crisis and Agrarian Change in Africa: A Review Essay', *African Studies Review* 27 (1984): 67–70, 85–9.
[19] Kotsonis, *Making Peasants*.
[20] David Moon, *The Russian Peasantry, 1600–1930* (London: Longman, 1996); David Moon, *The Plough that Broke the Steppe* (Oxford: Oxford University Press, 2014).

The absence of peasants made it possible to break with the European feudal heritage in a leap of freedom.[21] Nevertheless, just as in Russia at the turn of the twentieth century, farmers served to justify territorial expansion at the expense of nomads. At the two peripheries of the Western world we find a parallel between Tatars and Sioux, Russian peasants and American farmers.[22]

Fighting for or against ideal types. Peasant studies in the Cold War

Daniel Thorner and his wife Alice were already renowned Indianists when they moved to Paris at the very beginning of the 1960s. Their book, *Land and Labour in India*, was for generations an essential reference for those who studied the agrarian question in 'developing countries'.[23] At the International Conference on Economic History in Aix-en-Provence in 1962, Thorner proposed an innovative argument. Contrary to traditional Marxist theories, he believed that peasants and their social and economic organization were not transitory figures in the transition from feudalism to capitalism, but instead could be seen as a system in their own right. He used the examples of India, China, Latin America and Czarist Russia.[24] With regard to the latter, he cited an article written in German – by what was likely a Russian author, a certain Tchayanoff – which was published in 1924 in *Arkhiv für Sozialwissenschaft und Sozialpolitik*, a major review of the period directed by Alfred Weber, Emil Lederer and Joseph Schumpeter. This article shows how, contrary to the stages of development in Marxist theory, a peasant economic system is not only possible but also likely to help support the development of a merchant economy.[25] The work also presents a theory of demographic differentiation, which it opposes to the class differentiation of Marxist theory. According to this approach, the peasant community presents temporary forms of differentiation linked to the family cycle, to which communal distribution of land adapted. Although families with more children benefited from more land, this allocation was modified once the children left the paternal household. For Thorner, this theory provided a better explanation (in comparison to the dominant economic theories, both Marxist and liberal) of the behaviour and role of peasant farms in India, and especially their ability to take part in the process of economic growth.

This is where Thorner's interests joined up with those of his friend Basile Kerblay. The latter was studying the theory of planning at the time, but he began to take

---

[21] Allan Kulikoff, *From British Peasants to Colonial American Farmers* (Chapel Hill: University of North Carolina Press, 2000).
[22] Burbank and Cooper, *Empires*.
[23] Daniel and Alice Thorner, *Land and Labour in India* (Delhi: Oxford University Press, 1956).
[24] Daniel Thorner, 'Peasant as a Category in Economic History', *Deuxième conférence d'histoire économique*, vol. 2 (Aix-en-Provence, 1962): 287–300, reproduced in Theodor Shanin, *Peasants and Peasant Societies* (New York: Penguin, 1971): 202–17.
[25] A. V. Chayanov, 'Zur frage einer theorie der nichtkapitalistichen wirtschaftssysteme' (la théorie des systèmes économiques non-capitalistes), *Arkhiv für Sozialwissenschaft und Sozialpolitik* 51, no. 3 (1924): 577–618.

interest in peasant markets in the USSR.²⁶ Kerblay's argument was that networks other than the official one were operating concurrently, yet their quantitative importance and impact had to be demonstrated. These questions help explain why Kerblay, like Thorner, was interested in Chayanov's arguments, which offered interesting avenues for understanding the different forms of commercialization in peasant farming. Amid the silence of the official Soviet encyclopaedias of the time, Kerblay began to search for works by Chayanov in numerous Western libraries, including Paris, Berlin and New York, as well as collections belonging to public institutions (such as the National Institute of Statistics and Economic Studies), and even with private individuals. Among the latter, he had the foresight to contact Simon Kuznets, one of the major economists and statisticians of the century, especially famous for his theory linking economic growth and income distribution. According to Kuznets, the Marxist argument (increase in social and income differentiation with industrialization) is valid only during the early phases of industrialization; in the long term, these differences are reduced, and lower real incomes in particular close the gap with upper social strata.²⁷ Chayanov exerted a strong influence here, as did his theory of social differentiation and the debate between 1870 and 1930 in Russia and then the USSR. In fact, Kuznets was born in Russia to Jewish parents in 1901, and moved to the United States in 1922, where he completed (at Columbia University) the university studies he had begun in Russia. He therefore read Russian, and had in his library a number of works by Russian economists and statisticians, including Chayanov. This was an essential bridge in the economic and historiographical thought of the twentieth century, between the Russian experience and that of industrialized countries and new 'developing' countries. In any case, it was a matter of determining the impact of the industrialization process on social differentiation. We will return to this in the ensuing pages.

Since the 1960s, the work of the Polish historian Witold Kula has not only been a major reference for economic historians, but has also made it possible to establish a strong connection between the historiographical and political debates in the USSR, with those taking place during the same period in 'Socialist Republics' and with the renewal of European economic history. Kula discovered Chayanov in the late 1950s or early 1960s, and even though he could not openly cite him, he used Chayanov to advance a new historical and economic analysis of the resurgence of the servile system in Eastern Europe. An initial analysis of the transition from serfdom to capitalism in Poland, published in that country in 1955, appeared in French in 1960 through the Accademia polacca delle scienze a Roma under the title *Les débuts du capitalisme en Pologne dans la perspective de l'histoire comparée*. Shortly afterwards, in 1962, his economic theory of the feudal system was published in Poland; the translation of this book in France in 1970 was sought by Braudel, who found in it an exemplary

---

²⁶ Basile Kerblay. 'Entretiens sur la planification avec des économistes soviétiques', *Cahiers du Monde russe* 1, no. 1 (1959): 174–79.
²⁷ Simon Kuznets, 'Economic Growth and Economic Inequality', *American Economic Review* 45, no. 1 (1955): 1–28.

methodological synthesis between a sufficiently flexible 'model', and a historical dynamic that drove away any 'universal law of development'.

In an important article, which appeared in 1964 in the *Cahiers du monde russe et soviétique*, Kerblay was able to situate Chayanov's work in the context of research on the agrarian economy conducted in Russia between 1861 and the First World War, by providing a report on the situation of the peasant economy during the period. He detailed the activity of Chayanov and his group during the 1920s. Kerblay could not, and for good reason, precisely state what happened to Chayanov after his arrest in 1930.[28]

Shortly after his work of 1964, Kerblay edited with Thorner and R. Smith the very famous English translation of two works by Chayanov, the article on economic systems from 1924, and the theory of the peasant economy from 1925.[29] This last work, along with contact between Kerblay and Thorner, underscore that one of the reasons for the considerable success enjoyed by Chayanov's rediscovery was the fact that it took place in a specific historiographical and intellectual context, that of the debates surrounding the reforms in the USSR, development in 'the West' and the renewal of economic history. Beginning in 1954, and increasingly after the twentieth Congress of the Communist Party of the Soviet Union, there was a huge increase in studies on Russian economists and statisticians from the turn of the century. Of course, these works always began with the criticisms that Lenin had addressed to one or another 'bourgeois' economist, but this was often the only way of popularizing thought. Studies of the *zemstva*, investigations of the Gosplan and the Commissariat for Agriculture, the 'bourgeois' thought of N. D. Kondratiev and the 'petit-bourgeois' thoughts of Chayanov were explored at the time.[30]

The work of certain historians was strongly influenced by these thoughts – historians such as A. M. Anfimov and especially Danilov,[31] the latter of whom emphasized the force of the cooperative movement before the world war and especially during the 1920s, endeavouring like Kerblay to study the commercialization channels of peasant farms. The historiographical and political implications of this approach are important, as doubt is cast on Stalin's decision to abandon the NEP and to proceed with forced collectivization. On the contrary, the cooperative plan of Lenin and Bukharin (and, without citing him, of Chayanov) would have represented a viable solution enabling the reconciliation of economic growth with socialism. This renewal of the historiography on the basis of an underground circulation of forbidden authors was conducted for the well-defined purpose of 'reforming socialism'.

---

[28] Basile Kerblay, 'A.V. Cayanov. Un carrefour dans l'évolution de la pensée agraire en Russie de 1908 a 1930', *Cahiers du monde russe et sovietique* 4 (1964): 411–60.

[29] Chayanov, *On the Theory*.

[30] *Istoriia russkoi ekonomichesko mysly* (History of Russian Economic Thought), 3 vols (Moscow: Nauka), 1966; N. K. Figuroskaia, *Agrarnye problemy v sovetskoi ekonomicheskoi literature 20kh godov* (Agrarian Questions in the Soviet Economic Literature of the 1920s) (Moscow: Ekonomika, 1978).

[31] Viktor Petrovich Danilov, *Sovetskaia dokolkkoznaia derevnia* (The Soviet Countryside before the Collectivization), 2 vols (Moscow: Nauka, 1977, 1979).

In India, various authors – both Marxist and non-Marxist – tended to give priority to industrialization as the key to escaping from underdevelopment and poverty. Nevertheless, this approach came under sharper attack from the early 1960s onwards. Several elements were involved: the Khrushchev report, the denunciation of collectivization and Stalin's crimes, and the rediscovery of the NEP, Bukharin and Chayanov, and therefore peasant agriculture as a factor in economic development. Numerous authors used these elements to propose a solution midway between capitalism and socialism (the famous Third Way), consisting essentially of integrating the peasant world into an increasingly market-based economy. Numerous Marxist economists and anthropologists denied any possible long-term existence of a 'peasant mode of production', as this system would not offer support for the industrialization process, which is necessary to emerge from backwardness. A new group of economists thus began to argue that the true solution could be found in a development that is balanced and inscribed in the *longue durée*, one in which the peasant economy could gradually evolve toward a market economy, all while offering a safe landing for workers unable to find stable employment in cities.[32]

These approaches partially came to an end at the close of the 1960s when in the USSR the move towards reforming socialism was halted and collective farms were again at the forefront of economic policies. This attitude strongly influenced pro-soviet countries in the Global South, such as Tanzania, Ethiopia and Mozambique, where 'orthodox' Marxist-Leninist orientation sustained forced collectivization in the name of modernization.[33]

To sum up, the appropriation of knowledge by the town from the seventeenth century onward, its increasingly normative role and the difficulty of integrating the 'masses' in this erudite project, whether on national or colonial territory led to using statistics to impose a bureaucratic authoritarian rationalization of the economy and society as a whole. The question is how these intellectual and political discourses were influenced by and in turn influenced the actual behaviour of peasants and socio-economic dynamics. Peasants speak little; they act. Nevertheless, numerous sources offer access to their world. They just need to be cross-referenced. Studies on agriculture multiplied from the eighteenth century onward, while social inquiries became widespread in the nineteenth century, not only in urban settings (Le Play) but also in the countryside. Economic progress, social differentiation and inequalities were at the heart of these countless investigations and analyses featuring peasants. Associated with a wide variety of archives (land registries, parish records, urban employment, laws on poverty and vagrancy, birth/marriage/death registries, internal passports, landowners' and farmers' ledgers, petitions, military archives, rural inspection archives, etc.), often unexplored, especially at the local level, they have allowed us to revisit and update the history of the peasantry and the rural world. How so?

[32] Gunnar Myrdal, *Economic Theory and Underdeveloped Regions* (London: Duckworth, 1956); Paul Baran, *The Political Economy of Growth* (New York: John Calder, 1957).
[33] Goran Hyden, *Beyond Ujamaa in Tanzania: Underdevelopment and an Uncaptured Peasantry* (Berkeley: University of California Press, 1980); Allen Isaacman, *Cotton is the Mother of Poverty: Peasants, Work, and Rural Struggle in Colonial Mozambique, 1938-1961* (Portsmouth, NH: Heinemann, 1996); James Scott, *Seeing like a State* (New Haven: Yale University Press, 1998).

Peasants in history? Pluri-activity and multiple identities

In France and Britain, in Italy and Germany, traditional historiography has contrasted the inertia of the countryside with urban and industrial dynamism. For several decades now, this image no longer prevails, at least not in Western Europe. We now know that the famous 'agricultural revolution' of the eighteenth and nineteenth centuries constitutes a phase in a long process.[34] In terms of crop yields, techniques and the marketing of produce, if there was indeed a rupture it occurred both earlier – in the twelfth and thirteenth centuries – and later, after 1850 or even in the twentieth century with the mechanization and industrialization of agriculture. Naturally, this process did not manifest everywhere with the same intensity: certain regions of Britain, France, Italy, the Netherlands and China were affected more than others. It is no longer a question of contrasting British dynamism with French inertia. Centres of agrarian growth emerged, supported by demand from towns and by international trade or regional markets.

Since the eighteenth century, numerous observers have pointed out the role of enclosures in Britain. The privatization of common land, often carried out by force, led to the proletarianization of peasants but supported the rise of markets, towns and industry. Criticized by socialists, anarchists and populists of every stripe, this strategy is nevertheless considered by many others – from Arthur Young to current studies in economic history – as a necessary pre-condition for the emergence of a bourgeois, capitalist, industrial society.

However, in recent years, this formerly unanimous interpretation has been called into question thanks to the systematic examination of local archives. While a large number of enclosures did indeed take place in the seventeenth century, as shown by the archives, they were unexpectedly fewer in number between the eighteenth century and the beginning of the nineteenth, and finally experienced an uptick toward the middle of the nineteenth century.[35] The archives also show that enclosures had little impact on crop yields and productivity, with the exception of a few districts. In other words, agricultural growth in the United Kingdom was only partly due to privatization and innovation. Instead, it was built on a number of large estates, many small farms and techniques that had been developed several centuries earlier.

Similarly, in France, it was only after the Revolution that rural properties fragmented (until 1870), with large estates remaining more numerous in the north and smallholdings more widespread in Brittany, in the mountains and in the east. And, as in Britain, agrarian innovations were part of a long-term process. Given these

---

[34] Patrick O' Brien, 'Agriculture and the Industrial Revolution', *Economic History Review* 30, no. 1 (1977): 166–81; Gregory Clark, 'Productivity Growth without Technical Change in European Agriculture before 1850', *The Journal of Economic History* 47, no. 2 (June 1987): 419–32.

[35] Robert Allen, *Enclosure and the Yeoman* (Oxford: Clarendon Press, 1992); Robert Allen, 'Tracking the Agricultural Revolution in England', *Economic History Review* 52, no. 2 (1999): 209–35.

circumstances, it is hard to defend the thesis of the alleged gap between France and Britain in terms of property and agrarian techniques.[36]

The same goes for the gap between the so-called capitalist agriculture of Western Europe and that of Eastern Europe. Liberal, radical and Marxist historiography and such different authors as Kula, Wallerstein and North agree on this: in early modern times, Eastern Europe responded to the commercial, agrarian and then industrial expansion of the West by binding the peasantries to the land and its lords.[37] According to this view, the enserfment of the peasantry in the East contrasts with the rise of 'free' wage labour in the West. These dynamics are supposed to have accompanied an increasing international division of labour in which the periphery (Asia, Africa) and quasi-periphery (southern and Eastern Europe) were subordinated to the core (northern and western Europe). We may note that an increased dissemination of quitrent is recorded during the first half of the eighteenth century, followed by the greater success of labour services during the second half of this century. Finally, in the first half of the nineteenth century, the quitrent came back into prominence, although to a lesser degree than during the previous century. Within this overall framework, significant regional differences can be seen: forced labour was more widespread in the 'Black Earth' (the central, most fertile regions of European Russia), whereas the quitrent system was more widely practised near industrial areas.[38] Despite the better performances of big estates, overall data show quite good outcomes for the Russian economy as compared with most Western economies,[39] and this despite the well-known tendencies of statistics to underestimate products, yields and revenues. Both peasants and landlords entered the market in cereals as well as going in for proto-industrial activities and trade and transportation activities. Numerous 'serf-entrepreneurs' registered, on behalf of the landowner or sometimes quite independently, to start up businesses or even protoindustrial and industrial activities.[40] Serf-entrepreneurs often employed workers in their proto-industrial activity. They came from the same villages or from neighbouring districts. During and after the mid-eighteenth century, peasants bought an important share of protoindustrial products while benefiting from increasing incomes.[41] The

---

[36] George Grantham, 'Agricultural Supply during the Industrial Revolution: French Evidence and European Implications', *Journal of Economic History* 49, no. 1 (1989): 43–72; Giovanni Federico, *Feeding the World: An Economic History of Agriculture, 1800–2000* (Princeton: Princeton University Press, 2005).

[37] Immanuel Wallerstein, *The Modern World-System: Capitalist Agriculture and the Origins of the European World-Economy in the Sixteenth Century* (New York, London: Atheneum, 1974, 1976); Witold Kula, *An Economic Theory of the Feudal System* (London: New Left Books, 1976); Douglass North, *Structure and Change in Economic History* (New York: Norton, 1981).

[38] Vasilii I. Semevskii, *Krest'ianskii vopros v Rossii v XVIII i pervoi polovine XIX veka* (The Peasant Question in Russia in the Eighteenth to the First Half of the Nineteenth Century), 2 vols (Saint Petersburg, 1888).

[39] Carol Leonard, *Agrarian Reforms in Russia* (Cambridge: Cambridge University Press, 2011).

[40] Lidia S. Prokov'eva, *Krest'ianskaia obshchina v Rossii vo vtoroi polovine XVIII–pervoi polovine XIX v* (The Peasant Commune in Russia during the Second Half of the Eighteenth to the First Half of the Nineteenth Centuries) (Leningrad: Nauka, 1981).

[41] Alessandro Stanziani, *After Oriental Despotism: Eurasian Growth in Global Perspective* (London: Bloomsbury, 2014).

peasant economy under 'serfdom' corresponded neither to the Chayanovian model of a peasant willing to satisfy his family's needs and entering the market only when obliged, nor to Kula's model of peasants pushed to produce by the landlord, who took the entire product and sold it on the market. Peasants were already integrated into market activity, and protoindustry was not necessarily 'residual' (that is, an activity engaged in only after time and opportunities in agriculture had been fully exploited). Peasants' and nobles' integration into the market does not confirm the link between labour service and poor market development. 'Anti-economic' cultural values are used to oppose imaginary peasantries to proletarians, landlords to capitalists. In reality, Russian landlords and peasants were interested in profits and they were integrated into markets to various degrees. That they did not transform in accordance with some Western model does not mean that they were backward, but only that historical transformations of markets and societies may take different forms. Russian 'serfdom' was, in reality, a set of relatively flexible rules and norms that operated on a foundation of interacting landowners, managers, peasant elites (elders) and the rural community as a whole.

If noble privileges were not opposed to the market, then we can no longer study the history of pre-industrial worlds starting with ideal types such as the Junker, the *pomeshchik* (noble landowner), the *latifondista* or the *rentier*. Historians have claimed these actors were the opposite of English entrepreneurs and American farmers. Recent studies have shown, however, that the first group did not always use compulsory labour and was not made up solely of absentee landowners. In East Elbian Germany and Poland, Junkers and peasants took part in market development and innovation and their favourable attitude did not develop only after Napoleon and the French armies had passed through those territories. Since the eighteenth century, peasants and noble estate owners all across Europe, from France to Russia, had integrated markets and new economic dynamics.

A historiographical revolution has also begun in China. Until recently the shared ownership of land and the strength of the peasantry had been considered causes of backwardness or even revolutionary outbreaks. However, this was not the case; recent studies show that the peasant commune disappeared quickly, at least in the south Yangtze, where forms of well-protected property (better than in Britain) developed as early as the sixteenth century.[42] In other regions the situation was more complicated due to the multiplicity of statuses and forms of property that developed, though one cannot properly speak of peasant communes or self-sufficient consumption.

From Europe to China, the relations between the rural world and property are more complex than we are usually told.[43] The increase in crop yields was not necessarily linked to the privatization of land; the latter was more limited than previously believed in Britain, and much more accepted in China than is normally stated. Intermediate arrangements between pure property ownership and the commune were the most

---

[42] Pomeranz, *The Great Divergence*; Bin Wong, *China Transformed*.
[43] Stephen Broadberry and Bishnupriya Gupta, 'The Early Modern Great Divergence: Wages, Prices and Economic Development in Europe and Asia, 1500–1800', *The Economic History Review* 59, no. 1 (2006): 2–31.

widespread form in the nineteenth century and were what enabled the transformation of agriculture and rural societies between the seventeenth century and the end of the nineteenth.[44]

It is from this perspective that we can fully apprehend the work and multiple occupations taken on by peasants. The so-called 'populist' approaches have often emphasized the peasants' desire for self-sufficiency; they would not agree to sell their land nor engage in other activities unless forced. However, Marxists have always highlighted the rapid and inevitable dispersion of peasants, as well as their proletarianization brought on by the rise of capitalism. These two images need to be revised, at least for the period up to the end of the nineteenth century for certain regions of Europe, and much later for other regions and the rest of the world (except the USA).

In France, only 27.6 per cent of the population worked in the industrial sector in 1851 (16 per cent in 1815 and 21 per cent at the end of the 1830s). In the period 1855–64, small workshop production was still 1.6 times greater than that of industry. Market segmentation and multiple occupations were the rule. It was only between the 1860s and 1890s that the seasonal shift between agriculture and industry jobs began to decline. In 1860 around 500,000 workers (or quite possibly 800,000) would leave their job during the summer months. In 1890, seasonal workers numbered only 100,000. Seasonal migration, which accounted for 10 per cent of agricultural work in 1860, fell to 2 per cent thirty years later. Neither peasants nor proletarians, then, but worker peasants everywhere.[45]

Still, the boundaries between town and country or agriculture and industry were not the only fluid ones in France: that between land and sea was also fluid. Even at the beginning of the nineteenth century, fishermen near Lorient or Dunkirk were also called 'labourers' in everyday speech. In Dunkirk, Dieppe and Le Havre, fiscal sources reveal the low percentage of fishermen making a living exclusively from fishing.[46] In general, in coastal towns and villages, those dedicated fully or primarily to maritime activities made up a third of the inhabitants. The multiple-occupation model dominated everywhere. In one place fishermen grew hemp, in another they worked in vineyards or offered their services on the large grain farms of the Paris Basin. In general, from the turn of the eighteenth century onward, fishermen engaged in other work to complement their income. Daily-wage sailors, however, prioritized large-scale agricultural work and depended mainly on agricultural cycles.[47]

The rise of colonial commerce led to the development of new activities: tobacco factories and sugar refineries in Bordeaux, fish processing and packing in the main

---

[44] Philip C. C. Huang, 'Development or Involution in Eighteenth-Century Britain and China? A Review of Kenneth Pomeranz's "The Great Divergence: China, Europe, and the Making of the Modern World Economy"'; Kenneth Pomeranz, 'The Greater Divergence: China, Europe, and the Making of the Modern World Economy', *The Journal of Asian Studies* 61, no. 2 (2002): 501–38.

[45] Thierry Magnac and Gilles Postel-Vinay, 'Wage Competition between Agriculture and Industry in Mid-Nineteenth Century France', *Explorations in Economic History* 34 (1997): 1–26.

[46] Alain Cabantous, *Les citoyens du large – Les identités maritimes en France (XVII–XIXe siècles)* (Paris: Aubier, 1995).

[47] Alessandro Stanziani, *Sailors, Slaves, and Immigrants: Bondage in the Indian Ocean World* (New York: Palgrave Macmillan, 2014), chapter 2 in particular.

ports of the Atlantic coast, and shipbuilding. The multiple-occupation economy intensified: in Dunkirk the percentage of people dedicated exclusively to the sea dropped from 19 per cent in 1660 to 10 per cent under the first empire. And while the social reproduction of maritime professions concerned between a third and a quarter of the working population in large ports like Dunkirk, Le Havre, Bordeaux or Marseille, it was much higher in small ports like Saint-Valéry-sur-Somme or Arzon. Voyages to the Antilles, to Quebec and to the East Indies mostly drew sailors from the interior of the country as the risks were great (starvation, diseases, shipwrecks). Most often it was the youngest son or men who were not busy with agricultural work that were sent to the coastal towns.[48] Peasant artisan, peasant worker, peasant sailor, peasant day-labourer, peasant servant: the ideal peasant hardly existed. Could this be explained by some sort of 'French backwardness'?

Absolutely not, because it was the same in Britain where domestic servants and day labourers were just as hard to distinguish. These two categories belonged to a broader group, that of 'servants', which included apprentices and urban workers.[49] As seen above, in Britain during the eighteenth century and the first half of the nineteenth work remained seasonal, not only in agriculture but also in industry.

Thinkers from Marx and Weber, to Tawney and Sombart, to Douglass North, not to forget political scientists such as Barrington Moore, have all endeavoured to highlight the driving role of the bourgeoisie, especially the urban bourgeoisie, in the emergence of the modern world. According to this perspective, the landed aristocracy and peasantry were an impediment that slowed down the march toward progress. The case of Russia and Eastern Europe in general were used to demonstrate the validity of this theory. But these arguments fall apart when we discover that Russian and Polish nobles and peasants participated actively in the market and that they contributed to economic growth and 'modernization'. These conclusions join those of many historians of *ancien régime* France and of Prussia, likewise for the new discoveries concerning the rural worlds in China and Britain. The implications are important: multiple-occupation peasants everywhere supported the economic boom from the eighteenth century to the mid-nineteenth, while European landed aristocracies were much less absent than critics had affirmed in the eighteenth century. They all set in motion processes of modernization and market integration that preceded the official abolitions of serfdom and the great changes evoked by the rising bourgeoisie and its ideologues. This also lends support to Arno Mayer's thesis that the *ancien régime* in Europe was relatively flexible, that it was transformed in the eighteenth century, even more in the nineteenth, and did not finally collapse until the First World War. In terms of ruptures and continuities over the long term, the implications are important: the rural worlds demonstrated a real capacity for adaptation to institutional and economic upheavals in the eighteenth and nineteenth centuries. These capacities (and tensions) stem from the fact that they were never isolated: worker peasants, peasant merchants, peasant

---

[48] Cabantous, *Les citoyens*.
[49] Steinfeld, *The Invention*; Steinfeld, *Coercion, Contract*; Deakin and Wilkinson, *The Law of the Labor Market*.

sailors dominated the scene. This is a dynamic that eludes the social stereotypes that populists, liberals, socialists and Marxists have put forward over time.

Fissures that had appeared here and there between 1750 and 1870 would turn into veritable fractures with the transformations of the 1870–1914 period: great depression, internationalization of the economy, second industrial revolution, industrialization of agriculture and the First World War definitively swept away the ancient world. The tragedies of the first half of the twentieth century cannot be explained without taking into account this capacity for transformation of the rural societies and economies of preceding centuries and their collapse, occurring much later chronologically.

Are the United States an exception to this history made up of landed aristocracies and peasant workers? After all, the American myth was essentially founded on the absence of feudalism and peasantry.[50] Compared with Europe and Asia, American agriculture in the nineteenth century appears to have been concentrated and mechanized much sooner. Recent studies have revealed a considerable gap between Britain and the United States in terms of agricultural techniques and the organization of work.[51] At the same time, this image – however reassuring to the economic historian – does not hold up as well when one considers the differences between North and South. Until 1865, the South under slavery was much more capitalist than the North, which was made up of small producers in both agriculture and industry. Capitalism was on the side of forced labour rather than that of urban manufacturing. But the abolition of slavery changed the game. On the one hand, the North and the West mechanized and production became more concentrated. The South (Old South, New South), on the other hand, saw the beginning of very different transformations and, consequently, paths to 'modernization' that were just as diverse. This complexity remained in place during a large part of the twentieth century. The American exception therefore needs to be heavily qualified.[52]

In addition to the 'peasant' world's participation in economic and social upheavals between the middle of the seventeenth century and the end of the nineteenth, it also contributed to the transformation of societies and institutions through two other avenues: the army and colonization. Peasants were essential to the military revolution.[53] The peasant soldier was the very essence of this process, often considered one of the main instruments of European affirmation in the world. Without the massive recruitment of rural populations, the evolution of army and navy that began in the seventeenth century would not have been possible. The introduction of firearms

---

[50] H. J. Habakkuk, *American and British Technology in the Nineteenth Century* (Cambridge: Cambridge University Press, 1962).
[51] Kenneth L. Sokoloff and David Dollar, 'Agricultural Seasonality and the Organization of Manufacturing in Early Industrial Economies: The Contrast between England and the United States', *The Journal of Economic History* 57, no. 2 (1997): 288–321.
[52] Gavin Wright, *The Political Economy of the Cotton South: Households, Markets, and Wealth in the Nineteenth Century* (New York: Norton, 1978); Gavin Wright, *Old South, New South: Revolutions in the Southern Economy since the Civil War* (New York: Basic Books, 1986); Gavin Wright, *Slavery and American Economic Development* (Baton Rouge: LSU Press, 2006).
[53] Charles Tilly, *Coercion, Capital and European States. AD 990-1991* (Cambridge and Oxford: Blackwell, 1990); Geoffrey Parker, *The Military Revolution and the Rise of the West, 1500–1800* (Cambridge: Cambridge University Press, 1988).

and large ships enabled the de-specialization of war, while compulsory conscription and the creation of a standing army following the Napoleonic wars hit the rural world with full force.

This massive recruitment of peasant soldiers nevertheless entailed negotiations between the state and the landowners, families and employers who would be deprived of precious manpower.[54] And the results of these negotiations were far from identical. For example, the Polish magnates opposed the grand duke and the central power, which caused the conscription effort to fail, resulting in a financial disaster and the collapse of Poland-Lithuania.[55] The situation was different in Russia: long before Peter the Great, the state had centralized army recruitment and the supply of provisions, thus disarming the knights and nobility. Under Peter I, national conscription and the use of firearms were ramped up on an unprecedented scale – and this without resorting to massive borrowing, as was the case everywhere else in Europe, especially in Britain.[56] More than serfdom, it was the recruitment of peasants into the army that underpinned the strength of empire. And that was made possible not only by the central power's actions but also thanks to the increase in agricultural productivity initiated on the great estates.[57]

The British, for their part, recruited – or rather kidnapped – professional sailors as well as peasant sailors from the back country. The Navy introduced technical innovations that simplified tasks and thus facilitated this phenomenon. It was the same in France where peasant soldiers and peasant sailors made up most of the numbers.[58]

While peasants were enrolled as soldiers, soldiers and sailors were often mobilized to clear land in America, New France and Louisiana as well as in the Indies and the Mascarene Islands. Land clearers and day labourers from Normandy thus found themselves working not only on the great estates of Île-de-France but also aboard Breton ships and in the newly colonized regions.[59] A 'global Normandy' emerged whose history really ought to be traced one day.

In addition to this more or less forced military recruitment there was also that of candidates for migration to the colonies, also coerced. All of them were 'bound': an individual could be pressed into service in the army or as a 'migrant' and was subject to similar rules (e.g. punishment for desertion).[60] And all were peasants. For seven years they had to pay off the debt they had contracted to pay for the voyage. During

---

[54] Jeremy Black, *European Warfare, 1600–1815* (New Haven: Yale University Press, 1994).
[55] Stanziani, *After Oriental Despotism*.
[56] Simon Dixon, *The Modernization of Russia, 1676–1825* (Cambridge: Cambridge University Press, 1999).
[57] Alain Cabantous, *Dix mille marins face à l'océan. Les populations maritimes de Dunkerque au Havre (1660–1794)* (Paris: Publisud, 1991).
[58] Stanziani, *Sailors, Slaves*.
[59] Robert Mandrou, 'Vers les Antilles et le Canada au XVIe siècle', *Annales, Économies, Sociétés* 14 (1959): 667–75.
[60] Gabriel Debien, *Les engagés pour les Antilles 1634–1715* (Paris: Société de l'histoire des colonies françaises, 1952); Frédéric Mauro, 'French Indentured Servants for America, 1500–1800', in *Colonialism and Migration: Indentured Labour before and after Slavery*, edited by P. C. Emmer (Dordrecht, Boston and Lancaster: Martinus Nijhoff, 1986): 83–104.

this period these indentured men could be sold, they were not allowed to marry and all their time belonged to their master.⁶¹ Although the conditions for emigration during the seventeenth and eighteenth centuries and until the beginning of the nineteenth were the same in France and Britain, the results were different. British peasant migrants were much more numerous than French.⁶² There are several reasons for this: the use of coercion, which was much more systematic in Britain than in France where the impressment system never managed to take hold, the difficulties the French administration had in coordinating itself, and the incentives offered by the British authorities who quickly granted migrants the opportunity to take their families, even if it meant rapidly placing the children under a regime of forced apprenticeship – in reality forms of domestic servitude or workhouses in the colonies. Ireland, the first British colony, also helped to populate the New World.

It was a widespread phenomenon. From the seventeenth century onward, French and British peasants colonized the Americas. Their condition of servitude did not prevent them from occupying lands at the expense of native Americans. At the same time, Russia sent its peasants to occupy the steppes. Soldier colonists at first, then simply colonists thereafter. Peasants were displaced against the will of landowners in the central regions, but with the support of Russian military and civil authorities who wanted to occupy the new territories. This movement continued in the eighteenth century and accelerated in the nineteenth, especially after the abolition of serfdom, followed by more aggressive imperialism in Siberia and Central Asia. From the 1860s, Russia imitated the European empires and launched into a 'Russification' of the steppes.

The violence of Russian peasants against autochthonous people (and in particular against Jews) intensified, causing the disappearance of nomads from the steppes of Asia. The same happened almost simultaneously in America, where peasant immigrants were brought in to displace them. In this, the opposition between nomads and farmers was stark: a difference of civilization perhaps, different forms of violence certainly.

The same occurred in China: in the seventeenth century, the Qing occupied the northern frontier and Mongolian territories. As was done in other parts of the world, they sent Han peasants from the south and the coasts as soldier colonists.⁶³ In the nineteenth century, Manchuria in turn was targeted, with massive migrations from the coasts toward the inland territories. In addition to this, there were migrations abroad, encouraged by mid-century agricultural and social transformations. Peasants became 'coolies' and spread throughout the Indian Ocean, as far as Australia, while others crossed the Pacific in their millions to land in America.⁶⁴

Indian peasants moved about just as much. In the nineteenth century, when the British needed manpower for their tea plantations in Assam, intermediaries recruited

---

⁶¹ Alessandro Stanziani, *Labour in the Fringes of Empire* (New York: Palgrave, 2018).
⁶² Peter Moogk, 'Reluctant Exiles: Emigrants from France to Canada before 1760', *The William and Mary Quarterly* 46, no. 3 (1989): 463–505.
⁶³ Peter Perdue, *China Marching West: The Qing Conquest of Central Eurasia* (Cambridge, MA: Belknap Press, 2005): 350.
⁶⁴ Adam McKeown, *Melancholy Order. Asian Migration and the Nationalization of Borders* (New York: NYU Press, 2007).

them.[65] India was undergoing major economic and social transformations at that time; the British imposed changes in agricultural land ownership, famines struck the most fragile populations and harvests were unreliable. These circumstances encouraged migration, at first temporary and from the countryside into towns, before crossing borders. Indian 'coolies' dispersed throughout the Indian Ocean and to Britain, less so to the Americas. At the same time, the relation between agriculture and manufacturing was also evolving.[66] Recent studies have shown that the thesis whereby the East India Company caused the demise of Indian textile production needs to be nuanced.[67] Apart from the regions directly controlled by the company and then by the British crown, protoindustry and the multiple-occupation economy remained significant, to the point where, rather than deindustrialization, historians now speak of growth linked to domestic Indian demand and exports to China, these two destinations falling outside the scope of British statistical and economic data.

From 1870 on, we observe contradictory phenomena. Markets began to specialize, the peasant worker and peasant sailor tended to disappear, replaced by the proletarian and the professional sailor and a new, more specialized and mechanized agriculture. This process was accompanied by a major expulsion of peasants in France, Britain, Belgium, Italy and Spain, as well as in China and Japan. But only some of this manpower was absorbed by the towns, prompting the great migratory movement to the Americas and Australia. Although mobility became increasingly free and attained a massive, planetary scale, national borders began to close.[68] This was not only due to changes in markets and their saturation; it was also linked to the creation of a new welfare state. The welfare state nationalized resources and aid (previously done on a municipal or regional scale) and set in motion the process of isolation, indirectly encouraging hostility to new arrivals.

The situation was different in Brazil and Argentina where immigration remained significant: there was no state welfare in these countries and more land was still available. In Brazil, Polish peasant immigrants sought to reproduce the agriculture of their home country, shaping a dynamic and innovative peasant organization. It was more complicated for Italian immigrants, however: they arrived under contracts similar to indentured servitude, which the Italian government complained about. They would later work as labourers.[69]

Profound political changes accompanied these dynamics. In Europe, the right to vote was expanded, and the masses irrupted onto the political scene. It was not until the First World War, however, that universal (male) suffrage was introduced. In

---

[65] Jayeeta Sharma, *Empire's Garden: Assam and the Making of India* (Durham, NC: Duke University Press, 2011); Rana Behal, *One Hundred Years of Servitude: Political Economy of Tea Plantations in Colonial Assam* (New Delhi: Tulika Books 2014).
[66] Sugata Bose, *Peasant Labour and Colonial Capital: Rural Bengal since 1770* (Cambridge: Cambridge University Press, 1993).
[67] Thirtankar Roy, *The Economic History of India 1857–1947* (Delhi: Oxford University Press, 2000).
[68] McKeown, *Melancholy Order*.
[69] Melvin Ember, Carol Ember and Ian Skoggard, eds, *Encyclopedia of Diasporas* (New York: Springer, 2005): 255–9; Witold Kula, Marcin Kula and Josephine Wtulich, *Writing Home. Polish Immigrants in Brazil and the United States* (Boulder, CO: Westview, 1986).

Britain, suffrage was expanded just as the peasantry was disappearing. In France, it came at a time when the peasant worker was disappearing and small landowners were in difficulty. In recently reunified Italy and Germany, peasant access to voting was even more complicated due to the opposition of large landowners. In general, during the interwar period in Western Europe, peasants facing increasing economic difficulties were subjected to contradictory measures: while they enjoyed expanded political rights, their social rights were collapsing. The family and the village lost strength, while the new welfare state did not yet cover the rural world and workers in small businesses.[70] It was not until after the Second World War that rural people would enter the system of social protection and pensions, though often under special schemes.

It was different again in Russia where, despite significant growth between 1861 and 1914, the peasant worker remained an important actor. It was less the weakness of industry than the strength of the agrarian economy undergoing transformation that accounted for this phenomenon. This was not necessarily a question of 'backwardness', as proven by growth rates. The persistence of intensive protoindustrial forms of labour accompanied growth in Asia during a large part of the twentieth century. The economic 'worlds of possibilities' evoked by certain economists, sociologists and historians perfectly accounts for this phenomenon.[71] There was a growing gap between Western countries that based their growth on capital investment and parts of Eastern Europe and Asia that continued to develop through labour and that maintained strong economic ties between town and countryside.[72] The divergences between agrarian worlds, between European countries, between their regions and finally between 'Asia' and 'Europe' became more pronounced precisely at the turn of the twentieth century when markets were internationalizing.[73] The fragmentation of the peasantry and its multiple-occupation model produced diverse outcomes in the West and East in social, political and economic terms. While peasants in the West had access to political but not social rights, in China and Russia they lost both. In those countries it was the peasant worker – already vanished from the West but living through the first and second industrial revolutions in Asia – who led the great agrarian transformations in the form of violent collectivization.

These transformations of peasant worlds did not only occur in Europe and Asia. They were at the heart of colonialism at the end of the nineteenth century and into the twentieth, particularly in Africa. Representations of the European peasant accompanied the partition of Africa. For example, such representations provided the justification for a discourse advocating the abolition of local slavery in order to turn

---

[70] Henry Landsberger, ed., *Rural Protest: Peasant Movements and Social Change* (New York: Macmillan, 1973); Feliks Gross, ed., *European Ideologies: A Survey of Twentieth Century Political Ideas* (New York: Philosophical Library, 1948).

[71] Charles Sabel and Jonathan Zeitlin, *World of Possibilities* (Paris and Cambridge: MSH-Cambridge University Press, 1997).

[72] Kaouro Sugihara, 'Labour-Intensive Industrialisation in Global History', *Australian Economic History* 47, no. 2 (2007): 121–54; John Lee, 'Trade and Economy in Preindustrial East Asia, c. 1500–1800: East Asia in the Age of Global Integration', *The Journal of Asian Studies* 58, no. 1 (1999): 2–26.

[73] Thirtankar Roy, *Rethinking Economic Change in India. Labour and Livelihood* (London: Routledge, 2005).

Africans into employees (British side) or peasants (French side).[74] This led to major abuses, especially in the Congo. This process was an integral part of what the French and British called a civilizing mission that had to begin with work. In Zanzibar, the British tried to reproduce the distinction between proletarians and capitalists in a rural environment. In Kenya, they supported the formation of a class of African peasants – without success.

The French, for their part, condemned African feudalism with a view to transforming local communities into peasant villages. This ambition continued into the twentieth century. Like the British, and for the same reasons, they failed: African workers were not attracted to proletarianization, nor to the peasant ideal type that the colonial elites sought to impose on them. Multiple occupations and seasonal mobility remained the rule and would persist for a long time in the twentieth century, even after decolonization.

No doubt it was the dream of an ideal peasant that best expressed the gap between the perceptions and ambitions of the European colonizers and those of African populations. This same disparity has accompanied decolonization, and the ensuing violence and frustrations of the new African states and international organizations until the present.

---

[74] Frederick Cooper, *From Slaves to Squatters: Plantation Labour and Agriculture in Zanzibar and Coastal Kenya, 1890-1935* (New Haven and London: Yale University Press, 1980); Cooper, *Decolonization and African Society*; Andreas Eckert, 'Regulating the Social: Social Security Social Welfare, and the State in Late Colonial Tanzania', *The Journal of African History* 45, no. 3 (2004): 467–89.

7

What is a consumer? Identities and alterities in the stomach

Consumers seem nowadays to be at the very core of social, public and legal concerns: consumers' rights, consumption trends, social status and consumption, inequalities and consumption, global and local trends in consumption patterns are just a few of the many topics in discussion in academic journals, newspapers and media.[1] As several trends in sociology and historical sociology have expressed since the 1990s (Beck and Giddens among the best-known authors), in a post-industrial society, consumers and consumption have taken the place that 'bourgeois' and 'proletarians' had in the previous two centuries. 'A consumers' republic' has taken the place of workers' socialism.[2] But what exactly is a 'consumer'?

Interestingly enough, the word itself emerged slowly in common and academic language, especially legal terminology, during the second half of the nineteenth century. Before that it was more usual to speak of a 'purchaser'. Terminology was important insofar as, in a liberal unregulated society, there was no difference between the final consumer and any other purchaser, including a professional. It was only at the turn of the nineteenth and twentieth centuries that the word 'consumer' appeared in legal and institutional terms to designate the final consumer, distinguished from other purchasers, mostly professionals. This was because, at that time, consumers' rights were emerging: with the spread of chain stores and multiple chains of intermediaries, sophisticated items (chemical components, artificial fibres, industrial food, etc.), the final consumer was considered unable to really know what a product was made of. As the 'weaker party' in contracts, final consumers therefore deserved special protection, unlike other purchasers.[3]

---

[1] Just a few references: Frank Trentmann, *The Oxford Handbook of the History of Consumption* (Oxford: Oxford University Press, 2012); Maxine Berg, *Luxury and Pleasure in Eighteenth-Century Britain* (Oxford: Oxford University Press, 2008); Giorgio Riello, *Cotton: The Fabric that Made the Modern World* (Cambridge: Cambridge University Press, 2013); Carol Shammas, *The Pre-Industrial Consumer in England and the America* (Oxford: Oxford University Press, 1990); Alan Warde and Lydia Martens, *Eating Out: Social Differentiation, Consumption and Pleasure* (Cambridge: Cambridge University Press, 2000); Lendon Calder, *Financing the American Dream: A Cultural History of Consumer Credit* (Princeton: Princeton University Press, 1999).

[2] Cohen, *A Consumers' Republic*.

[3] Alessandro Stanziani, *Histoire de la qualité alimentaire* (Paris: Seuil, 2005).

Economists, too, were changing their argument: whereas, in the early eighteenth century, they mostly stressed the crucial role of consumption in economic dynamics, following the physiocrats in France and Adam Smith in Britain production was put at the core of economic reasoning. Consumption came back into economic theory with the neoclassical liberal approach during the last quarter of the nineteenth century: in this perspective, individual consumption drove individual and family choices on the labour market and the whole economy as well.[4]

Interestingly, Keynes, in so many respects hostile to marginalist theory and its laissez-faire attitude, put consumption at the very core of its theory, although from a macro and not micro perspective. Keynesianism and regulation considered that state intervention and not the market should guide investment and, from this perspective, consumption was crucial to making this strategy successful. Keynes cut the relationship between consumption and utility and instead stressed the link between consumption and liquidity (monetary availability, including credit) in the economy. However, 'consumers' were not further specified in this approach.

My aim here is not so much to discuss theories of consumption but rather to evaluate the tensions between these arguments and structural socio-economic dynamics. Following earlier chapters on workers, slaves and peasants, I do not intend to set 'theories' against 'facts', but rather to highlight their relationship in historical contexts. To that end, I shall not in a few pages add yet another 'short history' of consumers and consumptions to the many extremely valuable ones already available.[5] Instead, I follow a particular line of reasoning: I seek to 'open up' the historical notion of 'the consumer' by tracing social inequalities in food consumption. In particular, I will discuss the tension between famine, scarcity and opulent societies and the related clear-cut opposition between quality and quantity, food safety and food security. Quite often, these distinctions are placed in a quite rigid historical framework: quantities, scarcity and famines belong to pre-industrial societies only. I will contest this argument and stress instead their interaction in the long run, and, therefore, the role social inequalities in consumption play in early modern and modern societies. Social inequalities must be taken into consideration instead of speaking of consumers in general.[6] In this sense, 'modernity' has often been associated with the passage from luxury to mass consumption that was supposed to accompany

---

[4] Alessandro Stanziani, ed., *Dictionnaire de l'économie-droit* (Paris: LGDJ, 2007).
[5] For an introduction, see Trentmann, *The Oxford Handbook of the History of Consumption*; Brewer and Porter, *Consumption and the Worlds of Goods*; Sylvie Vabre, Martin Bruegel and Peter Atkins, eds, *Food History: A Feasts of the Senses in Europe, 1750 to the Present* (London: Routledge, 2021); Martin Bruegel, ed., *A Cultural History of Food in the Age of Empire* (London: Bloomsbury, 2015). For an introduction to the sociology of consumption, see Joel Stillerman, *The Sociology of Consumption: A Global Approach* (London: Polity Press, 2015); Peter Corrigan, *The Sociology of Consumption: An Introduction* (London: SAGE, 2012).
[6] Amartya Sen, *Poverty and Famines: An Essay on Entitlement and Deprivation* (Oxford: Clarendon Press, 1982); Andre Gunder-Frank and Barry Gills, *The World-Systems: Five Hundred Years or Five Thousands?* (London: Routledge, 1993).

industrialization while reducing inequalities.[7] However, the outcome of this process in terms of income distribution and well-being is unclear; let us take the case of food consumption. Conventional economic theories would argue that the share of food in a family's total expenses decreases when income increases. This argument does not take into consideration the central role luxury food plays in upper-class expenditure. Put into an historical perspective: according to one approach, pre-industrial societies combined strong social inequalities and unequal access to food (in both quality and quantity) for each social group. The nobility and upper classes had access to more food of better quality than lower classes. According to this view, market development would later lead to the democratization of tastes and goods and, thus, to increasing welfare for most people.[8] One variant of this approach argues that after an initial stage during which social inequalities increased, in the long run industrialization brought increasing welfare to the whole population.[9] Implicit in this view is the argument that food scarcity was mostly a concern of pre-industrial societies, while advanced economies are mostly concerned with problems of quality.[10]

Another view maintains that social inequalities, in particular with regard to food access, were not so pronounced under the *ancien régime* and did not disappear with industrialization, when they just affected other social groups and countries, in particular outside Europe. According to the world-system theory and its derivatives, disparities in food access persisted and even increased with industrialization and globalization.[11]

In these debates, product characteristics play a crucial role. According to the first view, product standardization sustains increasing supply and welfare.[12] In recent decades this view has been strongly challenged by the notions of industrious revolution and protoindustrialization, both putting the accent on demand rather than on supply.[13] Smith's, Marx's and Chandler's views have been questioned by those who have spoken of the coexistence of multiple worlds of production.[14] Criticism of standardization

---

[7] Some examples in a huge bibliography: Carlo Cipolla, *Before the Industrial Revolution* (New York: Norton, 1993); B. H. Slicher Van Bath, *De agrarische geschiedenis van West-Europa (500–1850)* (Utrecht: Het Spectrum, 1962); Wilhelm Abel, *Agricultural Fluctuations in Europe from the Thirteenth to the Twentieth Century* (London: Methuen, 1980; orig. 1935); Timothy Ashton, 'The Standard of Life of the Workers in England 1790–1830', *Journal of Economic History* 9 (1949): 19–38.

[8] Gregory Clark, *A Farewell to Alms* (Princeton: Princeton University Press, 2007); Angus Maddison, *Contours of the World Economy, 1–2030 AD* (Oxford: Oxford University Press, 2007).

[9] Kuznets, 'Economic Growth and Income Inequalities'.

[10] David Landes, *The Unbound Prometheus. Technological Change and Industrial Development in Western Europe from 1750 to the Present* (Cambridge: Cambridge University Press, 1969).

[11] Paul Bairoch, *Révolution industrielle et sous-développement* (Paris: Mouton, 1974); Immanuel Wallerstein, *The Modern World-System*, 2 vols (New York: Academic Press, 1974, 1980).

[12] Alfred Chandler, *Scale and Scope* (Cambridge, MA: Belknap Press, 1990); Joel Mokyr, *The Level of Riches* (Oxford: Oxford University Press, 1990).

[13] Jan de Vries, *The Industrious Revolution* (Cambridge: Cambridge University Press, 2008); Peter Kriedte, Hans Medick and Jürgen Schlumbhom, *Industrialisation before Industrialisation* (Cambridge: Cambridge University Press, 1981).

[14] Charles Sabel and Jonathan Zeitlin, *World of Possibilities* (Cambridge: Cambridge University Press, 1997); Robert Salais, *Les mondes de productions* (Paris: EHESS Éditions, 1992).

has equally been developed by those who link product standardization to loss of biodiversity and increasing inequalities between 'developed' and 'underdeveloped' areas.[15] Limits to industrialization and to more egalitarian access to food, and the controversial role of science, techniques and the persisting importance of local values have been fully developed.[16]

I will address these debates by examining their main categories and tenets. Is it true that quantity problems are relevant in pre-industrial societies while quality concerns intervene only with 'full stomachs'? Are famines only a problem in non-market and pre-industrial societies?[17] Is 'the consumer', with its choices, an actor only in 'opulent societies'? Are there not 'consumers' in pre-industrial societies? And are there still consumers in 'postmodern' contemporary societies?

Quantifying consumption and its roots: famines or speculation?

Older debates in the historiography opposed those who underlined the major break in terms of access to food, marked by the agrarian and industrial revolutions, to Marxist views stressing the persisting if not increasing inequalities in income and food distribution. In recent years, statistical assessments of both the production of food and its distribution among social groups in different countries and areas have made this puzzle much more complicated. Regional variations in food production and consumption are important in all countries and they have been related to several variables: the strength of peasant agriculture, much more embedded in markets than previously held; the increase of urban demand from the seventeenth century onwards; and technical improvements over the long run.[18] Detailed estimations of real income and timing of growth have been advanced for most countries.[19] Statistical assessments show that the growth in agricultural output began before the industrious revolution, in the twelfth century. According to this view, if the period usually defined as a break (mid-eighteenth to mid-nineteenth century) in fact reflected more accurately a steady but limited growth, major changes in agriculture yields, output and techniques occurred first in the seventeenth (the industrious revolution) and, then, in the twentieth century (second Industrial Revolution).[20]

---

[15] Bernard Jullien and Andy Smith, eds, *Industries and Globalization: The Political Causality of Difference* (London: Palgrave, 2008).
[16] Christopher Bayly, *The Birth of the Modern World, 1780–1914* (London: Blackwell, 2004).
[17] Sen, *Poverty and Famine*.
[18] Just two references in a huge bibliography: Robert Allen, 'The Growth of Labour Productivity in Early Modern English Agriculture', *Explorations in Economic History* 25, no. 2 (1988): 117–46; Paul Bairoch, *L'agriculture des pays développés 1800 à nos jours* (Paris: Economica, 1999).
[19] De Vries, *The Industrious Revolution*.
[20] Jan Luiten Van Zanden, *The Long Road to the Industrial Revolution* (Leiden: Brill, 2009); Gregory Clark, *A Farewell to Alms* (Princeton: Princeton University Press, 2007); George Grantham, 'Agricultural Supply during the Industrial Revolution: French Evidence and European Implications', *Journal of Economic History* 49 (1989): 43–72.

Conventional interpretations consider that the relationship between bad harvests, famine and speculation is specific to advanced capitalist economies. Until the mid-nineteenth century, bad harvests are considered to be a main origin of severe food distress, while after that period market speculation became the main cause of famine (together with wars). The Nobel Prize winner Amartya Sen made his fortune with this theory.

However, in recent decades, this interpretation has been corrected and a number of studies have pointed out the importance of markets, together with climatic variations, in the origin of famines from the twelfth century onwards. From this standpoint, there is no real break, but a slow decrease in the number of famines, at least in Western Europe and China, between the twelfth and nineteenth centuries.[21] One general implication is that it is no longer acceptable to contrast advanced market economies with barter economies: markets were important everywhere and only changed their meaning and structure, as Polanyi and Mauss clearly theorized. The gift is not an alternative to the market, but a part of it.

In terms of economic and social dynamics, this means that we cannot roughly associate the pre-industrial world with agricultural stagnation, food scarcity and famine, and the industrial world with abundance. Growth and increasing access to food occurred over the long run, while famines and bad harvests punctuated world history well after 1800. As several French historians showed decades ago,[22] there had never been so much wheat on the roads in modern France as in the years of presumably bad harvests. Scarcity was already reflecting a market failure rather than a simple collapse of production. The same conclusion has been drawn for other presumed non-market and 'stagnant' societies, such as nineteenth-century Eastern Europe, Asia and twentieth-century Africa.[23] Recent analyses testify to a relatively constant growth, for some areas comparable to that of Europe, which eventually changed only with the first or even the second Industrial Revolution.[24]

If market relationships were already on hand in pre-industrial France, Europe, Asia and parts of Africa, growth itself, on the other hand, did not eradicate problems of scarcity on food markets. In this perspective, scarcity was not linked to insufficient market development, stagnant societies and the like, but, on the contrary, to already developing market relationships. Despite long-run increasing production, speculation in food items and famines carry on well into the twentieth century and up to today.

---

[21] Jean Meuvret, *Le problème des subsistances à l'époque de Louis XIV* (Paris, La Haye: Mouton-EHESS, 1977); Massimo Montanari, *La fame e l'abbondanza* (Bari: Laterza, 1993); W. C. Jordan, *The Great Famine: Northern Europe in the Early Fourteenth Century* (Princeton: Princeton University Press, 1992).

[22] Meuvret, *Les problème des subsistances*.

[23] On Eastern Europe and Russia: Alessandro Stanziani, 'Revisiting Russian Serfdom: Bonded Peasants and Market Dynamics, 1600–1800', *International Labour and Working Class History* 78, no. 1 (2010): 12–27; Boris Mironov, 'Consequences of the Price Revolution in Eighteenth-Century Russia', *The Economic History Review* 45, no. 3 (1992): 457–78. On Africa: Gareth Austin, 'Reciprocal Comparison and African History Tackling Conceptual Eurocentrism in the Study of Africa's Economic Past', *African Study Review* 50, no. 3 (2007): 1–28.

[24] Kenneth Pomeranz, *The Great Divergence* (Princeton: Princeton University Press, 2000).

Since the 1870s, at the very moment when the West was recording considerable economic growth (the second Industrial Revolution, the *Belle Époque*), repeated famines hit several areas in Africa, Asia and Latin America. They had a devastating impact: 8–10 million victims in India between 1876 and 1879, another 10 million ten years later; 20 million victims in China between 1876 and 1879, a million in Brazil and 2 million ten years later.[25] These events provoked pandemics, typhus and cholera and a hecatomb in its literal sense. Livestock, poorly fed because of the lack of cereals, sick from worldwide zoonoses such as bovine tuberculosis, collapsed in numbers and contributed to the overall food scarcity. In India, between 1876 and 1878, 80 per cent of livestock was lost. Several bad harvests struck China as well between 1876 and 1878, to the point that missionaries wrote that local peasants ate parts their houses made of roots and wood, and then their dying children. Hundreds of thousands of people sold themselves into slavery or sold their children with the hope that the purchaser would feed them.[26] Several forces were at the origin of these global famines: global warming accelerated after the 1850s: this was the end of the Little Ice Age, only partly related to the first Industrial Revolution. Meanwhile, these events took place when the world surplus of cereals soared, due to the exponential growth of Russian, Canadian, Australian and US production, not to mention the impressive increase in yields in Europe. The result was a major fall of agricultural prices between the 1870s and the end of the century. If we add the major developments in transportation (train, steam boat), then it seems quite difficult to ignore the strong tie between famines in the Global South and speculation on world markets. Thus, in 1876, in India, drought in several areas did not stop the British accelerating the export of Indian cereals, which doubled from 1875 to 1876 and again the following year when it reached the record level of 6.4 millions hundredweight (1 cwt = 112 Imperial pounds, or 50.8 kg). The main British colonial administrative elites repeatedly stated that the market was ready to solve the emergency problem, mostly attributed to 'Indian laziness'; indeed, they claimed, humanitarian aid would not solve but only worsen the situation.[27] No measure of that sort was adopted, hence the millions of victims. These policies also had two other origins (beyond the liberal faith in markets): bad harvests in Britain and hence the urgent need for cereal imports to avoid tensions on the labour and consumption markets; pressures from Indian merchants involved in trade with the homeland and Europe.[28] These same arguments (lazy local population, need to galvanize it) were used in Egypt where, despite a major hunger, tax collectors still increased exports of cereals.

French colonial powers adopted a quite similar attitude in North Africa where, despite three years of drought and bad harvests, taxation and exports of cereals to

---

[25] Arap Maharatna, *The Demography of Famine* (Delhi: Oxford University Press, 1996); Davis, *Late Victorian*.
[26] Bohr, *Famine in China*.
[27] *British Parliamentary Papers, Report of the Indian Famine Commission*, part 1 (London, 1880).
[28] R. Neelakanteswara Rao, *Famines and Relief Administration: A Case Study of Coastal Andhra, 1858–1901* (Delhi: Oxford University Press, 1997); Tim Dyson, ed., *India's Historical Demography: Studies in Famine, Disease, and Society* (Cambridge: Cambridge University Press, 1989).

France did not stop.²⁹ At the turn of the century, again, the opening of a wheat market in Bamako, connected to world markets and intended to sustain exports and speculation, depleted local stocks of cereals and lay behind a major famine in 1899–1900, followed by a massive outmigration of the population.³⁰

This was a global phenomenon. Between the 1890s and 1914, in the interwar period and, again, in the 1950s, 1960s and 1970s, Europe and the US saw major speculative waves involving agriculture and food items mostly related to increasing internationalization, transportation and information (telegraph) progress and the growing power of produce exchanges.³¹ Quite recently, speculation in wheat has once again been a subject of public debate. All these speculative waves were much less a consequence of crop failures alone than of exploitation of perceived scarcity by markets. One might conclude that the so-called agrarian, commercial and industrial revolutions of the eighteenth and nineteenth centuries did not create or solve the problem of artificial (i.e. market) scarcity of food as opposed to crop failure. From the twelfth century up to today, speculative crises in food markets have been present. Market speculation in foodstuffs is not specific to advanced capitalism. This is not to deny the differences between thirteenth- and nineteenth-century Europe or between European, Asian and African areas, but it is important to avoid reasoning based on ideal types (peasant economies, capitalism) and taking them for historical realities. In the long run, market speculation in wheat and other items pertained to different worlds and not only to backward countries and pre-industrial Europe. The major break occurred only at the end of the nineteenth century, not before (first Industrial Revolution) nor after (present-day globalization). Indeed, the turn of the nineteenth century added a new dimension to speculation in foodstuffs; produce exchanges and their internal logic expressed the transition in a market economy from real to virtual trade. As a result of this transformation, transactions on wheat, flour and cooking oil markets were no longer solely concerned with supplying cities but became an integral part of capital trading. The real subject of the exchanges at produce exchanges and commodity markets was information about future products and transactions.

Then, after a break during the First World War, in the 1920s, global speculation and famine in the South increased again. In the West, monetary and financial transactions were again deregulated,³² despite Keynes's warnings from the mid-1920s on. Produce exchange and futures in raw materials and sources of energy strongly developed until the 1929 Crash. It is less well known that the crisis hit the Global South as well. Speculation had encouraged the growing of cocoa, rubber, cotton and sugar at the

---

[29] Charles-Robert Ageron, *Les Algériens musulmans et la France (1871–1919)* (Paris: Presses Universitaires de France, 1968); Laurent Heyberger, *Les corps en colonie. Faim, maladies, guerres et crises démographiques en Algérie au XIXe siècle* (Tempus: Presses Universitaires du Midi, 2019).

[30] Richard Roberts, 'The Emergence of a Grain Market in Bamako, 1883–1908', *Revue canadienne des études africaines/ Canadian Journal of African Studies* 14, no. 1 (1980): 55–81.

[31] Archives Nationales (henceforth AN), BB 18 6603-7 (illicit speculation). On speculation see also Stanziani, *Rules of Exchange*.

[32] Adam Tooze, *The Deluge: The Great War and the Remaking of the Global Order* (London: Penguin, 2015).

expense of local food cultures; with the crisis, the collapse of these markets produced massive hunger in several areas in Africa.

In France and the US, new regulatory policies were adopted in the 1930s; regulation and Keynesianism dominated national and international capitalist markets until the 1970s, when, again, deregulation won the day in most advanced countries. Hence the boom of speculation and futures down to the present.[33] In the 2000s, futures and speculation in raw materials and food items rose as never before; only 2 per cent of the transactions on the markets of raw materials correspond to exchanges of real products; almost the whole amount concerns virtual products most of which will never see the light of day. Speculators trade promises, and hunger. The rise in foodstuff prices in 2008 was so spectacular that it drove unrest in Haiti, Egypt and African cities (Conakry, Maputo) and countries (Burkina-Faso, Guinea and Cameroon), not to mention Yemen and Indonesia. The mass of 'consumers' in these countries still live in hunger and deprivation.

In short, we do not find any historical evidence of a passage from quantity to quality from a consumer's perspective; famines faded substantially in the Global North, but they increased in the Global South in the nineteenth and early twentieth century. The 'green revolution' of the last quarter of the twentieth century also brought increasing well-being and consumption in the Global South. Famines became rarer. At the same time, inequalities within each country increased, in both South and North, while the stress on planetary resources continues to grow. Consumer choice and its theory are sometimes still appropriate for manufactured goods, while it narrows for food as the whole planet progresses towards an apparently general opulence. It is now time to have a closer look at 'choice' and 'quality' in consumers' behaviour.

Quality in consumption: who defines it?

As many food historians have shown, concerns about quality of food have from early modern times on been widespread in France, Prussia, Italy, Britain, Russia, the USA and most Asian and African regions.[34] There is no clear historical confirmation of the (social-psychological) idea according to which quality matters only when the stomach is full. Quite the contrary, both quantity and quality concerns arise in the long run all over the world, and only their relationship changes over time and in different countries. In pre-industrial Europe up to the eighteenth century, for example, the process of defining quality reflected not only legal and economic concerns but also moral and religious ones. The quality of goods and its relation to a fair price played a central role in Thomistic thought. A fair price reflected a qualitative hierarchy of goods that referred to a given social hierarchy.[35] This hierarchical world was not exclusively

---

[33] Adam Tooze, *Crashed: How a Decade of Financial Crisis Changed the World* (London: Viking, 2018).
[34] Montanari, *La fame e l'abbondanza*; Michael French and Jim Phillips, *Cheated not Poisoned?* (Manchester: Manchester University Press, 2002).
[35] Jean-Yves Grenier, 'Une économie de l'identification. Juste prix et ordre des marchandises dans l'Ancien Régime', in *La qualité des produits en France, XVIIIe–XXe siècles*, edited by Alessandro Stanziani (Paris: Belin, 2003): 25–54.

defined by regulation. Regulated markets were certainly predominant, but they were not the only ones. Unregulated markets sprang up and were even officially or informally approved by the authorities.[36] Such formal and informal rules aimed at controlling markets, notably food markets, for a specific purpose: to ensure a sufficient quality of the product concerned, in precisely identified qualities and at fair prices.[37] This system does not correspond to the way it is described by its liberal critics: rules did not impede trade but rather provided a solid basis for it.[38] In this context, quantity and quality expertise and regulation were bound together: on the markets for foodstuffs as well as for manufactured goods, experts (so-called measurers) had to check that the quantity and quality of the wheat, meat, cotton and wine for sale corresponded to those which were claimed.[39] In this case, then, what did the 'liberal' nineteenth century bring to food and food markets?

While it is true that guild regulations were abolished at end of the eighteenth century, they had nevertheless not covered all goods.[40] Conversely, in the nineteenth century, trade associations introduced rules to define product quality prior to trade, and the definitions in the foodstuff markets often continued to be the result of municipal regulations. At the same time, market regulation was not specific to nineteenth-century France, Prussia or presumed corporate worlds. The assizes of bread were in use in Britain well into the nineteenth century[41] and anti-speculative attitudes and rules were adopted during the last quarter of the nineteenth century in most European countries and in the USA. Anglo-Saxon countries adopted strict regulation of food markets in the nineteenth and twentieth centuries.[42] If these rules are considered in detail, we may conclude that regulation was even stricter here than in France, while the principle of caveat emptor was more marked in France. In sum, between the eighteenth and the twentieth centuries, a wave of regulation of food quality traversed the West, which was linked to other common phenomena, viz. increasing intermediation, the development of national and international markets, the growing importance of chemistry in the agro-food sector, the raise of hygienist and public forums. Differences between countries appeared not so much in terms of regulation versus free market as in the specific contents of regulation. For example, French rules were adopted under pressure from both the wine lobbies and the hygienist movement, while in Britain, this was the case with milk. As a result, safety and germs played a much more important

---

[36] Steve Kaplan, *Le meilleur pain du Monde* (Paris: Fayard, 1996).
[37] Monica Martinat, *Le «juste » marché. Le système annonaire romain au XVIe et XVIIe siècles* (Rome: École française de Rome, 2005).
[38] Jean-Yves Grenier, *L'économie d'ancien régime* (Paris: Albin Michel, 1996).
[39] Alessandro Stanziani, *Histoire de la qualité alimentaire* (Paris: Seuil, 2005).
[40] Steve L. Kaplan and Philippe Minard, *La fortune du colbertisme* (Paris: Fayard, 2002).
[41] John Burnett and Derek Oddy, eds, *The Origins and Development of Food Policies in Europe* (London and New York: Leicester University Press, 1994).
[42] Frank Trentmann, ed., *Paradoxes of Civil Society: New Perspectives on Modern British and German History* (New York: Berghahn, 2000); Susan Strasser, Charles McGovern and Matthias Judt, eds, *Getting and Spending: European and American Societies in the Twentieth Century* (Cambridge: Cambridge University Press, 1998); Victoria De Grazia and Ellen Furlough, eds, *The Sex of Things: Gender and Consumption in Historical Perspective* (Berkeley: University of California Press, 1996); Ellen Furlough and Carl Strikwerda, eds, *Consumers against Capitalism? Consumer Cooperation in Europe, North America, and Japan, 1840–1990* (Lanham: Rowman & Littlefield, 1999).

role in British than in French rules (despite Pasteur).[43] The overall tendency to regulate even increased over time: from the early twentieth century on, the state, municipalities and European and business associations sought to provide appropriate definitions of foodstuffs and beverages. Hundreds of decrees defining wine, beer, pasta, wheat, milk, butter and so on were adopted in every country, were continuously updated and have ultimately been integrated into European rules which, far from creating bureaucratic management of agro-food and the economy in general, just confirmed previous trends and attitudes.

Regulation involves not only adulteration and quality in general but also signifiers of quality, i.e. labels, trademarks and brands. In this case as well, there is no confirmation of the old standing theory opposing guilds' labels to capitalist individual trademarks. On the one hand, under the *ancien régime*, collective trademarks and trademarks in general were not limited to high quality and luxury items and there was no direct link between legal protection and price or guilds and price, many items being produced outside guilds and sometimes with the support of these (on condition that cheap, non-certified products did not enter the same market segment as branded items).[44] On the other hand, in nineteenth- and twentieth-century Europe market prices and quality were not left to market forces only. Rules on trademarks were constantly at the core of public debates and business interests. Why was this so?

According to some scholars, as markets are imperfect and information does not circulate fully, then trademarks inform consumers and protect producers investing in quality. As such, trademarks reduce the cost of researching transaction costs and facilitate access to products.[45]

Others have replied that no such information is provided by trademarks, which therefore just seek to guarantee a producer's return. According to this view, trademarks redistribute income from final consumers to producers. Following Douglass North, an extremely widespread view asserts that the development of capitalism requires the full protection of private property. However, doubts may arise as to the historical soundness of this argument. First, despite a highly imperfect law on industrial property, registration of trademarks and brands continued to increase in the nineteenth century. Second, the lack of a presumably appropriate law on industrial and intellectual property did not compel market development.[46] Third, during most of the nineteenth century, American and British judges and political elites were strongly opposed to a firm recognition of industrial property, considered a form of monopoly.[47]

---

[43] Stanziani, *Histoire*.
[44] Gérard Béaur, Hubert Bonin and Claire Lemercier, eds, *Fraude, contrefaçon et contrebande de l'antiquité à nos jours* (Genève: Droz, 2006); Corine Maitte, *La trame incertaine, le monde textile de Prato au XVIIIe et XIXe siècles* (Villeneuve d'Ascq: Presses Universitaires du Septentrion, 2001).
[45] William Landes and Richard Posner, 'Trademark Law: An Economic Perspective', *Journal of Law and Economics* 30 (October 1987): 265–309; George Stigler, 'The Economics of Information', *Journal of Political Economy* 69 (1961): 213–25.
[46] Alessandro Stanziani, 'Negotiating Innovation in a Market Economy: Foodstuffs and Beverages Adulteration in Nineteenth-Century France', *Enterprise and Society* 8, no. 2 (2007): 375–412.
[47] Christine MacLeod, 'The Paradoxes of Patenting: Invention and its Diffusion in 18th- and 19th-Century Britain, France, and North America', *Technology and Culture* 32, no. 4 (1991): 885–910.

Luxury and capitalism

The passage from luxury to 'democratic' and then on to mass consumption constitutes a further tenet of the modernization paradigm.[48] I have already mentioned the fact that, roughly speaking, in the 'West' inequalities in real income and food access increased with industrialization and only fell in conjunction with the rise of welfare states, mostly during the second half of the twentieth century. Still, this overall picture needs to be refined. Common opinion contrasts the *ancien régime*, under which the social and legal status of the elites are said to echo the qualitative distinction between luxury and basic consumption, with industrial and modern societies in which only prices and the market determine social hierarchies.[49] I question this assertion and discuss, first, the identification of luxury and, then, the impact of market (price) and institutions (status, regulation) on social hierarchies.

Luxury has long been associated with *ancien régime* and so-called order/estate societies in which social hierarchies were based on blood and legal status. Enlightenment criticism of luxury is behind this interpretation, which has nevertheless found supporters among classical economists and, later, in Veblen and all those who associated luxury with leisure and unproductive activities.[50] However, as early as the eighteenth century, economists and philosophers made a distinction between 'bad' luxury (that of the unproductive classes) and good luxury, that is, consumption linked to increasing income, in turn due to working activity.[51] As a fruit of labour, consumption and luxury were legitimized. Right-wing and conservative parties nowadays still use this argument to justify their fiscal policies. Indeed, this argument is interesting insofar as it does not set consumption against growth. Supporters of the so-called industrious revolution also look favourably at luxury, not to mention recent approaches in global history[52] also featuring the particular significance of luxury consumption in Europe and Asia.[53] In this view, luxury was a powerful engine for accumulation and growth, rather than an obstacle to it. Once this point had been made for Western Europe,[54] then historical dynamics in other areas (Eastern Europe, China, Ottoman Empire, etc.) were reassessed as well.[55]

At the same time, these comparisons raise the major problem of the relative homogeneity of 'luxury' in different contexts and society. It is unfortunate that

---

[48] John Brewer and Roger Porter, eds, *Consumption and the World of Goods* (London: Routledge, 1993).
[49] William Reddy, 'The Structure of a Cultural Crisis: Thinking about Cloth in France before and after the Revolution', in *The Social Life of Things: Commodities in Cultural Perspective*, edited by Arjun Appadurai (New York: Cambridge University Press, 1986): 261–84.
[50] Thorstein Veblen, *The Theory of Leisure Class* (New York: Penguin, 1994; orig. 1899).
[51] Ferdinando Galiani, *Dialogues sur le commerce des blés* (Paris: Fayard, 1984; orig. 1770); Richard Cantillon, *Essai sur la nature du commerce en général* (Paris: INED, 1952; orig. 1755).
[52] Pomeranz, *The Great Divergence*.
[53] Roy Bin Wong, *China Transformed* (Ithaca: Cornel University Press, 1997).
[54] Maxine Berg and E. Eger, eds, *Luxury in the Eighteenth Century: Debates, Desires and Delectable Goods* (Basingstoke: Macmillan, 2003).
[55] B. S. Grewe and Karin Hofmeester, eds, *Luxury in Global Perspective: Commodities and Practices* (Oxford: Berg, 2010).

historians have often tried to follow sociologists in providing an ahistorical definition of luxury, since the distinctions between luxury, costly, ordinary, semi-luxury and cheap products change in different places and times. Thus, eighteenth- and nineteenth-century France provided different definitions of luxury, in turn quite different from those in vogue, say, in late Tsarist Russia, which were again quite different from those adopted in the USSR.[56]

Such differences exert a great influence on people's attitudes to luxury and income inequalities and ultimately on public policy. Analogous phenomena, such as the emergence of *nouveau riche* classes, increasing inequality and the distribution of luxury were not looked at in the same way in China and Russia during transforming periods, such as at the end of the nineteenth century or in the last twenty years.[57] Luxury and inequalities have provoked much more social tension in Russia than in China. Some have linked these different attitudes to the structure of the peasant commune, the relationship between peasants, nobles and state (in the nineteenth century),[58] or, nowadays, to post-communist social relations. Indeed, attitudes to luxury seem to be related also to the interplay between goods and their social meanings. Anthropologists have made interesting efforts in this direction; for example, more than twenty-five years ago, Appadurai suggested a definition of luxury in terms of five main features: restriction to elites, by price and/or by law; complexity of acquisition as distinct from scarcity; capacity to signal social messages; special knowledge required in consumption; close link to body, personality.[59] Can we empirically test these features?

Let us consider the first feature of luxury, as products restricted to elites, either by price or by law. Historians usually associate the former with capitalism and the latter with *ancien régime* societies. Indeed, some goods were certainly restricted to elites. However, this legal restriction involved not only luxury items, but most products, such as meat or clothes. In all these cases, legal determinants of product quality and hierarchy were supposed to reflect the social order. However, legal boundaries were easily overcome by social practice. This does not mean that institutions did not count, but only that they did not determine the whole social dynamics and that the market and exchange were equally important in pre-industrial societies. For example, if I take the case of meat, it is quite interesting that different historians of pre-industrial Europe have regarded it either as a luxury or a basic good.[60] Indeed, both interpretations are correct, insofar as the eighteenth-century French market for meat was separated into different markets, each of which was supposed to handle different qualities of meat. Social hierarchies were translated into clearly distinguished markets: a market for the

---

[56] Koleen Guy, *When Champagne Became French. Wine and the Making of National Identity* (Baltimore: John Hopkins University Press, 2003).
[57] Theda Skocpol, *States and Social Revolutions: A Comparative Analysis of France, Russia, and China* (Cambridge: Cambridge University Press, 1979).
[58] Among the forces which are said to influence attitudes to increasing inequalities: the structure of peasant commune, the relationship between peasants, nobles and state (in the nineteenth century) or, nowadays, post-communist social relations. Barrington Moore Jr, *The Social Origins of Dictatorship and Democracy* (Boston: Beacon Press, 1966).
[59] Appadurai, *The Social Life of Things*.
[60] Montanari, *La fame*.

elites and another for the people, a market for Paris, a second one for its outskirts and a third for the countryside. Different prices in each of these markets, and between them, were supposed to reflect product characteristics and, according to the doctrine of fair price, social order as well.[61] However, these boundaries were constantly transgressed, with low qualities being sold in the 'highest' market, and vice versa. This took place because markets and social dynamics were important in pre-industrial Europe and the correspondence between social hierarchies and qualities of food was continuously put to the test and eventually contested in social practices well before criticism from the Enlightenment and liberal philosophers. I may summarize this interaction between institutions and social practices by arguing (like Kopytoff)[62] that if classifications of things reflect the underlying social order, at the same time (unlike Durkheim's and Mauss's argument,[63] later refreshed by Mary Douglas)[64] the use of things and the circulation of commodities continuously contribute to reshaping the classification of things and the social order as well. If this is so, then what did the nineteenth century change in this story?

The usual answer is that luxury acquires a new meaning under capitalism: it expresses high prices of products sold to rich people. As such, luxury expresses a market convergence between high cost and quality items and people willing to spend on them. In this view, luxury under industrial and mature capitalism has nothing to do with legal boundaries as in early modern societies. Is that true? First, even in contemporary Europe, luxury has a legal definition: these are products for 'reserved markets', i.e. products that cannot be bought in supermarkets and ordinary retail shops.[65] The best perfumes are in *parfumeries* and not to be found in the supermarket; *haute couture* cannot be sold in ordinary *pret-à-porter* shops even if boutiques would like this. In short, for some products, legal distinctions and completely separate chains for luxury items are nowadays compulsory and more strictly enforced than they were in pre-industrial Europe. Contrary to common belief, luxury as a normative category is paradoxically more stringent nowadays than it was in the eighteenth century.[66]

Second, market development has not erased the connection between social order and hierarchies of goods. This coexistence of institutional, social and economic mechanisms gave rise to a perfectly coherent system in which each quality of meat related to the others. As Marvin Harris remarked several years ago, the best sirloin and

---

[61] Sidney Watts, *Meat Matters: Butchers, Politics, and Market Culture in Eighteenth-Century Paris* (New York: University of Rochester Press, 2006).
[62] Igor Kopytoff, 'The Cultural Biography of Things: Commoditization as Process', in Appadurai, *The Social Life*: 64–94.
[63] Émile Durkheim and Marcel Mauss, 'De quelques formes primitives de classification. Contribution à l'étude des représentations collectives', *L'année sociologique* 6 (1903), reprint in Marcel Mauss, *Essais de sociologie* (Paris: PUF, 1968), 162–230.
[64] Mary Douglas and Baron Isherwood, *The World of Goods: Toward an Anthropology of Consumption* (New York: Basic Books, 1979).
[65] Alain Bertrand, *Le droit des marques, des signes distinctifs et des noms de domaine* (Paris: Cedat, 2002).
[66] Alessandro Stanziani, ed., *Dictionnaire historique de l'économie-droit. XVIIIe–XXe siècles* (Paris: LGDJ, 2007).

luxury cuts can exist only if a wider public eats hamburger.[67] Their coexistence leads to the best exploitation of the animal's body. Exactly as it did the *ancien régime,* the market nowadays provides a close connection between social and product hierarchies whose stability is ensured by both market and legal rules.

At the same time, we must avoid confusing high-priced goods, luxury items (which are more than expensive: they circulate under special rules) and peculiar priceless products – the so-called singular goods. A Picasso painting or a Ferrari is not a luxury like spices were in pre-industrial times and expensive items are nowadays. Their price is so high, their characteristics are so peculiar that they enter another category: they are not only expensive because they are scarce or costly to produce; they are produced in extremely limited number, even if they are not unique. Thus, unlike luxury items, price is not even a relevant variable for singular goods.[68] These goods are outside the ordinary market mechanism and are better understood in the context of a gift economy. They enter the logic of reciprocity, selfishness and reputation, not that of market exchange. History is full of examples of gifts of singular goods. Chinese porcelain for French kings, French wine for Japanese emperors and Renoir's paintings for Rockefeller are quite common stories.[69]

However, distinction does not mean opposition. The fact that these items comply with a different logic than that of the common market does not mean that they are separated from the market as such. This is so because singular, unique goods and the gift economy in general express a peculiar form of reciprocity. Scholars (following Claude Lévi-Strauss) have too often contrasted gift and market, following a doubtful interpretation of Marcel Mauss. However, if one accepts Carlo Ginzburg's and others' (Marshall Sahlins[70]) interpretation of Mauss, then gift is not the opposite of market but is rather a peculiar form of exchange, in which obligations are even more compelling than under market exchange. This interpretation fits perfectly the logic of the unique extra luxury items we are dealing with.[71]

The implications for our analysis are considerable: if gift and market exchanges are not opposite but complementary worlds, then the so-called singular goods, on the one hand, and luxury, expensive and ordinary products, on the other, also constitute gradations of the same world. This is true not only in static, synchronous worlds but also in time: gift economy, luxury linked to status, laws, and institutions and luxury as an expression of price and market dynamics are variants of the same market economy. *Ancien régime* and the bourgeois world cannot be simply contrasted in a clear-cut and simplistic distinction between unproductive luxury and productive consumption as liberal philosophers and economists have asserted since the eighteenth century. A kind of 'economy of distinction' was at work; accurately

---

[67] Marvin Harris, *Good to Eat: Riddles of Food and Culture* (New York: Simon & Schuster, 1958).
[68] Lucien Karpik, *Valuing the Unique: The Economics of Singularities* (Princeton: Princeton University Press, 2010).
[69] Geoffrey Gunn, *First Globalization: The Eurasian Exchange 1500–1800* (Lanham: Rowman & Littlefield, 2003); Timothy Brook, *Vermeer's Hat: The Seventeenth Century and the Dawn of the Global World* (London: Profile Books, 2009).
[70] Marshall Sahlins, *Stone Age Economics* (Chicago and New York: Aldine Atherton, 1972).
[71] Carlo Ginzburg, 'Don et reconnaissance. Lecture de Mauss', *Annales, HSS* 6 (2010): 1303–20.

identified wines were associated with different prices. Distinction and links between markets and products were perfectly integrated with each other. If this is so, then, after examining the notion of 'luxury', we must turn to its complement, that is, mass production.

Standardization and mass consumption

Over decades, product standardization has been associated with increasing quantities, cheap products and even safe food.[72] This was particularly so between the early twentieth century and the 1970s, when standardized meat, milk and eggs were considered safe and, as such, opposed to unreliable products bought at the *open* market or the corner shop.[73] Recently, this attitude has been reversed (at least in Western countries), and supermarket standardized products are increasingly associated with low quality, if not considered harmful. Anti-global orientations identify in food standardization and food industrialization two of the main evils of the global era. In order to discuss food standardization, we are thus required to separate the issues related to the political economy of standardization from its factual contours. Questions on food industrialization and standardization appeared during the second half of the nineteenth century, when industry, with the help of chemistry, began penetrating the agro-food business. In this context, the 'normalization', that is 'stabilization', of food items was strongly supported by intermediaries and wholesale merchants who argued that 'the consumer wanted stable products'. This argument perfectly fitted their interests, insofar as wholesale traders blended different milk, wines and so on to obtain stable products. The more 'stable' and normalized the products, the greater their power. Unsurprisingly, wine-makers, cattle breeders and agrarian producers in general opposed this tendency. Opposition to merchant power became opposition to standardized products.[74] *Unstable* products soon became a guarantee of a 'natural' product, although ensuing decades would prove that this argument worked much better for wines than for milk and butter.

In the nineteenth-century debate on food normalization, forces other than producers and traders intervened, such as hygienists, consumers and public authorities. Most of these associated unstable products with fraud: adulterated wines, milk and butter were suspiciously regarded and often considered as proof of fraud. Hygienists ultimately adopted quite ambiguous attitudes, whereby on the one hand they criticized standardized food, while on the other hand they attacked unstable products. In the scientific debate a trade-off emerged: either instability with a higher sanitary risk or standardization with a lower risk.[75] The case of French cheeses perfectly reflects this trade-off.

---

[72] Alexander Nutzenadel and Frank Trentmann, eds, *Food and Globalization* (Oxford: Berg, 2008).
[73] Gilles Allaire and Robert Boyer, *La grande transformation de l'agriculture* (Paris: Inra, 1995).
[74] Stanziani, *Histoire de la qualité*.
[75] AN F 12 6872, 6873, 7417.

Throughout the twentieth century, therefore, the political economy of food standardization has led to the adoption and implementation of hundreds of rules, not only in France but in most Western countries and in the EU, aiming at identifying major products' characteristics. These lists are never complete and are continuously updated according to new techniques and the way these are adopted (or not) by main business associations.[76] This means that the institutional architecture of standardization seeks to provide consensual lists of the main features of each product. This is so because, in the real production of goods, standardization is far from being a universal and finished process. In some industries, such as that of wine, standardization has taken the form of normalization and stabilization through blending and intervention in the productive process in order to provide, year after year, wines with a similar taste and characteristics. Pasta offers a different outcome, in that the increasing mechanization launched at the beginning of the twentieth century appeals to standardization and mass production. However, these have encouraged an increasing differentiation of both the form of the product (long, wide, thin, curled, orecchiette, etc.) and its composition (different blends of wheat). Even at the height of mass production (between the 1950s and the 1970s), pasta produced in, say, northern or southern Italy, the USA or France barely shared the same technique of production or the same mix of flour. From the 1970s on, local producers in southern Italy in particular have even claimed a positive comeback on the market.[77]

In sum, normalization and standardization in the agro-food business are always partial: they involve some characteristics and techniques for each product, not all. There are not standardized products on the one hand and unique products on the other hand, but always a mix of standard and non-standard features. The impact of this process on price and social hierarchies depends on technical characteristics, social hierarchies of the industry concerned and the period under examination. From the nineteenth century onwards, the 'normalization' of agro-food has been a powerful tool in the hands of merchants against producers and, in part, retailers. Merchants have pushed product standardization in order to seize control of the industry concerned.[78]

The impact on final consumption has to be qualified: normalization has usually lowered prices and enlarged access to the product. Yet other forces have mitigated this outcome; first of all, the definition of the product itself has changed with standardization. Product differentiation and a huge difference between normalized and non-standardized products have increased over the twentieth century. This means that lower income groups have had access not to a generic product, say, milk or meat in general, but to a peculiar version of it, highly differentiated from top level wines or 'milk from the cow'. In this way, short-term advantages of food standardization have proved to be compensated by long-term negative effects in terms of health (cholesterol, or new cardiovascular diseases).[79] According to the available data, in

---

[76] Pierre-Marie Vincent, *Le droit de l'alimentation* (Paris: PUF, 1996).
[77] Silvano Serventi and François Sabban, *Les pâtes* (Arles: Actes Sud, 2001).
[78] Stanziani, *Histoire*.
[79] Tim Lang and Michael Heasman, *Food Wars: The Global Battle for Mouths, Minds, and Markets* (London: Earthscan, 2004).

post-industrial societies, this health trend mostly affects lower income groups. Finally, recent diffusion of standard features for top quality wines all around the world as shown in 'Mondovino' perfectly illustrates this tendency. Some techniques and inputs of production are transplanted into different areas and provided to specific producers. As such, uniform products and techniques are no more synonymous with low quality and mass-produced goods, but include high quality products as well.

For sure, there is a link between globalization and product standardization. The same clothes, toys and pizzas are produced and sold all over the world, and this trend has recently affected products such as wine, too.[80] Fears of a single world dominated by a few magnates and subjected to easy speculative attacks and decreasing biodiversity are major concerns. Yet one may question the extent of this process and its mechanisms. As we have seen, on the supply side, two major trends coexist in food markets over the long run: on the one hand, standardization enters the agro-food sector, in connection with the internationalization of markets; on the other hand, local and non-standardized products win increasing shares of markets, in particular in the most advanced countries.[81] As such, standardization in itself is not the main issue of the global era. The new consideration is the relationship between standardization and local societies. Appadurai and others have stressed that the invention of tradition in marketing strategies is a central corollary of globalization.[82] The more the world is global, the more traditions and localism are called into play in agro-food marketing. Indeed, this link has a long history. It was already present in the periods evoked above. For example, at the end of the nineteenth century, growing internationalization of the economy went hand in hand with the invention of tradition in agro-food and in general politics.[83] What is new today is the fact that this is happening not only in Europe and the USA but also in Latin America, Africa, Australia and some parts of Asia, and that these parts of the world are active actors in globalization. Indian, Brazilian and Chinese producers are able to compete with Western firms. Aggressive economic strategies and protectionism in the name of public health are no longer an exclusivity of the West. For example, Japanese producers, politicians and consumers (at least some of them), with the help of scientific argument, point out that obesity in Japan is linked to the new consumption of Western food.[84] Even if well founded, this argument cannot mask the increasing consumption of Japanese food per capita, its impact on body weight and the strong interest of Japanese lobbies in preserving the domestic market. As in the West, institutions, and schools in particular, are called on to intervene in this process and provide 'good' food education.

---

[80] Kym Anderson, *The Worlds Wine Market: Globalization at Work* (Aldershot: Ashgate, 2005).
[81] Food and Agriculture Organization (FAO), *The State of Agricultural Commodity Markets 2004* (Rome: FAO Press, 2004).
[82] Arjun Appadurai, *Modernity at Large: Cultural Dimensions of Globalization* (Indianapolis: University of Minnesota Press, 1996).
[83] Guy, *Champagne*.
[84] Yumi Matsushita, Nobuo Yoshiike, Fumi Kaneda, Katsushi Yoshita and Hidemi Takimoto, 'Trends in Childhood Obesity in Japan during Last 25 Years from the National Nutrition Survey', *Obesity Research* 12 (2004): 205–14.

Similar trends are occurring in Brazil and China. Local and national food is considered as the best adapted to local tastes and, thus, to public health.[85] Yet this tendency is not completely new. As we have seen, from the seventeenth century on, the increasing supply of food and agricultural produce was a feature not only of Western Europe but also beyond. The agrarian revolution has to be incorporated into a long-term evolution. Increasing demand and major market development outside and prior to industrial capitalism have played a major role in world history since the modern era.[86] As such, multi-polar globalization is not entirely new. Multi-centrism is particularly clear in food history, in which, for several centuries, supply and consumption have been local and global at the same time. Western anti-global actors and scholars give too much importance to the West and deliberately ignore the increasing power of other parts of the world, past and present.

Indeed, one may wonder whether the standardization of tastes really follows that of products. Colin Campbell and Arjun Appadurai have already criticized the excessive stress historians such as Brewer and Porter have placed on the imitation effect.[87] Not only is this effect overestimated and barely proven – except for the elites – it also ignores the persistent strength of habits and repetition in consumption in general and food in particular. This phenomenon is not new; all the histories of travellers in modern times taken up by Braudel and many others show the importance of local food habits, even in a transnational context. Nowadays, pizza and Chinese food are to be found all over the world. At the same time, they vary profoundly from one country to another according to the origins of emigrants and the way they identify local preferences.[88] One may complain about this, but the fact is that fusion, rather than standardized food, is the dominant trend in kitchens and recipes around the world.[89] Historical and anthropological studies on pizza, Chinese or Indian food confirm this phenomenon.[90] Resistances to exotic food are strong and they are overcome with the help of institutions, local communities, diasporas and, last but not least, trade policies (free entry or not of Chinese food, for example). Neither the West nor China is completely globalizing the world; interaction between cultures is more responsible for this than the standardization of taste.

An analogous conclusion can be drawn for the link between globalization and scarcity. We have seen that quantity–quality problems have been linked over the long run and that one cannot speak of a passage from quantity to quality in accordance with the modernization paradigm. As I have shown, globalization and speculation

---

[85] Xingang Zhang, Zhaoqing Sun, Xinzhong Zhang, Liqiang Zheng, Shuangshuang Liu, Changlu Xu, Jiajin Li, Fenfen Zhao, Jue Li, Dayi Hu, et al., 'Prevalence and Associated Factors of Overweight and Obesity in a Chinese Rural Population', *Obesity Research* 16 (2007): 168–71; C. A. Monteiro, M. H. Benicio, W. L. Conde and B. M. Popkin, 'Shifting Obesity Trends in Brazil', *European Journal of Clinical Nutrition* 54, no. 4 (2000): 342–6.

[86] Bayly, *The Birth*; Appadurai, *Modernity*.

[87] Colin Campbell, *The Romantic Ethic and the Spirit of Modern Consumerism* (Oxford: Blackwell, 1987).

[88] Alberto Capatti, *Le goût nouveau, origine de la modernité alimentaire* (Paris: Albin Michel, 1989).

[89] Jean-Loup Amselle, *L'Occident décroché. Enquête sur le post-colonialisme* (Paris: Pluriel, 2010).

[90] Sylvie Sanchez, *Pizza Connexion* (Paris: CNRS éditions, 2007).

in foodstuffs are not limited to the present. From this standpoint, the rise of virtual markets at the end of the nineteenth century marked a break in history for it provoked a major, persistent divergence between increasing production of food in some areas and its scarcity in many other parts of the globe. Virtual products were an invention of the turn of the nineteenth century. Nowadays speculation in raw materials and foodstuffs is not new by virtue of the speculative mechanism itself, but with regard to its size and the actors involved. Global speculation is not only a fact of Western actors but also of major firms and traders in China, Brazil and Russia. The 'West' can protest against these attitudes but it can hardly condemn them, not only because Western speculators are involved but also because EU agricultural policies encourage protectionism and speculation and contribute to increasing inequalities in food access.[91]

Conclusion: Part 3

The emergence of the notion of worker, before and beyond that of proletarian, was not particularly related to that of class, at least not as Marx conceived it. Instead, it emerged in a mutual, slow process of correspondence and rejection at the same time as other categories: slave, artisan and peasant. Most labouring people in eighteenth- and the first half of nineteenth-century Britain (and even more in France and other European countries) only temporarily sold their labour force on the urban market: they were seasonally peasants, seamen, tradesmen and some craftsmen. These identifications and self-identifications were temporary and referred to each other. Thus, the identification of the slave and that of the free worker went hand in hand, to the point that the legal qualification of slaves in the Americas involved a definition of what a 'free man' was in the American colonies (in turn different from Britain).[92] The definition of worker evolved before (there were servants), during and after the abolition of slavery. 'We are not slaves' was a slogan that meant different things at these different stages: servants vis-à-vis slaves were different from wage earners and employees vis-à-vis former slaves. Solidarity with the slaves was one possibility, but not the only one among British workers. And this ambivalent attitude was all the more widespread because many workers went back to their countryside homes for their main agricultural activities. They did not want to be slaves, but did not want to be proletarians either.

'Classes' consolidated only after the 1870s, at least in the 'West': the second Industrial Revolution brought with it the end of pluri-activity and many peasants turned into proletarians. But, contrary to Marx's prediction, this shift took place when labour was more protected (with the welfare state) not less. The 'real' proletarians, as a class and as a labour activity emerged when, thanks to the welfare state, their well-being began to improve well above subsistence level. This transformation of the workers and their consciousness also radicalized their contrast with other labouring groups; peasants, confronted with the great transformation, strengthened their 'rural

---

[91] Stanziani, *Capital terre*.
[92] Steinfeld, *The Invention of Free Labor*.

consciousness'. Fascism, Nazism and to some extent communism emerged in the twentieth century precisely as a reaction of rural classes confronted with the second Industrial Revolution. Peasants were not protected by the new welfare state. And the same was true for the former slaves in the colonies: they were excluded from the welfare state in the homeland. Workers and their unions nationalized welfare. In the twentieth century, class consciousness among the workers was national, not international, and even hostile to national peasants and migrants from the colonies. Not by accident, the emergence of the category of 'consumer' also took place in the twentieth century, when the working class benefited from increasing incomes. From this standpoint, the presumed 'bourgeois' attitudes of the working class, so often associated with the last quarter of the twentieth century, were actually co-substantial with the rise of the welfare state. Whereas, in the nineteenth century, class consciousness among peasant workers was mostly a utopia among some intellectuals and political leaders, in the twentieth century it turned into the hostility of some working people and their unions towards peasants and colonial immigrants. The fight against capitalists was real, but it could not be separated from these other issues. These ambiguities still pervade the positions workers and unions in advanced countries take up on the political chessboard. Class consciousness needs to be really global or it cannot exist at all, as capital, not labour, perfectly proves today.

With this issue in mind, we can now move to the last section of our journey: after disclosing the intellectual and social origins of historical artefacts, archives, data and social identities, what can we perhaps salvage from the main theories of social dynamics?

Part Four

The quest of universality: values, theories and the European model

So far, we have discussed the artefacts of social history (archives and data) and the historical construction and evolution of the main social categories. It is starting from this standpoint that we look with fresh eyes at some theories of social historical dynamics. If so-called empirical observation and its main presuppositions are socially and historically situated, then how were social theories also fully integrated into the history of societies?

8

Societies and their evolution: from the Enlightenments to Marxisms

In previous chapters, we have discussed the various attitudes Enlightenment authors adopted vis-à-vis archives, statistics and social classifications. Archives entered the debate between erudition and antiquarianism on the one hand and philosophical history on the other hand. Despite their overall scepticism about archives, many eighteenth-century authors made use of figures, in particular when discussing topics such as slavery and its efficiency or agriculture and productivity. In turn, these orientations were grounded on new notions of social groups, estate and classes. We need now to understand how all these components entered broader considerations of history and social dynamics. In their multiple approaches, Enlightenment authors advanced multiples notions of 'history' and of 'community', but both were identified at the crossroads of multiple worlds, not just France, Scotland or Prussia.[1] Reflection on history, its methods and its relationship to philosophy, religion, law and the social sciences took place not only in Enlightenment Europe, but in other areas, particularly Asia. In every instance, these reflections were a response to structural transformations in states, societies and economies and the growing importance of trade, consumption and protoindustrial activity. 'Enlightenment' thinking developed in response to these global dynamics: encounters with other worlds no longer fuelled the exoticism and wonderment of previous centuries, but instead raised questions about which values, economic systems and types of warfare could dominate and whether or not this new order of priorities was acceptable.[2] Were the main social actors as identified in philosophical histories of the eighteenth century a mere expression of Europe?

---

[1] Antoine Lilti, *L'héritage des Lumières* (Paris: Seuil, EHESS, 2019); J. G. A. Pocock, *Barbarism and Religion*, 5 vols (Cambridge: Cambridge University Press, 1999–2011); Karen O'Brien, *Narratives of Enlightenment: Cosmopolitan History from Voltaire to Gibbon* (Cambridge: Cambridge University Press, 1997); Guido Abbattista, 'The Historical Thought of the French Philosophes', in the *Oxford History of Historical Writing*, edited by Daniel Woolf, 5 vols (Oxford: Oxford University Press, 2011–5), vol. 3, 401–27; Hugh Trevor-Roper, *History and the Enlightenment* (New Haven: Yale University Press 2010); Jonathan Israel, *Enlightenment Contested: Philosophy, Modernity, and the Emancipation of Man, 1670–1752* (Oxford: Oxford University Press, 2008); Sebastian Conrad, 'Enlightenment in Global History: A Historiographical Critique', *American Historical Review* 117, no. 4 (October 2012): 999–1027.

[2] Kontler László, Antonella Romano, Silvia Sebastiani and Borbala Szuszanna Török, eds, *Negotiating Knowledge in Early Modern Empires: A Decentered View* (New York: Palgrave Macmillan, 2014).

Nowadays the dominant view among historians considers Enlightenment as an intellectual movement that radiated outwards from its source in Europe. Some present it as a source of progress, others a source of dependence and exploitation of the 'subaltern'.[3] And yet, the Enlightenment was not just a French, but a European[4] – if not global – phenomenon.[5]

Instead, European thought changed precisely in response to contacts with other worlds, whether appreciating or criticizing them.[6] Transformations occurred not just in Europe, but all across the continents.[7] Thus, although a number of *philosophes* were caught up in the widespread fascination with China and its civilization, Voltaire rejected any connection between these ideas in his *Essai sur les moeurs,* on the grounds that Chinese philosophers were disciples of 'natural religion'.[8] Although he criticized certain aspects of Chinese society, he also wrote a partly erroneous defence of China's examination-based social hierarchy compared with the French social hierarchy based on rank.

It is important to note that these positions did not necessarily imply a belief in Western superiority: some believed in it (Voltaire and Cornelius de Pauw) but others did not even take a position on this point (Guillaume Raynal in the first editions of the *l'Histoire philosophique et politique des établissements et du commerce des Européens dans les deux Indes* [*Philosophical and Political History of the Two Indies*]). A third group, including thinkers such as Diderot and Rousseau, argued that non-European areas could in fact be superior to a corrupt Europe.[9]

As most Enlightenment authors were intent on writing universal histories, the issue of source reliability was especially crucial.[10] The travel literature and first-hand accounts of missionaries were well known; these works were found in the personal libraries of Voltaire, Raynal, Diderot and Turgot.[11] Abbé Prevost was one of the first to question the trustworthiness of these narratives.[12] In his view, the boundary line between history and fiction was blurred because they depended on the same sources. Rousseau adopted a similar approach in the notes to his *Second discours*, insisting

---

[3] Gayatri Chakravorty Spivak, *A Critique of Postcolonial Reason: Toward a History of the Vanishing Present* (Cambridge, MA: Harvard University Press, 1999).
[4] Franco Venturi, *Settecento riformatore*, 5 vols (Turin: Einaudi, 1966–90); Israel, *Enlightenment Contested*; Silvia Sebastiani, *The Scottish Enlightenment* (London: Palgrave Macmillan, 2013).
[5] Pocock, *Barbarism and Religion*; *Multiple Modernities*, Special Issue, *Daedalus* 129, no. 1 (2000).
[6] Sankar Muthu, *Enlightenment against Empire* (Princeton: Princeton University Press, 2003); Jennifer Pitts, *A Turn to Empire: The Rise of Imperial Liberalism in Britain and France* (Princeton: Princeton University Press, 2006).
[7] Armitage and Subrahmanyam, *The Age of Revolutions in Global Context*; Felicity Nussbaum, ed., *The Global Eighteenth Century* (Baltimore: Johns Hopkins University Press, 2003).
[8] Voltaire, François-Marie and Arouet, *Essai sur les mœurs et l'esprit des nations* (Paris: Lefèvre, 1756).
[9] Guillaume-Thomas Raynal, *Histoire philosophique et politique des établissements et du commerce des Européens dans les deux Indes*, 2nd ed. (Genève: Pellet, 1780).
[10] Michèle Duchet, *Anthropologie et histoire au siècle des Lumières* (Paris: Albin Michel, 1971).
[11] Guillaume-Thomas Raynal, *Histoire philosophique et politique des établissements et du commerce des Européens dans les deux Indes* (La Haye: Gosse fils, 1774).
[12] Antoine-François Prevost, *Histoire générale des voyages ou nouvelle collection de toutes les relations de voyage par mer et par terre qui ont été publiées jusqu'à présent dans les différentes langues*, 15 vols (Paris: Didot, 1746–59), in particular vol. 14.

that although 'for three or four hundred years, the inhabitants of Europe have been flooding across the rest of the globe and constantly publishing new accounts of travels and encounters, I am convinced that the only men we know are Europeans'.[13]

This scepticism towards travel literature was common among *philosophes*; some distinguished the writings of genuine travellers from the second-hand accounts; others criticized Western prejudices, e.g. those of the Spanish compared with those of British, etc.[14] They therefore found a solution not in history – like the erudite authors they criticized – but in philosophy. According to many of them, the reliability of sources could not be guaranteed, and therefore only philosophical precepts could orient knowledge. From this standpoint, it was not even necessary to know languages and local cultures.[15] David Hume, for example, challenged the authenticity of the Ossian fragments and oral traditions, which he dismissed as myths. Gibbon adopted a similar approach in writing his general work on the decline of the Roman Empire.[16]

On the opposite side, Rousseau defended the value of 'uncontaminated' oral sources; Adam Ferguson[17] and Giambattista Vico[18] viewed such traditions as a way of learning about what was 'different' without relying on the accounts of European observers. These 'young' and 'savage' civilizations 'could show the way' to Europe, which was 'corrupted' (in the sense of 'degraded').

In sum, the age of Enlightenment by no means formed a homogeneous whole; Eurocentric attitudes increased compared to previous periods, but their content and scope varied widely according to the author, time and place. In this context, the study of society was at once a philosophical and anthropological exercise. The meaning of society was to be found in general philosophical principle, not empirical observation. This approach engendered two main heritages: insisting on the knowledge of the 'other' the better to civilize it, and an attitude close to anthropology and the preservation of local 'specificities'. The former attitude was normative, the second was descriptive and invited one to imagine the multiple options accessible to humans.

These ambiguities in the relationships between history, philosophy and society were particularly clear in the ways Enlightenment authors identified the social classes and sought in particular to distinguish slaves from 'free men'. A shared way of thinking developed around the status of labour: a group of authors of differing backgrounds looked into slavery in the colonies, serfdom in Russia and guild labour in France in order to prove a 'natural right' to freedom and, for some, the unprofitability of unfree forms of labour.[19] Historical narrative became an increasingly common form of justification for these analogies. According to Montesquieu and several others, in France, serfdom to the land belonged to the past. Likewise, the slave in the colonies

---

[13] Jean-Jacques Rousseau, *Oeuvres politiques*, vol. 3 (Paris: Éditions de la Pleiade, 1967): 212.
[14] Cornelius de Pauw, *Recherches philosophiques sur les Américains*, 2 vols (Berlin: Decker, 1768–9).
[15] Duchet, *Anthropologie*.
[16] Edward Gibbon, *The Decline and Fall of the Roman Empire* (London: Strahan and Cadell, 1776).
[17] Adam Ferguson, *An Essay on the History of Civil Society* (Edinburgh, 1767).
[18] Giovambattista Vico, *La scienza nuova* (Napoli, 1725).
[19] Steven L. Kaplan, *La fin des corporations* (Paris: Fayard, 2001); Gilbert Faccarello and Philippe Steiner, *La pensée économique pendant la révolution française* (Grenoble: Presses universitaires de Grenoble, 1990).

and the Russian serf would soon become vestiges of the past, though at that time they remained justified by the backwardness of the colonies and Russia.[20]

It was only in the 1780s that some French philosophers changed their minds and celebrated revolutionary 'changes from below' rather than enlightenment from above. From the 1780s on, Diderot and Condillac associated their scepticism about enlightened despotism[21] with a more general criticism of European civilization. Concomitantly, another development became apparent: the priority given to economic over political and ethical considerations, previously held only by a few physiocrats, became widespread. From that point on, more and more economists and *philosophes* accorded a cognitive and normative priority to pure economic calculation; however, this association came quite late and was not representative of eighteenth-century economic and philosophical thought. In contradiction to the retrospective image created from the nineteenth century on, almost all of these authors, aside from a few physiocrats, still linked economics and ethics.[22] This link will increasingly vanish during the nineteenth century.

Marx's social actors in global context

We have already reminded how Marx and his followers identified the main social actors and the use and misuse they made of archives (very little) and data. It is now time to understand how and whether these artefacts of history entered the overall interpretations of social dynamics. Said, and after him Chakrabarty, did not intend to replace Marx with another thinker but to show the gap between him, his derivative in India and Indian realities. Both criticized Marx's Eurocentrism and Orientalism. I would suggest a different approach: I will not embark in a kind of short history of Marxism, not even of its multiple conceptions of history. Instead of asking whether Marx is appropriate to understand a non-Western reality, I will consider two points: how Marx identified the social actors and how his theory interacted with non-European realities. Usual postmodernist and subaltern interpretations of Marx insist presume that Marxist theory was valid for Europe, not elsewhere. However, we have shown in Chapter 6 that peasants or proletarians as Marx identified them actually did not exist in Europe. Peasant workers were the most widespread social category in Europe until the end of the nineteenth century, if not the mid-twentieth century in some areas. As such, proletarians were rare even in Europe. Marx's social imagination, already pronounced for Europe, was even less adapted to catch non-European realities.

The 'cases' of India and Russia obliged Marx to confront realities different from Germany or Britain; as we will see, he had to decide whether his theory of historical development was universally acceptable. At the same time, these confrontations with

---

[20] A. R. J. Turgot, *Oeuvres et documents le concernant*, 5 vols, edited by Gustave Schelle (Paris: Félix Alcan, 1913–23), vol. 2: 375.
[21] Duchet, *Anthropologie et histoire*: 134 f.
[22] Perrot, *Histoire intellectuelle de l'économie politique*.

the 'others' differed in two main ways: first, Russia was not properly 'European' or a form of Asiatic despotism; placed between Asia and Europe, Russia was difficult to put into a box, much more than idealized India. Second, Russian intellectuals directly interacted with Marx and contributed to shaping his views. Initially, in his letters on India published in the *Daily Tribune* in the early 1850s, Marx attacked British colonialism, but also acknowledged that it had brought about some improvements, for example, by introducing private property and the struggle against castes.[23] In all likelihood under the influence of Hegel, he viewed Indian townships and villages as the underlying reason for Indian immobilism.[24] Marx began to revise his opinion after the Sepoy rebellion in 1857–78. These troops formed the core of the EIC army in India, combining local military expertise with British techniques to further the company's gradual expansion in India. In 1857, however, the Meerut garrison rebelled against their commander's orders, and the revolt soon spread to most of British-controlled northern and central India. Public opinion and the press were shocked by the events, which they viewed as a sign of ingratitude for Britain's civilizing efforts and the resources it had contributed to India. Marx joined in the debate, declaring that, on the contrary, the revolt was the consequence of authoritarian British colonial policies and exploitation.[25] At the time, he was completing the *Grundrisse*; unlike his previous works, this new book argued that several different historical dynamics could conceivably bring about the transition from pre-capitalist systems to capitalism. He introduced the notion of an Asian system of production.[26] In this same perspective, in the so-called 'Economic Manuscript' (in fact, the first sketch of *Das Kapital* in 1861–3), Marx contradicted his former theses, concluding that the Indian township and village were not necessarily the sources of the country's immobilism.[27] He added that British rule had destroyed the Indian village without introducing capitalism.[28]

The Russian edition of *Das Kapital* confirmed the major issues involved in Marx's theory when faced with non-European areas. Like India, Russia too raised analytical problems for Marx; but even more than mid-century India, Russia produced local reactions and local followers of Marx. The interaction between Marx and Russian intellectuals strongly impacted both sides' visions of what constituted progress, development, history and universalism. In Russia, the opposition between Slavophiles and Westernizers in nineteenth-century Russia stemmed precisely from the issue that concerns us here: Eurocentrism in its epistemological and historical dimensions. In Russia, starting in the 1840s, first the Slavophiles and then the Westernizers such as Herzen saw the Russian peasant commune as a historical singularity that might allow the country to move directly into modernity without going through a capitalist phase

---

[23] Kevin Anderson, *Marx at the Margins: On Nationalism, Ethnicity, and Non-Western Societies* (Chicago: University of Chicago Press, 2010).
[24] Karl Marx and Friedrich Engels, *Collected Works*, 50 vols (New York: International Publishers, 1975–2004), vol. 12: 132, 217–18; vol. 39: 333–4.
[25] Marx and Engels, *Collected Works*, vol. 15: 297–305.
[26] Karl Marx, *Grundrisse*, translated by Martin Nicolaus (New York: Penguin, 1973).
[27] Marx and Engels, *Collected Works*, vol. 31: 236.
[28] Marx and Engels, *Collected Works*, vol. 34: 118–19.

of development.²⁹ The debate over the peasant commune was inseparable from the comparison between Russia and the West; this comparison became the keystone in the tensions between Slavophiles and Westernizers and later between populists and Marxists. The issue was precisely whether there was a global tendency at work in economies and societies or whether historical singularities could shape its direction. This debate was at once ideological (the role of the peasantry in the revolution), empirical (how to prove the arguments used) and methodological (how to make comparisons).³⁰ That is why this debate inevitably ended up being combined with the debate over method in the science of society. Unlike the more or less idealized Indians, the Russian case immediately appeared more problematic to Marx, for two main reasons: first, Russia was not properly 'Europe' but it was not 'Asiatic despotism' either. Where was it to be put? Second, the Russian intelligentsia directly interacted with Marx and contributed to shaping his thought; this was not the case in India.

In 1869, Mikhailovsky claimed that the evolution of humankind was not the result of necessity but of individual will. That is why the methods of the natural sciences cannot be applied to the science of society and, in general, progress is not expressed in the division of labour and specialization but, on the contrary, in non-differentiation and cooperation. Mikhailovsky criticized the division of labour and the market in order to attack the specialization of knowledge. 'Specialization prevents us from grasping the connections between the various aspects of a phenomenon.' Among the forms of social and economic organization, the peasant commune was best suited to comply with this principle.³¹

But how were these conclusions to be reconciled with the Marxist thought these authors associated themselves with? Could Marxist categories properly account for reality in Russia? From the early 1870s, Tkachev, Mikhailovsky and Vera Zasulich questioned Marx and Engels about the commune and the 'laws of development': was it possible to follow a different development path from the one in the West and thus achieve socialism without going through a capitalist stage?

In a letter to Vera Zasulich, Marx acknowledged that the peasant commune was the basis for social regeneration of Russia.³² In the same letter, Marx recalled that he had changed his mind about the impact of British colonialism on India; in the 1850s (*Grundrisse* [Critique of Political Economy]), he had maintained that the introduction of private land ownership was a considerable improvement. Now he concluded, on the contrary, that this measure had impoverished India.

Thus, by turning his focus towards Russia and Asia, Marx ultimately cast doubt on his previous conclusions and seemed to provide a less universal and deterministic

---

²⁹ Nikolai G. Chernyshevskii, 'Ob Obshchinnom vladenii' (On Community Ownership), 1858, reproduced in *Sochineniia*, Works, vol. 2 (Geneva: Elpidine, 1879).

³⁰ Alessandro Stanziani, *L'économie en révolution, le cas russe. 1870–1930* (Paris: Albin Michel, 1998).

³¹ Mikhail Mikhailovskii, 'Chto takoe progress' (What is Progress), 1869; 'Analogicheskii metod v obshchestvennoi nauke' (The Analogical Method in Social Science), 1869; 'Bor'ba za individual'nost'' (The Struggle for Individuality), in *Sochineniia*, vol. 1 (Saint Petersburg: Izdanie Russkoe Bogatstvo, 1909).

³² For the letters between Marx and the Russians: Theodor Shanin, ed., *Late Marx and the Russian Road, Marx and the 'peripheries of capitalism'* (New York: Monthly Review Press, 1983).

approach to history. Yet this evolution remained extremely cautious and part of a political and normative approach: revolution and the advent of socialism were Marx's main concerns. It is no accident that Engels always refused to take into consideration the French and the Russian editions of *Das Kapital* and referred to the German one in order to encourage further translations and 'preserve' Marx's thought.

Yet, the political philosophy of history in the USSR had the difficult task of integrating both the Bolshevik Revolution and Soviet imperialism in its new scheme. How could this possibly be justified? How could one reconcile theory with empirical investigation? This time it was not, as for Marx, the compatibility of India or Russia with his general theory, but that of revolutionary Russia with one 'Marxism' or another.

These debates had major political implications. The identification of a society's mode of production was essential: if it was classified as 'feudal', then it was legitimate to make alliances with local 'bourgeoisie'; on the contrary, if the concerned area was considered as 'capitalist', then its elite must be fought. In 1920, the Baku Congress of Peoples of the East expressed its hostility to the necessity of the colonial world passing through the capitalist stage. This guideline did not solve the problem of knowing whether, for example, Turkmenistan was in the feudal stage only, or in an early capitalist period, and whether an 'Asiatic mode of production' existed. Transformations in China also influenced this debate. Although the most pressing political question underlying this debate was the strategy to be pursued by the Chinese Communist Party in relation to the nationalist Kuomintang, its conclusions had potentially serious implications for the colonial world in general. If the Asiatic mode of production was accepted as 'Marxist', then places like China, Iran and Egypt could possibly be qualified as such. This meant that these economically stagnant countries were incapable of generating the economic surplus required to produce a bourgeoisie and therefore revolutionary change. However, during the 1920s, Stalin gradually characterized this theory as being close to Trotskyism and therefore the so-called *Aziatchiki* were politically and ideologically defeated and the theory removed from the Soviet Marxist canon.[33] Unlike Indian and other nationalisms in the interwar period, the dichotomy lay at the heart of Soviet Marxist analysis.[34]

Soviet-style universal history was therefore part of a discipline that sought to take all aspects of human beings into consideration, while subordinating 'culture' and the superstructure of economic dynamics. It was also a history that strove to reconcile socialism in a single country with the aim of 'showing the way' to the rest of humanity. In spite of its contradictions, this conception of history had considerable influence on Marxists all over the world. We now know that, despite the Cold War, East–West contacts were considerable and significant, not only through the Communist International but also via scholarly conferences.

This ferment spread to countries in the socialist block, such as Poland and Hungary, where economic history often enabled new interpretations, partly due to its legitimacy from a Marxist viewpoint, and partly due to the possibility of connecting with Western

---

[33] Dunn, *The Fall and Rise*; Fogel, 'The Debates over the Asiatic Mode of Production'.
[34] Michael Kemper, 'Red Orientalism: Mikhail Pavlovich and Marxist Oriental Studies in Early Soviet Russia', *Die Welt des Islams* 50 (2010): 435–76.

approaches pursuing a 'technical' approach – statistics and regressions – that attracted less censorship. Witold Kula in Poland and Györgi Ranki and Ivan Berend in Hungary produced works that would also influence their Western colleagues for a long time. The same was true of historians interested in social history (such as Bronislaw Geremek) and intellectual history (Andrzej Walicki), who were quickly translated, and later welcomed in France and the United States.

These multiple paths to capitalism and/or socialism animated debate in India, as seen in the chapter on peasant studies. In this context, Indian historians maintained a privileged dialogue with the (especially English-speaking) Western world, encouraged by the Indian intellectual diaspora in the United States and Britain. The references were Marx and E. P. Thompson, along with Gramsci. During the 1950s, Marxist historiography gave rise, especially in Brazil, to increased studies of economic dependence. The *coup d'état* of 1964 and repression were followed by both an increase in the number of universities in Brazil, and the rise of a US-educated Brazilian intellectual diaspora, which over time exerted growing influence within the United States. Argentina presents a history that is partly similar, with the rise and fall of Peronism, and then a new dictatorship beginning in 1966. In addition to the nationalist history that was under the control of censors, this period saw two primary influences: Marxism (and the influence of Maurice Dobb, Pierre Vilar and Witold Kula in particular) and the Annales School through the intermediary of Ruggiero Romano.

As a result, Marxism and economic analysis were profoundly transformed by theories of dependence developed in the Latin American context, while Western postcolonial thought was influenced by Indian research. The categories of analysis themselves were affected, as notions such as power, dependence, liberty, subaltern, peasant, state, economy-world, globalization, market and capitalism, among others, were profoundly changed by these debates and the reflections of authors from the 'Global South'. The global history of our time, whatever its tendencies, would not have been possible without these works.

It is important to distinguish between the evolution of historiography in Russia and that in China, where Marxist historians since the 1950s, such as Guo Moruo, have endeavoured to show Chinese history's conformity to Stalin's stages of historical development. Dynastic history was thus transformed into Western periodization, with ancient, medieval (feudal), early modern (colonialism and capitalism) and modern (communism) periods. This standardization was emphasized with the purges of the late 1950s. The new historiography combines Chinese nationalism and globality in the Stalinist sense of the term (universality of historical laws).[35] In this instance, in both the 1950s and 1960s, the tension centred on the relationship between national history, national revolution and global dynamics. Some historians were attacked solely because of the attention they gave to sources, and their critique of them: the party issued reminders that this perspective was that of historians of Imperial China and

---

[35] Helwig Schmidt-Glintzer, Achim Mittag and Jörn Rüsen, eds, *Historical Truth, Historical Criticism and Ideology: Chinese Historiography and Historical Culture from a New Comparative Perspective* (Leiden: Brill: 2005).

capitalism. With the exception of one Marxist historian, Fan Wenlan, all of the others attacked the traditional tools of historiography. Thus, unlike the USSR, historians were unable to hide behind the sources and their supposed objectivity, but on the contrary were supposed to take up a position for or against the revolution, and show the biased nature of anti-revolutionary sources.[36] The press seized upon the debate, which prompted a multitude of reactions, including that of the philosopher Feng Youlan, who believed that history, unlike the natural sciences, could not identify general laws but only singularities. This was a way of supporting heterodox historians. The official reaction was vehement, with the party reminding those concerned that Marxism and Leninism were historical sciences with their own laws. This line of reasoning was imposed even more during the Cultural Revolution.

The debate over the uniqueness of Chinese history and sources spread under Deng Xiaoping, who advanced the notion of 'historical truth' framed by 'four [fundamental] principles' in conformity with Marxist doctrine. In the early 1980s, the debate between 'facts' and 'theory' was taken up again, as some still sought a compromise with Marxist doctrine, while others pressed further (Li Xin in particular), and invoked the priority of 'facts' over (Marxist) theory. Beginning in the 1990s, Chinese historiography covered subjects that were as varied as those in the West, including historical interpretations seeing the light of day that contrasted with the official versions of preceding decades. This openness also had its limits. There was censorship – particularly for political subjects (democracy and its history, for example) – as well as the hostility of Chinese historians, not dissimilar from that of their Russian colleagues, to deconstructionism and postmodernism, partly for the same reasons, namely the importance of arriving at a reconstruction of facts after the 'lies' in history. The revision of the 'cultural revolution' was achieved in this perspective.

In this context, Bozhong Li, anticipating the works of Wong and Pomeranz, demonstrated the dynamism of the economy and markets in China until the late eighteenth century: China was not 'backward' until that time. Wang and Pomeranz reinstated this argument, but from a Weberian, rather than a neo-Marxist, perspective. However, most 'Sinologists', in both China and the West, preferred to keep alive the conventional historiographical periodization in dynasties: even if this approach seems odd compared to the now-established criticism in the Western historiography of histories written according to kings' lives, for China it seems different: it sounds like an alternative to the official Marxist regime periodization.

Neo-Marxism and the 'social turn'

Great Britain, which did not carry the burden of the Nazi legacy, presents a partly different evolution compared to Germany, Italy and also to some extent France: post-war history and historiography expressed conservative attitudes with regard to

---

[36] Merle Goldman, 'The Unique Blooming and Contending of 1961–2', *China Quarterly* 37 (1969): 54–83.

method and content. Resistance to the rise of the USSR and the collapse of the Russian Empire did not encourage British historians to open up, at least initially. British history remained central; that of other worlds, such as Asia and Africa, was developed at SOAS in particular, and remained in the minority as well as separate in the curriculum, as in university institutions where history was identified with that of Great Britain, and perhaps the West. After 1945, historical works showed more than ever the exceptional role of England and Great Britain as a precursor and bulwark of democracy and capitalism. The Glorious Revolution of 1688, the Industrial Revolution and the English role during the world wars became the keystones of a history associating England with modernity. British history was always presented as being connected to but distinct from that of Europe, which was associated with despotism – from Napoleon to Hitler – and economic regulation.[37] As in Germany, it took until 1960s for social groups to have broader access to higher education and university, as well as for history to be diffused in the curriculum and for a new generation of frequently Marxist historians to arrive on the scene, such as Eric Hobsbawm and E. P. Thompson. We have already mentioned this attitude towards quantitative social history. In 1963 Thompson published *The Making of the English Working Class* in which he targeted deterministic Marxism as expressed by Althusser; he also strongly attacked Durkheim and his use of history presented as static.[38] To this, he opposed history from below, where ordinary people played a role – social, political and intellectual. Most of the representatives of the social turn made large use of statistics; to their eyes this was a way of opposing intellectual history but also giving a form of objectivity to their arguments. Quantification was seen as a major tool to produce a history from 'bottom up', and compensate for the fact that marginal and subaltern people were relatively absent in the archives. Following the Marxist approach, social history also insisted on the role of structures in determining the historical course. Of course, this attitude was easily criticized by all those (including previous social quantitative historians) who advocated a cultural turn.[39]

Thompson shared Geertz's critique of functionalism and his preference for uncovering the meanings of rituals. To a given extent, history from below produced its major filiation not only in the West but also in India, where Gramsci, and thus Thompson, inspired the first wave of subaltern studies, before they shifted towards a cultural turn much inspired by Foucault and Said instead. Beside Thompson, authors such as Charles Tilly (who trained as a sociologist), Theda Skocpol (a political scientist) and James Scott, all converged around history from below.[40] In this wake, Lawrence Stone and Peter Burke also urged historians to reject functionalism.[41] Joan Scott,

---

[37] Michael Bentley, *Modernizing England's Past: English Historiography in the Age of Modernism, 1870–1970* (Cambridge: Cambridge University Press, 2005).
[38] E. P. Thompson, *The Poverty of Theory and Other Essays* (London: Merlin, 1979).
[39] Christoph Conrad, 'Social History', in *The International Encyclopedia of the Social and Behavioural Sciences*, edited by James Wright, 2nd ed., vol. 22 (Elsevier, 2015): 307–22.
[40] Tilly, 'Three Visions of History and Theory'; Skocpol, *Visions and Method*; James Scott, *Domination and the Art of Resistance* (New Haven: Yale University Press, 1990).
[41] Burke, *History and Social Theory*.

Lynn Hunt and William Sewell therefore contested the social structural determinism and, instead, they insisted on the codetermination of societies, economies and ideas. However, if some followed Thompson and found in the anthropology of Clifford Geertz their new reference, others performed their cultural turn in the wake of literary or philosophical studies (Derrida and Foucault *imprimis*). Finally, at the end of the 1990s, both Sewell and Hunt praised a synthesis of social and cultural history.[42]

Hayden White wrote a four-page discussion of Thompson's *Working Class*. He saw in it a sequence of tropisms in which Thompson identified class consciousness through a construction of both sources and historical reality. The presumed 'real historical context' actually was that of Thompson and, according to White, the sequence of chapters of the *Working Class* actually expressed the progressive making of Thompson's own self-consciousness.[43]

This criticism is not incompatible with Chakrabarty: when discussing the meaning of working class, labour and work in the Indian context, he reached the conclusion that either one had to praise the universality of these concepts or their relativism based upon an idea of culture exceptionalism. According to him, Thompson praised the latter interpretation as against Marxist determinism. Chakrabarty sought to overcome both these interpretations, stressing the cultural appropriation of these meanings and practices in the Indian context. To a given extent this was a consequence of the Gramscian approach inspiring the subaltern studies, but it is also worth noting that in the case of Chakrabarty, unlike Guha, there is less the effort to underline the peasant resistance to proletarianization than the cultural hegemony of the 'West', both liberal and Marxist. We have already discussed at length these issues in previous chapters when we have uncovered the identification of labour and working people in Britain –not exactly a 'working class' – while stressing the interplay between India and Britain in the identification of labour. We turn now to historians' representations of the social. Chakrabarty devoted a full chapter to the problem of the relationship between individual time and social time in life, and again these were deeply different in various contexts. In fact, during the 1970s and early 1980s, this debate took place not only in Britain and India but also in France, where the so-called third generation of the *Annales* attacked the *longue durée*. It was a reaction to 1968 in politics, and to structuralism in historical epistemology.

Since 1989, few attempts have been made to adapt Marx and his thought to this new context; a few of them were advanced by well-known Marxist authors such as Negri, Arrighi, Amin or Wallerstein. These works did not move an inch compared to previous ones – by these same or other authors in the same vein. It was only in the aftermath of

---

[42] Sewell, 'The Political Unconscious'; Victoria Bonnell and Lynn Hunt, eds, *Beyond the Cultural Turn* (Berkeley: University of California Press, 1999).

[43] Hayden White, *Tropics of Discourse: Essays in Cultural Criticism* (Baltimore: Johns Hopkins University Press, 1978); Hayden White, *The Content of the Form: Narrative Discourse and Historical Representation* (Baltimore: Johns Hopkins University Press, 1987); Dominick LaCapra, *History, Politics, and the Novel* (Ithaca: Cornell University Press, 1987); Dominick LaCapra, *Rethinking Intellectual History: Texts, Contexts, Language* (Ithaca: Cornell University Press, 1983); Dominick LaCapra, *History and Criticism* (Ithaca, NY: Cornell University Press, 1985).

the crisis of 2008 that a return to Marx became clear on a wider scale. Some already well-known historians such as Kocka, van der Linden and Haupt insisted on the necessity of relying on Marx to enhance global history.[44] These attempts maintained nevertheless some postulates of Marxist orthodoxy: capitalism is identified exclusively with wage-labour (despite dozens and dozens of works proving the importance of slavery and coerced labour, in the past as nowadays, for capitalism) and the nation-state is still considered as a central institutional player. Meanwhile a new generation of scholars sought to include Marxism into a wider context: Moyn and Sartori stressed its relevance for a renewed global intellectual history,[45] while Sven Beckert and several other authors of the so-called New History of Capitalism adopt a Marxist approach to explain the role American slavery played in the rising of Anglo-American capitalism.[46] It is not by chance that Subrahmanyam qualified these approaches as Eurocentric.[47]

As such, Marxist approaches have met strong difficulties in explaining so many central features of historical development, such as the persistence of the peasant worker in Europe during much of the nineteenth and twentieth centuries, that of forced labour all around the world until today, the strength of land aristocracies in Europe until the First World War, the absence of revolutions in the West and their importance outside it, not to forget the transmutations of capitalism despite its huge crises in 1929 and 2008. Are there other approaches available to understand past and current social tensions?

---

[44] Haupt and Kocka, *Comparative and Trans-national History*.
[45] Samuel Moyn and Andrew Sartori, eds, *Global Intellectual History* (New York: Columbia University Press, 2013).
[46] Beckert, *Empire of Cotton*.
[47] Sanjay Subrahmanyam, *Aux origines de l'histoire globale* (Paris: Collège de France/ Fayard, 2014).

9

Weberian worlds

Among the countless authors who undertook a similar kind of analysis in the late nineteenth and early twentieth centuries, one reference is at least as important as Marx: Max Weber. We have already mentioned his influence on the identification of the main social actors. We need now to better include this point into Weber's wider conception of social history. I do not intend to engage in a genuine analysis of Weber's thought, any more than of Marx's theory, but rather to review the way Weber has been and can be used in social and economic history. Weber has had crucial and lasting impact on several currents of global history, notably those that emphasize comparison.[1] Whether they confirm Weber's importance – as in the case of Charles Tilly – or criticize him – as in the case of Pomeranz – the German author remains an inescapable reference.[2] We also need carefully to distinguish Weber's thought from the many approaches more or less inspired by him. Weber certainly had a Eurocentric approach, as had Marx before him. For sure, Weber sought to explain the success of the West; but, at the same time, his explanation was far more complex, as were those of dozens of authors who explicitly or implicitly claimed Weber's inspiration. Some recent critics addressed to Weber actually are correct for 'weberians', authors inspired by Weber, rather than for Weber himself.[3] Weber used comparison as his main tool of investigation. His aim was to account for different historical trajectories;[4] the crucial element in this process lay in the choice of fields and variables. Fields were society, religion and the economy; they entered Weberian architecture to provide a fully integrated analysis of society. Then, within each field, Weber selected what he considered the relevant variables. For example, the comparison between Britain and China was made by focusing on private property or the role played by science in technological innovation, power struggles between entrepreneurs, capitalists and wage earners, and so on.[5] Capitalism was distinguished by the pursuit of profit and the rational organization of production factors.[6] For

---

[1] Pierre Bourdieau, Jean-Claude Chamboredon and Jean-Claude Passeron, *Le métier de sociologue: préalables épistémologiques* (Berlin and New York: Mouton de Gruyter, 1968), particularly 169 ff.
[2] Osterhammel, *The Transformation of the World*; Haupt and Kocka, *Comparative and Transnational History*; Wong, *China Transformed*.
[3] J. M. Blaut, *Eight Eurocentric Historians* (New York: Guilford Publications, 2000).
[4] Stephen Karlberg, *La sociologie historique comparative de Max Weber* (Paris: La Découverte, 2002).
[5] Innerk Bruhns, 'Max Weber, l'économie et l'histoire', *Annales HSC* 51, no. 6 (1996): 1259–87.
[6] Max Weber, *Wirtschaft und Gesellschaft* (Tübingen: Mohr, 1922, 1925); English translation, *Economy and Society* (Cambridge, MA: Harvard University Press, 2019).

example, Confucianism and Hinduism did not lend themselves readily to capitalist development because they condemn greed. The same distinction was found in Europe between Catholicism and Protestantism.[7] In Weber's view, what differentiated Asia from Europe was, together with religion, the absence of politically autonomous cities controlled by merchants and the lack of a precise legal order and private property.[8]

This approach was adopted by political scientists and sociologists as well as by several global economists and historians. The important point here is the relationship Weber maintained between comparison and ideal types;[9] this link was crucial to incorporating historical analysis into a sociological perspective. Comparison requires constant terms; without them, it becomes impossible. According to Weber, this is the price to pay for reconciling logical rigour with empirical analysis.

He shared with Marx the identification of capitalism with profit seeking and the constitution of a 'proletarian army'. However, unlike Marx, Weber never predicted the end of capitalism. These different hypotheses on social historical dynamics reflected their respective reasoning. Marx progressed by extension and generalization; he started from a more or less idealized British experience and suggested that this path would spread all around the globe. Weber did not follow this path, and instead his reasoning was based on comparison. He, too, started from the British ideal type, but then he compared it to other more or less historicized ideal types. That is why Marx had to confront non-European cases and evaluate whether or not they fitted into his scheme; Weber did not have this problem, and insisted on specificities instead. These are two different kinds of Eurocentrism, as Chakrabarty and Goody each argue in their own way:[10] Marx sought to extend to the whole planet a model identified with the British case, while Weber judged the non-European world in the light of a stylized capitalism and society in Britain. In both cases, these authors praised a 'global' perspective, in the sense that society had to be studied under its multiple angles; and this included also knowledge, politics and the economy.[11] However, Weber characterized the non-European world through their forms of knowledge, while Marx insisted on economic structures.[12]

To some extent, these two approaches are still widespread in global history today: one identifies the global with the history of globalization and studies this last in its expansion from the 'core' to the 'periphery'; the other interprets global history as a fundamental contrast between areas and, possibly, 'civilizations'. Weberian-style

---

[7] Wolfgang Mommsen, *Max Weber and German Politics, 1890–1920* (Chicago: University of Chicago Press, 1984).

[8] Pamela Kyle Crossing, *What Is Global History?* (Cambridge: Polity Press, 2008).

[9] Wolfgang Mommsen and Jürgen Osterhammel, eds, *Max Weber and His Contemporaries* (London and New York: Routledge, 1986).

[10] Chakrabarty, *Provincializing*; Jack Goody, *The East in the West* (Cambridge: Cambridge University Press 1996).

[11] Derek Sayer, *Capitalism and Modernity: An Excursus on Marx and Weber* (London: Routledge, 1991); Philippe Raynaud, *Weber et les dilemmes de la raison moderne* (Paris: PUF, 1987).

[12] Mark Gould, 'Marx and Weber and the Logic of Historical Explanation: The Rise of Machine Capitalism', *Journal of Classical Sociology* 16, no. 4 (2016): 321–48. See also Norman Birnbaum's classic work, 'Conflicting Interpretations of the Rise of Capitalism: Marx and Weber', *British Journal of Sociology* 4 (1953): 125–41.

analyses have been extremely widespread right up to today. Most of them have involved economic and sociological comparisons between Europe and Asia based on ideal types. Even when these approaches have employed empirical analysis, it has not been with a view to questioning the initial hypotheses but rather to confirm them. Let us take one example among others: religion. A serious proof has never been found to substantiate the favourable connection between Protestantism and capitalism or the tensions between Catholicism and Confucianism, on the one hand, and capitalism on the other. Yet these elements continue to be evoked as if there were established truths – except when they are reversed entirely nowadays, and Confucianism is invoked to explain China's economic success.[13]

Another Weberian concern was the relationship between history, social dynamics and comparative paths. Alexander Gerschenkron is justly famous for *Economic Backwardness in Historical Perspective*. This work was part of a broad debate in the 1950s and 1960s: with decolonization, economists raised the problem of (under) development and what should be done to remedy it. In the context of the Cold War, this issue was inseparable from the question of which economic and political form the new states would take: capitalism or socialism. The components of this debate were globalized; observers not only compared the economic achievements of the USSR to those of the West but also the trajectories of China, India and the countries in the Americas, Africa and Asia that acquired their independence at the time. A number of economists emphasized the need to put these debates in 'historical perspective'. This position warrants reflection. What exactly does it mean to study economic development in a historical perspective?

Like Max Weber, Gerschenkron began by drawing up the list of Western characteristics on which his comparison would be based; he too emphasized cities, the bourgeoisie, markets and private property. Yet unlike Marx and to some extent Weber, he thought it was possible to arrive at industrialization (but not capitalism) without a bourgeoisie. In place of this component, 'backward' countries (to use the jargon of the 1960s and 1970s) such as Prussia and Russia had 'substituting factors', notably the state. This is a very clever solution to the problem raised by the need to reconcile particular features, historical specificities and general dynamics. If backwardness and diversity go together, then it is possible to conceive of alternative paths.[14] His model postulates that the more backward an economy is at the outset of economic development, the more likely a bourgeois, middle entrepreneurial class will be lacking and the more institutional substitutes will be required. In particular, taking the example of Germany and Russia, Gerschenkron argues that the lack of a bourgeoisie was compensated for by the major role of the state. In late-comer countries, capital-intensive industries and large-size units, instead of agriculture and consumption units, take the lead. However, contrary to appearances, like Weber, Gerschenkron does not compare Russia

---

[13] Jan Rehmann, *Max Weber: Modernization as Passive Revolution. A Gramscian Analysis* (Leiden: Brill, 2013); Peter Ghosh, *Max Weber and the Protestant Ethic: Twin Histories* (Oxford: Oxford University Press, 2014).

[14] Alexander Gerschenkron, *Economic Backwardness in Historical Perspective* (Cambridge, MA: Harvard University Press, 1962).

to England in specific historical contexts. Instead, he contrasts an ideal image of the West (and of England in particular) with an equally ideal image of nineteenth-century Russia. English economic development is associated with the early introduction of a parliament, privatization of the commons and hence the formation of a proletariat available for agriculture and industry. In contrast, Russia is associated with market towns – and therefore with a bourgeoisie – as well as the presence of an absentee landed gentry living off serfdom. The debate over modernization, in fact the very use of this concept, implied a strongly determinist philosophy of history, Eurocentric categories and postulates and, ultimately, circular explanatory arguments.[15]

Gerschenkron put great faith in the economic and statistical research produced in Russia between 1870 and 1930. He never sought to develop a critical understanding of figures and how they were produced. We have already discussed this; as shown, the economic and social statistics produced in Russia at the turn of the century were, for the most part, the work of intellectuals, specialists and sometimes merely activists employed by the *zemstvo*, local self-government organizations. These authors were quick to reveal the inadequacies of the reforms, the limits of autocracy and the impoverishment of the peasantry. Above and beyond their considerable differences, 'Marxists' and 'populists' agreed on this aspect. They selected typical cases and variables to confirm their hypotheses. These were the sources Gerschenkron used in his work. Gerschenkron doubly decontextualized Russian data: first, he took out contextual turn-of-the-century sources, which in turn were the result of a particular empirical clarification, and, second, he believed that these studies were relevant insofar as 'third world' challenges after the Second World War were similar to those of Russia at the end of the nineteenth century. This double decontextualization, of both sources and historical periods, was crucial. All the authors that made use of this approach were eager to distinguish themselves from the Stalinist-Soviet variant and planners oriented towards a *tabula rasa* approach and a radical rethinking of society and the economy. Gerschenkron put forward an important element: the examples of Russia and Prussia showed that backward countries could take another path, founded more on the state than on the bourgeoisie. It was less a question of the peasant economy or of promoting alternative paths for moving forward than of historical necessity. In other words, he retained the Hegelian approach that underpinned Marx, but in a substantially modified version with several possible paths of development, all of them justified by the laws of history and economics. However, his two terms – the notion of backwardness and historical temporalities – were not readily compatible. In reality, economic backwardness referred to logical time; it was a question of proposing a scale of comparison to account for both economic growth and so-called blocking factors. The schema of comparison was constructed from a list of elements drawn from a Western ideal type. The analyses gained in contemporary relevance but lost

---

[15] Dearn Tipps, 'Modernization Theory and the Comparative Study of Societies: A Critical Perspective', *Comparative Studies in Society and History* 15 (1973): 199–226; Frederick Cooper, Allen Isaacman, Florencia Mallon, William Roseberry and Steve Stern, *Confronting Historical Paradigms: Peasants, Labour, and the Capitalist World System in Africa and Latin America* (Madison: University of Wisconsin Press, 1993).

their historical depth. The comparisons were more atemporal than anachronistic. Despite his criticism of Weber, Gerschenkron nevertheless retained several of his methodological postulates and even some of his content (the Industrial Revolution and its origins). Ahistorical comparison, Eurocentrism and the transformation of sources into data fit well together. Herein lies the essential connection between Weber, Gerschenkron and development economics: these studies, often centred on the twin notions of backwardness and progress, reflected issues that were not only intellectual but also political and therefore normative. In this context, the misusing of data, essentially to confirm preconceived theories, was not a necessary implication of quantitative economic and social history, but mostly of its normative aim and ambition. History had to prove the path to 'modernization'. This same approach runs through the revolutions of the eighteenth and early nineteenth centuries, economic and social transformations, the Russian Revolution, the tragedies of the twentieth century and finally the Cold War and decolonization, as shown by the case of Gerschenkron and the debate over modernization in the 1950s–1970s. Thus, Walt Rostow put forward his theory of stages of growth in open opposition to socialism: he showed that the stages of growth were universal and that it was impossible to follow a path imposed from on high as in the USSR. Rostow delivered a more radical critique of state planning. History served to validate the Western-style itinerary and the arrow of time moved in only one direction. Paradoxically, Rostow reproduced Marx's argument according to which the most advanced countries showed the way and the future to backward countries. This universalist approach did not win unanimous support within development economics in the 1950s and 1960s. The responses put forward reveal a distinct evolution; during the 1950s, the various authors – both Marxist and non-Marxist – tended to give priority to industrialization as the key to escaping from underdevelopment and poverty. In this context, the rural peasant economy was seen as conducive to backwardness insofar as it had a limited ability to commercialize its production or supply workers for industry.[16] The various identifications of the peasantry discussed above belonged to this questioning.

In this context, the identification of the state and the nation-state in particular is equally important. The comparative history and the sociology of state construction have often taught us to think in terms of nation-states. Even if an author like Charles Tilly declares at the outset that we must avoid projecting recent constructions on the past, he cannot help doing so himself.[17] That is one of the consequences of studying the past in order to find the origins of the present. Tilly divides states into three groups: tribute-making empires; city-states, mainly Italian; and nation-states. These three categories corresponded to different gradations of capital and coercion. City-states were distinguished by maximal capital and minimal coercive power; at the opposite

---

[16] Among the proponents of this approach, see Paul Rosenstein-Rodan, 'Problems of Industrialization of Eastern and Souteastern Europe', *Economic Journal* 53 (June–September 1943): 202–11; Ragnar Nurske, *Problems of Capital Formation in Underdeveloped Countries* (Oxford: Basil Blackwell, 1953); W. A. Lewis, *The Theory of Economic Growth* (London: Allen and Unwin, 1955).

[17] Charles Tilly, *Coercion, Capital and European States. AD 990–1991* (Cambridge and Oxford: Blackwell, 1990).

extreme, again according to Tilly, in Asian empires like Russia and China, lack of capital was compensated by maximum coercion. Finally, only the European nation-states are said to have achieved the right mix of capital and coercion. This combination is said to have given birth to modern states, along with their armies, as well as the Industrial Revolution and urbanization.

This reasoning raises two types of questions: it starts from the results and assumes the chronological antecedents were 'causes', even though there is no evidence, for example, that the growth of England was actually linked to the adoption of the Bill of Rights in 1689 or that Venice lost its power because it was unable to produce a state like France. Capitalism often developed without granting many civil rights; indeed, history is full of examples to the contrary. In the end, even the development of capitalism in nineteenth-century Europe was based on considerable restriction of civil and political rights, which were reserved for a minority of landowners. The link between democracy and capitalism is no doubt politically correct but it is not necessarily true. It is therefore important to look for capitalism outside current liberal, democratic countries.

Conversely, the Asian states in the modern period were hardly as despotic and had more capital than Tilly and others assert. It is true, as these authors have emphasized, that the Mongol and Turkic powers of Central Asia left their mark on major Asian states like China and Russia. Yet the Mongol and Turkic powers were far less nomadic and plundering than is usually claimed. They possessed a well-established territorial organization, tax system and conscription system that they passed on to their Eurasian successors. The Empire of Chinggis Khan was among the largest, if not *the* largest, in history, and we now know that the Mongols were anything but mere nomadic pillagers. In short, we should not suppose that these countries were held together solely by a great deal of coercion or that they had no capital.[18]

In other words, Weber's and Weberians' notions of the state are mostly anachronistic and Eurocentric. The lack of languages and archives and the strong normative ambition of these studies lay at the origin of these limitations. Are there solutions to these shortcomings?

Nicolas di Cosmo tried to go further than Tilly by proposing a theory of state construction in Central Asia. He made use of local archives and criticized the opposition between nomad and sedentary populations and put an emphasis on 'crisis' situations to explain the origin of territorial powers in Central Asia. Initially, political entities in Central Asia were organized into clans corresponding to extensive use of the territory. Later on, di Cosmo claimed, the depletion of resources gave rise to a crisis affecting both the economy and the legitimacy of clan chiefs, which could only be overcome by consolidating the territory and creating a tax system and a regular army. This theory goes beyond the nomad-sedentary opposition and has the virtue of introducing the Central Asian powers on the stage of world history.[19] At the same time, the author's approach ends up legitimizing a historical construction by imagining a

---

[18] Nicola Di Cosmo, *Ancient China and Its Enemies: The Rise of Nomadic Power in East Asian History* (Cambridge: Cambridge University Press, 2002).
[19] Nicola Di Cosmo, 'State Formation and Periodization in Inner Asian History', *Journal of World History* 10, no. 1 (1999): 1–40.

'crisis' at its origin: if a change occurred, that meant a crisis must have taken place. Reinhart Koselleck had already criticized the use of the notion of crisis: a crisis for whom and mentioned by whom?[20] How much profit was accumulated and how many powers took hold during so-called 'crisis' periods?

The relevance of this argument applies to every period and historical configuration: no doubt it is still valid today when the media and politicians invoke a 'crisis' to gain acceptance for certain changes; it is even more valid in history. Prior to di Cosmo, famous historians like Steensgaard, Hobsbawm and many others continually spoke of a 'crisis' in the seventeenth century that would have prompted the shift from the late medieval world to the capitalist world.[21] Braudel endeavoured to criticize this supposed break, which to his mind was used not so much to account for historical dynamics than to confirm the stages of capitalism as seen by Marxists as well as the liberal vulgate. Considering crisis as a factor of change meant ignoring the *longue durée*, the persistence of structures, the slow evolution of the economy and, above all, institutions.[22] And, as the political scientist Barrington Moore sensibly asked as early as the 1960s: what reasons do we have for thinking that change causes crises, whereas we take stability for granted? What about the struggles engaged to keep a way of life, a belief or an institution alive?[23]

We must therefore try to integrate the moments of rupture into long-term, historical trajectories without imposing any necessity. It is always possible, with hindsight, to explain a historical phenomenon by one necessity or another. This approach prevents us from seeing the possible outcomes of a given moment as well as historical bifurcations. If we cannot point to a crisis or tension between coercion and capital, how can we explain the evolutions of these territorial formations in Eurasia? Where is the boundary separating Europe from other worlds? In the case of Russia, in particular, when can we use European categories and when should we reject them? Is there a difference between the state, law, a profit-based economy and economic ethics in Russia and in Europe? Are those values homogeneous throughout an area called 'Europe'? All these questions remained unsolved in comparative and Weberian-like approaches.

The great divergence: Weber on his head?

The debate over the great divergence, inspired by the title of Kenneth Pomeranz's book, has profoundly influenced global history, particularly the form that pays greater attention to economic aspects, which has developed over the last fifteen years. It is of

---

[20] Koselleck, *Future Past*.
[21] Eric Hobsbawm, 'The General Crisis of the European Economy in the Seventeenth Century', *Past & Present* 6, no. 1 (1954): 33–53; Niels Steensgaard, *The Asian Trade Revolution of the Seventeenth Century: The East India Company and the Decline of the Caravan Trade* (Chicago: University of Chicago Press, 1975).
[22] Fernand Braudel, *Civilisation matérielle, économie et capitalisme*, 3 vols (Paris: Armand Colin, 1977–9).
[23] Barrington Moore, *The Social Origins*.

particular relevance here because Pomeranz's book includes all the topics discussed here: the use of local archives, statistics, social categories and models. How does it mobilize them?

This approach begins with a critique of Eurocentrism and Weberian-style comparisons. The proponents of the great divergence therefore used this as their starting point to dispute the absence of growth in Asia and China prior to the nineteenth century.[24] In Pomeranz's approach, the great divergence is mainly related to colonial expansion and factor endowments: while Western Europe benefited from its American colonies, and then from American markets and resources, Russian despotism and power limited Asian, mainly Chinese, expansion. Of course, as Pomeranz pointed out several times, we should not confuse global history, which focuses on broad yet determined spaces, with world history. If we accept this distinction, the next step is to grasp what these syntheses contribute compared with comparative global history and conventional approaches. The problem lies in the difficulty of confirming these interpretations empirically; the environmental component and Europe's use of colonial resources correspond more to the colonizers' aims than to historical realities. Similarly, the history of Asia is punctuated with wars just as much as that of Europe.[25] In all these cases, the subsequent imperial constructions were often unexpected historical results that need to be explained. Unlike the debates during the 1970s and 1980s, the discussions pertaining to the great divergence lack any reflexivity in the sense that they do not look carefully at the origin of their sources, but rather restrict themselves to examining the representativeness of a particular region, profession or activity, how the data should be aggregated, etc. Debates focus on measurement and econometrics, not on the historical origin of the data themselves. This leads to the second limitation in this debate: by its very subject – per capita income, growth rate – all the studies surrounding the great divergence blithely ignore distribution and inequalities. What sort of income distribution accompanied British growth and how did it differ from distribution in China during the same period?

Information pertaining to distribution in Britain in the eighteenth century and above all the nineteenth century has been widely explored and published, but it is still a matter of guesswork with regard to India and China in the same period. Hence the question: what is the point of focusing solely on a few economic indicators – growth rate, per capita income – and ignoring distribution?

This approach was asserted by liberal Western intellectual orthodoxy after 1991 but it was already on the rise in the 1970s. It maintains the Weberian approach and relies entirely on European categories – markets, efficiency and rational economic organization. Finally, research work on the great divergences is also problematic from the standpoint of political philosophy: how long will economic history – whether global or not – have to focus exclusively on growth and on 'who was first'?

---

[24] Bozhong Li, *Agricultural Development in Jiangnan* (New York: St. Martin's Press, 1998).
[25] Broadberry and Gupta, 'The Early Modern Great Divergence'; Patrick O'Brien, 'Ten Years of Debates on the Origin of the Great Divergence', http://www.history.ac.uk/reviews/review/1008.

In other words, in the debate about the great divergence we are apparently at the other end of the spectrum from classical Weberian approaches: instead of trying to fit the data into a model, here the data are used to confirm or disprove earlier studies without any pre-judgement. To be sure, these approaches do not fall into the trap of facile comparison mentioned earlier; they also avoid celebrating the West and, like every other global history approach, the ones used by proponents of the great divergence also propose important solutions to the question of how the singularities of the various parts of the world are linked to each other and how they are connected to a larger whole (e.g. the comparison between the Yangzi Delta and Lancashire leads to a reassessment of European and Chinese dynamics as a whole). But what about the model itself?

Pomeranz explains the Chinese dynamic according to the same criteria used for Europe: demographic growth, the protection of private property and the commercial and protoindustrial dynamic.[26] In other words, like Weber, Landes, Polanyi, Marx and so many others before him, Pomeranz retains the idealized British model of privatization of common lands, proletarianization, industrialization, bourgeois and individualist mentality, etc., and then extends it to China.

He opted for this approach, despite the fact that this ideal type had been challenged during the decades before his work: the privatization of common lands was less important and decisive than was generally believed, like the role of parliament or protection of private property or even the influence of the Industrial Revolution itself.[27] Pomeranz acted as if the historiography of the British economy had not budged since the 1960s; he then took the underlying model and observed that it was more valid in China (or at least in Yangzi) than in Britain itself, where market imperfections continued to exist. This is a complete reversal of the customary association between an ideal market (and its institutions) and Britain; this association is said to have been historically less present in Britain than in China or at least some of its regions. At first glance, the great divergence is a way of calling into question Eurocentrism and Great Britain's role as the historical driving force. In reality, the British Industrial Revolution found new justification in colonialism and American resources, whereas China's decadence was associated with the absence of a colonial empire and of exploitable resources like those on the American continent. The whole debate over the great divergence actually is the result of the neoliberal Western intellectual orthodoxy and the fall of the Berlin Wall: according to this theory, markets and capitalism dominate the last few centuries of world history; institutions, eventually factors endowments influence historical outcomes, not 'mentalities' or different economic attitudes (as anthropologists had expressed them). Is there any possible alternative to this approach?

---

[26] Pomeranz, *The Great Divergence*.
[27] Postel-Vinay, 'The Dis-integration'; Allen, *Enclosure and the Yeoman*; Robert Allen, *The British Industrial Revolution in Global Perspective* (Cambridge: Cambridge University Press, 2009); Prisannan Parthasarathi, *Why Europe Grew Rich and Asia Did not: Global Economic Divergence, 1600–1850* (Cambridge: Cambridge University Press, 2011).

Durkheim and the Annales School

In the late nineteenth and early twentieth centuries, a debate erupted in France following the publication of works on sociological method: first *The Rules of Sociological Method* (1895) by Durkheim, and later *The Historical Method Applied to the Social Sciences* (1901) and *A Political History of Contemporary Europe Since 1814* by Seignobos.[28] Seignobos's position was quite simple: history is the study of human beings in their individual and social complexity and therefore cannot claim to be a science. Seignobos reacted to the scientific positivism of the sociologists with his own positivism of sources. In his view, the sources are justified in themselves; the only questions historians are entitled to raise are those found in the sources themselves; otherwise, they would be preaching anachronism and simplification, as was often the case in sociology. Durkheim opposed this conclusion and descriptive history.[29] Without causal explanation, Durkheim concluded, history is purely descriptive and has no social function. In this context, he considered comparison indispensable for bringing to fruition the project of unifying the social sciences. We find here the same tensions between sources and data, social categories and models discussed in the previous chapters. Was there any novelty?

In part, this is the same problem that Marx, Weber and Schmoller faced, though the answers were not necessarily the same. Along with these authors, Durkheim showed the same determination to identify the causalities and laws of society and shared the same aim of unifying the social sciences. However, what was specific to the French debate at the turn of the century was the critique – absent in Weber – of events in favour of structural variables. The debate was more concerned with the relations between singularity and generality over time than in space, as had been the case with Weber. Durkheim was less interested in the 'unknown factors' than in the very conditions of social action in its historical dimension. Durkheim tried to achieve a unified vision of the social sciences. He was not the only one. The historian's profession, according to Bloch, consisted precisely in reconciling these elements.[30] They were seeking the global in the connections between several levels of history rather than in a political project for society.

And yet, Bloch's approach was greatly embedded in the particular context in which he lived, Strasburg, at the frontier between France and Germany. Marc Bloch took for granted the relevance of similarities among societies in Western Europe. Of all his positions, this is perhaps the one that was most influenced by the interwar context; the tensions within European space motivated Bloch's desire to claim its homogeneity despite the First World War and the conflict between France and Germany. These were indeed major challenges, especially when viewed from Strasbourg where Bloch lived.

---

[28] Charles Seignobos, *La méthode historique appliquée aux sciences sociales* (Paris: Alcan, 1901). On these debates: Gérard Noiriel, 'Pour une approche subjectiviste du social', *Annales ESC* 6 (1989): 1435–59.

[29] Émile Durkheim, 'Débat sur l'explication en histoire et en sociologie', *Extrait du Bulletin de la société française de philosophie* 8 (1908): 229–45. Reproduced in Émile Durkheim, *Textes. 1. Éléments d'une théorie sociale* (Paris: Éditions de Minuit, 1975): 199–217.

[30] Marc Bloch, *Écrire la société féodale. Lettres à Henri Berr, 1924–1943*. Texts compiled by Jacqueline Pluet-Despatin (Paris: Institut mémoires de l'édition contemporaine, 1992).

As a result, contrary to his own method, he assumed far more than demonstrated the homogeneity of Europe and its relevance to making suitable comparisons.

Thus, Bloch was led to exclude Russia *a priori* from European space, a choice every bit as questionable as that of identifying Europe without the Mediterranean. He was confusing the historian's skills with analytical relevance: no doubt within the community of historians, as it was understood in France and in Europe and which Bloch defended in his work, the knowledge of languages was assumed to be indispensable to study a region and produce comparisons and/or circulatory analyses. The refusal to make comparisons for reasons of 'language' or 'civilization' is just as weak as making comparisons based on generalist models. This is a persistent problem: the singularity of area studies or of civilizations is always evoked and almost never made explicit.[31] For example, the role of the state, despotism and hostility to private property as well as 'big space' are thought to identify Russia's presumed singularity.[32] Similarly, China is characterized by the weight of the state and its bureaucracy, trade, the very long-term nature and presumed stability of its institutions,[33] whereas Africa is distinguished by the weakness of the state.[34] And so forth. Most often the reasoning is circular (the state accounts for the state, space justifies space, etc.). Sometimes, singularity is even translated into uniqueness: a given region is said to be *sui generis* and therefore incomparable because unlike any other. Nevertheless, any justification of this position would require an explicit comparison[35] whereas this practice is rejected in the name precisely of the specificity and uniqueness of one area or another.

Such 'singularity' is also associated with the *longue durée*. Persistent features account for the singularity of a civilization: its environment, its culture, its language, its religion and its state.[36] In defining civilizations and area studies, the *longue durée* approach turns into a boomerang: what began as a heuristic tool (how to justify Europe instead of the Mediterranean? China instead of the Han culture?) becomes an intellectual prison.[37]

---

[31] Robert H. Bates, 'Area Studies and the Discipline: A Useful Controversy?' *PS: Political Science & Politics* 30, no. 2 (June 1997): 166–70.

[32] John Le Donne, *Absolutisms and Ruling Class: The Formation of the Russian Political Order, 1700–1825* (Oxford: Oxford University Press, 1991). See also the three recent volumes of the *Cambridge History of Russia*.

[33] For a discussion on this point: Arthur Waldron, *The Great Wall of China: From History to Myth* (Cambridge: Cambridge University Press, 1990); Leo Shin, *The Making of the Chinese State: Ethnicity and Expansion on the Ming Bordeland* (Cambridge: Cambridge University Press, 2006).

[34] Frederick Cooper, 'Conflict and Connections: Rethinking Colonial African History', *American Historical Review* 99, no. 5 (1994): 1516–45.

[35] Michael Werner and Bénédicte Zimmermann, *De la comparaison à l'histoire croisée* (Paris: Seuil, 2004).

[36] A few examples among countless others regarding the specificities of Russia or China: Marc Raeff, 'Un Empire comme les autres?', *Cahiers du monde russe* 30, no. 4 (1989): 321–7; André Berelowitch, *La hiérarchie des égaux. La noblesse russe d'ancien régime* (Paris: Seuil, 2001); Pierre-Étienne Will, 'Présentation' of 'Économie et technique en Chine', *Annales HSC* 49, no. 4 (1999): 777–81; Bin Wong, Pierre-Étienne Will, *Nourish the People* (Ann Arbor: University of Michigan Press, 1993), see introduction in particular with the singularities of China compared with Europe.

[37] Wong, 'Entre monde et nation'; Sanjay Subrahmanyam, 'Connected Histories. Notes Towards a Reconfiguration of Early Modern Eurasia', *Modern Asian Studies* 31, no. 3 (1997): 735–62 for critiques on these approaches.

Bloch and Febvre insisted on the priority of structures – social structures in particular – over short-term micro dynamics. Yet neither dared to incorporate these analyses in an approach that transcended French or possibly Franco-Germanic space. The first Annals schools was in principle far from Weber and close to Durkheim. But, in fact, it preserved conventional historiography's tools such as erudition and philology although in discussion with social sciences.

The issue is that the identification of social actors was mostly based on erudition and philology rather than on social theory, and it had some major consequences: on the one hand, the quest of complexity stands for historical explanation against the presumed 'simplification' of social sciences; on the other hand, non-European worlds and the global connections stand out of these investigations. In particular, the *Annales* had nothing or very few to say about colonialism. Yet, this attitude was shared also by sociologists of the Durkheim's school.[38]

Social structures and the *longue durée*

Bloch stressed erudition and the archives but, despite his formal announcements, he put sociology and social sciences to the background of his investigation, with the above-mentioned shortcomings (the identification of Europe, for instance). On the contary, Braudel borrowed much from social sciences, anthropology, geography and partly economic history, but he did not hesitate to write about areas of the world where he did not know the languages and the archives. In fact, Braudel's global history grew out of the convergence of two different traditions: Durkheim and his sociology and the first generation of the Annales School, on the one hand, and the Historical School, especially Sombart, on the other. Like the other founders of the Annales School, Braudel took from Durkheim his criticism of descriptive history and his interest in a form of 'total history' in which structures dominated events and not the other way round. Durkheim had tried to achieve a unified vision of the social sciences; Braudel persisted along this way but his ambition was to give priority to history among social sciences.[39] His demonstration was inspired less by Weber's schema than by Sombart:[40] this legacy is visible in his definition of capitalism. The association between capitalism and monopoly, capitalism and finance, and the role played by Italy and its international trading networks is present in Braudel and Sombart. However, when it was a matter of explaining the economic dynamics of other worlds, Braudel based himself on Europe as a model; Chinese capitalism would thus have obstacles and limits in relation to European capitalism, English capitalism in particular. In this way, the synthesis

---

[38] Fuyuki Kurosawa, 'The Durkheimian School and Colonialism', in Steinmetz, *Sociology and Empire*: 188–212.

[39] Maurice Aymard, 'La longue durée aujourd'hui. Bilan d'un demi siècle, 1958–2008', in *From Florence to the Mediterranean and Beyond. Essays in Honor of Anthony Molho*, edited by Diogo Ramada Courto, Eric Dursteller, Julius Kirshner and Francesca Trivellato (Firenze: Olschki, 2009): 558–79.

[40] Joseph Tendler, *The Palgrave Macmillan Opponents of the Annales School* (New York: Palgrave Macmillan, 2013).

remained fundamentally Eurocentric, as Braudel sought to explain Western expansion, and neglected the strength of Asia. This attitude was profoundly influenced by the Cold War and European construction with regard to politics. It was a particular yet nevertheless well-consolidated Eurocentrism, which provided sometimes surprising divisions: on the one hand, his effort to propose a Mediterranean in which Islam was an integral part of Europe was a courageous act, but on the other, Russia, which was also identified as a separate civilization, remained outside Europe despite the intense relations and transfers – cultural, economic, political – between the Russian world and Europe over the *longue durée*, which Braudel even knew all too well.[41] The division of spatial scales remained a central preoccupation for Braudel and his followers, and is so in global history today. Braudel included other worlds in his approach, but did so using secondary sources, and did not hesitate to recruit historians and especially anthropologists from non-European worlds. At the same time, these other worlds were almost solely seen according to European expansion, and took on consistency only in relation to Europe. For Braudel, modernity was a European affair, although he did not go all the way in Wallerstein's direction, as he relied on the notion of an economy-world but in a more flexible way than his American colleagues, with no historical determinism or Marxism for support.

Critiques have been made of the identification of the primary Braudelian civilizations. In the Braudel approach, civilizations defined themselves through spaces (territory), societies (the existence of cities), economies (the need for a system of exchange) and collective mentalities (a religion). It is important that these elements endure over time, even though Braudel was ready to admit that exchange and circulation, along with colonialism, reshuffled the deck and modified civilizations over time. Critics were tough: in the case of Islam, for instance, the debate over whether an Islamic community (Islamicate) existed at a specific period was (and is) lively. Some have responded in the affirmative,[42] others in the negative.[43] In similar fashion, Braudel's identification of an African civilization was welcomed by some as a recognition of this continent, and renewed discussion regarding the written sources of early modern territorial powers as the sole foundation and legitimacy of history. Yet it is hard to identify a unified 'Africa' separate from other civilizations as such.[44] This distinction is relatively recent and is in large part a result of decolonization. Much ink continues to be spilled regarding African identity, and with it any form of comparison and distinction. Although Cooper criticizes the very category of identity, it is strongly affirmed in the studies of Africanists, especially in African Studies departments.

Seen from other regions of the world, the Braudelian chronology (roughly from the twelfth to the eighteenth century) was not necessarily relevant. For instance, Sinologists and Indianists proposed a division that did not at all coincide with that of the West. For some, modernity began two thousand years ago – or with Mao (depending on the

---

[41] Fernand Braudel, *Grammaire des civilisations* (Paris: Arthaud, 1987).
[42] Marshall Hodgson, *Rethinking World History* (Cambridge: Cambridge University Press, 1993).
[43] Alam, *The Languages of Political Islam*.
[44] Joseph Millar, 'History and Africa/Africa and History', *American Historical Review* 104, no. 1 (1999): 1–32.

historiography)⁴⁵ – and for others with the British occupation.⁴⁶ These chronological frameworks are different, although not necessarily incompatible with the Western approach, especially in the case of nationalist historiographies. This is particularly true of India, where the periodization into pre-colonial, colonial and postcolonial generally confirms rather than invalidates British and Western domination. The presumed 'specificity' of a particular area is most often associated with *temps longs*, with enduring elements making up the specificity of an area.⁴⁷ This was, for instance, the case with the importance of the state in Russia and the USSR: the *longue durée* thus turned into a boomerang, from an heuristic tool into an intellectual prison.

The connection between economy-worlds was central. The historical dynamics of capitalisms, in Europe as well as elsewhere, thus found a possible explanation, and it was not the only one. Let us consider the case of Asia. What is the pertinent space? China, South-east Asia, the entire Indian Ocean?

Each of these responses stands up, and can be justified: taking inspiration from Braudel, Bin Wong speaks of China as an economy-world,⁴⁸ Chaudhuri does the same for India and the Indian Ocean,⁴⁹ Di Cosmo for Central Asia,⁵⁰ Denys Lombard and others for South-east Asia.⁵¹ The determination of the pertinent scale depends on the question being asked: maritime commerce invites one to gather in a single world regions stretching from China to East Africa, whereas land-based commerce relates, for example, to the Silk Road.⁵²

Yet this immediate solution – the division depends on the question being asked – is not enough, for it is an externalist and overarching approach that says nothing about how the actors themselves considered these divisions. In other words, in the common contrast between external spatial-temporal divisions – stemming from a particular outline from the social sciences – and divisions claiming to be internal to the sources, certain elements, and not insubstantial ones at that, remain in the background: the production of models on the one hand, and of sources on the other. Both are taken as givens instead of being subjected to a reflexive approach and an empirical test for validating or rejecting them. This is why these approaches struggle to provide a reflexive and empirical analysis of a category that underpins them – that of the specificity or uniqueness of the area or domain studied. This element is often mentioned but hardly

---

⁴⁵ Frederick Mote and Denis Twichett, eds, *The Cambridge History of China*, vol. 7, parts 1 and 2 (Cambridge: Cambridge University Press, 1988).
⁴⁶ Subrahmanyam, 'Connected Histories'.
⁴⁷ Bin Wong and Will, *Nourish the People*.
⁴⁸ Roy Bin Wong, 'Entre monde et nation. Les régions braudeliennes en Asie', *Annales HSC* 56, no. 1 (2001): 5–41.
⁴⁹ Kirti N. Chaudhuri, *Trade and Civilization in the Indian Ocean* (Cambridge: Cambridge University Press, 1985).
⁵⁰ Nicola Di Cosmo, 'State Formation and Periodization in Inner Asian History', *Journal of World History* 10, no. 1 (1999): 1–40.
⁵¹ Denys Lombard, *Le Carrefour javanais. Essai d'histoire globale* (Paris: EHESS, 1992); Michael Pearson, *The Indian Ocean* (London and New York: Routledge, 2003).
⁵² Stephen Dale, *The Muslim Empires of the Ottomans, Safavids and Mughals* (Cambridge: Cambridge University Press, 2010).

ever clarified.⁵³ One possible solution is no longer to imagine entities called China, Africa and India as atemporal realities. This approach is similar to that of Denys Lombard, who uses multiple sources to explore the multifarious constructs of space-times in the Java archipelago, its opening up to the exterior, slow transformations and accelerations.⁵⁴

Taken together, these works show the importance of combining a number of elements: the reflexive interaction between history and the social sciences, as well as the search for appropriate categories of analysis, in such a way as to decentralize not only the subject of the study and its conclusions but also the categories of analysis themselves. Historians need reflexivity in order to open up the epistemological presuppositions of Western historiographies.

Back to anthropology?

Starting in the 1970s, comparative economic and social history in its most economist form has been the constant target of critics who brought out the fundamental differences between societies and thus the impossibility of using a single model to explain different socio-economic dynamics in time and space.⁵⁵ This trend did not resolve in opposing presumed local societies to capitalist economies; several authors insisted on the process of hybridization: Gilberto Freyre in Brail, Mauss's students in France and, to a given extent, Lévi-Strauss as well. Finally, Bourdieu stressed that the Kabyle society had been continuously reshaped by Arab and European influences. This argument was joined to a more general one consisting of revealing the irreducible difference between history and the social sciences on the one hand, and natural sciences on the other. This approach was widely acclaimed by those who thought that proposed modalities of development had to be suited to each country. Economic and social policies should be adapted to the local 'context'.⁵⁶ Unlike general economic models, these approaches relied upon anthropology and sought to identify local conditions and to orient development policies. This relativism, in large part anti-imperialist, but also anti-industrialist, had a twofold advantage over the approaches mentioned earlier: it avoided taking a mythical West as model and reintroduced a 'superstructure' in the objects of comparative analysis.

---

⁵³ Bates, 'Area Studies'.
⁵⁴ Lombard, *Le Carrefour javanais*.
⁵⁵ Just a few references among a huge literature: in economic anthropology: Appadurai, *The Social Life of Things*; Philip Curtin, *Cross-Cultural Trade in World History* (Cambridge: Cambridge University Press, 1984); George Dalton, ed., *Research in Economic Anthropology* (Greenwich, CT: JAI Press, 1983). In France: Bernand Lepetit, 'Une logique du raisonnement historique', *Annale ESC* 5 (1993): 1209–19; special issue 'Histoire et sciences sociales', *Annales ESC* 38, no. 6 (1983); Passeron, *Le raisonnement sociologique*.
⁵⁶ Par Arndt, *Economic Development. The History of an Idea* (Chicago: University of Chicago Press, 1987); Gerald Meier, James Rauch, *Leading Issues in Development Economics* (Oxford: Oxford University Press, 2000); Deepak Lal, *The Poverty of Development Economics* (Boston: MIT Press, 2000).

However, against this relativism, neo-institutional economics, developed in the 1970s by Douglass North among others, became the dominant paradigm in comparative economic history.[57] Instead of evoking an ideal competitive market, like liberal, neoclassical theory, neo-institutional thought took seriously the criticism of those who viewed the market economy as a particular historical construction. It incorporated institutional phenomena in the neoliberal approach, maintaining that institutions were efficient insofar as they offered a means to cope with 'market imperfections'. Thus, the commons, which had been criticized since the eighteenth century as a source of inefficiency, were viewed as a safeguard against risk at a time when the markets were still so imperfect they prevented rapid compensation for poor harvests in one region by the surplus from other regions.[58] In this way, 'market imperfections' were the explanation for Russian peasant settlements and serfdom in Eastern Europe.[59] In other words, there is a rationale for every institution present in the history of humanity.

Such approaches were not abandoned when colonialism and the Cold War came to an end; on the contrary, those historical processes even encouraged their use. The 'transition' to capitalism in the former Soviet-bloc countries as well as in Latin America and, of course, China and India became the inevitable outcome of an economic model considered to be valid everywhere. The same model and presumed historical pattern have been applied to all sorts of historical experiments, including in Russia and the USSR. Joseph Stiglitz, a Nobel Prize winner in economics, revealed the limits of free market equilibrium along with the distortions produced by the Soviet bureaucracy and by managed economies in general.[60] He thus suggests that appropriate institutions can correct and help the market without suffocating it.

We may observe that, in these approaches, the same model is employed to talk about the market in nineteenth-century Africa, serfdom in Russia or fairs in Europe in the modern period: it is no accident that neo-institutional economics speaks less about capitalism than about the market economy. This approach calls into question the classifications of economic systems proposed by traditional neoclassical and Marxist literatures (capitalism, peasant economy, feudalism, etc.). Instead, we find a typology of organizations that evolve strictly in relation to the institutional context. Hence, the approach cannot explain the relationship between institutional changes and forms of market organization: are institutions the result or the source of economic behaviour? In the case of the USSR, did economic weakness cause political decline or, on the contrary, did Soviet institutions close the market and thereby bring about its inevitable collapse?

---

[57] Douglass North and Robert Thomas, *The Rise of Western Civilization: A New Economic History* (Cambridge: Cambridge University Press, 1973).
[58] Donald McCloskey, 'The Open Fields of England: Rent, Risk, and the Rate of Interest, 1300–1815', in *Markets in History: Economic Studies of the Past*, edited by David Galenson (Cambridge: Cambridge University Press, 1989), 5–51; Randall Nielsen, 'Storage and English Government Intervention in Early Modern Grain Markets', *The Journal of Economic History* 57, no. 1 (1997): 1–33.
[59] Tracy K. Dennison, 'Did Serfdom Matter? Russian Rural Society, 1750–1860', *Historical Research* 79 (2003): 74–89.
[60] Joseph Stiglitz, *Whither Socialism?* (Cambridge, MA: MIT Press, 1994).

This question, which may seem innocuous to historians, was important for development policy insofar as the debate, especially in the 1990s, was focused on knowing whether, in post-socialist countries in particular, it was first necessary to set up market institutions and a democratic political system in order to have a market, or conversely whether the market would give rise through its very development to adequate institutions.[61] The issue appears to have been resolved since then because, contrary to the politically correct arguments that always sought to link capitalism to democracy, the experiences in China and Russia in recent years confirm that this equation is by no means obvious from the standpoint either of political philosophy or historical observation.

The end of decolonization brought with it the end of development economics as it had been conceived until then. With the BRICS (Brazil, Russia, India, China and South Africa) and the crisis of the North, the issue of development transcended the division between North and South. In this context, more and more authors specializing in non-European regions began to advocate a point of view diametrically opposed to cultural relativism. Using mentalities to explain underdevelopment became synonymous with racism; however, if economic rationality was indeed one and the same throughout the world, it became possible to attribute the causes of poverty to local institutions and corruption.

This increasing rift between history and economics was enlarged by the gradual decline of economic anthropology. Unlike sociology and most historical investigations grounded in so-called 'area studies' or their opposite (subaltern studies), anthropology deconstructed the 'us' and the 'other' and overcame the comparison, or indeed the contrast, between essentialized 'cultures' and 'area studies'. Instead, circulation and translations are part of the comparison itself. Anthropology, by putting under scrutiny the very notion of 'culture', caused comparative historians, and historians more generally, to redefine their reasoning in terms of well-identified 'cultures' or 'civilizations'. No 'culture' is isolated from the others, and its representations and self-representations go well beyond the conventional opposition between 'realities' and 'representations' so dear to economic and some social historians. It is no accident that anthropologists are usually highly critical of the very notion of 'area studies' as ahistorical, essentialist cultural identities.[62] And yet, the radical relativism and indistinction of subject and object, so dear to Geertz and his followers, no longer enjoys unanimous consensus among anthropologists, which in turn opens the way to further interaction with social and economic anthropologists and historians.[63] The interface between postmodernist and postcolonialist deconstructivism and new reflexive, critical reconstruction of the past found many examples, strongly inspired by anthropology, including Ginzburg's

---

[61] Grigory Yavlinsky, *Laissez-Faire versus Policy-Led Transformation, Lessons of the Economic Reforms in Russia* (Moscow: Center for Economic and Political Research, 1996); Shafiqul Islam and Michael Mandelbaum, eds, *Making Markets Economic Transformations in Eastern Europe and the Post-Soviet States* (New York: Council of Foreign Relations, 1993).

[62] Jane Guyer, 'Anthropology in Area Studies', *Annual Review of Anthropology* 33 (2004): 499–523; Philippe Descola, *Par delà nature et culture* (Paris: Gallimard, 2005, English translation, Chicago, 2013); Geertz, *The Interpretation of Cultures*.

[63] Sahlins, *Stone Age Economics*; George Steinmetz, ed., *The Politics of Methods in the Human Sciences* (Durham, NC: Duke University Press, 2005).

historical morphologies, Stoler's ethnography in and of the archives and Zemon Davis and Luedtke's historical anthropology.[64]

From the early twentieth century on, economic anthropology sought within this overall framework to indicate a different relationship with history and other social sciences than that of mainstream economics.[65] From Malinowski and Mauss (already discussed in the chapter on consumption), passing through Polanyi, Firth and Sahlins, Geertz again, and Godelier and Goody, and down to Zalizer, Appadurai, Comaroff and Graeber, to cite only the 'usual suspects', hundreds of anthropological historical studies were published on local communities and their 'economic' behaviour all around the world. Naturally one must distinguish at least three main periods: until the end of the Second World War, economic anthropology mostly engaged with 'primitive economies', strongly inspired by ethnography and contrasting them with Western advanced economies.[66] The force of this exploration lay in openly opposing the mainstream economic trends, both classical liberal and Marxist, deeply embedded in European and US notions and historical experiences, while showing that possible alternative economic behaviours still persisted around the world. The two main problems raised by this approach were the essentialization of 'primitive' economies, and their positioning outside time and possible change. However, these same criticisms, strongly supported by cultural anthropology during the second half of the twentieth century (Geertz in particular) need also to be nuanced: as Carlo Ginzburg stressed in his discussion of the author, Mauss did not set the gift against market economics, as is usually stated, but, on the contrary, revealed their strong hierarchical relationship. Gift was anything but spontaneous and this explains why it was reappropriated by capitalist economies and societies.

During the Cold War, economic anthropology gave rise to intense debates about 'multiple economic rationalities', and, to some extent, it was the refusal of any presumably economic relationships independent from cultural and social features that marked this major trend during much of the twentieth century. In part as a response to the Cold War, in part as a consequence of the increasing specialization and compartmentalization of knowledge, anthropology, and economic anthropology in particular, became more relativistic and set specificities against presumed universalisms. During the Cold War and decolonization, these were not merely theoretical debates: concrete policies to be adopted in 'developing countries' were a major issue: did 'Africans' or 'Indians' have to act like Londoners at the Stock Exchange to escape from poverty? Most interesting for us was that this attitude ultimately led to questions about economic behaviours, and the boundaries between economic, social and cultural life in 'advanced' countries themselves. According to many anthropologists, optimizing agents, as mainstream

---

[64] Ginzburg, *Clues, Myths*; Stoler, *Along the Archival Grain*; Zemon Davis, *Fiction in the Archives*; Alf Luedtke, *History of Everyday Life* (Princeton: Princeton University Press, 1995).

[65] Raymond Firth, *Primitive Economics of the New Zealand Maori* (London: Routledge, 1929); Edward Evans-Pritchard, *The Nuer: A Description of the Modes of Livelihood and Political Institutions of a Nilotic People* (Oxford: Oxford University Press, 1940); Marcel Mauss, *Essai sur le don* (édition Paris: PUF, 2012; orig. 1924).

[66] For a synthesis, Chris Hann and Keith Hart, *Economic Anthropology* (New York: Polity Press, 2011).

economics calls them, were non-existent everywhere.[67] In short, the presumed 'local' was not only connected to other 'local' entities and therefore to the global, but it forced scholars to reframe theories and interpretations of the 'West' itself. Decade after decade, historians, especially those close to microhistory, seemed extremely sensitive to this argument.[68] It was a way of reconciling criticism of positivistic Eurocentrism with the concrete modus operandi of the economies both in the 'West' and outside it.

Finally, after 1989, economic anthropology was quite shattered and seemed to be swept away by the general faith in market economies. 'Politically correct' attitudes no longer consisted of opposing the World Bank paradigm, pushing any state and actor in the world to act according to neoclassical economic theory, but, quite the contrary, in arguing that Chinese or Africans were no less keen on profits and the market than Europeans and only 'bad' institutions (including postcolonial domination) prevented them from acting accordingly (Acemoglu and Austin adopted this line of reasoning). During these years, economic anthropology was often attracted by economics and occasionally converged with evolutionary anthropology. This last actually expressed a convergence of biology and economics, where 'optimizing agents' responded to 'natural selection', and vice versa. To some extent this was the very end of economic anthropology as an alternative to mainstream economics. Nowadays, economic anthropology is slowly returning, drawn by the distortions of neocapitalism, as Graeber and Hart's works show. Methodologically, this latest turn marks the desired convergence between field work, very locally embedded, and global history. Anthropology offers a key to penetrate all the different perspectives studied in this book: the historical anthropology of the archive buildings and data settings leads us to overcome the opposition between the emic and the etic, 'us' and 'the other', while the historical and economic anthropology identifying the main social actors makes it possible to overcome the other tension discussed between fixed classes and multiple class identifications with no other social specification. Finally, anthropology helps overcome the notion of area studies without falling into the trap of an undefined globalization with scarce, if no, explanatory power.

Conclusion: Part 4

The global revolutions of the years 1780–1820 were the consequence and extension of structural transformation of the world economies as well as regional, transregional and imperial social and political dynamics.

Independentism in Latin America, the Haitian Revolution and tensions in Southeast Asia accompanied the better-known revolutions in France and the United States. These connected events decisively influenced historical practices, as history became

---

[67] Appadurai, *The Social Life of Things*; Clifford Geertz, Hildred Geertz and Lawrence Rosen, *Meaning and Order in Moroccan Society* (Cambridge: Cambridge University Press 1979); David Graeber, *Toward an Anthropological Theory of Value: The False Coin of Our Own Dreams* (New York: Palgrave, 2001); Maurice Godelier, *Rationalité et irrationalité en économie* (Paris: Maspero, 1968); Claude Meillassoux, *L'anthropologie économique des Gouro de Côte d'Ivoire* (Paris: Mouton, 1964).

[68] Giovanni Levi, *Le pouvoir au village* (Paris: Gallimard, 1989).

a key political issue aiming to deny or, on the contrary, to support the revolutionary enterprise. The social sciences and philosophy of the nineteenth century contributed as much as historians – if not more – to the consolidation of the Eurocentric view of the world, as these thinkers presented categories and analyses that were potentially valid for part or all of Europe as universal truths. The proletariat in motion found little confirmation in England itself, and even less outside it; democracy struggled to affirm itself in Europe, and was even less successful elsewhere.

These tensions between Eurocentric universalisms and national histories gave rise to important contradictions that intensified beginning in the 1870s and especially with the First World War. The end of *anciens régimes* and empires in Europe accompanied the rise of radical nationalisms. While philosophy and universal history examined the decline of the West (Spengler) or its role in relation to other civilizations (Toynbee), the interactions between history and the social sciences were renewed in a different project, notably in France, with the *Annales*. However, these approaches struggled to match up with the influence of nationalism in Europe (the central political role of history in totalitarian states), but also in the Americas and Asia – with tensions, for example, in India and China surrounding history and its political role and content. This serves as an important warning for our current debates.

Decolonization, the Cold War and the welfare state dominated the post-war political landscape. This was a major turning point indeed, as colonial empires collapsed against the backdrop of the Cold War. The tools of politics, sociology and anthropology were broadly used by historians, and inversely history was considered indispensable in economics, the social sciences and politics. The history of 'underdevelopment' accompanied that of the system-worlds of Braudel and Wallerstein. Although these approaches sought to be global, they still preserved a profoundly Eurocentric epistemological and conceptual framework. That is the most important legacy of colonialism, along with economic dependence.

The decomposition of this world beginning in the 1970s, and even more so after 1989, opened the way for our current globalization, of which global history is a reflection. Postcolonial studies offer an invitation to rethink history by drawing on non-Western categories, although this approach does not rule out the danger of new Sinocentrisms, Indocentrisms or nationalisms in Africa. This danger became a reality when the success of capitalism, so celebrated after 1989, led to a paradoxical result: the West won the Cold War but lost peace, as the speculative and political crises of recent years bear witness. The strength and limits of global history reflect those of the post-1989 world and, like it, invite one to think globally and give a voice to non-European worlds.

General conclusion

Global trends

In the early 1970s, Eric Hobsbawm argued for a shift from social history to the history of society. By this he meant not only a move beyond conventional British historiography but also and more generally that any history is social history. He was probably right, and the previous chapters are much indebted to this claim. Since then, however, the intellectual and social landscape has radically changed. First, the cultural turn challenged the 'materialistic' view of history and the positivism of sources and data. Then, Chakrabarty and many other postcolonial authors contested the Eurocentric views found in the social sciences and social history. Finally, non-European, connected and global historiographies raised doubts about the very notion of society and social history that Hobsbawm had in mind in terms of its concepts and methods.

This book follows a different path, seeking to move beyond the dichotomies that have oriented conventional as well as postmodernist and postcolonial approaches: the dichotomy between social history and the history of intellectual and political 'discourses'; that between sources and data, between history (and social sciences) rooted in the archives/qualitative sources and quantitative history; and that between the notions and practices prevailing in Western historiography and those followed elsewhere. I have tried instead to understand the social and historical origins of these dichotomies, while highlighting the interrelations between the various elements. This is neither a purely methodological and epistemological discussion, nor a history of historiography and its methods, but a global and connected social history of social history and its component parts. Intellectual history is social history in the sense that it is not confined to a discussion of categories in a vacuum, but reveals their social origins and implications, including those of the actors and institutions that produce and use them. For the same reason, sources and data are neither an invention (deconstruction posture) nor a photo of reality (positivist approach). The production of statistics and sources is a social process, both upstream during the production of documents or inquiries that generate data, then in their classification and presentation, and finally in their interpretation and transposition in time and space.

This same attitude may be adopted for interpretive models and social categories, which likewise are neither pure ideology, nor a mere reflection of their time, but tools for understanding and for social action. The normativity of categories and social models has been a constant since the eighteenth century. However, it must be explained in historically situated social processes, which cannot be confined to the West, but must be apprehended on a transnational and global level. Admittedly, the principal models and frameworks employed in the social sciences that have inspired social history, from the Enlightenment thinkers to Marx, Weber, decolonization and right up to the present day have mostly been produced by Western authors. But does that make them Eurocentric?

The influences of non-European worlds have been decisive for all the authors discussed. For the Enlightenment thinkers, the ambition to civilize was combined with a real interest in non-European worlds, to the point where some authors considered that Europe had much to learn from those other worlds. However, nineteenth-century positivism promoted images of social realities that were increasingly inspired by Europe – or an ideal image of it – sometimes in Britain (Marx), sometimes in Germany (Hegel, Weber).

From that time on and almost up to the present day, the inability of both liberal and Marxist thinking to overcome historical determinism is a reflection of their Eurocentrism and their normativity. The social sciences are supposed to change society, and in so doing they interpret other worlds using European categories. Nevertheless, outside Western Europe these reflections have produced original syntheses, in Russia for example, but also in India, transforming Marx or Weber into something else. It would be quite reductionist to interpret these simply as the impact of the centre on the periphery.

Interconnected local, regional and global socio-economic and political dynamics interacted with the qualification and using of sources, data and social categories. These artefacts evolved together; in the eighteenth century, while global revolutions impacted Europe and Asia, then Latin America in the early nineteenth century, archives were rejected as 'antiquarianism', while philosophy and statistical data became tools to sustain reforms. The very same identification of 'revolution' and 'class' confirmed this overall trend: these notions evolved together with social dynamics. And yet, this trend was far from being universal: the emancipation of the bourgeoisie and the criticism of estates and social groups in *ancien régime* society coexisted with the legal, social and intellectual qualification of 'the slave' in the colonies, while being hardly understandable, at least in the same terms, outside Western Europe.

During the nineteenth century, when archives turned into nationalist and eventually anti-revolutionary tools, social statistics became the arena of political confrontation between different ideals of 'modernization'. Archives and written documents gradually became the only 'true' source of historical knowledge, as opposed to traditional stories and oral sources that historians like Ranke reserve for 'people without history' and hence anthropologists. In turn, this same ambivalence was reflected in the tensions upon social categories and the main interpretative models. Working class and peasants rigidified into opposite statistical, social and political entities, despite their extreme fluidity in social behaviours, while the abolition of slavery made the boundary with 'free' workers even more vague. In the twentieth century, most of these categories, epistemological tools and historical artefacts were shuttered by several disruptive events: two world wars, the Bolshevik and the Chinese revolutions, decolonization and the Cold War. If, without the French Revolution, there would be no national archives in France, then, without the Russian Revolution, there would be no archives of the triumphant proletariat and the single party. Archives, statistics, social models and categories became political weapons as never before. 'Truth' in archival memory, genocides, colonization and decolonization, totalitarianism, data on these same events, but also on employment, GDP and all the other economic variables orienting public policies, social and intellectual debates on who is the worker, the capitalist, etc., not to forget the sometimes violent debates on the 'laws of history' animated the twentieth century.

Local dynamics and the social construction of historical artefacts

At the same time, the main aim of 'controlling' historical memories through archives and influencing political debates with the help of statistics and social categories had to confront with the multiplicity of actors, values and judgements. For example, we have seen that, despite any effort to adopt the 'principle of origin', the classification of archives was modified over time in relation to institutional dynamics. These changes blur the initial message: did the French Revolution really shatter the aristocratic order? Did the Russian Revolution actually give the reins of power to the proletariat or to the single party?

And then there is the social life of the documents themselves, when various actors ascribe meanings to them and harness them for social purposes which are constantly being modified. Although censorship has been quite strong at times – as it was in the USSR – it was unable to stifle these interpretations that rippled through Soviet society and even beyond.

These tensions extend to the colonial archives, which in principle were the expression of the colonial power, but in reality a reflection of its lack of coordination. Decolonization was marked by major battles between the former colonizing countries and the emerging new states to safeguard and control the colonial memory, to organize it in order to write – each in their own way – the 'true history' of colonization. Rather than reproduce the debates that continue to the present day between colonial archives as an expression of the governing power (and therefore unusable) and colonial archives as an expression of resistance by the colonized, we have shown how these archives were jointly although unequally written by actors who, although they possessed very different powers, all participated in the creation and classification of documents. The social history of colonial archives (and archives in general) confirms this overlap and the lack of differentiation between 'practices' and 'discourse'.

Thus, universities and history textbooks are wrong to present archival science, erudition and philology as 'auxiliary disciplines', as techniques to be distinguished from interpretation or, better still, to orient it in an 'objective' way. Documents and the way they are classified have a social life that involves writing, conservation, cataloguing and interpretation. The history of certain fundamental events in recent centuries – the French Revolution, the Russian Revolution, decolonization – is both a factual history and a history of the documents and signs that make it intelligible. The battle for the archives, their production and control, accompanies and contributes to the construction of the world.

Likewise, the construction of statistical data applied to society immediately raises the question of categories and social models. For decades, discussions centred on whether an instrument considered to be technical, such as correlation, could be distinguished from the social categories to which it is applied and therefore whether statistics is a purely technical tool or a discipline. Once again, these discussions have taken place in a connected way in several regions of the world. Quantitative social history was first challenged in Russia, India and Latin America at the end of the nineteenth century, then reinstated in the middle of the twentieth century on the condition that 'local' social categories be used. In return, these discussions have influenced the way social statistics are conceived and practised even in the West. For example, the time budgets of Russian statisticians have been used as a model for similar instruments developed in Europe. Is that sufficient reason to call socio-economic statistics 'pure invention' and to contrast them to 'true social history' based on the archives?

Even though a great many historians have advanced this conclusion, it is not correct. The history of statistics, like that of the archives, shows that figures are produced jointly by investigators and elites on one hand and the actors who are the subject of study on the other. Peasants, craftsmen and workers all influence the construction of data in their own way. It is therefore fundamental to identify these interactions in the archives of statistical investigations and inquiries. All these investigations have their commissioners and users. And they are used and reused, influencing political decisions. For example, the social policies implemented in Europe and in Russia at the turn of the nineteenth and twentieth centuries express a common concern: the collapse of the ancient world dominated by peasants and small producers, and the establishment of a new industrial and urban world – Polanyi's 'great transformation'. On both sides of the Urals, the establishment of both state and local institutional organizations aimed to energize public action which, animated by positivism, claimed to be scientific. The use and misuse of statistics met this requirement, which nevertheless concealed a fundamental ambiguity between those who commissioned the inquiries – public authorities and local elites – and those who conducted and produced them – statisticians and economists, who were often radical if not revolutionary. The local elites commissioned inquiries to support fiscal claims against the central power, while the latter sought to guide and stabilize social change. By contrast, the investigators saw the inquiries as an instrument to express their political discontent. And all of them were confronted with the people who were the subject of these inquiries: mainly peasants and workers, who found themselves placed in pigeonholes – sometimes ill-fitting, but which they had contributed to shaping. The production and use of statistical investigations were spawned by the interaction between these elements. This is why these inquiries are neither an objective reflection of society nor a pure invention of the elites, but both at once, and contribute for this very reason to social dynamics. Social history and the history of these inquiries are but one.

These cases reveal the use of quantitative knowledge by public authorities and also by social actors following clear dynamics: the transformation of the agrarian world and the food supply in France and Western Europe; social inequalities and the transformation of rural worlds in Russia and also to a certain extent in France and Europe; the establishment of international networks for trade and human migration; the various attempts to gain some measure of control over the vagaries of climate for reasons of social stability and also for transportation and communication, especially in the colonial world.

From this point of view, the opposition between sources and data, between archives and statistics serves no purpose. In both cases, they are the building blocks for knowledge and social and political action. Nor is it a question of contrasting objective reality with fallacious interpretations, but rather the co-production and social use of these tools.

In this perspective, the identification of social actors is done both upstream and downstream from the archives and data. For example, the construction of the peasant is part of the history of administrations and of rural and urban worlds. By defining themselves as isolated actors, on one hand, but also as holding multiple occupations (and which ones), peasants take part in these games of social identification and self-identification. The same goes for other actors: workers, capitalists, merchants and consumers. In all these cases, identifying these social categories is an intellectual, political, discursive (if you will) and real process. There is no reason to separate these dimensions. Nor is there any reason to formulate a definition of the worker or peasant in Europe in contrast to those in Russia, India or Brazil. Such a way of seeing things overlooks the fact that the identification of these actors has been done at the intersection of several worlds, with albeit unequal though real interactions. The connected history of the 'peasant' category highlights a fundamental element: ever since the eighteenth century, what perturbs social theories the most is the in-between state; peasant but also proletarian, slave *and* wage earner, capitalist and consumer at the same time. Liberal and Marxist approaches have sought to avoid these awkward scenarios and have remained entrenched in 'pure' cases – peasant or proletarian – which are more useful for normative and political purposes. For liberal theorists and Marxists alike, a proletarian peasant or a wage earner slave constitutes a problem for the theory of social classes and for that of individual and 'free' actors. There are two striking elements in the long history of peasants: first, the plasticity of their definition – ranging from anti-revolutionaries to protectors of the environment to opponents of capitalism – and, second, the complexity of the social realities where, barring rare exceptions, those who are defined or who define themselves as peasants are also in reality farmers, merchants, employees, soldiers and sailors.

The same goes for the world of work and the uncertain boundary between free and forced labour. Conflicting definitions have been given for slaves, and not only in relation to today's academic debates and international disagreements – the condemnation of child slavery in Africa or in South Asia, for example. Similar debates took place at the end of the eighteenth century. Slave owners, companies and certain workers associations argued that the proletarian was the true slave and that Blacks in reality lived in good conditions. This argument was reprised much later in the middle of the postcolonial debates when the question was whether forms of slavery existed in Africa and India before and under the colonial yoke, but anchored in local societies.

We have retraced the history of these debates by following the experiences of well-known utilitarian theorists in India: Jeremy Bentham, James and John Stuart Mill. Even more than for Marx, their approaches to freedom, labour, law and sovereignty were put to the test when they were confronted with the realities in India. What occurred in reality was a mix of the two, but following very particular perspectives. The situation in India prompted a new discussion about the definition of slavery, but also that of free (uncoerced) and wage labour. Considering the various forms of dependence in India as slavery or as family relations has implications not only for the regulation of labour in India but also in Great Britain. The extension of the Masters and Servants Act to India led Henry Sumner Maine to push for its abrogation in Britain was based on the assumption that the same norms and categories could not possibly apply to such different contexts. Paradoxically, these attitudes were in accordance with those of unions and worker movements, which for decades had been calling for the repeal of penal sanctions against British workers in the home country.

The archives and databases on employees and slaves are part of this same movement: these categories have been negotiated, unequally, among the people concerned. For example, an employee being classified as a servant in Great Britain or as a 'lender of service' in France meant that they would not have access to any real legal or social protection until near the end of the nineteenth century. While this does not make these employees slaves, they were still not salaried employees in the modern sense and would only be defined as such at the turn of the twentieth century in most of Europe.

Similarly, the fact that the classification of slavery only included chattel slaves gave historic preponderance to the Atlantic and enabled the production of magnificent databases accounting for all the slaves taken from Africa over nearly four hundred years. However, because of this, other forms of slavery in Africa, Asia and in the Indian Ocean continue to pose a problem: are debt bondage, forced marriage and concubinage forms of slavery even though they do not constitute chattel slavery? Fierce debates have divided researchers, politicians, observers and institutions all around the world.

What now?

Following the crisis of social history and the advent of the cultural turn, i.e. since the early 1980s, we have witnessed the decline of the welfare state and the end of decolonization and the Socialist Bloc. Regarding historiographical approaches, these decades have seen the criticism of positivism in the social sciences, then a revival of interest, and finally a clash between postmodernist approaches and neo-positivist approaches. To this we must add the conflicts between postcolonial and subaltern approaches and Eurocentric approaches. The so-called 'clash of civilizations' was a reactionary project and ultimately not very credible when it was formulated in the early 1990s. Yet over time it has been transformed not only into a real attitude, but a dominant one, mainly in the West, but also elsewhere. The reasons are simple: the West won the Cold War and then lost the peace by imposing unbridled neoliberalism, which led to the happiness of some, euphoria, and then the sharp decline of most other inhabitants of the planet. Globalization could have been harnessed to heal the fractures of decades and centuries of history. The reality has been the opposite: the frenetic dispossession of the planet and its inhabitants by a handful of actors. The result is the return of nationalism in politics and history – in Europe, Eastern Europe,[1] the United States, Russia and the former Soviet countries,[2] but also in Africa[3] and Asia.[4]

Faced with this turn of events, history and the social sciences have their role to play. It is possible to develop analyses – and university programmes – founded on three pillars: history; decentralized, reflexive social sciences (including economics); languages and multiple worlds. The existing academic programmes, at every level, are never built on all three pillars at once. Often we find history as a humanity pitted against the social sciences. At times it is national history against the history of cultural areas. Other times it is 'scientific' economics against the sociologists and the historians. Knowledge and its teaching are fragmented, whereas they should be global in the sense that we have shown throughout this book: a strong interaction between disciplines and worlds. Until now such a synthesis has never been possible, but it has never been so close. It is time to use this heuristic to shape a world made of encounters rather than confrontations between 'civilizations'.

---

[1] László Deme, 'Liberal Nationalism in Hungary, 1988–1990', *East European Quarterly* 32, no. 1 (1998): 57–82; François Fejtö and Ewa Kulesza-Mietkowski, eds, *La fin des démocraties populaires: les chemins du post-communisme* (Paris: Seuil, 1997).

[2] See, in particular, the writings of Marlène Laruelle on Central Asia and its identity. Also: Muzzafar Suleymanov, 'The Role of History in the Creation of National Identities in Central Asia: Uzbekistan and Kyrgyzstan Case Studies', *Peace and Conflict Review* 1, no. 1 (2008): 1–33.

[3] Terence Ranger, 'Nationalist Historiography, Patriotic History, and the History of the Nation: The Struggle over the Past in Zimbabwe', *Journal of Southern African Studies* 30, no. 2 (2004): 215–34.

[4] John Zavos, 'Searching for Hindu Nationalism in Modern Indian History: Analysis of Some Early Ideological Developments', *Economic and Political Weekly* 34, no. 32 (7–13 August 1999): 2269–76.

References

Archives

AN (National Archives, Paris):
  BB 18 6603 through 6607 (illicit speculation)
  F 12 6872, 6873, 7417
ANOM (Colonial Archives, Aix-en-Provence):
  FM SG/Reu c124 d 931, 932, 934, 935, 937, 941, 942, 945, 947
  FM SG/Reu c 454, d 5042 to 5074.
BL (British Library) MSS Brit. Emp. S 2o, E2/4 (Anti-Slavery Papers, minute book of the Committee of the Anti-Slavery Society)
IOR (Indian Office Records), John Stuart Mill, Political dispatch to Bombay, 18 October 1843, E/4/1074: 54–6
RGIA (Russian Imperial Archives), fond 1290, opis 2, delo 430, 456. 628
The National Archives (TNA), Kew, CO (Colonial Office), 318/116

Select Bibliography

Abbott, Andrew, *Chaos of Disciplines* (Chicago: University of Chicago Press, 2001).
Abel, Wilhelm, *Agricultural Fluctuations in Europe from the Thirteenth to the Twentieth Century* (London: Methuen, 1980; orig. 1935).
Abercromby, Ralph, *Weather: A Popular Exposition of the Nature of Weather Changes from Day to Day* (London: Kegan Paul, 1887).
Abioye, Abiola, 'Fifty Years of Archives Administration in Nigeria: Lessons for the Future', *Record Management Journal* 17, no. 1 (2007): 52–62.
Adelman, Jeremy, *Sovereignty and Revolution in the Iberian Atlantic* (Princeton: Princeton University Press, 2006).
Adelman, Jeremy, *Worldly Philosopher. The Odyssey of A.O. Hirschman* (Princeton: Princeton University Press, 2013).
Ageron, Charles-Robert, *Les Algériens musulmans et la France (1871–1919)* (Paris: Presses Universitaires de France, 1968).
Alam, Muzzafar, *The Languages of Political Islam, 1200–1800* (Chicago: University of Chicago Press, 2004).
Alatortseva, A. I. and Galina D. Alekseeva, eds, *50 let sovetskoi istoricheskoi nauka: Khronika nauchnoi zhizni, 1917–1967* (50 Years of Soviet Historical Science: Chronicles of the Scientific Life, 1917–1967) (Moscow: Gosizdat, 1971).
Allaire, Gilles and Robert Boyer, *La grande transformation de l'agriculture* (Paris: Inra, 1995).
Allen, Richard, *European Slave Trade in the Indian Ocean, 1500–1850* (Athens: Ohio University Press, 2015).

Allen, Robert, *The British Industrial Revolution in Global Perspective* (Cambridge: Cambridge University Press, 2009).
Allen, Robert, *Enclosure and the Yeoman* (Oxford: Clarendon Press, 1992).
Allen, Robert, 'The Growth of Labour Productivity in Early Modern English Agriculture', *Explorations in Economic History* 25, no. 2 (1988): 117–46.
Allen, Robert, 'Tracking the Agricultural Revolution in England', *Economic History Review* 52, no. 2 (1999): 209–35.
Amin, Shahid, *Event, Metaphor, Memory: 1922–1992* (Berkeley: University of California Press, 1995).
Amselle, Jean-Loup, *L'Occident décroché. Enquête sur le post-colonialisme* (Paris: Pluriel, 2010).
Anderson, Benedict, *Imagined Communities* (London: Verso, 1991).
Anderson, Katharine, *Predicting the Weather. Victorians and the Science of Meteorology* (Chicago: University of Chicago Press, 2005).
Anderson, Kevin, *Marx at the Margins: On Nationalism, Ethnicity, and Non-Western Societies* (Chicago: University of Chicago Press, 2010).
Anderson, Kimberly, 'The Footprint and the Stepping Foot: Archival Records, Evidence, and Time', *Archival Science* 13, no. 4 (2013): 349–71.
Anderson, Kym, *The Worlds Wine Market: Globalization at Work* (Aldershot: Ashgate, 2005).
Anstey, Roger, *The Atlantic Slave Trade and British Abolition* (London: Macmillan, 1975).
Anstey, Roger, 'Capitalism and Slavery: A Critique', *Economic History Review* 21 (1968): 307–20.
Appadurai, Arjun, *Modernity at Large: Cultural Dimensions of Globalization* (Indianapolis: University of Minnesota Press, 1996).
Appadurai, Arjun, ed., *The Social Life of Things: Commodities in Cultural Perspective* (New York: Cambridge University Press, 1986).
Arendt, Hannah, *On Revolution* (New York: Viking Press, 1963).
Arès, Florence, *Rapport final sur le développement des archives nigériennes* (ONU, 1991).
Armitage, David, *The Ideological Origins of the British Empire* (Cambridge: Cambridge University Press, 2000).
Armitage, David and Sanjay Subrahmanyam, eds, *The Age of Revolutions in Global Context, c. 1760–1840* (New York: Palgrave Macmillan, 2010).
Arndt, Par, *Economic Development: The History of an Idea* (Chicago: University of Chicago Press, 1987).
Arsenault, Raymond, 'The Public Storm: Hurricanes and the State in Twentieth Century America', in *American Public Life and the Historical Imagination*, edited by Wendy Gamber, Michael Grossberg and Hendrick Hartog (Notre Dame: University of Notre Dame Press, 2003): 201–32.
Asante, Molefi Kete, *The Afrocentric Idea* (Philadelphia: Temple University Press, 1987).
Ashton, Timothy, 'The Standard of Life of the Workers in England 1790–1830', *Journal of Economic History* 9 (1949): 19–38.
Atiyah, Patrick, *The Rise and Fall of Freedom of Contract* (Oxford: Oxford University Press, 1979).
Austin, Gareth, 'Reciprocal Comparison and African History Tackling Conceptual Eurocentrism in the Study of Africa's Economic Past', *African Study Review* 50, no. 3 (2007): 1–28.
Axel, Brian, ed., *From the Margins: Historical Anthropology and Its Future* (Durham, NC: Duke University Press, 2005).

Aymard, Maurice, 'La longue durée aujourd'hui. Bilan d'un demi siècle, 1958–2008', in *From Florence to the Mediterranean and Beyond. Essays in Honor of Anthony Molho*, edited by Diogo Ramada Courto, Eric Dursteller, Julius Kirshner and Francesca Trivellato (Firenze: Olschki, 2009): 558–79.

Baàr, Monika, *Historians and Nationalism: East-Central Europe in the Nineteenth Century* (Oxford: Oxford University Press, 2010).

Bairoch, Paul, *L'Agriculture des pays développés 1800 à nos jours* (Paris: Economica, 1999).

Bairoch, Paul, *Révolution industrielle et sous-développement* (Paris: Mouton, 1974).

Baker, Keith Michael and Dan Edelstein, eds, *Scripting Revolution: A Historical Approach to Comparative Study of Revolution* (Stanford: Stanford University Press, 2015).

Balakrishnan, Gopal, ed., *Mapping the Nation* (London: Verso, 1998).

Banerjee, Abhijit and Esther Duflo, *Poor Economics: A Radical Rethinking of the Way to Fight Global Poverty* (New York: Public Affairs, 2011).

Banerjii, Rakhal D., *The Age of the Imperial Guptas* (Benares: Benares Hindu University, 1933).

Bankoff, Greg, *Cultures of Disaster: Society and Natural Hazard in the Philippines* (London: Routledge, 2003).

Baran, Paul, *The Political Economy of Growth* (New York: John Calder, 1957).

Barber, John, *Soviet Historians in Crisis, 1928–1932* (New York: Holmes and Meier, 1981).

Barber, Richard, and Michael Glantz, *Currents of Change: El Niño's Impact on Climate and Society* (Cambridge: Cambridge University Press, 1996).

Barker, Joanne, *Native Act Law, Recognition and Cultural Authenticity* (Durham, NC: Duke University Press, 2011).

Barrett, Thomas, *At the Edge of Empire: The Terek Cossacks and the North Caucasus Frontier, 1700–1860* (Boulder, CO: Westview Press, 1999).

Bastian, Jeannette, 'Reading Colonial Records through Colonial Lens: The Provenance of Place, Space, and Creation', *Archival Science* 6 (2006): 267–84.

Bastian, Jeannette, 'Whispers in the Archives: Finding the Voices of the Colonized in the Records of the Colonizer', in *Political Pressure and the Archival Record*, edited by Margareth Procter, Michael Cook and Caroline Williams (Chicago: Society of American Archivists, 2006): 25–43.

Bates, Robert H. 'Area Studies and the Discipline: A Useful Controversy?' *PS: Political Science & Politics* 30, no. 2 (June 1997): 166–70.

Bayly, Christopher, *The Birth of the Modern World, 1780–1914* (London: Blackwell, 2004).

Bayly, Christopher, *Empire and Information: Intelligence Gathering and Social Communication in India, 1780–1870* (Cambridge: Cambridge University Press, 1996).

Beattie, James, Emily O'Gorman and Matthew Henry, *Climate, Science, and Colonization: Histories from Australia and New Zealand* (Basingstoke: Palgrave Macmillan, 2014).

Beaud, Jean-Pierre and Cláudia Damasceno Fonseca, 'Le chiffre et la carte. Pratiques statistiques et cartographiques en Amérique latine (du milieu du XVIII e au milieu du XX e siècle)', *Histoire & Mesure* 32, no. 1 (2017): 3–8.

Béaur, Gérard, Hubert Bonin and Claire Lemercier, eds, *Fraude, contrefaçon et contrebande de l'antiquité à nos jours* (Genève: Droz, 2006).

Béchu, Claire, ed., *Les Archives nationales. Des lieux pour l'histoire de France. Bicentenaire d'une installation, 1808–2008* (Paris: Archives nationales-Éditions Somogy, 2008).

Beckert, Jens, *Imagined Futures: Fictional Expectations and Capitalist Dynamics* (Cambridge, MA: Harvard University Press, 2016).

Beckert, Sven, 'Emancipation and Empire: Reconstructing the Worldwide Web of Cotton Production in the Age of the American Civil War', *American Historical Review* 109, no. 5 (2004): 1405–38.

Beckert, Sven, *Empire of Cotton* (New York: Knopf, 2014).
Beckert, Sven and Christine Desan, *American Capitalism: New Histories* (New York: Columbia University Press, 2018).
Behal, Rana, *One Hundred Years of Servitude: Political Economy of Tea Plantations in Colonial Assam* (New Delhi: Tulika Books, 2014).
Bell, Andrew, John Swenson-Wright and Karin Tybjerg, eds, *Evidence* (Cambridge: Cambridge University Press, 2008).
Bender, Thomas, *Intellectual and Public Life: Essays on the Social History of Academic Intellectuals in the United States* (Baltimore: Johns Hopkins University, 1993).
Bentham, Jeremy, *Works of Jeremy Bentham*, edited by J. Bowring (Edinburgh: William Tait, 1838–43).
Bentley, Gilbert, *The Evolution of National Insurance in Great Britain: The Origins of the Welfare State* (London: Joseph, 1966).
Bentley, Michael, *Modernizing England's Past: English Historiography in the Age of Modernism, 1870–1970* (Cambridge: Cambridge University Press, 2005).
Berelowitch, André, *La hiérarchie des égaux. La noblesse russe d'ancien régime* (Paris: Seuil, 2001).
Berg, Maxine, *The Age of Manufactures, 1700–1820* (London: Routledge, 1985).
Berg, Maxine, *Luxury and Pleasure in Eighteenth-Century Britain* (Oxford: Oxford University Press, 2008).
Berg, Maxine and E. Eger, eds, *Luxury in the Eighteenth Century: Debates, Desires and Delectable Goods* (Basingstoke: Macmillan, 2003).
Berger, Stefan, Linas Eriksonas and Andrew Mycock, eds, *Narrating the Nation: Representations in History, Media and the Arts* (New York and Oxford: Berghahn Books, 2008).
Berlière, Jean-Marc, 'Richesse et misère des archives policières', *Les cahiers de la sécurité intérieure* 3 (1990–1): 165–75.
Bernard, H. Russell, *Research Methods in Anthropology: Qualitative and Quantitative Approaches*, 6th ed. (Lanham: Rowman & Littlefield, 2018).
Bernier, François, *Un libertin dans l'Inde Moghole* (Paris: Chandeigne, 2008).
Bernstein, Peter, *Against the God: The Remarkable Story of Risk* (New York: Wiley, 1996).
Bertrand, Alain, *Le droit des marques, des signes distinctifs et des noms de domaine* (Paris: Cedat, 2002).
Bertrand, Romain, *L'Histoire à parts égales* (Paris: Seuil, 2011).
Betts, Alexander, ed., *Global Migration Governance* (Oxford: Oxford University Press, 2011).
Bhattacharya, Sabyasachi, ed., *Towards a New History of Work* (Delhi: Tulika Book, 2014).
Bin Wong, Roy, *China Transformed* (Ithaca: Cornel University Press, 1997).
Bin Wong, Roy, 'Entre monde et nation. Les régions braudeliennes en Asie', *Annales HSC* 56, no. 1 (2001): 5–41.
Bin Wong, Roy and Pierre-Étienne Will, *Nourish the People* (Ann Arbor: University of Michigan Press, 1993).
Birnbaum, Norman, 'Conflicting Interpretations of the Rise of Capitalism: Marx and Weber', *British Journal of Sociology* 4 (1953): 125–41.
Black, Jeremy, *European Warfare, 1600–1815* (New Haven: Yale University Press, 1994).
Blackstone, William, *Commentaries on the Laws of England*, 4 vols (London: Strahan, Woodfall, 1793–5).
Blaut, J. M., *Eight Eurocentric Historians* (New York: Guilford Publications, 2000).
Bloch, Marc, *Apologie pour l'histoire ou métier d'historien* (Paris: Colin, 1993; orig. 1949).

Bloch, Marc, *Écrire la société féodale. Lettres à Henri Berr, 1924–1943*. Texts compiled by Jacqueline Pluet-Despatin (Paris: Institut mémoires de l'édition contemporaine, 1992).
Blouin, Francis and William Rosenberg, eds, *Processing the Past: Contesting Authorities in History and the Archives* (New York: Oxford University Press, 2013).
Blum, Alain and Martine Mespoulet, *L'anarchie bureaucratique. Statistique et pouvoir sous Staline* (Paris: La découverte, 2003).
Blum, Françoise, ed., *Genre de l'archive. Constitution et transmission des mémoires militantes* (Paris: Codhos éditions, 2017).
Bohr, Paul, *Famine in China* (Cambridge, MA: Harvard University Press, 1972).
Bonnell, Victoria and Lynn Hunt, eds, *Beyond the Cultural Turn* (Berkeley: University of California Press, 1999).
Bonneuil, Christophe and Jean-Baptiste Fressoz, *The Shock of the Anthropocene* (London: Verso, 2017).
Borgé, Jacques and Nicolas Viasnoff, *Archives de l'Indochine* (s. l., M. Trinckvel, 1995).
Bose, Sugata, *Peasant Labour and Colonial Capital: Rural Bengal since 1770* (Cambridge: Cambridge University Press, 1993).
Bouk, Daniel, *How Our Days Became Numbered: Risk and the Rise of the Statistical Individual* (Chicago and London: University of Chicago Press, 2015).
Bourdieu, Pierre, Jean-Claude Chamboredon and Jean-Claude Passeron, *Le métier de sociologue: préalables épistémologiques* (Berlin and New York: Mouton de Gruyter, 1968).
Boyer, Christopher, *Becoming Campesinos: Politics, Identity, and Agrarian Struggle in Postrevolutionary Michoacán, 1920–1935* (Stanford: Stanford University Press, 2003).
Brading, D. A., *The First America: The Spanish Monarchy, Creole Patriots and the Liberal State, 1492–1867* (Cambridge: Cambridge University Press, 1991).
Brass, Tom and Marcel van der Linden, eds, *Free and Unfree Labour: The Debate Continues* (Berne: Peter Lang, 1997).
Braudel, Fernand, *Civilisation matérielle, économie et capitalisme*, 3 vols (Paris: Armand Colin, 1977–9).
Braudel, Fernand, *Grammaire des civilisations* (Paris: Arthaud, 1987).
Braudel, Fernand, *La Méditerranée et le monde méditerranéen à l'époque de Philippe II* (Paris: Flammarion, 1949).
Bréard, Andrea, *Reform, Bureaucratic Expansion and Production of Numbers: Statistics in Early 20th Century China*, Habilitationsschrift (Berlin: Technische Universität Berlin, 2008).
Breman, Jan, *Timing the Coolie Beast* (Delhi: Oxford University Press, 1989).
Brewer, John and Roger Porter, eds, *Consumption and the World of Goods* (London: Routledge, 1993).
Brian, Eric, *La mesure de l'État* (Paris: Albin Michel, 1996).
Bridet, Hilaire Gabriel, *Étude sur les ouragans de l'hémisphère austral. Manœuvres à faire pour s'en éloigner et se soustraire aux avaries qu'ils peuvent occasionner* (Saint-Denis, La Réunion: Rambosson, 1861).
Broadberry, Stephen and Bishnupriya Gupta, 'The Early Modern Great Divergence: Wages, Prices and Economic Development in Europe and Asia, 1500–1800', *The Economic History Review* 59, no. 1 (2006): 2–31.
Brook, Timothy, *Vermeer's Hat: The Seventeenth Century and the Dawn of the Global World* (London: Profile Books, 2009).
Brower, Daniel R. and Edward J. Lazzerini, eds, *Russia's Orient: Imperial Borderlands and Peoples, 1700–1917* (Bloomington: Indiana University Press, 1997).

Brown, Delmer and Ichiro Ishida, trans. and eds, *The Future and the Past: A Translation and Story of the Gukansho, an Interpretative History of Japan, Written in 1219* (Berkeley: University of California Press, 1979).
Brown, Ian, *The School of Oriental and African Studies: Imperial Training and the Expansion of Learning* (Cambridge: Cambridge University Press, 2016).
Browne, Walter, *The Moon and the Weather*, 2nd ed. (London: Balliere, Tyndall and Cox, 1886).
Bruegel, Martin, ed., *A Cultural History of Food in the Age of Empire* (London: Bloomsbury, 2015).
Bruhns, Innerk, 'Max Weber, l'économie et l'histoire', *Annales HSC* 51, no. 6 (1996): 1259–87.
Buckley, Brendan, Roland Fletcher, Shi-Yu Simon Wang, Brian Zottoli and Christophe Pottier, 'Monsoon Extremes and Society over the Past Millennium on Mainland South-East Asia', *Quaternary Science Review* 95 (2014): 1–19.
Bulle, P., 'François Bernier and the Origins of the Concept of Race', in *The Color of Liberty: Histories of Race in France*, edited by Sue Peabody and T. Stovall (Durham, NC and London: Duke University Press, 2003): 11–27.
Burbank, Jane and David L. Ransel, eds, *Imperial Russia: New Histories for the Empire* (Bloomington: Indiana University Press, 1998).
Burbank, Jane, Mark von Hagen and Anatolyi Remnev, eds, *Russian Empire: Space, People, Power, 1700–1930* (Bloomington: Indiana University Press, 2008).
Burds, Jeffrey, *When Russia Learned to Read* (Princeton: Princeton University Press, 1985).
Burgess, John, *Reconstruction and Constitution* (New York: Scribner's Son, 1902).
Burke, Edmund, *The Works of the Right Honourable Edmunde Burke* (London: Bell, 1889).
Burke, Peter, *History and Social Theory* (Ithaca, NY: Cornell University Press, 1992).
Burnard, Trevor and Giorgio Riello, 'Slavery and the New History of Capitalism', *Journal of Global History* 15, no. 2 (2020): 225–44.
Burnett, John and Derek Oddy, eds, *The Origins and Development of Food Policies in Europe* (London and New York: Leicester University Press, 1994).
Bush Michael, ed., *Serfdom and Slavery: Studies in Legal Bondage* (Manchester: Manchester University Press, 1996).
Byrnes, Robert, 'Creating the Soviet Historical Profession, 1917–1934', *Slavic Review* 50, no. 2 (1991): 297–308.
Cabantous, Alain, *Les citoyens du large – Les identités maritimes en France (XVII–XIXe siècles)* (Paris: Aubier, 1995).
Cabantous, Alain, *Dix mille marins face à l'océan. Les populations maritimes de Dunkerque au Havre (1660–1794)* (Paris: Publisud, 1991).
Calder, Lendon, *Financing the American Dream: A Cultural History of Consumer Credit* (Princeton: Princeton University Press, 1999).
Campbell, Colin, *The Romantic Ethic and the Spirit of Modern Consumerism* (Oxford: Blackwell, 1987).
Campbell, Gwyn, ed., *Bondage and the Environment in the Indian Ocean World* (New York: Palgrave, 2018).
Campbell, Gwyn and Alessandro Stanziani, eds, *Debt and Bondage in the Indian Ocean World* (London: Pickering & Chatto, 2013).
Campos Boralevi, Lea, *Bentham and the Oppressed* (Berlin and New York: Walter de Gruyter, 1984).
Cantillon, Richard, *Essai sur la nature du commerce en général* (Paris: INED, 1952; orig. 1755).

Capatti, Alberto, *Le goût nouveau, origine de la modernité alimentaire* (Paris: Albin Michel, 1989).
Catterall, Helene T., ed., *Judicial Cases Concerning American Slavery and the Negro*, 5 vols (Washington: Carnegie Institution, 1926–37).
Cerutti, Simona and Isabelle Grangaud, 'Sources and Contextualization: Comparing Eighteenth Century North-Africa and Western European Institutions', *Comparative Studies in Society and History* 59, no. 1 (2017): 5–33.
Chakrabarty, Dipesh, *The Calling of History: Sir Jadunath Sarkar and His Empire of Truth* (Chicago: University of Chicago Press, 2015).
Chakrabarty, Dipesh, *Provincializing Europe* (Princeton: Princeton University Press, 2000).
Chandler, Alfred, *Scale and Scope* (Cambridge, MA: Belknap Press, 1990).
Chandra, Satish, *State, Pluralism, and the Indian Historical Tradition* (Oxford: Oxford University Press, 2008).
Charlton, Thomas, Lois Myers and Rebecca Sharpless, eds, *History of Oral History* (Lanham: Altamira Press, 2007).
Chatterjee, Indrani, *Gender, Slavery, and Law in Colonial India* (New Delhi: Oxford University Press, 1999).
Chatterjee, Indrani and Richard Eaton, eds, *Slavery and South Asian History* (Bloomington: Indiana University Press, 2006).
Chaudhuri, Kirti N., *Trade and Civilization in the Indian Ocean* (Cambridge: Cambridge University Press, 1985).
Chayanov, Aleksandr, *On the Theory of Peasant Economy* (Homewood: Illinois, 1966).
Chayanov, Aleksandr, 'Zur frage einer theorie der nichtkapitalistichen wirtschaftssysteme (la théorie des systèmes économiques non-capitalistes)', *Arkhiv für Sozialwissenschaft und Sozialpolitik* 51, no. 3 (1924): 577–618.
Chenoweth, Michael, 'A Reassessment of Historical Atlantic Basin Tropical Cyclone Activity, 1700–1855', *Climate Change* 76 (2006): 169–240.
Chernov, A. V., *Istoriia organizatsiia arkhivnogo dela SSSR. Kratkii ocherk* (History and Organization of Archives in the USSR. Small Essay) (Moscow: Gosizdat, 1940).
Chernyk, Viktor A., 'Tsentr izucheniia minuvshikh vremen: k 50-letiiu Arkeograficheskoi komissii RAN' (The Center of Study of "Small Affairs": 50 Years of the Archaeographical Commission of the Academy of Science), *Vestnik Rossiskoi Akademii Nauk* 76, no. 9 (2006): 837–42.
Chernyshevskii, Nikolai, *Sochineniia* (Works) (Geneva: Elpidine, 1879).
Chudakova, M. S., 'Organy politicheskogo syska nakanune i v period Fevral'skoi revoliutsii' (The Political Investigation Organs on the Eve and during the February Revolution), *Vestnik KGU im. N. A. Nekrasova* 3 (2006): 132–7.
Chuprov, Aleksandr I., *Kurs Politicheskoi ekonomik* (Handbook of Political Economy) (Moscow, 1885; 1924 ed., Moscow: Gozizdat).
Cipolla, Carlo, *Before the Industrial Revolution* (New York: Norton, 1993).
Clair, Sylvie, 'Le Centre des Archives d'Outre-Mer', *La Gazette des archives* 142–3 (1988): 5–17.
Clark, Gregory, *A Farewell to Alms* (Princeton: Princeton University Press, 2007).
Clark, Gregory, 'Agriculture and the Industrial Revolution, 1750–1850', in *The British Industrial Revolution: An Economic Perspective*, edited by Joel Mokyr (Boulder, CO: Westview Press, 1993), 227–66.
Clark, Gregory, 'Productivity Growth without Technical Change in European Agriculture before 1850', *The Journal of Economic History* 47, no. 2 (June 1987): 419–32.

Clifford, James, *The Predicament of Culture: Twentieth-Century Ethnography, Literature, and Art* (Cambridge, MA: Harvard University Press, 1988).
Coeuré, Sophie, 'Le siècle soviétique des archives', *Annales HSS* 74, no. 3 (2019): 657–86.
Coeuré, Sophie and Vincent Duclert, *Les archives* (Paris: La découverte, 2011).
Cohen, Elizabeth, *A Consumers' Republic* (New York: Knopf, 2003).
Colten, Crain, *Perilous Place, Powerful Storms: Hurricane Protection in Coastal Louisiana* (Jackson: University Press of Mississippi, 2009).
Comaroff, Jean and John, *Ethnography and the Historical Imagination* (Boulder, CO: Westview Press, 1992).
Congbin, Fu and J. Fletcher, 'Large Signals of Climatic Variation over the Ocean in the Asian Monsoon Region', *Advances in Atmospheric Sciences* 5, no. 4 (1988): 389–404.
Conrad, Christoph, 'Social History', in *The International Encyclopedia of the Social and Behavioural Sciences*, edited by James Wright, 2nd ed., vol. 22 (Amsterdam: Elsevier, 2015): 307–22.
Conrad, Sebastian, 'Enlightenment in Global History. A Historiographical Critique', *American Historical Review* 117, no. 4 (October 2012): 999–1027.
Cook, Eli, *The Pricing of Progress: Economic Indicators and the Capitalization of American Life* (Cambridge, MA: Harvard University Press, 2017).
Cook, Terry, 'Fashionable Nonsense or Professional Rebirth: Postmodernism and the Practice of Archives', *Archiv* 51 (2001): 14–35.
Cooper, Frederick, *Citizenship between Empire and Nation* (Princeton: Princeton University Press, 2014).
Cooper, Frederick, 'Conflict and Connections: Rethinking Colonial African History', *American Historical Review* 99, no. 5 (1994): 1516–45.
Cooper, Frederick, *Decolonization and African Society: The Labor Question in French and British Africa* (Cambridge: Cambridge University Press, 1996).
Cooper, Frederick, *From Slaves to Squatters: Plantation Labour and Agriculture in Zanzibar and Coastal Kenya, 1890–1935* (New Haven and London: Yale University Press, 1980).
Cooper, Frederick and Anne Laura Stoler, eds, *Tensions of Empire* (Berkeley: University of California Press, 1997).
Cooper, Frederick, Allen Isaacman, Florencia Mallon, William Roseberry and Steve Stern, eds, *Confronting Historical Paradigms: Peasants, Labour, and the Capitalist World System in Africa and Latin America* (Madison: University of Wisconsin Press, 1993).
Coquery-Vidrovitch, Catherine, 'A l'origine de l'historiographie africaine de langue française', *Présence africaine* 173, no. 1 (2006): 77–90.
Coquery-Vidrovitch, Catherine and Odile Goerg, *Des historiens africains en Afrique* (Paris: L'Harmattan, 1998).
Corrigan, Peter, *The Sociology of Consumption: An Introduction* (London: SAGE, 2012).
Cox, John, *Storm Watchers: The Turbulent History of Weather Prediction from Franklin's Kite to El Niño* (Hoboken, NJ: John Wiley and sons, 2002).
Coyle, Diane, *GDP: A Brief but Affectionate History* (Princeton: Princeton University Press, 2014).
Crossley, Pamela Kyle, *A Translucent Mirror: History and Identity in Qing Imperial Ideology* (Berkeley: University of California Press, 1999).
Cunningham, Henri and P. Viazzo, *Child Labour in Historical Perspective, 1800–1985: Historical Studies from Europe, Japan, and Colombia* (Florence: European University Press, 1996).
Curtin, Philip, *Cross-Cultural Trade in World History* (Cambridge: Cambridge University Press, 1984).

Dahan Dalmedico, Amy, 'History and Epistemology of Models: Meteorology (1946–1963) as a Case Study', *Archive for History of Exact Science* 55 (2001): 395–422.

Dale, Andrew, *A History of Inverse Probability* (New York: Springer, 1999).

Dale, Stephen, *The Muslim Empires of the Ottomans, Safavids and Mughals* (Cambridge: Cambridge University Press, 2010).

Dalton, George, ed., *Research in Economic Anthropology* (Greenwich, CT: JAI Press, 1983).

Danilov, Viktor Petrovich, *Sovetskaia dokolkkoznaia derevnia* (The Soviet Countryside before the Collectivization), 2 vols (Moscow: Nauka, 1977, 1979).

Darity, William, 'The Number Game and the Profitability of the British Trade in Slaves', *Journal of Economic History* 45 (1985): 693–703.

Darity, William, 'Profitability of the British Trade in Slave once Again', *Explorations in Economic History* 26 (1989): 380–4.

Daudin, Guillaume, 'Comment calculer les profits de la traite?', *Outre-mer* 89, no. 336–7 (2002): 43–62.

Daudin, Guillaume, *Commerce et prospérité: la France au XVIIIe siècle* (Paris: PUPS, 2005).

Daudin, Guillaume, 'Profitability of Slavery and Long-Distance Trading in Context: The Case of Eighteenth-Century France', *The Journal of Economic History* 64, no. 1 (2004): 144–71.

Davis, David Brion, *The Problem of Slavery in the Western Culture* (New York: Oxford University Press, 1966).

Davis, Mike, *Late Victorian Holocausts* (London: Verso, 2000).

De Ferry, Féréol, 'Les archives en Indochine', *Gazette des archives* 8 (1950): 33–41.

De Grazia, Victoria and Ellen Furlough, eds, *The Sex of Things: Gender and Consumption in Historical Perspective* (Berkeley: University of California Press, 1996).

De Pauw, Cornelius, *Recherches philosophiques sur les Américains*, 2 vols (Berlin: Decker, 1768–9).

De Sismondi, Jean-Charles Léonard Simon, *Nouveaux principes d'économie politique* (Paris: Delanauy, 1819).

De Vito, Christian and Anne Garritsen, *Micro-Spatial Histories of Global Labour* (London: Palgrave, 2018).

de Vries, Jan, *The Industrious Revolution* (Cambridge: Cambridge University Press, 2008).

Deakin, Simon and Frank Wilkinson, *The Law of the Labor Market* (Oxford: Oxford University Press, 2005).

Debien, Gabriel, *Les engagés pour les Antilles 1634–1715* (Paris: Société de l'histoire des colonies françaises, 1952).

Dejung, Christophe, David Motadel and Jürgen Osterhammel, eds, *The Global Bourgeoisie: The Rise of the Middle Classes in the Age of the Empire* (Princeton: Princeton University Press, 2019).

Delsalle, Paul, *Une histoire de l'archivistique* (Saint-Foie: Presses Universitaires du Québec, 2000).

Deme, László, 'Liberal Nationalism in Hungary, 1988–1990', *East European Quarterly* 32, no. 1 (1998): 57–82.

Demidova Natalia F., ed., *Materialy po istorii russko-mongol'skikh otnoshenii: russko-mongol'skie otnosheniia, 1654–1685 sbornik dokumentov* (Materials for the History of Russian-Mongol Relations: Russian-Mongol Relations, 1654–1685, Collection of Documents) (Moscow: Izdatel'skaia Firma Vostochnaia Literatura, 1995, 1996, 2000).

Demidova, Natalia F. and Viktor S. Miasnikov, eds, *Russko-kitaiskie otnosheniia v xvii veke: materialy i dokumenty* (Russian-Chinese Relations in the Seventeenth Century: Materials and Documents), 2 vols (Moscow: Nauka, 1969–72).

Dennison, Tracy K., 'Did Serfdom Matter? Russian Rural Society, 1750–1860', *Historical Research* 79 (2003): 74–89.
Deringer, William, *Calculated Values: Finance, Politics, and the Quantitative Age* (Cambridge, MA and London: Harvard University Press, 2018).
Deringer, William, 'Compound Interest Corrected: The Imaginative Mathematics of the Financial Future in Early Modern England', *Osiris* 33, no. 1 (October 2018): 109–29.
Desan, Suzanne, Lynn Hunt and William Max Nelson, eds, *The French Revolution in Global Perspective* (Ithaca, NY and London: Cornell University Press, 2013).
Descola, Philippe, *Par-delà nature et culture* (Paris: Gallimard, 2015. English translation, 2015).
Desrosières, Alain, *Gouverner par les nombres* (Paris: Presses des Mines, 2008).
Desrosières, Alain, *La politique des grands nombres* (Paris: La découverte, 1993).
Dew, Nicholas, *Orientalism in Louis XIV's France* (Oxford: Oxford University Press, 2009).
Di Cosmo, Nicola, *Ancient China and Its Enemies: The Rise of Nomadic Power in East Asian History* (Cambridge: Cambridge University Press, 2002).
Di Cosmo, Nicola, 'State Formation and Periodization in Inner Asian History', *Journal of World History* 10, no. 1 (1999): 1–40.
Di Costanzo, Giuseppe, ed., *La cultura storica italiana tra Otto e Novecento* (Napoli: Liguori, 1990).
Diamond, Jared, *Collapse* (New York: Viking Press, 2005).
Diamond, Jared, *Guns, Germs, and Steel* (New York: W. W. Norton, 1997).
Diawara, Mamadou, and others, eds, *Historical Memory in Africa* (New York: Columbia University, 2010).
Dicey, Albert V., *Lectures on the Relation between Law and Public Opinion in England during the Nineteenth Century* (London: Richard Vandewetering, 1905).
Dirks, Nicholas, Geoff Eley and Sherry Ortner, eds, *Culture, Power, History: A Reader in Contemporary Social History* (Princeton: Princeton University Press, 1994).
Dirlik, Arif, Vinay Bahl and Peter Gran, eds, *History after the Three Worlds: Post-Eurocentric Historiographies* (Oxford: Oxford University Press, 2000).
Dixon, Simon, *The Modernization of Russia, 1676–1825* (Cambridge: Cambridge University Press, 1999).
Dod, C. R., *Electoral Facts 1832–1853 Impartially Stated*, edited by H. J. Hanham (London: Harvester Press, 1972).
Dossé, François, *La marche des idées: histoire des intellectuels, histoire intellectuelle* (Paris: La découverte, 2003).
Douglas, Mary, *How Institutions Think* (Syracuse: Syracuse University Press, 1986).
Douglas, Mary and Baron Isherwood, *The World of Goods: Toward an Anthropology of Consumption* (New York: Basic Books, 1979).
Douwe Van der Ploeg, Jan, *The New Peasantries: Struggles for Autonomy and Sustainability in an Era of Empire and Globalization* (London: Earthscan, 2008).
Dove, Henry, *The Law of Storms Considered in Connection with the Ordinary Movement of the Atmosphere* (London: Longman, 1886).
Dronin, Nikolai M. and Edward G. Bellinger, *Climate Dependence and Food Problems in Russia 1900–1990: The Interaction of Climate and Agricultural Policy and Their Effect on Food Problems* (Budapest and New York: CEU Press, 2005).
Du Toit, André, 'La Commission Vérité et Réconciliation sud-africaine. Histoire locale et responsabilité face au monde', *Politique africaine* 92, no. 4 (2003): 97–116.
Duchet, Michèle, *Anthropologie et histoire au siècle des Lumières* (Paris: Albin Michel, 1971).

Dunn, Stephen, *The Fall and Rise of the Asiatic Mode of Production* (London: Routledge & Kegan Paul, 1982).

Dunning, William, *Reconstruction, Political and Economic, 1865–1877* (New York: Harper, 1907).

Durkheim, Émile and Marcel Mauss, 'De quelques formes primitives de classification. Contribution à l'étude des représentations collectives', *L'année sociologique* 6 (1903), reprint in Marcel Mauss, *Essais de sociologie* (Paris: PUF, 1968): 162–230.

Dyson, Tim, ed., *India's Historical Demography: Studies in Famine, Disease, and Society* (Cambridge: Cambridge University Press, 1989).

Echevarria, Roberto Gonzalez, *Myth and Archive: A Theory of Latin American Narrative* (Cambridge: Cambridge University Press, 1990).

Eckert, Andreas, ed., *Global Histories of Work* (Oldenburg: De Gruyter, 2016).

Eckert, Andreas 'Regulating the Social: Social Security, Social Welfare, and the State in Late Colonial Tanzania', *The Journal of African History* 45, no. 3 (2004): 467–89.

Ecormier, Jean, *Cyclones tropicaux du Sud-ouest de l'Océan Indien, le cas de l'Ile de la Réunion* (La Réunion: S.M.R., 1992).

Edelman, Marc, *Peasants against Globalization: Rural Social Movements in Costa Rica* (Stanford: Stanford University Press, 1999).

Eggleston, Edward, *The Beginning of a Nation, a History of the Sources and Rise of the Earliest Settlements in America, with Special Reference to the Life and Character of People* (New York: Appleton, 1896).

Ellis, Frank, *Peasant Economics: Farm Households in Agrarian Development* (Cambridge: Cambridge University Press, 1988).

Eltis, David, *Economic Growth and the Ending of Transatlantic Slave Trade* (New York: Oxford University Press, 1987).

Eltis, David, Stephen D. Behrendt, David Richardson and Herbert S. Klein, *The Trans-Atlantic Slave Trade: A Database on CD-ROM* (Cambridge and New York: Cambridge University Press, 1999).

Ember, Melvin, Carol Ember and Ian Skoggard, eds, *Encyclopedia of Diasporas* (New York: Springer, 2005).

Emmanuel, Kerry, *Divine Wind: The History and Science of Hurricanes* (Oxford: Oxford University Press, 2005).

Engerman, Stanley, ed., *Terms of Labor. Slavery, Freedom and Free Labor* (Stanford: Stanford University Press, 1999).

Engerman, Stanley, 'The Slave Trade and British Capital Formation in the Eighteenth Century: A Comment on Williams Thesis', *Business History Review* 46 (1972): 430–43.

Epstein, Catherine, *A Past Renewed: A Catalogue of German Speaking Refugee Historians in the United States* (Cambridge: Cambridge University Press, 1993).

Escobar, Arturo, *Sentipensar con la tierra* (Medellin, Colombia: Ediciones Unaula, 2014).

Escudier, Alexandre, 'Temporalisation et modernité politique: penser avec Koselleck', *Annales HSS* 64, no. 6 (2009): 1269–1301.

Espagne, Michel, 'Sur les limites du comparatisme en histoire culturelle', *Genèse* 17, no. 1 (1994): 112–21.

Etkind, Alexander, *Internal Colonization: Russia's Imperial Experience* (Cambridge: Polity Press, 2011).

Evans-Pritchard, Edward, 'Social Anthropology: Past and Present, The Marett Lecture, 1950', *Social Anthropology and Other Essays* (New York: Free Press, 1951): 112–24.

Evans-Pritchard, Edward, *The Nuer: A Description of the Modes of Livelihood and Political Institutions of a Nilotic People* (Oxford: Oxford University Press, 1940).

Eve, Prospère, *Ile à peur, La peur redoutée ou récupérée à La Réunion des origines à nos jours* (Saint André, La Réunion: éd. Graphica, 1992).
Fabian, Johannes, *Time and the Others: How Anthropology Makes Its Object* (New York: Columbia University Press, 1983).
Faccarello, Gilbert and Heinz Kurz, eds, *Handbook of the History of Economic Analysis* (Cheltenham: Edward Elgar online, 2016) https://doi.org/10.4337/9781785366642
Faccarello, Gilbert and Philippe Steiner, eds, *La pensée économique pendant la révolution française* (Grenoble: Presses universitaires de Grenoble, 1990).
Fagan, Brian, *Floods, Famines and Emperors: El Niño and the Fate of Civilization* (New York: Basic Books, 1999).
Falola, Toyin, *Sources and Methods in African History: Spoken, Written, Unearthed* (Rochester, NY: University of Rochester Press, 2002).
FAO, *The State of Agricultural Commodity Markets 2004* (Rome: FAO Press, 2004).
Farge, Arlette, *Le goût de l'archive* (Paris: Seuil, 1989).
Farrell, Stephen, Melanie Unwin and James Walvin, eds, *The British Slave Trade: Abolition, Parliament and People* (Edinburgh: Edinburgh University Press, 2007).
Favier, Jean and Lucie, *Archives Nationales. Quinze siècles d'histoire* (Paris: Nathan, 1988).
Favier, Lucie, *La mémoire de l'État. Histoire des Archives nationales* (Paris: Fayard, 2004).
Federico, Giovanni, *Feeding the World: An Economic History of Agriculture, 1800–2000* (Princeton: Princeton University Press, 2005).
Fejtö, François and Ewa Kulesza-Mietkowski, eds, *La fin des démocraties populaires: les chemins du post-communisme* (Paris: Seuil, 1997).
Ferdinand, Malcom, *Une écologie décoloniale* (Paris: Seuil, 2019).
Ferguson, Adam, *An Essay on the History of Civil Society* (Edinburgh, 1767).
Figuroskaia, N. K., *Agrarnye problemy v sovetskoi ekonomicheskoi literature 20kh godov* (Agrarian Questions in the Soviet Economic Literature of the 1920s) (Moscow: Ekonomika, 1978).
Filatova, Irina, 'Indoctrination or Scholarship? Education of Africans at the Communist University of the Toilers of the East in the Soviet Union, 1923–1937', *Paedagogica Historica: International Journal of the History of Education* 35, no. 1 (1999): 41–66.
Fink, Leon, *In Search of the Working Class: Essays in American Labor History and Political Culture* (Champaign, IL: University of Illinois Press, 1994).
Fink, Leon, *Sweatshops at Sea: Merchant Seamen in the World's First Globalized Industry, from 1812 to the Present* (Chapel Hill: University of North Carolina Press, 2011).
Finnegan, Ruth, *Literacy and Orality* (London: Callender Press, 2014).
Firth, Raymond, *Primitive Economics of the New Zealand Maori* (London: Routledge, 1929).
Fleming, James Rodger, *Meteorology in America, 1800–1870* (Baltimore: Johns Hopkins University Press, 1990).
Fogel, Joshua, 'The Debates over the Asiatic Mode of Production in Soviet Russia, China and Japan'. *American Historical Review* 93, no. 1 (1988): 56–79.
Fogel, Robert, Enid Fogel, Marc Guglielmo and Nathaniel Grotte, *Political Arithmetic: Simon Kuznets and the Empirical Tradition in Economics* (Chicago: University of Chicago Press, 2013).
Foucault, Michel, *L'archéologie du savoir* (Paris: Gallimard, 1969; English translation 2002).
Fouéré, Marie-Aude, 'L'Effet Derrida en Afrique du Sud. Jacques Derrida, Verne Harris et la notion d'archive(s) dans l'horizon post-apartheid', *Annales HSS* 74, no. 3 (2019): 745–78.

Fouéré, Marie-Aude, *Remembering Julius Nyerere in Tanzania: History, Legacy, Memory* (Dar es Salaam: Mkuki na Nyota, 2015).

Fouéré, Marie-Aude and Lotte Hughes, 'Heritage and Memory in East Africa Today: A Review of Recent Developments in Cultural Heritage Research and Memory Studies', *Azania: Archaeological Research in Africa* 50, no. 4 (2015): 542–58.

Fowler, William, *Mozley and Tyndall on Miracles* (London: Longman and Green, 1868).

Franke, Wolfgang, *An Introduction to the Source of Ming History* (Kuala Lumpur: University of Malaya Press, 1968).

Franzmann, Tom, 'Antislavery and Political Economy in the Early Victorian House of Commons: A Research Note on "Capitalist Hegemony"', *Journal of Social History* 27, no. 3 (1994): 579–93.

Freches, José, 'François Bernier, philosophe de Confucius au XVIIe siècle', *Bulletin de l'Ecole française d'Extrême-Orient* 60 (1973): 385–400.

French, Michael and Jim Phillips, *Cheated not Poisoned?* (Manchester: Manchester University Press, 2002).

Fu, C. and J. Fletcher, 'Large Signals of Climatic Variation over the Ocean in the Asian Monsoon Region', *Advances in Atmospheric Sciences* 5, no. 4 (1988): 389–404.

Fukuyama, Francis, *The End of History and the Last Man* (New York: Free Press, 1992).

Furlough, Ellen and Carl Strikwerda, eds, *Consumers against Capitalism? Consumer Cooperation in Europe, North America, and Japan, 1840–1990* (Lanham: Rowman & Littlefield, 1999).

Furner, Mary O. and Barry Supple, eds, *The State and Economic Knowledge: The American and British Experiences* (Cambridge: Cambridge University Press, 1990).

Galiani, Ferdinando, *Dialogues sur le commerce des blés* (Paris: Fayard, 1984; orig. 1770).

Gallegati, Mauro and Domenico Mignacca, 'Jevons, Sunspots Theory and Economic Fluctuations', *History of Economic Ideas* 2, no. 2 (1994): 23–40.

Galton, Francis, *Metereographica* (London: Macmillan, 1863).

Garnier, Emmanuel and Jérémy Desarthe, 'Cyclones and Societies in the Mascarene Islands, Seventeenth–Twentieth Centuries', *American Journal of Climate Change* 2 (2013): 1–13.

Gautam, Meena, 'History of Archives and Archival Sciences from 1950 onwards Based on Indian Practices', *Atlanti* 23 (2013): 135–47.

Geertz, Clifford, *Local Knowledge* (London: Basic Books, 1985).

Geertz, Clifford, Hildred Geertz and Lawrence Rosen, *Meaning and Order in Moroccan Society* (Cambridge: Cambridge University Press, 1979).

Geraci, Robert and Michael Khodarkovsky, eds, *Of Religion and Empire: Missions, Conversion, and Tolerance in Tsarist Russia* (Ithaca and London: Yale University Press, 2001).

Gérard, Gabriel, *Un grand créole, Joseph Hubert, 1747–1825* (Saint-Denis, La Réunion: éditions Azalée, 2006).

Gerbeau, Herbert, 'Quelques aspects de la traite illégale des esclaves à Bourbon au XIXe siècle', in *Mouvements de populations dans l'Océan indien*, Association historique internationale de l'Océan indien (Paris: Imprimerie Champion, 1979): 273–96.

Gerschenkron, Alexander, *Economic Backwardness in Historical Perspective* (Cambridge, MA: Harvard University Press, 1962).

Gershoni, Israel and Amy Singer, and Y. Hakan Erdem, eds, *Middle East Historiographies: Narrating the Twentieth Century* (Seattle: University of Washington Press, 2006).

Ghosh, Arunabh, *Making It Count: Statistics and Statecraft in the Early Republic of China* (Princeton: Princeton University Press, 2020).

Ghosh, J. K., P. Maiti, Talluri Rao and B. K. Sinha, 'Evolution of Statistics in India', *International Statistics Review* 67, no. 1 (2007): 13–34.

Ghosh, Peter, *Max Weber and the Protestant Ethic: Twin Histories* (Oxford: Oxford University Press, 2014).

Gibbon, Edward, *The Decline and Fall of the Roman Empire* (London: Strahan and Cadell, 1776).

Gilbert, Erik and Jonathan Reynolds, *Africa in World History from Prehistory to the Present* (Upper Saddle River, NJ: Pearson, 2004).

Ginzburg, Carlo, 'Don et reconnaissance. Lecture de Mauss', *Annale, HSS* 6 (2010): 1303–20.

Ginzburg, Carlo, *Miti, emblemi e spie* (Torino: Einaudi, 1986). English translation: *Clues, Myths and the Historical Method* (Baltimore: Johns Hopkins University Press, 1989).

Giomi, Fabio, Celia Keren and Morgane Labbé, eds, *Public and Private Welfare in Modern Europe: Productive Entanglements* (London: Routledge, 2022).

Godelier, Maurice, *Rationalité et irrationalité en économie* (Paris: Maspero, 1968).

Goldman, Merle, 'The Unique Blooming and Contending of 1961–2', *China Quarterly* 37 (1969): 54–83.

Golinski, Jan, *British Weather and the Climate of Enlightenment* (Chicago: University of Chicago Press, 2007).

Goody, Jack, *The Domestication of the Savage Mind* (Cambridge: Cambridge University Press, 1977).

Goody, Jack, *The East in the West* (Cambridge: Cambridge University Press, 1996).

Goody, Jack, *The Interface between the Oral and the Written* (Cambridge: Cambridge University Press, 1987).

Gorshenina, Svetalana, 'Krupneishie proekty kolonial'nykh arkhivov Rossii: utopichnost' ekzostivnoi Turkestaniki general- gubernatora Konstantina Petrovicha fon Kaufmana', *Ab Imperio* 3 (2007): 291–35.

Gould, Mark, 'Marx and Weber and the Logic of Historical Explanation: The Rise of Machine Capitalism', *Journal of Classical Sociology* 16, no. 4 (2016): 321–48.

Goulemot, Jean-Marie, *Le règne de l'histoire* (Paris: Albin Michel, 1996).

Graeber, David, *Toward an Anthropological Theory of Value: The False Coin of Our Own Dreams* (New York: Palgrave, 2001).

Grafton, Anthony, *Defenders of the Text: The Traditions of Scholarship in the Age of Science, 1450–1800* (Cambridge, MA: Harvard University Press, 1991).

Grafton, Anthony, *What Was History? The Art of History in Early Modern Europe* (Cambridge: Cambridge University Press, 2006).

Grantham, George, 'Agricultural Supply during the Industrial Revolution: French Evidence and European Implications', *Journal of Economic History* 49, no. 1 (1989): 43–72.

Grenier, Jean-Yves, *L'Économie d'ancien régime* (Paris: Albin Michel, 1996).

Grenier, Jean-Yves, 'Une économie de l'identification. Juste prix et ordre des marchandises dans l'Ancien Régime', in *La qualité des produits en France, XVIIIe–Xxe siècles*, edited by Alessandro Stanziani (Paris: Belin, 2003), 25–54.

Grewe, B. S. and Karin Hofmeester, eds, *Luxury in Global Perspective: Commodities and Practices* (Oxford: Berg, 2010).

Grimsted, Patricia, *Archives of Russia Five Years After: 'Purveyors of Sensations' or 'Shadows Cast to the Past'* (Amsterdam: International Institute of Social History, 1997).

Guha, Sumit, 'Speaking Historically: The Changing Voices of Historical Narration in Western India', *American Historical Review* 109, no. 4 (2005): 1084–1103.

Guilane Jean, *Abel, Caïn, Ötzi. L'héritage néolithique* (Paris: Gallimard, 2011).

Gunn, Geoffrey, *First Globalization: The Eurasian Exchange 1500–1800* (Lahnam: Rowman & Littlefield, 2003).
Guy, Koleen, *When Champagne Became French: Wine and the Making of National Identity* (Baltimore: Johns Hopkins University Press, 2003).
Guyer, Jane, 'Anthropology in Area Studies', *Annual Review of Anthropology* 33 (2004): 499–523.
Habakkuk, H. J., *American and British Technology in the Nineteenth Century* (Cambridge: Cambridge University Press, 1962).
Habermas, Jürgen, *The Structural Transformation of the Public Sphere* (Cambridge: Polity, 1989; orig. 1962).
Hacking, Ian, *The Social Construction of What?* (Cambridge, MA: Harvard University Press, 1999).
Hai Xu, Y. Hong and B. Hong, 'Decreasing Asian Summer Monsoon Intensity after 1860 AD in the Global Warming Epoch', *Climatic Dynamics* 39 (2012): 2079–88.
Hamilton, Carolyn, Verne Harris, Michèle Pickover, Graeme Reid and Razia Saleh, eds, *Refiguring the Archive* (Dordrecht: Kluwer Academic, 2002).
Hann, Chris and Keith Hart, *Economic Anthropology* (New York: Polity Press, 2011).
Harbi, Mohammed and Benjamin Stora, *La guerre d'Algérie, 1954–2004. La fin de l'amnésie* (Paris: Laffont, 2004).
Harrigan, Michael, 'Seventeenth-Century French Travellers and the Encounter with Indian Histories', *French History* 28, no. 1 (2014): 1–22.
Harris, Jose, *Unemployment and Politics: A Study in English Social Policy, 1886–1914* (Oxford: Clarendon Press, 1972).
Harris, Marvin, *Good to Eat: Riddles of Food and Culture* (New York: Simon & Schuster, 1958).
Harris, Verne, *Archives and Justice: A South African Perspective* (Chicago: Society of American Archivists, 2007).
Harris, Verne, *National Archives of South Africa* (Pretoria: National Archives, 2000).
Harrison, John, ed., *New Lights on Early Medieval Japanese Historiography* (Gainsville, FL: University of Florida Press, 1959).
Harrison, Mark, *Climate and Constitution: Health, Race, Environment and British Imperialism in India, 1600–1850* (Delhi: Oxford University Press, 1999).
Harrison, Peter, 'Prophecy, Early Modern Apologetics and Hume's Argument against Miracles' *Journal of the History of Ideas* 60 (1999): 241–56.
Haupt, Heinz-Gerhard and Jürgen Kocka, *Comparative and Trans-national History* (New York: Berghahn, 2009).
Hawkins, Sean, *Writing and Colonialism in Northern Ghana: The Encounter between the LoDagaa and 'the World of Paper'* (Toronto: University of Toronto Press, 2002).
Hay, Douglas and Paul Craven, eds, *Masters, Servants, and Magistrates in Britain and the Empire, 1562–1955* (Chapel Hill: University of North Carolina Press, 2004).
Herbst, Jeffrey, *States and Power in Africa: Comparative Lessons in Authority and Control* (Princeton: Princeton University Press, 2000).
Herschel, John, *Meteorology* (Edinburgh: Black, 1862).
Heyberger, Laurent, *Les corps en colonie. Faim, maladies, guerres et crises démographiques en Algérie au XIXe siècle* (Tempus: Presses Universitaires du Midi, 2019).
Hickey, Kieran, ed., *Advances in Hurricane Researches. Modelling, Meteorology, Preparedness, and Impact* (Rijeka: In tech, 2012).
Hirsch, Francine, *Empire of Nations: Ethnographic Knowledge and the Making of the Soviet Union* (Ithaca, NY: Cornell University Press, 2005).

Hobsbawm, Eric, 'The General Crisis of the European Economy in the Seventeenth Century', *Past & Present* 6, no. 1 (1954): 33–53.
Hodgson, Marshall, *Rethinking World History* (Cambridge: Cambridge University Press, 1993).
Hosking, Geoffrey, *Russia: People and Empire, 1552–1917* (Cambridge, MA: Harvard University Press, 1997).
House of Commons, *Papers in Explanation of the Condition of the Slave Population*, 5 November 1831, *Parliamentary Papers*, 1830–1 (230), 16.1: 59–88.
Hulme, Mike, *Weathered: Cultures of Climate* (London: SAGE, 2016).
Huntington, Samuel, *The Clash of Civilizations* (New York: Simon & Schuster, 2011: orig. article 1993).
Huret, Romain, *Katrina, 2005. L'ouragan, l'État et les pauvres aux États-Unis* (Paris: EHESS, 2010).
Hyden, Goran, *Beyond Ujamaa in Tanzania: Underdevelopment and an Uncaptured Peasantry* (Berkeley: University of California Press, 1980).
Ianson, Iulii, *Teoriia statistiki* (Statistical Theory), 3rd ed. (Saint Petersburg: Landau, 1886).
Iggers, Georg and Edward Wang, Supriya Mukherjee, *A Global History of Modern Historiographies* (New York: Routledge, 2008).
ILO, *Every Child Counts: New Global Estimates on Child Labour* (Geneva: BIT Press, 2002).
ILO, *International Labour Conference, Papers and Proceedings, 89th Session* (Geneva: ILO Press, 2001).
ILO, *La fin du travail des enfants: un objectif à notre porté* (Geneva : OIT, 2006).
Inikori, Joseph, *Africans and the Industrial Revolution in England* (Cambridge: Cambridge University Press, 2002).
Inikori, Joseph, 'Market Structures and the Profits of the British African Trade in the Late Eighteenth Century. A Rejoinder', *Journal of Economic History* 43 (1983): 723–8.
Institut International de Statistique, VI Session de l'Institut International de Statistique. Saint-Pétersbourg, 1897, *Bulletin de l'Institut International de Statistique*, XI (Saint Petersburg, 1899); XI Session, Copenhagen, 1908 in vol. 17 (Copenhagen, 1908).
IPCC (Intergovernmental Panel on Climate Change), 'Managing the Risks of Extreme Events and Disasters to Advance Climate Change Adaptation', *Special Report of Intergovernmental Panel on Climate Change* (Cambridge: Cambridge University Press, 2012).
Isaacman, Allen, *Cotton Is the Mother of Poverty: Peasants, Work, and Rural Struggle in Colonial Mozambique, 1938–1961* (Portsmouth, NH: Heinemann, 1996).
Isaacman, Allen, 'Peasants and Rural Social Protests on Africa', *African Studies Review* 33 (1990): 1–120.
Islam, Shafiqul and Michael Mandelbaum, eds, *Making Markets Economic Transformations in Eastern Europe and the Post-Soviet States* (New York: Council of Foreign Relations, 1993).
Israel, Jonathan, *Enlightenment Contested: Philosophy, Modernity, and the Emancipation of Man, 1670–1752* (Oxford: Oxford University Press, 2008).
Jankovic, Vladimir, *Reading the Sky: A Cultural History of English Weather* (Manchester: Manchester University Press, 2000).
Jevons, William, *The Theory of Political Economy* (London: Macmillan, 1979).
Jordan, W. C., *The Great Famine: Northern Europe in the Early Fourteenth Century* (Princeton: Princeton University Press, 1992).

Jullien, Bernard and Andy Smith, eds, *Industries and Globalization: The Political Causality of Difference* (London: Palgrave, 2008).
Kablukov, Nikolai A., *Posobie pri mestnyh statisticheskikh obsledovaniiakh* (Methods for Local Statistical Investigations) (Moscow, 1910).
Kahn-Freund, Otto, 'A Note on Status and Contract in British Labour Law', *Modern Law Review* 30 (1967): 635–44.
Kaplan, Steven, *La fin des corporations* (Paris: Fayard, 2002).
Kaplan, Steven, *Le meilleur pain du Monde* (Paris: Fayard, 1996).
Kaplan, Steven and Philippe Minard, *La fortune du colbertisme* (Paris: Fayard, 2002).
Kaplan, Vera, 'Two Archives of the Russian Revolution', *Archival Science* 20 (2020): 361–80.
Kappeler, Andreas, *Rußland als Vielvölkerreich: Entstehung, Geschichte, Zerfall* (Munich: C. H. Beck, 1992).
Kapteijns, Lidwien, *African Historiography Written by Africans, 1955–1973* (Leiden: Brill, 1973).
Karabell, Zachary, *The Leading Indicators: A Short History of the Numbers That Rule the World* (New York: Simon & Schuster, 2014).
Karlberg, Stephen, *La sociologie historique comparative de Max Weber* (Paris: La Découverte, 2002).
Karpik, Lucien, *Valuing the Unique: The Economics of Singularities* (Princeton: Princeton University Press, 2010).
Kearney, Michael, *Reconceptualizing the Peasantry: Anthropology in Global Perspective* (Boulder, CO: Westview Press, 1996).
Kemper, Michael, 'Red Orientalism: Mikhail Pavlovich and Marxist Oriental Studies in Early Soviet Russia', *Die Welt des Islams* 50 (2010): 435–76.
Kemper, Michael and Stephan Conermann, eds, *The Heritage of Soviet Oriental Studies* (London: Routledge, 2011).
Kerblay, Basile, 'A.V. Cayanov. Un carrefour dans l'évolution de la pensée agraire en Russie de 1908 a 1930', *Cahiers du monde russe et sovietique* 4 (1964): 411–60.
Khalid, Adeeb, 'Russian History and the Debate over Orientalism', *Kritika: Explorations in Russian and Eurasian History* 1, no. 4 (2000): 691–9.
Khalid, Adeeb, 'Searching of Muslim Voices in Post-Soviet Archives', *Ab Imperio* 4 (2008): 302–12.
Khalidi, Tarif, *Historical Thought in the Classical Period* (Cambridge: Cambridge University Press, 1994).
Khlevniuk, Oleg V., *Stalinskoie Politburo v 30-ye gody* (Stalin Politburo during the 1930s) (Moscow: Airo-XX, 1995).
Khorkhordina, Tat'iana, *Istoriia otechestva I arkhivy: 1917–1980-e gg* (History of the Nation and the Archives, 1917–1980) (Moscow: RGGU, 1994).
Khorkhordina, Tat'iana, *Rossiiskaia nauka ob arkhivakh: Istoriia. Teoriia. Liudi* (The Russian Archival Science: History, Theory and People) (Moscow: RGGU, 2003).
Klein, Judy L., *Statistical Visions in Time: A History of Time Series Analysis, 1662–1938* (Cambridge: Cambridge University Press, 1997).
Klein, Judy L. and Mary S. Morgan, eds, *The Age of Economic Measurement* (Durham, NC: Duke University Press, 2001).
Kliuchevskii, Vasilii, *Kurs russkoi istorii* (Lessons of Russian History) (Moscow: Tipografiia Lissnera i Sobko, 1904–21).
Knapp, Georg Friedrich, *Theorie des Bevölkerungs-Wechsels: Abhandlungen zur Angewanden Mathematik* (Braunschweig: Friedrich Vieweg und Sohn, 1874).

Knight, Nathaniel, 'Grigor'ev in Orenburg, 1851–1862: Russian Orientalism in the Service of Empire?' *Slavic Review* 59, no. 1 (2000): 74–100.
Kocka, Jürgen, *Arbeitsverhältnisse und Arbeiterexistenzen. Grundlagen der Klassenbildung im 19. Jahrhundert* (Bonn: Dietz, 1990).
Kocka, Jürgen, 'New Trends in Labour Movement Historiography: A German Perspective', *International Review of Social History* 42 (1997): 67–78.
Kocka, Jürgen, *White Collar Workers in America 1890–1940: A Social Political History in International Perspective* (London: SAGE, 1980).
Korneev, Vladimir E. and Olga N. Kopylova, 'Arkhivisty na sluzhbe totalitarnogo gosudarstva 1918-nachalo 1940-kh godov' (Archivists at the Service of the Totalitarian State, 1918–Beginning of the 1940s), *Otechestvennye Arkhivy* 1 (1992): 13–24.
Koselleck, Reinhart, *Futures Past: On the Semantics of Historical Time* (Cambridge, MA: MIT Press, 1985; orig. German 1979).
Koselleck, Reinhart, 'Revolution', in *Geschichtliche Grudbegriffe: Historisches Lexicon zur Politisch-Soziale Sprache in Deutschland*, edited by Otto Brunner, Werner Conze and Reinhart Koselleck, 9 vols (Stuttgart: Ernst Klett Verlag, 1972–90), vol. 4: 653–788.
Kotkin, Stephen, 'The State-Is It Us? Memoirs, Archives, and Kremlinologists', *The Russian Review* 61, no. 1 (2002): 35–51.
Kotsonis, Yanni, *Making Peasant Backward* (New York: St. Martin's Press, 1999).
Kriedte, Peter, Hans Medick and Jürgen Schlumbhom, *Industrialisation before Industrialisation* (Cambridge: Cambridge University Press, 1981).
Krishnamurti, T. N., Lidia Stefanova and Vasubandhu Misra, eds, *Tropical Meteorology: An Introduction* (New York: Springer, 2013).
Kula, Witold, *An Economic Theory of the Feudal System* (London: New Left Books, 1976).
Kula, Witold, *Les mesures et les hommes* (Paris: EHESS, 1985).
Kula, Witold, Marcin Kula and Josephine Wtulich, *Writing Home: Polish Immigrants in Brazil and the United States* (Boulder, CO: Westview, 1986).
Kulikoff, Allan, *From British Peasants to Colonial American Farmers* (Chapel Hill: University of North Carolina Press, 2000).
Kumar, Sunil, *The Emergence of the Delhi Sultanate, 1192–1286* (New Delhi: Permanent Black, 2007).
Kussmaul, Ann, *Servants in Husbandry in Early Modern England* (Cambridge: Cambridge University Press, 1981).
Kutzbach, Gisela, *The Thermal Theory of Cyclones: A History of Meteorological Thought in the Nineteenth Century* (Boston: American Meteorological Society, 1979).
Kuznets, Simon, 'Economic Growth and Economic Inequality', *American Economic Review* 45, no. 1 (1955): 1–28.
Kyle Crossing, Pamela, *What Is Global History?* (Cambridge: Polity Press, 2008).
Labbé, Morgane, *La Nationalité, une histoire de chiffres. Politique et statistiques en Europe centrale (1848–1919)* (Paris: Presses de SciencesPo, 2019).
LaCapra, Dominick, *History and Criticism* (Ithaca: Cornell University Press, 1985).
LaCapra, Dominick, *History, Politics, and the Novel* (Ithaca: Cornell University Press, 1987).
LaCapra, Dominick, *Rethinking Intellectual History: Texts, Contexts, Language* (Ithaca: Cornell University Press, 1983).
Lal, Deepak, *The Poverty of Development Economics* (Boston: MIT Press, 2000).
Lal, Vinay *The History of History: Politics and Scholarship in Modern India* (Delhi: Oxford University Press, 2003).

Landes, David, *The Unbound Prometheus: Technological Change and Industrial Development in Western Europe from 1750 to the Present* (Cambridge: Cambridge University Press, 1969).
Landes, William and Richard Posner, 'Trademark Law: An Economic Perspective', *Journal of Law and Economics* 30 (October 1987): 265–309.
Landsberger, Henry, ed., *Rural Protest: Peasant Movements and Social Change* (New York: Macmillan, 1973).
Lang, Tim and Michael Heasman, *Food Wars: The Global Battle for Mouths, Minds, and Markets* (London: Earthscan, 2004).
Laroche, Charles, 'Les archives de l'expansion française outre-mer conservées en métropole', *La gazette des archives* 55 (1966): 235–52.
Laroui, Abdallah, *Islam et histoire* (Paris: Albin Michel, 1999).
Larson, Erik, *Isaac's Storm: A Man, a Time and the Deadliest Hurricane in History* (New York: Crown, 1999).
Laslett, Peter, *The World We Have Lost*: *England before the Industrial Age* (London: Methuen, 1965).
László, Kontler, Antonella Romano, Silvia Sebastiani and Borbala Szusanna Török, eds, *Negotiating Knowledge in Early Modern Empires: A Decentred View* (New York: Palgrave Macmillan, 2014).
Latour, Bruno, *We Have Never Been Modern* (Cambridge, MA: Harvard University Press, 1992).
Laurent, Sébastien, ed., *Archives 'secrètes', secrets d'archives? Historiens et archivistes face aux archives sensibles* (Paris: CNRS Éditions, 2003).
Le Cour Grandmaison, Olivier, *Le 17 Octobre 1961. Un crime d'État à Paris* (Paris: La dispute, 2001).
Le Donne, John, *Absolutisms and Ruling Class: The Formation of the Russian Political Order, 1700–1825* (Oxford: Oxford University Press, 1991).
Le Goff, Jacques, 'Comment écrire une biographie historique aujourd'hui?', *Le débat* 54, no. 2 (1989): 48–53.
Lee, John, 'Trade and Economy in Preindustrial East Asia, c. 1500–1800: East Asia in the Age of Global Integration', *The Journal of Asian Studies* 58, no. 1 (1999): 2–26.
Lee, Thomas, ed., *The New and the Multiple: Song Senses of the Past* (Hong Kong: Chinese University Press, 2005).
Lefebvre, Camille and M'hamed Oualdi, 'Remettre le colonial à sa place. Histoires enchevêtrées des débuts de la colonisation en Afrique de l'Ouest et au Maghreb', *Annales HSS* 72, no. 4 (2017): 937–43.
Leonard, Carol, *Agrarian Reforms in Russia* (Cambridge: Cambridge University Press, 2011).
Lepenies, Phillip, *The Power of a Single Number: A Political History of GDP* (New York: Columbia University Press, 2016).
Lepetit, Bernand, 'Une logique du raisonnement historique', *Annale ESC* 5 (1993): 1209–19.
Lepore, Jill, *If Then: How the Simulmatics Corporation Invented the Future* (New York: Liveright, 2020).
Levi, Giovanni, *Le pouvoir au village* (Paris : Gallimard, 1989).
Levi, Giovanni, 'Les usages de la biographie', *Annales ESC* 44, no. 6 (1989): 1325–36.
Levi, Scott, *The Indian Diaspora in Central Asia, 1550–1900* (Leiden: Brill, 2002).
Lévi-Strauss, Claude, *La pensée sauvage* (Paris: Plon, 1962). New English translation, Chicago University Press, 2021.
Levy, Jonathan, *Freaks of Fortune: The Emerging World of Capitalism and Risk in America* (Cambridge, MA: Harvard University Press, 2014).

Lewis, Simon and Mark Maslin, 'Defining the Anthropocene', *Nature* 519 (2015): 171–80.
Lewis, W. A., *The Theory of Economic Growth* (London: Allen & Unwin, 1955).
Li, Bozhong, *Agricultural Development in Jiangnan* (New York: St. Martin's Press, 1998).
Lieven, Dominic, ed., *The Cambridge History of Russia, Vol. 2. Imperial Russia, 1689–1917* (Cambridge: Cambridge University Press, 2006).
Lilti, Antoine, *L'héritage des Lumières* (Paris: Seuil, EHESS, 2019).
Lindert, Peter and Jeffrey Williamson, 'English Workers' Living Standards during the Industrial Revolution: A New Look', *Economic History Review* 36, no. 1 (1983): 1–25.
Lindert, Peter and Jeffrey Williamson, 'Revising England's Social Tables, 1688–1867', *Explorations in Economic History* 19, no. 4 (1982): 385–408.
Livingstone, David, 'Reading the Heavens, Planting the Earth: Cultures of British Science', *History Workshop Journal* 54 (2000): 236–41.
Lloyd, Christopher, *The Structures of History* (Oxford: Blackwell, 1993).
Locher, Fabien, *Le savant et la tempête. Étudier l'atmosphère et prévoir le temps au XIXe siècle* (Rennes: Presses Universitaires de Rennes, 2008).
Lombard, Denys, *Le Carrefour javanais. Essai d'histoire globale* (Paris : EHESS, 1992).
Lovett, Verney, *A History of the Indian Nationalist Movement* (London: Murray, 1920).
Lucassen, Leo, 'Working Together: New Directions in Global Labour History', *Journal of Global History* 11, no. 1 (2016): 66–87.
Luedtke, Alf, *History of Everyday Life* (Princeton: Princeton University Press, 1995).
MacLeod, Christine, 'The Paradoxes of Patenting: Invention and Its Diffusion in 18- and 19th-Century Britain, France, and North America', *Technology and Culture* 32, no. 4 (1991): 885–910.
Maddison, Angus, *Contours of the World Economy, 1–2030 AD* (Oxford: Oxford University Press, 2007).
Magnac, Thierry and Gilles Postel-Vinay, 'Wage Competition between Agriculture and Industry in Mid-Nineteenth Century France', *Explorations in Economic History* 34 (1997): 1–26.
Maharatna, Arap, *The Demography of Famine* (Delhi: Oxford University Press, 1996).
Mahony, Martin, 'For an Empire of "All Types of Climate": Meteorology as an Imperial Science', *Journal of Historical Geography* 51 (2016): 29–39.
Maine, Henry Sumner, *Ancient Law: Its Connection with the Early History of Society, and Its Relation to Modern Ideas* (London: John Murray, 1861).
Maine, Henry Sumner, *Village-Communities in the East and the West* (London: Murray, 1876).
Maitte, Corine, *La trame incertaine, le monde textile de Prato au XVIIIe et XIXe siècles* (Villeneuve d'Ascq: Presses Universitaires du Septentrion, 2001).
Maksakov, V., *Historiia i organizatsiia arkhivnogo dela SSSR 1917–1945 gg.* (History and Organization of Archives in the USSR, 19217–1945) (Moscow: Nauka, 1969).
Maksakov, V. 'Piat let Arkhiva Oktiabr'skoi revoliiutsii, 1920-sentiabr' 1925 g.' (Five Years of Revolutionary Archives, October 1920–September 1925), *Arkhivnoe delo* 5–6 (1926): 3–13.
Mandrou, Robert, 'Vers les Antilles et le Canada au XVIe siècle', *Annales, Économies, Sociétés* 14 (1959): 667–75.
Mantena, Rama Sundari, *The Origins of Modern Historiography in India* (New York: Palgrave Macmillan, 2012).
Markwick, Roger, *Rewriting History in Soviet Union: The Politics of Revisionist Historiography, 1956–1974* (New York: Palgrave, 2001).
Marlow, Louise, *Hierarchy and Egalitarianism in Islamic Thought* (Cambridge: Cambridge University Press, 1997).

Martinat, Monica, *Le juste marché. Le système annonaire romain au XVIe et XVIIe siècles* (Rome: École française de Rome, 2005).

Marx, Karl and Friedrich Engels, *Collected Works*, 50 vols (New York: International Publishers, 1975–2004).

Marx, Karl, *Grundrisse*, translated by Martin Nicolaus (New York: Penguin, 1973).

Masood, Ehsan, *The Great Invention: The Story of GDP and the Making and Unmaking of the Modern World* (New York: Pegasus Books, 2016).

Matsushita, Yumi, Nobuo Yoshiike, Fumi Kaneda, Katsushi Yoshita and Hidemi Takimoto, 'Trends in Childhood Obesity In Japan during Last 25 Years From the National Nutrition Survey', *Obesity Research* 12 (2004): 205–14.

Matsuzato, Kimitaka, *Imperiology: From Empirical Knowledge to Discussing the Russian Empire* (Sapporo: Slavic Research Center, 2007).

Mauro, Fréderic, 'French Indentured Servants for America, 1500–1800', in *Colonialism and Migration: Indentured Labour before and after Slavery*, edited by P. C. Emmer (Dordrecht, Boston and Lancaster: Martinus Nijhoff Publishers, 1986): 83–104.

Mauss, Marcel, *Essai sur le don* (édition Paris: PUF: 2012; orig. 1924).

Mayda, Anna Maria, 'International Migration: A Panel Data Analysis of the Determinants of Bilateral Flows', *Journal of Population Economics* 23 (2010): 1249–74.

Mazour, Marc, *The Writing of History in the Soviet Union* (Stanford: Stanford University Press, 1971).

Mban, Albert, *Les problème des archives africaines. À quand la solution?* (Paris: L'Harmattan, 2007).

Mbaye, Ousmane, 'Le Cao m: un centre d'archives partagées?' *Afrique et Histoire* 7, no. 1 (2009): 291–9.

McCall, Daniel, *Africa in Time Perspective: A Discussion of Historical Reconstruction from Unwritten Sources* (Boston: Boston University Press, 1964).

McCloskey, Deidre, *Bourgeois Dignity: Why Economics Can't Explain the Modern World* (Chicago: University of Chicago Press, 2011).

McCloskey, Donald, 'The Open Fields of England: Rent, Risk, and the Rate of Interest, 1300–1815', in *Markets in History: Economic Studies of the Past*, edited by David Galenson (Cambridge: Cambridge University Press, 1989): 5–51.

McKemmish, S. and others, eds, *Archives: Recordkeeping in Society* (Wagga Wagga, NSW: Center for Information Studies, Charles Sturt University, 2005).

McKendrick, Neil, 'Josiah Wedgwood and Factory Discipline', *The Historical Journal* 4 (1961): 30–55.

McKeown, Adam, *Melancholy Order: Asian Migration and the Nationalization of Borders* (New York: NYU Press, 2007).

McLaren, Lauren, Anja Neundorf and Ian Paterson, 'Diversity and Perceptions of Immigration: How the Past Influences the Present', *Political Studies* 1 (2020) https://doi.org/10.1177%2F0032321720922774.

Mehl, Margaret, *History and the State in Nineteenth-Century Japan* (New York: St. Martin's Press, 1998).

Meier, Gerald and James Rauch, *Leading Issues in Development Economics* (Oxford: Oxford University Press, 2000).

Meillassoux, Claude, *Anthropologie de l'esclavage* (Paris: PUF, 1986).

Meillassoux, Claude, *L'anthropologie économique des Gouro de Côte d'Ivoire* (Paris: Mouton, 1964).

Mendras, Henri, *Les sociétés paysanne s: éléments pour une théorie de la paysannerie* (Paris: Gallimard, 1995).

Mendras, Henri, 'L'invention de la paysannerie. Un moment de l'histoire de la sociologie française d'après-guerre', *Revue française de sociologie* 41, no. 3 (2000): 539–52.
Merivale, Herman, *Lectures on Colonization and Colonies* (London: Orme, Brown, Green and Longmans, 1841).
Mespoulet, Martine, *Statistiques et révolution en Russie un compromis impossible (1880–1930)* (Rennes: PUR, 2001).
Meuvret, Jean, *Le problème des subsistances à l'époque de Louis XIV* (Paris and La Haye: Mouton-EHESS, 1977).
Miers, Suzanne, 'Contemporary Forms of Slavery', *Canadian Journal of African Studies* (Special Issue on Slavery and Islam in African History: A Tribute to Martin Klein) 34, no. 3 (2000): 714–47.
Miers, Suzanne and Igor Kopytoff, eds, *Slavery in Africa: Historical and Anthropological Perspectives* (Madison, WI: University of Wisconsin Press, 1977).
Mikhailovskii, Mikhail, *Sochineniia* (Works) (Saint Petersburg: Izdanie Russkoe Bogatstvo, 1909).
Mill, John Stuart, *Collected Works of John Stuart Mill*, edited by John Robson and Stefano Collini (Toronto: University of Toronto Press, 1984).
Millar, Joseph, 'History and Africa/Africa and History', *American Historical Review* 104, no. 1 (1999): 1–32.
Millas, José Carlos and Leonard Perdue, *Hurricanes of the Caribbean and Adjacent Regions, 1492–1800* (Miami: Academy of the Arts and Sciences of the Americas, 1968).
Miller, Aleksei, ed., *Rossiiskaia imperiia v sravnitel´noi perspektive: Sbornik statei* (Moscow: Novoe izdatel´stvo, 2004).
Miller, Alexei and Alfred J. Rieber, eds, *Imperial Rule* (Budapest: Central European University Press, 2004).
Mimura, N. and others, 'Small Islands', in *Climate Change: Impacts, Adaptation and Vulnerability: Contribution of Working Group II to the Fourth Assessment Report of the Intergovernmental Panel on Climate Change*, edited by M. L. Parry et al. (Cambridge: Cambridge University Press, 2007): 687–716.
Mintz, Sidney, 'A Note on the Definition of Peasantries', *Journal of Peasant Studies* 1, no. 1 (1973): 91–106.
Mironov, Boris, 'Consequences of the Price Revolution in Eighteenth-Century Russia', *The Economic History Review* 45, no. 3 (1992): 457–78.
Mnjama, Nathan, 'Dealing with Backlog Accumulation of Archival Materials in Eastern and Southern Africa', *Information Development* 22, no. 1 (2006): 48–56.
Mokyr, Joel, *The Level of Riches* (Oxford: Oxford University Press, 1990).
Mommsen, Wolfgang, *Max Weber and German Politics, 1890–1920* (Chicago: University of Chicago Press, 1984).
Mommsen, Wolfgang and Jürgen Osterhammel, eds, *Max Weber and His Contemporaries* (London and New York: Routledge, 1986).
Montanari, Massimo, *La fame e l'abbondanza* (Bari: Laterza, 1993).
Monteiro, C. A., M. H. Benicio, W. L. Conde and B. M. Popkin, 'Shifting Obesity Trends in Brazil', *European Journal of Clinical Nutrition* 54, no. 4 (2000): 342–6.
Moogk, Peter, 'Reluctant Exiles: Emigrants from France to Canada before 1760', *The William and Mary Quarterly* 46, no. 3 (1989): 463–505.
Moon, David, *The Plough That Broke the Steppe* (Oxford: Oxford University Press, 2014).
Moon, David, *The Russian Peasantry, 1600–1930* (London: Longman, 1996).
Mooney, Chris, *Storm World: Hurricanes, Politics and the Battle over Global Warming* (Orlando: Harcourt, 2007).

Moore, Barrington, *Social Origins of Dictatorship and Democracy: Lord and Peasant in the Making of the Modern World* (Boston: Beacon Press, 1966).

Morrison, Alexander, 'Applied Orientalism in British India and Tsarist Turkestan', *Comparative Studies in Society and History* 51, no. 3 (2009): 619–47.

Morrison, Alexander, *Russian Rule in Samarkand, 1868–1910: A Comparison with British India* (Oxford: Oxford University Press, 2008).

Mote, Frederick and Denis Twichett, eds, *The Cambridge History of China*, vol. 7 (Cambridge: Cambridge University Press, 1988).

Moyn, Samuel and Andrew Sartori, eds, *Global Intellectual History* (New York: Columbia University Press, 2013).

Mugnai, Paolo Francesco, 'Ricerche su François Bernier filosofo e viaggiatore (1620–1688)', *Studi filosofici* 7 (1984): 53–115.

Mukherjee, Supriya, 'Indian Historical Writing since 1947', in *The Oxford History of Historical Writing*, edited by Alex Schneider and Daniel Woolf (Oxford: Oxford University Press), vol. 5: 515–38.

Mukhia, Harbans, *Historians and Historiography during the Reign of Akbar* (New Delhi: Vikha Publishing House, 1976).

Mulcahy, Matthew, *Hurricanes and Society in the British Greater Caribbean, 1624–1783* (Baltimore: Johns Hopkins University Press, 2006).

Murname, R. J. and K.-B. Liu, *Hurricanes and Typhoons: Past, Present and Future* (New York: Columbia University Press, 2004).

Murphy, Peter, ed., *Evidence, Proof and Facts: A Book of Sources* (New York: Oxford University Press, 2003).

Murr, Sylvia, 'Bernier et les gassendistes', *Corpus* 20–1 (1992): 115–35.

Muthu, Sankar, *Enlightenment against Empire* (Princeton: Princeton University Press, 2003).

Myrdal, Gunnar, *Economic Theory and Underdeveloped Regions* (London: Duckworth, 1956).

Neale, Caroline, *Writing Independent History: African Historiography, 1960–1980* (Westport, CT: Greenwood Press, 1985).

Nérard, François-Xavier, 'Quelles archives soviétique s? Réflexion sur la constitution des archives du pouvoir stalinien', *Territoires contemporains* 2 (2011) http://tristan.u-bourgogne.fr/CGC/publications/historiographie/FX_Nerard.html

Ng, On-cho and Edward Wang, *Mirroring the Past: The Writing and Use of History in Imperial China* (Honolulu: Hawaii University Press, 2005).

Nielsen, Randall, 'Storage and English Government Intervention in Early Modern Grain Markets', *The Journal of Economic History* 57, no. 1 (1997): 1–33.

Nora, Pierre, *Les lieux de mémoire. II. La nation* (Paris: Gallimard, 1986).

Norinaga, Motoori, *Gunsho ruiju* (Great Collection of Old Documents), comp. Hanawa Hokiichi, 30 vols (Tokyo: Kanseikai, 1959–60).

North, Douglass, *Structure and Change in Economic History* (New York: Norton, 1981).

North, Douglass and Robert Thomas, *The Rise of Western Civilization: A New Economic History* (Cambridge: Cambridge University Press, 1973).

Northrop, Douglas, *Veiled Empire* (New Haven: Yale University Press, 2016).

Nurske, Ragnar, *Problems of Capital Formation in Underdeveloped Countries* (Oxford: Basil Blackwell, 1953).

Nussbaum, Felicity, ed., *The Global Eighteenth Century* (Baltimore: Johns Hopkins University Press, 2003).

Nutzenadel, Alexander and Frank Trentmann, eds, *Food and Globalization* (Oxford: Berg, 2008).

O'Brien, Karen, *Narratives of Enlightenment: Cosmopolitan History from Voltaire to Gibbon* (Cambridge: Cambridge University Press, 1997).
O'Brien, Patrick, 'Agriculture and the Industrial Revolution', *Economic History Review* 30, no. 1 (1977): 166–81.
Ong, Walter, *Orality and Literacy: The Technologizing of the World* (New York: Methuen, 1982).
Otero, Hernán, 'Socio-History of Statistics on Latin America. A Review', *Histoire et mesure* 33, no. 2 (2018): 13–32.
Pajot, Elie, *Simples renseignements sur l'Ile Bourbon* (Paris: Challanel Ainé, Librairie Coloniale, 1887).
Palmer, Bryan, *Descent into Discourse: The Reification of Language and the Writing of Social History* (Philadelphia: Temple University Press, 1990).
Pantaleon, Jorge, *Una nación a medida. Creencia económica y estadística en la Argentina (1918–1952)* (Buenos Aires: Ediciones al Margen, 2009).
Parker, Geoffrey, *The Military Revolution and the Rise of the West, 1500–1800* (Cambridge: Cambridge University Press, 1988).
Parthasarathi, Prisannan, *Why Europe Grew Rich and Asia Did Not: Global Economic Divergence, 1600–1850* (Cambridge: Cambridge University Press, 2011).
Passeron, Jean-Claude, *Le raisonnement sociologique* (Paris: Nathan, 1991).
Patnaik, Utsa and M. Dingwaney, eds, *Chains of Servitude: Bondage and Slavery in India* (Hyderabad: Sangan Books, 1985).
Patterson, Orlando, *Slavery and Social Death* (Cambridge: Cambridge University Press, 1982).
Pearson, Michael, *The Indian Ocean* (London and New York: Routledge, 2003).
Perdue, Peter, *China Marching West: The Qing Conquest of Central Eurasia* (Cambridge, MA: Belknap Press, 2005).
Perrot, Jean-Claude, *Histoire intellectuelle de l'économie politique* (Paris: EHESS, 1992).
Philips, C. H., ed., *Historians of India, Pakistan and Ceylon* (New York: Oxford University Press, 1961).
Philipsen, Dirk, *The Little Big Number: How GDP Came to Rule the World and What to Do about It* (Princeton: Princeton University Press, 2015).
Piddington, Henri, *The Sailor's Horn-book for the Law of Storms* (London: Smith/Elder, 1848).
Piketty, Thomas, *Capital in the 21st Century* (Boston: Harvard University Press, 2014).
Pitts, Jennifer, *A Turn to Empire: The Rise of Imperial Liberalism in Britain and France* (Princeton: Princeton University Press, 2006).
Platonov, Sergei F., *Ocherki po istorii smuty v Moskvoskom gosudarstve XVI–XVII v* (Studies on the Times of Trouble in the Muscovite State, Sixteenth–Seventeenth Centuries) (Saint Petersburg, 1899, new ed., Vremia, 1923).
Pocock, J. G. A., *Barbarism and Religion*, 5 vols (Cambridge: Cambridge University Press, 1999–2011).
Pokrovskii, Mikhail, 'Obshchestvennye nauki v SSSR za 10 let' (Social Sciences in the USSR in the Past Ten Years), *Vestnik kommunisticheskoi akademii* 26 (1928): 3–30.
Pollock, Sean, 'Historians and Their Sources: Discourses of Russian Empire and Islam in Eurasian Archives', *Ab Imperio* 4 (2008): 234–52.
Pollock, Sheldon, Benjamin Elman and Ku-ming Kevin Chang, eds, *World Philology* (Boston, MA: Harvard University Press, 2015).
Pomeranz, Kenneth, *The Great Divergence* (Princeton: Princeton University Press, 2000).
Pomian, Krzysztof, *Sur l'histoire* (Paris: Gallimard, 1999).

Poovey, Mary, *A History of Modern Fact* (Chicago: University of Chicago Press, 1998).
Porter, Theodor, *The Rise of Statistical Thinking, 1820–1900* (Princeton: Princeton University Press, 1986).
Porter, Theodor, *Trust in Numbers: The Pursuit of Objectivity in Science and Public Life* (Princeton: Princeton University Press, 1995).
Postel-Vinay, Gilles, 'The Dis-integration of Traditional Labour Markets in France: From Agriculture and Industry to Agriculture or Industry', in *Labour Market Evolution*, edited by George Grantham and Mary MacKinnon (London and New York: Routledge, 1994), 64–83.
Prakash, Gyan, 'Subaltern Studies as Postcolonial Criticism', *American Historical Review* 99, no. 5 (1994): 1475–90.
Preiswerk, Roy and Dominique Perrot, *Ethnocentrism and History: Africa, Asia and Indian America in Western Textbooks* (New York: Nok. Print. 1978).
Prevost, Antoine-François, *Histoire générale des voyages ou nouvelle collection de toutes les relations de voyage par mer et par terre qui ont été publiées jusqu'à présent dans les différentes langues*, 15 vols (Paris: Didot, 1746–59).
Price, Richard, *Convict and the Colonel: A Story of Colonialism and Resistance in the Caribbean* (Boston: Beacon Press, 1998).
Prokov'eva, Lidia S., *Krest'ianskaia obshchina v Rossii vo vtoroi polovine XVIII-pervoi polovine XIX v* (The Peasant Commune in Russia during the Second Half of the Eighteenth to the First Half of the Nineteenth Centuries) (Leningrad: Nauka, 1981).
Prozorova-Thomas, Victoria, 'Le classement selon le principe de pertinence comme reflet de la commande d'État: les archives soviétiques', *Matériaux pour l'histoire de notre temps* 82, no. 2 (2006): 58–64.
Quetelet, Adolphe, *Du système social et des lois qui le régissent* (Paris: Guillaumin, 1848).
Quinn, Sholeh, *Historical Writing during the Reign of Shah Abbas: Ideology, Imitation and Legitimacy in Safavid Chronicles* (Salt Lake City: University of Utah Press, 2000).
Raj, Kapil, *Relocating Modern Science* (Basingstoke: Macmillan, 2007).
Ralph, Michael, 'Value of Life: Insurance, Slavery, and Expertise', in *American Capitalism: New Histories*, edited by Sven Beckert and Christine Desan (New York: Columbia University Press, 2018), 257–81.
Raman, Kartik Kalyan, 'Utilitarianism and the Criminal Law in Colonial India: A Study of the Practical Limits of Utilitarian Jurisprudence', *Modern Asian Studies* 28, no. 4 (1994): 739–91.
Ranger, Terence, 'Nationalist Historiography, Patriotic History, and the History of the Nation: The Struggle over the Past in Zimbabwe', *Journal of Southern African Studies* 30, no. 2 (2004): 215–34.
Ranke, Leopold, *Die Römischen Päpste in den letzten vier Jahrhunderten*, 3 vols (Leipzig: Duncker und Humblot, 1834–6).
Rao, R. Neelakanteswara, *Famines and Relief Administration: A Case Study of Coastal Andhra, 1858–1901* (Delhi: Oxford University Press, 1997).
Rao, Velcheru Narayana, David Shulman and Sanjay Subrahmanyam, *Textures of Time; Writing History in South India, 1600–1800* (Delhi: Permanent Black, 2001).
Raynal, Guillaume-Thomas, *Histoire philosophique et politique des établissements et du commerce des Européens dans les deux Indes* (Genève: Pellet, 1780).
Rehmann, Jan, *Max Weber: Modernization as Passive Revolution: A Gramscian Analysis* (Leiden: Brill, 2013).
Reid, William, *An Attempt to Develop the Law of Storms* (London: John Weale, 1838).

Rice, Alan and Martin Crawford, eds, *Liberating Sojourn: Frederick Douglass and Transatlantic Reform* (Athens: Ohio University Press, 1999).
Richards, Thomas, *The Imperial Archive: Knowledge and the Fantasy of Empire* (London and New York: Verso, 1993).
Richardson, David, 'Accounting for "Profits in the British Trade in Slaves: Reply to William Darity', *Explorations in Economic History* 26 (1989): 492–9.
Richardson, David, 'Market Structures and the Profits of the British African Trade in the Late Eighteenth Century. A Comment', *Journal of Economic History* 43 (1983): 713–21.
Riello, Giorgio, *Cotton: The Fabric That Made the Modern World* (Cambridge: Cambridge University Press, 2013).
Riot-Sarcey, Michèle, 'Questionner l'histoire à rebrousse-poil', *Espace Temps* 82–3 (2003): 17–27.
Robbins, Richard G. Jr., *Famine in Russia 1891–1892. The Imperial Government Responds to a Crisis* (New York and London: Columbia University Press, 1975).
Roberts, Richard, 'The Emergence of a Grain Market in Bamako, 1883–1908', *Revue canadienne des études africaines/Canadian Journal of African Studies* 14, no. 1 (1980): 55–81.
Roche, William, 'Evidence of Evidence Is Evidence under Screening-Off', *Episteme* 11, no. 1 (2014): 119–24.
Rohland, Eleonora, *Changes in the Air* (New York: Berghahn, 2018).
Rönnbäck, Klass, 'On the Economic Importance of the Slave Plantation Complex to the British Economy during the Eighteenth Century: A Value-Added Approach', *Journal of Global History* 13, no. 3 (2018): 308–27.
Rosen, Fred, *Bentham, Byron and Greece: Constitutionalism, Nationalism, and Early Liberal Political Thought* (Oxford: Clarendon Press, 1992).
Rosenstein-Rodan, Paul, 'Problems of Industrialization of Eastern and Souteastern Europe', *Economic Journal* 53 (June–September (1943): 202–11.
Rosenthal, Franz, *A History of Muslim Historiography* (Leiden: Brill, 1968).
Rothschild, Emma, *The Inner Life of Empires* (Princeton: Princeton University Press, 2011).
Rousseau, Jean-Jacques, *Oeuvres politiques*, III (Paris: Éditions de la Pleaide, 1967).
Rousseau, Jean-Yves and Carole Couture, eds, *Les fondements de la discipline archivistique* (Québec: Presses Universitaires du Québec, 1994).
Roy, Thirtankar, *The Economic History of India 1857–1947* (Delhi: Oxford University Press, 2000).
Roy, Thirtankar, *Rethinking Economic Change in India. Labour and Livelihood* (London: Routledge, 2005).
Rubiés, Joan-Pau, 'Race, Climate and Civilization in the Works of François Bernier', in *L'Inde des Lumières: Discourse, histoire, savoirs (XVIIe–XIXe siècle)*, edited by Marie Fourcade and Ines Zupanov (Paris: EHESS, 2013), 53–78.
Rubiés, Joan-Pau, 'Oriental Despotism and European Orientalism: Botero to Montesquieu', *Journal of Early Modern History*, 9 (2005): 106–80.
Rüsen, Jan, ed., *Western Historical Thinking: An Intercultural Debate, Making Sense of History*. Studies in Historical Culture and Intercultural Communication (New York: Berghahn, 2002).
Russell, Lynette, 'Indigenous Knowledge and Archives: Accessing Hidden History and Understandings', *Australian Academic and Research Libraries* 36, no. 2 (2013): 161–71.
Sabel, Charles and Jonathan Zeitlin, *World of Possibilities* (Cambridge: Cambridge University Press, 1997).

Sabol, Steven, *The Touch of Civilization: Comparing American and Russian Internal Colonization* (Boulder, CO: University Press of Colorado, 2017).
Sahlins, Marshall, *Stone Age Economics* (Chicago and New York: Aldine Atherton, 1972).
Salais, Robert, *Les mondes de productions* (Paris: EHESS Éditions, 1992).
Salomoni, Antonella, 'Un savoir historique d'État. Les archives soviétiques', *Annales HSS* 50, no. 1 (1995): 3–27.
Samoshenko Viktor, N., *Istoriia arkhivnogo dela v dorevoliutsionnoi Rossii* (History of Archives in Pre-revolutionary Russia) (Moscow: Vysshaia Shkola, 1989).
Sanchez, Sylvie, *Pizza Connexion* (Paris: CNRS éditions, 2007).
Sara, Berry, 'The Food Crisis and Agrarian Change in Africa: A Review Essay', *African Studies Review* 27 (1984): 67–70, 85–9.
Sarkar, Jadunath, *Fall of the Mughal Empire* (Calcutta: Patna, 1932–50).
Sarkar, Jadunath, *History of Aurangzeb*, 5 vols (Calcutta: Sarknar, 1912–52).
Sarkar, Sumit, *Writing Social History* (Delhi: Oxford University Press, 1997).
Sarma Sen, A. K., 'Henry Piddington (1797–1858): A Bicentennial Tribute', *Weather* 52, no. 6 (2012): 187–93.
Say, Jean-Baptiste, *Cours d'économie politique* (Bruxelles: Meline, Cans et Compagnie, 1843).
Sayer, Derek, *Capitalism and Modernity: An Excursus on Marx and Weber* (London: Routledge, 1991).
Schaffer, Simon, 'Les cérémonies de la mesure', *Annales HSS* 70, no. 2 (2015): 409–35.
Schaffer, Simon, 'Self-Evidence', *Critical Inquiry* 18, no. 2 (1992): 327–62.
Schmidt-Glintzer, Helwig, Achim Mittag and Jörn Rüsen, eds, *Historical Truth, Historical Criticism and Ideology: Chinese Historiography and Historical Culture from a New Comparative Perspective* (Leiden: Brill: 2005).
Schuler, Monica, 'The Recruitment of African Indentured Labourers for European Colonies in the Nineteenth Century', in *Colonialism and Migration: Indentured Labour before and after Slavery*, edited by Petr Emmer (Dordrecht, Boston and Lancaster: Martinus Nijhoff, 1986), 125–61.
Schurer, Andrew, Gabriele Hegerl, Michael Mann, Simon Tett and Steven Phipps, 'Separating Forces from Chaotic Climate Variability over the Past Millennium', *Journal of Climate* 26 (2013): 6954–73.
Schwartz, Joan and Terry Cook, 'Archives, Records, and Power: The Making of Modern Memory', *Archival Science* 2 (2002): 1–19.
Scott-Smith, Tom, *On an Empty Stomach: Two Hundred Years of Hunger Relief* (Ithaca and London: Cornell University Press, 2021).
Scott, James, *Domination and the Art of Resistance* (New Haven: Yale University Press, 1990).
Scott, James, *The Moral Economy of the Peasant: Rebellion and Subsistence in Southeast Asia* (New Haven: Yale University Press, 1976).
Scott, James, *Seeing like a State* (New Haven: Yale University Press, 1998).
Scott, James, *Weapons of the Weak: Everyday Forms of Peasant Resistance* (New Haven: Yale University Press, 1985).
Sebastiani, Silvia, *The Scottish Enlightenment* (London: Palgrave Macmillan, 2013).
Seignobos, Charles, *La méthode historique appliquée aux sciences sociales* (Paris: Alcan, 1901).
Semevskii, Vasilii I., *Krest'ianskii vopros v Rossii v XVIII i pervoi polovine XIX veka* (The Peasant Question in Russia in the Eighteenth to the First Half of the Nineteenth Century), 2 vols (Saint Petersburg, 1888).

Sen, Amartya, *Poverty and Famines: An Essay on Entitlement and Deprivation* (Oxford: Clarendon Press, 1982).
Sen, Siva Pada, ed., *Historians and Historiography in Modern India* (Calcutta: Institute of Historical Studies, 1973).
Senra, Nelson, *História das Estatísticas Brasileiras: 1822–2002*, 4 vols (Rio de Janeiro: IBGE, 2006–9).
Serventi, Silvano François Sabban, *Les pâtes* (Arles: Actes Sud, 2001).
Servigne, Pablo and Raphaël Stevens, *Comment tout peut s'effondrer* (Paris: Seuil, 2015).
Sewell, William, *Gens de métier et révolution. Le langage du travail de l'Ancien régime à 1848* (Paris: Aubier, 1983).
Sewell, William, *Logics of History: Social Theory and Social Transformation* (Chicago: University of Chicago Press, 2005).
Sewell, William, 'The Political Unconscious of Social and Cultural History, or, Confessions of a Previous Quantitative Historian', in *The Politics of Method*, edited by George Steinmetz (Durham, NC: Duke University Press, 2005): 173–206.
Shammas, Carol, *The Pre-Industrial Consumer in England and the America* (Oxford: Oxford University Press, 1990).
Shanin, Theodor, *The Awkward Class; Political Sociology of Peasantry in a Developing Society: Russia 1910–1925* (Oxford: Clarendon Press, 1972).
Shanin, Theodor, *Defining Peasants: Essays Concerning Rural Societies, Expolary Economies, and Learning from Them in the Contemporary World* (Oxford: Blackwell, 1990).
Shanin, Theodor, ed., *Late Marx and the Russian Road, Marx and the 'Peripheries of Capitalism'* (New York: Monthly Review Press, 1983).
Shanin, Theodor, *Peasants and Peasant Societies* (New York: Penguin, 1971).
Sharma, Jayeeta, *Empire's Garden: Assam and the Making of India* (Durham, NC: Duke University Press, 2011).
Sheynin, O. B. 'On the History of Statistical Method in Meteorology', *Archive for History of Exact Science* 31 (1984): 53–95.
Shin, Leo, *The Making of the Chinese State: Ethnicity and Expansion on the Ming Borderland* (Cambridge: Cambridge University Press, 2006).
Shteppa, Konstantin, *Russian Historians and the Soviet State* (New Brunswick: Rutger University Press, 1962).
Sidorova, Liubov, *Ottepel' v istoricheskoi nauke: sovetskaia istoriograpfiia pervogo poslestalinskogo desiatiletiia* (The Thaw of the Historical Science: The Soviet Historiography during the First Decade after Stalin) (Moscow: Pamiatniki istoricheskoi mysli, 1997).
Singavarelou, Pierre, 'Des historiens sans histoire? La construction de l'historiographie coloniale en France sous la Troisième République', *Actes de la Recherche en Sciences sociales* 184, no. 5 (2010): 30–43.
Skidmore, James, *The Trauma of Defeat: Ricarda Huch's Historiography during the Weimer Republic* (Berne: Peter Lang, 2005).
Skinner, Jonathan, ed., *The Interview: An Ethnographic Approach* (London: Bloomsbury, 2013).
Skocpol, Theda, *States and Social Revolutions: A Comparative Analysis of France, Russia, and China* (Cambridge: Cambridge University Press, 1979).
Skocpol, Theda, *Visions and Method in Historical Sociology* (Cambridge: Cambridge University Press, 1985).
Slicher Van Bath, B. H., *De agrarische geschiedenis van West-Europa (500–1850)* (Utrecht: Het Spectrum, 1962).

Smith, Anthony, *The Ethnic Origins of Nations* (Oxford: Blackwell, 1986).
Sokoloff, Kenneth and David Dollar, 'Agricultural Seasonality and the Organization of Manufacturing in Early Industrial Economies: The Contrast between England and the United States', *The Journal of Economic History* 57, no. 2 (1997): 288–321.
Solow, Barbara, 'Caribbean Slavery and British Growth: The Eric Williams Hypothesis', *Journal of Development Economics* 17 (1985): 99–115
Sonenscher, Michael, *Work and Wages: Natural Law, Politics and the Eighteenth-Century French Trades* (Cambridge: Cambridge University Press, 1989).
Spivak, Gayatri Chakravorty, *A Critique of Postcolonial Reason: Toward a History of the Vanishing Present* (Cambridge, MA: Harvard University Press, 1999).
Spivak, Gayatri Chakravorty, 'The Rani of Sirmur: An Essay in Reading the Archives', *History and Theory* 24, no. 3 (1985): 247–72.
Stanziani, Alessandro, *After Oriental Despotism: Eurasian Growth in Global Perspective* (London: Bloomsbury, 2014).
Stanziani, Alessandro, *Bâtisseurs d'Empires. Russie, Inde et Chine à la croisée des mondes* (Paris: Liber, 2012).
Stanziani, Alessandro, *Capital terre. Une histoire longue du monde d'après* (Paris: Payot, 2021).
Stanziani, Alessandro, ed., *Dictionnaire de l'économie-droit* (Paris: LGDJ, 2007).
Stanziani, Alessandro, *Eurocentrism and the Politics of Global History* (New York: Palgrave, 2018).
Stanziani, Alessandro, *Histoire de la qualité alimentaire* (Paris: Seuil, 2005).
Stanziani, Alessandro, *L'Economie en révolution, le cas russe. 1870–1930* (Paris: Albin Michel, 1998).
Stanziani, Alessandro, *Labor in the Fringes of Empire* (New York: Palgrave, 2018).
Stanziani, Alessandro, *Les entrelacements du monde* (Paris: CNRS éditions, 2018).
Stanziani, Alessandro, 'Negotiating Innovation in a Market Economy: Foodstuffs and Beverages Adulteration in Nineteenth-Century France', *Enterprise and Society* 8, no. 2 (2007): 375–412.
Stanziani, Alessandro, 'Revisiting Russian Serfdom: Bonded Peasants and Market Dynamics, 1600–1800', *International Labor and Working Class History* 78, no. 1 (2010): 12–27.
Stanziani, Alessandro, *Rules of Exchange: French Capitalism in Comparative Perspective, Eighteenth-Twentieth Centuries* (Cambridge: Cambridge University Press, 2012).
Stanziani, Alessandro, *Seamen, Migrants and Workers: Bondage in the Indian Ocean World, Eighteenth–Nineteenth Centuries* (New York: Palgrave Macmillan, 2014).
Stanziani, Alessandro, 'Statistics', in *Encyclopedia of Europe, 1789–1914*, edited by John Merriman and J. M. Winter (New York: Scribner, 2006).
Steensgaard, Niels, *The Asian Trade Revolution of the Seventeenth Century: The East India Company and the Decline of the Caravan Trade* (Chicago: University of Chicago Press, 1975).
Stein, Alex, *Foundations of Evidence Law* (Oxford: Oxford University Press, 2005).
Steinberg, Marc, 'Capitalist Development, the Labor Process, and the Law', *American Journal of Sociology* 109, no. 2 (2003): 445–95.
Steinfeld, Robert, *Coercion, Contract, and Free Labor in the Nineteenth Century* (Cambridge: Cambridge University Press, 2001).
Steinfeld, Robert, *The Invention of Free Labor: The Employment Relation in English and American Law and Culture, 1350–1870* (Chapel Hill: North Carolina University Press, 1991).

Steinmetz, George, ed., *The Politics of Methods in the Human Sciences* (Durham, NC: Duke University Press, 2005).
Steinmetz, George, ed., *Sociology and Empire* (Durham, NC and London: Duke University Press, 2013).
Steinmetz, Willibald, 'Nachruf auf Reinhart Koselleck (1923–2006)', *Geschichte und Gesellschaft* 32–3 (2006): 412–32.
Steinmetz, Willibald, ed., *Private Law and Social Inequality in the Industrial Age: Comparing Legal Cultures in Britain, France, Germany and the United States* (Oxford: Oxford University Press, 2000).
Steinmetz, Willibald, Michael Freeden and Javier Fernandez-Sebastian, eds, *Conceptual History in the European Space* (New York: Berghahn, 2017).
Stigler, George, 'The Economics of Information', *Journal of Political Economy* 69 (1961): 213–25.
Stigler, Stephen, *The History of Statistics: The Measurement of Statistics before 1900* (Boston: Belknap Press, 1990).
Stiglitz, Joseph, Amartya Sen and Jean-Paul Fitoussi, *Mismeasuring Our Lives: Why GDP Doesn't Add Up* (New York: New Press, 2010).
Stiglitz, Joseph, *Whither Socialism?* (Cambridge, MA: MIT Press, 1994).
Stillerman, Joel, *The Sociology of Consumption: A Global Approach* (London: Polity Press, 2015).
Stites, Richard, *Serfdom, Society, and the Arts in Imperial Russia* (New Haven: Yale University Press, 2005).
Stoke, Eric, *The English Utilitarians and India* (Oxford: Oxford University Press, 1959).
Stoler, Ann Laura, *Along the Archival Grain* (Princeton: Princeton University Press, 2009).
Stoler, Ann Laure, *Capitalism and Confrontation in Sumatra's Plantation, 1870–1979* (Ann Arbor, 1995).
Stoler, Ann Laura, 'Colonial Archives and the Art of Governance', *Archival Science* 2 (2002): 87–109.
Strasser, Susan, Charles McGovern and Matthias Judt, eds, *Getting and Spending: European and American Societies in the Twentieth Century* (Cambridge: Cambridge University Press, 1998).
Studenski, Paul, *The Income of Nations, Part One: History* (New York: New York University Press, 1958).
Subrahmanyam, Sanjay, *Aux origines de l'histoire globale* (Paris: Collège de France/ Fayard, 2014).
Subrahmanyam, Sanjay, *The Career and Legend of Vasco da Gama* (New York: Cambridge University Press, 1997).
Subrahmanyam, Sanjay, 'Connected Histories. Notes Towards a Reconfiguration of Early Modern Eurasia', *Modern Asian Studies* 31, no. 3 (1997): 735–62.
Subrahmanyam, Sanjay, 'Du Tage au Gange au XVIe siècle. Une conjoncture millénariste à l'échelle eurasiatique', *Annales. Histoire, Sciences Sociales* (2001): 51–84.
Sugihara, Kaouro, 'Labour-Intensive Industrialisation in Global History', *Australian Economic History* 47, no. 2 (2007): 121–54.
Suleymanov, Muzzafar, 'The Role of History in the Creation of National Identities in Central Asia: Uzbekistan and Kyrgyzstan Case Studies', *Peace and Conflict Review* 1, no. 1 (2008): 1–33.
Taillemite, Etienne, 'Les archives de la France d'outre-mer', *La Gazette des archives* 22 (1957): 6–22.

Taleb, Nassim Nicholas, *The Black Swann: The Impact of the Highly Improbable* (New York: Random House, 2010).
Tannenbaum, Frank, 'Contract versus Status', *Political Science Quarterly* 65, no. 2 (1950): 181–92.
Tendler, Joseph, *The Palgrave Macmillan Opponents of the Annales School* (New York: Palgrave Macmillan, 2013).
Tenishev, V. N., *Byt velikorusskikh krest'ian-zemlepashtsev* (The Life of Grand Russian Peasants) (Saint Petersburg: Izdatel'stvo evropeicheskogo doma, 1993).
Testart, Alain, *L'esclave, la dette et le pouvoir* (Paris: Éditions errance, 2001).
Thénault, Sylvie, *Une drôle de justice: les magistrats dans la guerre d'Algérie* (Paris: La Découverte, 2001).
Thiesse, Anne-Marie, *La création des identités nationales: Europe XVIIIe–XIXe siècle* (Paris: Seuil, 1999).
Thompson, E. P., *The Poverty of Theory and Other Essays* (London: Merlin, 1979).
Thompson, E. P., 'Time, Work Discipline, and Industrial Capitalism', *Past & Present* 38 (1967): 56–97.
Thorner, Daniel and Alice, *Land and Labour in India* (Delhi: Oxford University Press, 1956).
Tilly, Charles, *Coercion, Capital and European States, AD 990–1991* (Cambridge and Oxford: Blackwell, 1990).
Tilly, Charles, 'Three Visions of History and Theory', *History and Theory* 46 (2007): 299–307.
Timiriatsev, D. A., 'Rapport sur l'unification de l'enregistrement de la statistique des récoltes', *Bulletin de l'Institut International de Statistique* 11 (1899): 142–8.
Timmer, Charles, 'The Turnip, the New Husbandry, and the English Agricultural Revolution', *Quarterly Journal of Economics* 83 (1969): 375–95.
Tinker, Hugh, *A New System of Slavery: The Export of Indian Labour Overseas 1830–1920* (London: Hansib, 1974).
Tipps, Dearn, 'Modernization Theory and the Comparative Study of Societies: A Critical Perspective', *Comparative Studies in Society and History* 15 (1973): 199–226.
Todorova, Maria, 'Does Russian Orientalism Have a Russian Soul? A Contribution to the Debate between Nathaniel Knight and Adeeb Khalid', *Kritika: Explorations in Russian and Eurasian History* 1, no. 4 (2000): 717–27.
Tolz, Vera, *Russia's Own Orient: The Politics of Identity and Oriental Studies in the Late Imperial and Early Soviet Periods* (Oxford: Oxford University Press, 2011).
Tooze, Adam, *Crashed: How a Decade of Financial Crisis Changed the World* (London: Viking, 2018).
Tooze, Adam, *Statistics and the German State, 1900–1945* (Cambridge: Cambridge University Press).
Tooze, Adam, *The Deluge: The Great War and the Remaking of the Global Order* (London: Penguin, 2015).
Tough, Alistair, 'Archives in Sub-Saharan Africa Half a Century after Independence', *Archival Science* 9, no. 3 (2009): 187–201.
Trentmann, Frank, *The Oxford Handbook of the History of Consumption* (Oxford: Oxford University Press, 2012).
Trentmann, Frank, ed., *Paradoxes of Civil Society: New Perspectives on Modern British and German History* (New York: Berghahn, 2000).
Trevor-Roper, Hugh, *History and the Enlightenment* (New Haven: Yale University Press, 2010).

TsSK, *Veroiatnyi sbor khlebov v … godu* in *Ezhegodnik Rossii* (Saint Petersburg, 1904–17).
Tugan-Baranovskij, Mikhail I., *Osnovy politicheskoi ekonomii* (Fundamentals of Political Economy) 2 vols (Saint Petersburg: Ministry of Internal Affairs, 1905–11, reprint Moscow: Rosspen, 1998).
Turgot, A. R. J., *Oeuvres et documents le concernant*, 5 vols, edited by Gustave Schelle (Paris: Félix Alcan, 1913–23), 2: 375.
Turner, Frederick Jackson, 'The Significance of the Frontier in American History', reprint in *Frontier and Section: Selected Writings of F.J. Turner* (Englewood Cliffs, NJ: Prentice Hall, 1961).
Twining, William, *Rethinking Evidence: Exploratory Essays* (Cambridge: Cambridge University Press, 1994).
Tyrrell, Ian, *Historians in Public: The Practice of American History, 1890–1970* (Chicago: University of Chicago Press, 2005).
Unicef, *The State of the World's Children* (Oxford: Oxford University Press, 1991).
Vabre, Sylvie, Martin Bruegel and Peter Atkins, eds, *Food History: A Feasts of the Senses in Europe, 1750 to the Present* (London: Routledge, 2021).
Van der Linden, Marcel, ed., *Workers of the World* (Leiden: Brill, 2008).
Van Zanden, Jan Luiten, *The Long Road to the Industrial Revolution* (Leiden: Brill, 2009).
Vansina, Jan, *De la tradition orale: essai de méthode historique* (Tervuren: Musée royal de l'Afrique centrale, 1961).
Veblen, Thorstein, *The Theory of Leisure Class* (New York: Penguin, 1994; orig. 1899).
Venturi, Franco, *Settecento riformatore*, 5 vols (Turin: Einaudi, 1966–90).
Verdery, Katherine and Ivo Banac, eds, *National Character and National Ideology in Interwar Eastern Europe* (New Haven: Yale Center For International and Area Studies, 1995).
Vincent, Pierre-Marie, *Le droit de l'alimentation* (Paris: PUF, 1996).
Voltaire, François-Marie, Arouet, *Essai sur les mœurs et l'esprit des nations* (Paris: Lefèvre, 1756).
Von Hagen, Mark, 'The Archival Gold Rush and Historical Agendas in the Post-Soviet Era', *Slavic Review* 52, no. 1 (1993): 96–100.
Vucinich, Wayne, ed., *The Zemstvo in Russia: An Experiment in Local Self-Governement* (Cambridge: Cambridge University Press, 1982).
Wahrman, Dror, *The Making of the Modern Self: Identity and Culture in Eighteenth-Century England* (New Haven: Yale University Press, 2004).
Waldron, Arthur, *The Great Wall of China: From History to Myth* (Cambridge: Cambridge University Press, 1990).
Wallerstein, Immanuel, *The Modern World-System: Capitalist Agriculture and the Origins of the European World-Economy in the Sixteenth Century* (New York and London: Atheneum, 1974, 1976).
Wang, Edward, *Inventing China through History* (New York: State University of New York Press, 2001).
Warde, Alan and Lydia Martens, *Eating Out: Social Differentiation, Consumption and Pleasure* (Cambridge: Cambridge University Press, 2000).
Watts, Sidney, *Meat Matters: Butchers, Politics, and Market Culture in Eighteenth-Century Paris* (Rochester, NY: University of Rochester Press, 2006).
Weber, Eugène, *Peasants into Frenchmen* (Stanford: Stanford University Press, 1976).
Weber, Jacques, 'L'Émigration indienne à la Réunion: "contraire à la morale" ou "utile à l'humanité"', in *Esclavage et abolition dans l' Océan Indien, 1723–1869*, edited by Edmond Maestri (Paris: L'Harmattan, 2002): 309–28.

Weber, Max, *Wirtschaft und Gesellschaft* (Tübingen: Mohr, 1922, 1925). English translation, *Economy and Society* (Cambridge, MA: Harvard University Press, 2019).
Webster, Peter and Song Yang, 'Monsoon and ENSO: Selective Interactive Systems', *Quarterly Journal of the Royal Meteorological Society* 118, no. 507 (1992): 877–926.
Weis, Tony, *The Global Food Economy: The Battle for the Future of Farming* (London: Zed Books, 2007).
Weitz, Richard, *From Peasant to Farmer* (New York: Columbia University Press, 1971).
Werner, Michael and Bénédicte Zimmermann, dir, *De la comparaison à l'histoire croisée* (Paris: Seuil, 2004).
Werner, Michael and Bénédicte Zimmermann, *De la comparaison à l'histoire croisée* (Paris: Seuil, 2004).
Werth, Nicolas, 'De la soviétologie en général et des archives russes en particulier', *Le Débat* (November–December 1993): 127–44.
Wescoat, James, 'Water, Climate and the Limits of Human Wisdom: Historical-Geographic Analogies between Early Mughal and Modern South Asia', *Professional Geographer* 66, no. 3 (2014): 382–9.
Wheatcroft, Stephen G., 'The 1891–92 Famine in Russia: Towards a More Detailed Analysis of Its Scale and Demographic Significance', in *Economy and Society in Russia and the Soviet Union, 1860–1930, Essays for Olga Crisp*, edited by Linda Harriet Edmondson and P. Waldron (New York: St. Martin's Press, 1992): 44–64.
Wheeler, Roxann, *The Complexion of Race: Categories of Difference in Eighteenth-Century British Culture* (Philadelphia: University of Pennsylvania Press, 2002).
White, Hayden, *The Content of the Form: Narrative Discourse and Historical Representation* (Baltimore: Johns Hopkins University Press, 1987).
White, Hayden, *Tropics of Discourse: Essays in Cultural Criticism* (Baltimore: Johns Hopkins University Press, 1978).
Williams, Eric, *Capitalism and Slavery* (Chapel Hill: North Carolina University Press, 1944).
Williamson, Fiona, 'Weathering the Empire: Meteorological Research in the Early British Straits Settlements', *The British Journal for the History of Science* 48, no. 3 (2015): 475–92.
Winks, Robin, *The Historiography of the British Empire-Commonwealth: Trends, Interpretations, and Resources* (Durham, NC: University of North Carolina Press, 1966).
Wolf, Eric, *Peasants* (Englewood Cliffs, NJ: Prentice Hall, 1966).
Wolf, Eric, *Peasant Wars of the Twentieth Century* (New York: Harper & Row, 1969).
Wolf, Eric, *Europe and the People without History* (Berkeley: University of California Press, 1982).
Woolf, Daniel, *A Global History of History* (Cambridge: Cambridge University Press, 2011).
Woolf, Daniel, ed., *The Oxford History of Historical Writing*, 5 vols (Oxford: Oxford University Press, 2011–15).
Wright, Gavin, *Old South, New South: Revolutions in the Southern Economy since the Civil War* (New York: Basic Books, 1986).
Wright, Gavin, *The Political Economy of the Cotton South: Households, Markets, and Wealth in the Nineteenth Century* (New York: Norton, 1978).
Wright, Gavin, *Slavery and American Economic Development* (Baton Rouge: LSU Press, 2006).

Xu, H., Y. Hong and B. Hong, 'Decreasing Asian Summer Monsoon Intensity after 1860 AD in the Global Warming Epoch', *Climatic Dynamics* 39 (2012): 2079–88.

Yates, Frances, *The Art of Memory* (Chicago: University of Chicago Press, 1966).

Yavlinsky, Grigory, *Laissez-Faire versus Policy-Led Transformation: Lessons of the Economic Reforms in Russia* (Moscow: Center for Economic and Political Research, 1996).

Yekelchyk, Serhy, *Stalin's Empire of Memory* (Toronto: University of Toronto Press, 2004).

Zakim Michael and Gary John Kornblith, eds, *Capitalism Takes Command: The Social Transformation of Nineteenth-Century America* (Chicago and London: University of Chicago Press, 2012): 223–47.

Zalasiewicz Jan et al., 'When Did the Anthropocene Begin? A Mid-Twentieth Century Boundary Level Is Stratigraphically Optimal', *Quaternary International* 383, no. 5 (2015): 196–203.

Zavos, John, 'Searching for Hindu Nationalism in Modern Indian History: Analysis of Some Early Ideological Developments', *Economic and Political Weekly* 34, no. 32 (7–13 August 1999): 2269–76.

Zelnik, Reginald, *Perils of Pankratova: Some Stories from the Annals of Soviet Historiography* (Seattle: University of Washington Press, 2005).

Zemon Davis, Natalie, *Fiction in the Archives* (Stanford: Stanford University Press, 1990).

Zemon Davis, Natalie, *The Return of Martin Guerre* (Cambridge, MA: Harvard University Press, 1983).

Zhang Wenxian, 'Dang An: A Brief History of the Chinese Imperial Archives and Its Administration', *Journal of Archival Organization* 2, no. 1/2 (2004): 17–38.

Zhang, Xingang and Zhaoqing Sun, Xinzhong Zhang, Liqiang Zheng, Shuangshuang Liu, Changlu Xu, Jiajin Li, Fenfen Zhao, Jue Li, Dayi Hu, et al., 'Prevalence and Associated Factors of Overweight and Obesity in a Chinese Rural Population', *Obesity Research* 16 (2007): 168–71.

Index

agronomy 125
Algeria 51, 52
anthropology 17, 22, 48, 53, 58, 69, 103, 123, 153, 165, 173, 186, 189, 191, 192, 193, 194, 203, 210, 211, 212, 213, 216, 218
apprentice, apprenticeship 109, 110, 115, 116, 134, 137
archaebotanics 85
area studies 7, 10, 47, 185, 189, 191, 193, 204, 216, 233
astronomy 12, 21, 24, 77

Barbados 89
Bayesian (probability) 66, 78, 79
Beaufort, Francis 79, 89
Bengal 25, 27, 44, 90, 117, 138, 206
Bentham, Jeremy 113, 114, 116, 117, 118, 119, 121, 200, 205, 207, 227
Bernier, François 23, 24, 25, 27, 205, 207, 214, 224, 227
Bertillon, Jacques 64
Bloch, Marc 17, 184, 185, 186, 205, 206
Bolshevik 6, 8, 23, 33, 37, 44, 169,196
Bombay 90, 202
Bourgeoisie 13, 104, 123, 124, 134, 169, 177, 178, 196, 210
Braudel, Fernand 17, 22, 74, 127, 158, 181, 188, 194, 205, 206
Brazil 138, 146, 157, 158, 159, 170, 199, 219, 223
bureaucrat 9, 10, 30, 41, 65, 69, 70, 98, 129, 150

Calcutta 44, 45, 89, 90, 228, 229
capitalism 1, 3, 8, 9, 10, 11, 13, 14, 15, 17, 22, 34, 37, 46, 56, 58, 59, 60, 61, 63, 65, 67, 69, 71, 73, 74, 75, 79, 80, 98, 102, 104, 108, 114, 115, 124, 126, 127, 129, 133, 135, 147, 149, 150, 151, 152, 153, 158, 167, 168, 169, 170, 172, 174, 175, 176, 177, 180, 181, 183, 186, 188, 190, 191, 193, 194, 203, 205, 206, 207, 214, 215, 220, 226, 228, 229, 230, 232, 234
captive 110
census 64, 67, 84, 107, 111
Central Asia 40, 41, 43, 137, 180, 188, 201, 220, 231
Chakrabarty, Dipesh, 4, 13, 16, 44, 47, 104, 120, 166, 173, 176, 195, 208
Chayanov, Alexandr' 124, 125, 126, 127, 128, 129, 132, 208
children 103, 107, 108, 109, 110, 116, 126, 137, 146, 233
China 3, 11, 25, 26, 27, 40, 46, 54, 71, 80, 88, 98, 124, 126, 130, 132, 133, 134, 137, 138, 139, 145, 146, 151, 152, 158, 159, 164, 169, 170, 171, 175, 177, 180, 182, 183, 185, 188, 189, 190, 191, 194
Chuprov, Aleksandr 66, 125, 208
civilization 2, 5, 7, 14, 24, 39, 53, 71, 74, 85, 105, 118, 119, 120, 125, 164, 165, 166, 176, 185, 187, 188, 190, 191, 194, 200, 201, 208, 213, 217, 224, 227, 228, 195
class 2, 3, 4, 13, 14, 17, 34, 36, 47, 65, 72, 86, 102, 104, 108, 111, 115, 126, 140, 143, 145, 151, 152, 159, 160, 163, 165, 172, 173, 177, 185, 193, 196, 199, 213
classification 1, 6, 7, 13, 20, 23, 26, 27, 28, 29, 30, 31, 34, 35, 36, 37, 47, 48, 49, 50, 51, 53, 54, 55, 56, 79, 80, 86, 88, 99, 108, 123, 153, 163, 169, 190, 197, 200, 212
climate 11, 12, 76, 79, 80, 84, 85, 86, 90, 92, 94, 96, 199, 204
Cold War 7, 16, 17, 38, 123, 126, 169, 177, 179, 187, 190, 192, 194, 197, 200

colonial 3, 4, 6, 7, 8, 11, 13, 14, 20, 24, 29, 30, 31, 38, 39, 40–56, 74, 77, 80, 81, 84, 86, 87, 88, 92, 94, 95, 96, 98, 99, 107, 108, 112, 115, 118, 120, 121, 126, 129, 133, 136, 139, 140, 146, 160, 164, 167–170, 182, 183, 185–188, 190, 191, 193, 194, 195, 197, 199, 200
colonial law 56, 112
common lands 103, 124, 130, 183
commons 178, 190
comparison 16, 17, 20, 39, 50, 63, 71, 83, 103, 113, 126, 145, 151, 168, 175, 176, 178, 179, 182–187, 191, 203, 224
Comte, Auguste 66
cooperative 69, 115, 125, 128
copy (document) 30
correlation 11, 75, 77, 83, 97, 198
cultural anthropology 58, 192
custom, customary 43, 53, 68, 71, 85, 95, 97
cyclone 85–96, 208, 212, 214, 219

decolonization 6, 8, 9, 18, 20, 23, 33, 45, 46, 47, 49, 51, 52, 53, 54, 55, 72, 123, 140, 177, 179, 187, 191, 192, 194, 196, 197, 200, 209
Derrida, Jacques 7, 8, 38, 47, 173
Diderot, Denis 164, 166
Dobb, Maurice 170
Durkheim, Emile 2, 17, 153, 172, 184, 186, 212

Eastern Europe 17, 80, 127, 131, 134, 139, 145, 151, 179, 190, 191, 201, 217, 233
empire 22, 25, 27, 29, 31, 39, 40, 41, 42, 43, 44, 45, 47–50, 54, 60, 61, 80, 86, 91, 92, 104, 134, 136, 137, 151, 165, 172, 179, 180, 183, 185, 194
enclosure 103, 109, 130
eurocentric, eurocentrism ii, 3, 13, 16, 21, 22, 27, 42, 43, 50, 54, 73, 105, 145, 165, 166, 167, 174, 175, 176, 178, 179, 180, 182, 183, 187, 193, 194, 195, 196, 200

famine 12, 73, 76, 80–82, 85, 89, 96, 138, 142, 144, 145, 146, 147, 148

fishermen 133
food 87, 93, 95, 96, 123, 125, 141, 143–151, 153, 155–159, 199
forecast 11, 12, 66, 76–81, 84, 85, 86, 91, 98
Foucault, Michel 7, 8, 29, 38, 47, 117, 172, 173

Galton, Francis 77, 91
Gauss, Carl Friedrich 77, 78, 79
Gershenkron, Alexander 177
GDP 197, 209
Geertz, Clifford 22, 117, 172, 173, 191, 192
great divergence 17, 105, 132, 133, 181–183
green revolution 148

harvest 11, 12, 69, 77, 79, 80, 82–89, 92–96, 111, 138, 145, 146, 190
Hubert, Joseph 90, 150
Hume, David 64, 76, 165, 216
hurricane 79, 86, 88–91, 94, 203

Ianson, Iulii 66, 217
identity 118, 123, 152, 187, 201, 206
India 1, 3, 4, 5, 6, 7, 11, 12, 13, 14, 16, 21, 24, 25, 26, 29, 31, 43–47, 53–55, 65, 72, 77, 79, 80, 81, 84, 85–88, 90, 91, 94, 95, 96, 97, 104, 105, 108, 117–121, 126, 129, 137, 138, 146, 157, 158, 166–173, 177, 182, 187, 188, 189, 190, 192, 194, 196, 198, 199, 200, 201, 202
Indian ocean 12, 14, 79, 84, 85, 86, 87, 88, 89, 90, 92, 96, 112, 137, 138, 188, 200
Indochina 50, 51, 88
industrial revolution 17, 22, 59, 60, 61, 64, 73, 108, 110, 111, 130, 131, 135, 139, 143, 144, 145, 146, 147, 159, 160, 172, 179, 180, 183
industrious revolution 143, 144, 151
inequalities 1, 5, 14, 61, 72, 73–79, 84, 97, 99, 107, 108, 121, 129, 141, 142, 143, 144, 148, 151, 152, 159, 182, 199
insurance 86, 93, 98, 120, 121
Islam, Islamic 25, 26, 40, 107, 187, 191

Japan 26, 40, 43, 79, 88, 107, 138, 149, 154, 157
Jevons, Stanley 77, 81, 124
Junker 132

Kerblay, Basile 126–128
Knapp, Georg Friederich 65
Koselleck, Reinhardt 3, 4, 21, 22, 24, 181, 212
Kula, Witold 69, 127, 131, 132, 138, 170
Kuznets, Simon 10, 127, 143

Laplace, Pierre Simon 64, 66, 77
large numbers (law) 64, 66
Latin America 72, 80, 97, 126, 146, 157, 170, 190, 193, 196, 198
Lederer, Emile 126
legal status 14, 107, 108, 109, 112, 120, 151
Lenin, Vladimir Ilich 6, 34, 36, 37, 39, 67, 124, 128, 129, 131, 169, 170, 171
Lexis, Wilhelm 65
liberalism 55, 72, 73, 200
luxury 142, 143, 150–155

Madagascar 51, 88
Madras 90
Maine, Henry Sumner 13, 107, 108, 119, 120
Malthus, Thomas 113
Manchuria 137
Marathas, Marathi 25, 27, 45
marriage 51, 102, 103, 109, 129, 200
Marx, Karl 69, 102, 108, 111, 115, 124, 125, 143, 159, 166, 167, 168, 169, 170, 171, 172, 174, 175, 176, 177, 179, 183, 184, 196, 200
Marxist 65, 67, 102, 103, 104, 126, 127, 129, 134, 135, 144, 163, 166, 168, 169, 170, 171, 172, 173, 175, 179, 181, 187, 190, 192, 196, 199
Masters and Servants Acts 109, 110, 114, 120
Mauritius island 85, 87, 89, 92, 96
Mauss, Marcel 17, 145, 153, 154, 189, 192
merchants 80, 108, 126, 134, 146, 155, 156, 176, 199
Merivale, Herman 115, 223
microhistory 17, 103, 104, 193
Mill, John Stuart 77, 200, 202

Ming 25, 26
modernization (theory) 15, 17, 73, 74, 81, 86, 98, 99, 129, 134, 135, 151, 158, 178, 179, 196
monsoon 12, 80, 81, 85, 87, 88, 95, 96
Mughal 3, 23, 24, 25, 27, 45, 86
Muslim 25, 27, 40, 41, 42

nation state 54, 55, 99, 179
neoliberalism 14, 200
New History of Capitalism 1, 60, 174

oral, orality 6, 23, 39, 42, 43, 45, 46, 50, 53, 54, 55, 69, 148, 165, 196
Orientalism 7, 24, 39, 44, 120, 166, 169
Ottoman 6, 43, 54, 151, 188

Pankratova, Anna 37
Pearson, Karl 64
Persian 3, 25, 26, 27, 40
Petty, William 64
philology 186, 197
Piddington, Henry 89, 90
Platonov, Serguei 34
Pokrovskii, Mikhail 34, 36
Polanyi, Karl 17, 108, 145, 183, 192
Poor Laws 113, 114, 116
populist 37, 67, 125, 130, 133, 135, 168, 178
postcolonial 3, 6, 7, 8, 30, 39, 41, 42, 45, 47, 50, 52, 53, 56, 120, 164, 170, 188, 191, 193, 194, 195, 199, 200
probability 11, 24, 58, 64, 66, 77, 78, 91
produce exchange 80, 147
property 11, 90, 109, 110, 115, 131, 132, 150, 167, 175, 176, 183, 185
protoindustry 11, 67, 131, 132, 138, 139, 163, 183

Quetelet, Adolphe 64, 66, 77

random, randomly (sampling) 66, 67, 68, 78
recruitment 92, 110, 135, 136
Reid, William 43, 89, 90
Reunion island 51, 85–92
revolution 3, 6, 8, 9, 17, 20, 21, 22, 23, 24, 25, 27, 28, 33, 34, 35, 36, 37, 39, 40, 44, 49, 51, 54, 55, 59, 60, 61, 64, 65,

66, 69, 73, 99, 104, 108, 110, 111, 115, 123, 124, 130, 131, 132, 135, 139, 143, 144, 145, 146, 147, 148, 151, 158, 159, 160, 166, 168, 169, 171, 172, 174, 179, 180, 183, 193, 194, 196, 197, 198, 199
rights 14, 29, 71, 103, 108, 109, 110, 112, 113, 121, 125, 139, 141, 180
risk 75, 78, 85, 93, 96, 102, 120, 134, 155
Rousseau, Jean-Jacques 164, 165
Russia 33–43, 47, 54, 55, 65, 66, 67, 68, 69, 70, 71, 79, 80, 81, 82, 83, 84, 97, 98, 107, 113, 117, 124, 125, 126, 127, 128, 131, 132, 134, 136, 137, 139, 145, 146, 148, 149, 152, 159, 163, 165, 166, 167, 168, 169, 170, 171, 172, 177, 178, 179, 180, 181, 182, 185, 187, 188, 190, 191, 196, 197, 198, 199, 201

Said, Edward 16, 39, 47, 54, 117, 120, 196, 172
sailor 88, 90, 133, 134, 135, 136, 138, 199
Saint-Domingue 21
sample, sampling 64, 65, 67, 83, 84
Sarkar, Jadunath 44, 45
Say, Jean-Baptiste 115
Schumpeter, Peter 126
selection (in sampling) 64, 66, 67
Senegal 52
Serfdom 65, 66, 107, 112, 113, 127, 132, 134, 136, 137, 145, 165, 178, 190
servant 13, 95, 103, 109, 110, 113, 114, 115, 117, 120, 134, 159, 200
service 51, 84, 102, 109, 110, 114, 131, 132, 133, 136, 200
Siberia 137
slave, slavery 1, 2, 10, 13, 14, 16, 31, 52, 59, 60, 61, 92, 93, 95, 99, 104–131, 133, 135, 136, 139, 140, 142, 146, 159, 160, 163, 165, 174, 196, 199, 200
soldier 64, 135, 136, 137, 199
solidarity 17, 98, 159
song 25
speculation 77, 80, 81, 84, 124, 144, 145, 146, 147, 148, 158, 159
Spivak, Gayatri Chakravorty 46, 47, 164
Stalin, Joseph 6, 10, 37, 38, 125, 128, 129, 169, 170, 171, 178

standard, standardisation 60, 69, 78, 79, 80, 91, 95, 99, 115, 117, 143, 144, 156, 157, 158
Statute of Artificers 109, 110
Stewart, Dugald 64
subaltern (studies) 8, 13, 16, 41, 42, 45, 47, 50, 52, 56, 105, 117, 164, 166, 170, 172, 173, 191, 200
sugar 87, 92, 93, 95, 96, 97, 133, 147
survey 61, 66, 67, 83, 157

Tarle, Yevgeny 34
taxonomy 104
temporal, temporality 22, 26, 33, 178, 179, 188, 189
Thompson, E.P. 13, 22, 58, 69, 170, 172, 173
Thorner, Alice 126
Thorner, Daniel 126, 127, 128
time (linear, cyclical, labour, etc) 21, 22, 29, 43, 45, 69–71, 74, 82, 98, 104, 109, 110, 111, 114, 178–179, 189, 192, 195, 198
totalitarian 6, 20, 30, 33, 35, 38, 98, 194, 197
traders 60, 68, 79, 80, 155, 159

United States 28, 29, 47, 52, 53, 59, 81, 83, 84, 107, 108, 127, 135, 170, 193, 201
utilitarian(ism) 102, 113, 115, 118, 119, 121, 124, 200

Vandervelde, Emile 125

wage, wage labour. 14, 31, 48, 95, 103, 104, 107, 109–117, 120, 121, 131, 132, 133, 159, 174, 175, 199, 200
Wallerstein, Immanuel 17, 131, 174, 187, 194
Walras, Léon 66
warming 1, 5, 73, 85, 86, 92, 96, 97, 146
Williams, Eric 220, 234
women 103, 108, 109 121

Zasulich, Vera 168
Zolla, Daniel 125

www.ingramcontent.com/pod-product-compliance
Lightning Source LLC
Chambersburg PA
CBHW062142300426
44115CB00012BA/2014